WILD BILL & BUFFALO BILL

HICKOK CODY

Wild Bill Hickok and Buffalo Bill Cody

WILD BILL
HICKOK
& BUFFALO BILL
CODY

PLAINSMEN
OF THE
LEGENDARY WEST

BILL MARKLEY

TWODOT®

Essex, Connecticut
Helena, Montana

A · TWODOT® · BOOK

An imprint of Globe Pequot, the trade division of
The Rowman & Littlefield Publishing Group, Inc.
4501 Forbes Blvd., Ste. 200
Lanham, MD 20706
www.rowman.com

Distributed by NATIONAL BOOK NETWORK

British Library Cataloguing in Publication Information available

Library of Congress Cataloging-in-Publication Data

Names: Markley, Bill, 1951- author.
Title: Wild Bill Hickok and Buffalo Bill Cody : plainsmen of the legendary
    West / Bill Markley.
Description: Guilford, Connecticut : TwoDot, [2022] | Includes bibliographical
    references and index. | Summary: "In this new joint biography of these two great
    plainsmen of the Old West, author Bill Markley offers a thoughtful and entertaining
    examination of these two soldiers, scouts, and showmen who left a lasting legacy"
    — Provided by publisher.
Identifiers: LCCN 2022006851 (print) | LCCN 2022006852 (ebook) | ISBN
    9781493048427 (paper ; alk. paper) | ISBN 9781493048434 (electronic)
Subjects: LCSH: Hickok, Wild Bill, 1837-1876. | Buffalo Bill, 1846-1917. | Pioneers—
    West (U.S.)—Biography. | United States marshals—West (U.S.)—Biography. | Frontier
    and pioneer life—West (U.S.) | West (U.S.)—Biography. | West (U.S.)—History—
    1860–1890.
Classification: LCC F594 .M113 2022 (print) | LCC F594 (ebook) | DDC
    978/.020922 [B]—dc23/eng/20220222
LC record available at https://lccn.loc.gov/2022006851
LC ebook record available at https://lccn.loc.gov/2022006852

♾™ The paper used in this publication meets the minimum requirements of American
National Standard for Information Sciences—Permanence of Paper for Printed Library
Materials, ANSI/NISO Z39.48-1992.

"My friend, Long Hair [Buffalo Bill Cody] gave me this hat. I value it very highly, for the hand that placed it upon my head had a friendly feeling for me."
—SITTING BULL, HUNKPAPA LAKOTA LEADER, WHEN A PERSON WORE HIS HAT WITHOUT HIS PERMISSION

"Bill and I were the best of friends."
—BUFFALO BILL CODY SPEAKING OF WILD BILL HICKOK AFTER HIS DEATH

CONTENTS

ILLUSTRATIONS LIST

INTRODUCTION

When people hear the names Wild Bill and Buffalo Bill they associate them with the Old West. Wild Bill Hickok and Buffalo Bill Cody were and still are bigger than life characters. They were considered heroes and the greatest plainsmen of their time.

Today, people may know a little about them, a mixture of truth and myth. They might know Wild Bill Hickok was a gunfighter. They might think Calamity Jane and he were lovers. They might have heard Jack McCall shot him in the back of the head in a Deadwood saloon. People might have heard Buffalo Bill rode for the Pony Express and shot enough buffalo to get his nickname. They might know he was a great showman, taking his Wild West exhibition across the country and to Europe. Is all this correct, is it false, or is it a combination of truth and fiction?

Wild Bill and Buffalo Bill were top-notch plainsmen. They knew where to locate water, grass for livestock, sheltered campsites, and game for hunting. They knew how to survive the blistering heat and terrific thunderstorms of summer and the subzero blizzards of winter. They could avoid Indians or act as trackers following the trails of Indians and desperados. They were expert marksmen and didn't back down from a fight. They rushed in when others hesitated. Their stories are complicated and intertwined. They were good friends and had adventures together. James Butler Hickok became known as Wild Bill, and William Frederick Cody became known as Buffalo Bill.

Mention of their names can be confusing, because there were many Wild Bills and Buffalo Bills. It was even hard for the newspapers to keep them all straight. The March 1, 1870 edition of the

Leavenworth Times reported, "Geo. A. Parker of Fort McPherson informs us that it was Joe Lane, and not Buffalo Bill, who was recently killed. William is alive and kicking, and very expert in hunting antelope and buffalo. We believe there is now a 'Buffalo Bill' or a 'Wild Bill' in every county in every Western State and Territory. It is, therefore, easy to kill him, and easy for William to still live."[1]

Just to complicate things, they were both masters of tall tales. Wild Bill had a vivid imagination and was a real leg-puller. Buffalo Bill loved to embellish his stories. Dime novels and so-called true histories encrusted their lives with fictional adventures. When I include stories about them I believe stand on shaky historical ground, I'll let you know.

As I researched both Bills, I grew to like them. They were usually kind and generous to people. They took a man or woman at their word, unless crossed. They certainly weren't perfect, but they stood for what they thought was right.

I have written what I believe is true and correct about Wild Bill and Buffalo Bill, but I may have gotten some things wrong. I may have missed a piece of information, or something new may come to light confirming or disproving what we know now.

By August 1876, Hickok was dead, and that September, Cody's scouting for the Army ended. Cody outlived Hickok by forty years and became one of the greatest showmen the world has ever seen. That story would fill several volumes and can't be covered in this book.

This book compares Wild Bill Hickok and Buffalo Bill Cody's lives side by side; and Jim Hatzell's illustrations visually add to their stories.

So, are you ready? Let's enter the frontier world of Wild Bill Hickok and Buffalo Bill Cody to learn why they were the greatest plainsmen.

CHAPTER 1
EARLY LIFE (1837–1857)

The family of James Butler Hickok, who would become known as Wild Bill, had been in America a long time. Originally from England, the Hickoks arrived in New England in 1635. James's great-grandfather enlisted in the Continental Army and fought in the Revolutionary War. His grandfather fought for the United States and was killed during the War of 1812.[1]

William Hickok, James's father, was born in 1801, on Lake Champlain, at North Hero, Vermont. While studying to be a Presbyterian minister at Vermont's Middlebury College, William met Polly Butler, and they married on June 23, 1829. Polly's father had been one of Ethan Allen's Green Mountain Boys during the Revolution, and she was an aunt to Benjamin Butler, who would become a well-known Civil War general and Radical Republican.[2]

William contracted typhoid fever. He survived but in a weakened condition and with complete amnesia. Giving up the ministry, he opened a store in Broome County, New York. In 1830, Polly and William had their first child, Oliver. The next year, a second son Lorenzo was born, but he did not live long. In 1832, they had another son naming him Lorenzo.[3]

In 1833, the Hickoks moved to Illinois where their son Horace was born in 1834. They lived in several locations, finally settling at

Homer (present-day Troy Grove) in 1836 where William opened a store.[4]

On May 27, 1837, James Butler Hickok was born. His parents named him after Polly's father. William and Polly's joy over James's birth must have been short-lived. That same month, the United States was hit by a financial crisis that sent the country into a depression named the Panic of 1837. Losing their store and home, the Hickoks had just enough funds to buy land north of town and begin farming.[5]

Two more children were added to the Hickok family, Celinda in 1839 and Lydia in 1842. The Hickok children received some education and helped with chores around the farm; free time was spent roaming the woods. James enjoyed reading frontier adventure stories. The children received Christian religious instruction at the local church in Homer and William added to it by telling his children they needed to think for themselves and form their own conclusions.[6]

As James grew older, the boys built and lived in a log cabin separate from their parents. After completing their family obligations, the boys worked for neighboring farmers. James saved his money and, at the age of eight, bought a single-shot flintlock pistol with which he became proficient.[7]

The Hickoks were against slavery. Putting their beliefs into action, they became part of the Underground Railroad network that hid and assisted escaped slaves. The work was dangerous. Local law enforcement officers were obligated to return escaped slaves. Bounty hunters, who tracked down slaves and returned them to their masters, and kidnappers, who captured Blacks and sold them into slavery, were active in the area. As part of the Underground Railroad, the Hickoks hid, cared for, and transported escaped slaves. Alongside the cellar under the Hickok house was a second secret cellar where slaves hid until it was time for them to continue on their journey.[8]

The Hickoks helped hundreds of slaves in their escape to freedom. One woman named Hannah remained with the Hickoks for

Underground Railroad escape

many years.[9]

Bounty hunters and kidnappers would shoot at William and others thought to be transporting escaped slaves. One night, William was driving his wagon along the road. James and Horace sat alongside him on the wagon seat while escaped slaves hid in the wagon bed. A group of men came upon them and fired their weapons to force them to stop. William pushed his sons back into the wagon bed and raced his team of horses down the road. Outdistancing their pursuers, William drove the wagon down a side road, eluding their attackers.[10]

In 1851, Oliver left to make his fortune in California. He had been working for a neighboring farmer named Carr who hired James to take Oliver's place. One day, James and a gang of boys were swimming in a fast-flowing stream on Carr's farm. One of the boys, James Wylie, could not swim. An older boy bullied the younger boys, dunking them under water. The bully pushed Wylie into deep water, and he went under. James jumped in and brought Wylie safely to the streambank. The bully had rapidly left the water and dressed. James grabbed him and threw him into the stream.[11]

James spent his free time in the woods. When he was fourteen years old, he bought a good pistol and purchased a rifle with his father's assistance. Wolves were such a problem that Illinois offered a bounty on them. James shot many wolves collecting the bounties.[12]

William had been in poor health and died on May 5, 1852. James was fifteen years old at the time. Lorenzo, Horace, and James worked the farm, and James supplemented the family food supply by hunting.[13]

The Hickok family bought a house in Homer and moved back to town. James became bored with town life and wanted to follow brother Oliver west, but Lorenzo and Horace convinced him to stay until their mother and sisters were better situated.[14]

In 1854, seventeen-year-old James went to Utica, Illinois, where he was hired as a tow-path driver on the Illinois and Michigan Canal, connecting Lake Michigan to the Mississippi River. Teams of draft horses or mules were hitched to the canal boats and were driven to walk along the side of the canal on a towpath pulling the boats loaded with cargo or passengers.[15]

One day, James caught his boss, Charles Hudson, abusing a team of draft animals. The two of them got into a fistfight. Hudson was larger and more muscular than James, but James stood his ground. The fight went on quite a while. As Hudson and James grappled and fought, they wound up in the canal. The fight ended when Hudson had to be pulled out of the water. James was fired on the spot.[16]

By 1856, nineteen-year-old James had grown into a six-foot-tall, slim, muscular, young man. He was skilled in the use of a gun and knew how to be self-sufficient. He was quiet and self-confident. He believed in freedom and equality for all and was taught to care for the less fortunate. James enjoyed music, playing the fiddle, singing, and whistling; and he loved to dance. He had a vivid imagination, enjoying a good practical joke and pulling

James Hickok's canal fight

someone's leg. His sister Lydia said he enjoyed trying "to scare us to death" with tall tales.[17]

That year, the federal government opened Kansas Territory to settlers, and Lorenzo and James decided to head there to investigate homesteading possibilities. It was a violent time in Kansas. The Kansas-Nebraska Act of 1854 allowed the residents of Kansas and Nebraska Territories to determine whether they would ban slavery or allow it. Confrontations between pro- and antislavery supporters were on the rise.

It was probably June 1856 when Lorenzo and James set off on foot for St. Louis, Missouri, where they planned to seek passage on a westbound Missouri River steamboat. Neighbors were sad to see the brothers leave, especially the McLaughlin sisters, Sarah and Josephine, both of whom may have had romantic interests in James. The brothers walked along the Illinois River and then cut cross-country to St. Louis.[18]

The city was a beehive of activity. The Hickok boys had never seen so many people in one place. Lorenzo did not care for the hustle and bustle. The brothers went to the post office where they found letters from home. The news was not good; their mother was in poor health. Lorenzo decided to return; but James was determined to proceed to Kansas to establish a homestead for the family. Lorenzo gave James the Hickok family money to invest in farmland and headed home while James booked passage on a Missouri River steamboat to Leavenworth, Kansas.[19]

For whatever reason, the Hickok family had given Lorenzo the nickname "Billy Barnes." Some of the men who headed upriver with James had overheard James call Lorenzo "Bill," and they applied the moniker to James calling him "Bill" and "Shanghai Bill." The nickname "Bill" stuck.[20]

It was most likely later in June 1856 when the steamboat reached the landing at Leavenworth.[21] A proslavery mob wouldn't allow any passengers to disembark but did allow the cargo to be unloaded. Pretending to be one of the workmen, James grabbed a load, walked off the boat, and disappeared into the crowd.[22]

James worked as a plowman and at various other jobs. He met John Owens, an abolitionist and early Kansas settler who lived near Monticello on Mill Creek in Johnson County southwest of Kansas City, Missouri. James impressed the residents of Mill Creek with his shooting ability. Using a dragoon revolver, he could hit tin cans at a hundred yards.[23]

Owens introduced young Hickok to James Lane, leader of the Free State Army, an abolitionist militia engaged in violent confrontations with proslavery militias. Hickok won first place in a Free State Army shooting contest and, along with Owens, may have acted as a bodyguard for Lane.[24]

Later in 1857, the freighting firm Russell, Majors & Waddell[25] hired James as a bullwhacker. Things were heating up between the federal government and the Mormons in Utah. The firm had a contract with the US Army to send bull trains hauling wagon loads of supplies to Fort Bridger in Wyoming. Russell, Majors & Waddell also hired an eleven-year-old boy named Billy Cody.[26]

The family of William Frederick Cody, who would become known as Buffalo Bill, had been in America for a long time. Originally from Jersey, one of the English Channel Islands, the Cody ancestors were living in Beverly, Massachusetts, by 1698. William's father, Isaac, was born in Peel County, Upper Canada, in 1811. When Isaac was seventeen, the family moved to a farm near Cleveland, Ohio. In 1834, he married Martha O'Connor, who died after the birth of their daughter Martha in 1835. Isaac married Rebecca Sumner, and she died soon after their marriage.[27]

In 1839, Isaac's older brother Elijah and his family began a journey to Missouri where they planned to settle. Isaac went with them, traveling by boat on the Ohio River. When the Codys stopped in Cincinnati, Isaac met Mary Ann Bonsell Laycock. They were infatuated with each other. After the Codys reached Missouri, Isaac returned to Ohio where he and Mary were married in 1840.[28]

Mary's mother's ancestors were from Derbyshire, England, and by 1690, they had settled in Darby, Pennsylvania.[29] Mary's mother died in 1830. Her father remarried and was lost at sea. When her stepmother remarried, Mary went to Cincinnati to live with her brother. Three years after her arrival, she met Isaac Cody and they married.[30]

Isaac, Mary, and his daughter Martha were soon heading by boat down the Ohio River to the Mississippi River and then up that river to Davenport, Iowa Territory, where Isaac established a business trading with Indians. A year later, he had accumulated enough money to buy a house near LeClaire, Iowa, and at the same time established a homestead claim on property two miles west of town where he built a four-room log house.[31]

Mary and Isaac had a son Samuel born February 22, 1841, followed by daughter Julia Melvina born March 28, 1843. William Frederick was born on February 26, 1846.[32]

In 1847, William Brackenridge, an absentee landowner, hired Isaac Cody to develop a six-hundred-acre farm ten miles northwest of LeClaire. Isaac hired twenty-five men to clear the land, plow and plant crops, quarry stone, and build a ten-room, two-story stone house. Once the house was built, Isaac and his family moved in, and he continued as farm manager.[33]

The fall of that year, Isaac hired Miss Helen Goodrige to teach school for twelve children in a log cabin. Two students were the older Cody children, who took young Willie with them.[34] After finishing chores and schoolwork, Willie enjoyed roaming the fields and woods with the Cody family dog Turk.[35]

Isaac resigned managing Brackenridge's property in 1849, moved the family back to their LeClaire home, and contracted to drive a wagon between Davenport, Iowa, and Chicago, Illinois, hauling mail and passengers. In 1852, Isaac sold his transportation business and went back to work for William Brackenridge managing his property at Walnut Grove on the road from Davenport to Dubuque, Iowa.[36]

Tragedy struck the Codys in September 1853. Twelve-year-old Samuel and seven-year-old Willie were on horseback herding cows. Samuel was mounted on Betsy, a mare who was known for throwing her riders. They were herding the cows down the road in front of the schoolhouse just as school let out. Betsy acted up. Rearing back, she fell on Samuel, crushing him. Willie was sent to get Isaac, who was at a political rally a mile away. Samuel was carried to the closest house, where he lingered through the night and died the next day.[37]

By April 1854, Isaac was ready to move on. He resigned from his Walnut Grove manager job, and the Codys sold their Iowa land. They hired a driver and loaded their belongings and trade goods into two wagons, while Mary and the children rode in a large carriage with three bench seats. The number of children had increased over the years. In addition to Martha, Julia, and William, there was Eliza Alice born in 1848, Laura Ella[38] born in 1850, and Mary Hannah who was six months old.[39]

The Cody family's destination was Weston, Missouri, where Isaac's older brother Elijah lived. Elijah farmed, operated a general store, and exported hemp. Elijah owned slaves to help in his business ventures.[40]

The Cody family headed southwest, Mary and her daughters in the carriage followed by the two wagons hauling their goods. Willie rode a pony with Turk tagging alongside. The trip was pleasant and took about a month. Instead of camping at night, they stayed in hotels or private homes. When they crossed into Missouri, a slave state, it was the first time the children had seen Black or enslaved people. When they reached Weston, Elijah gave them the use of a vacant house on his farm.[41]

The Cody brothers knew Congress was working to organize the territory directly west of the Missouri River into Kansas Territory and Nebraska Territory. The territories would then be open for settlement. Elijah knew it was good land. He and his wife planned to visit and trade with the Potawatomi Indians eighty miles to the west and invited Isaac and Mary along. They took Willie with them.[42]

After being ferried across the Missouri River, the Codys stopped at Fort Leavenworth. Built in 1827, it was one of a series of forts ranging north to south established to protect settlers on the frontier and to keep Indian tribes from attacking each other. An additional mission for the troops stationed at the fort was to provide protection for commerce on the Santa Fe Trail.[43]

While at Fort Leavenworth, Willie saw covered wagons heading west as well as infantry, artillery, and mounted dragoons conducting drills.[44] Frontier characters fascinated him, especially members of the Kickapoo, Potawatomi, Delaware, Choctaw, and other tribes. Isaac and Mary viewed the land along Salt Creek as good and selected where they wanted to live once the territory was open for settlement.[45]

The Codys continued westward to the Potawatomi reservation. While his uncle and father traded with the Potawatomis, the Indians allowed Willie to ride their ponies. Isaac traded for a little four-year-old pony for Willie. Willie named him Prince. The pony was untrained, and Isaac told Willie it was his responsibility to train him. Prince repeatedly bucked off Willie, but he always climbed back on.[46]

On their return to Weston, Isaac and Elijah stopped at Fort Leavenworth where they met with the quartermaster. Isaac made a deal with the quartermaster that he would provide hay for the fort in exchange for allowing him to pasture his horses in the Salt Creek Valley and build a cabin there. The location, which would become the Cody homestead was three miles west of Fort Leavenworth on the south side of the Oregon and Mormon wagon road in what would become Kickapoo Township in Leavenworth County.[47]

Willie remained behind with Isaac in the Salt Creek Valley while the rest of the Codys returned to Weston. There, Isaac and Willie chanced to meet Horace Billings, a nephew of Isaac. Horace was helping drive a horse herd east after having spent time in California and Hawaii. He had many adventurous experiences, including riding in a circus. During his brief stay with the Codys, Horace helped Willie with Prince's training and taught Prince to kneel and other tricks. Horace gave Willie riding instructions and showed off his circus skills such as standing on top of a running horse.[48]

On May 30, 1854, President Franklin Pierce signed the Kansas-Nebraska Act into law, splitting the unorganized territory into Kansas Territory and Nebraska Territory and opening the land for settlement. Isaac learned about it on June 10, and after surveying his Salt Creek property, filed a claim. He hired workmen to help build a seven-room log house that the family would live in and rent out rooms.[49]

One of the provisions of the Kansas-Nebraska Act was that residents of the two territories could determine if they were a free territory or a slave territory. Many people assumed Isaac was pro-slavery since his brother Elijah was a slaveowner, but Isaac was not, and when asked, he stated his opposition to it. Those who opposed slavery were called abolitionists and also free soilers. Those who were proslavery would later be called border ruffians, since many of them were from Missouri and crossed the border to support slavery. Additional settlers flocked into the Salt Creek Valley, many of them proslavery.[50]

The same day Isaac learned he could file a claim on his land, proslavery residents drafted and signed the Salt Creek Valley Resolutions. Two of the provisions were: "That we recognize the institution of slavery as always existing in this Territory and recommend that slaveholders introduce their property as soon as possible," and "That we afford protection to no Abolitionists as settlers of Kansas Territory."[51]

Isaac Cody and his family went about their business developing their farmland and cutting hay and firewood to sell to Fort Leavenworth. Willie played with neighboring Kickapoo children, learning their language. The freighting company of Russell & Majors had won an Army contract to haul supplies to the western forts and established its headquarters at Fort Leavenworth. Willie was fascinated with the freight wagons drawn by six yoke of oxen and the men involved with freighting—wagon masters, bullwhackers, and others. By the end of 1854, Willie knew them all.[52]

M. Pierce Rively had a store in Salt Creek Valley where he traded with the Kickapoos, Delawares, and Cherokees. Reverend Joel Grover was a missionary to those tribes. Rively, Grover, and Isaac Cody threw a Fourth of July barbecue for whites and Indians alike. Over two hundred Indian men, women, and children attended. The feast included two roasted beeves and a wagonload of food. The whites gave patriotic speeches and the Indians danced. Together, they played games and competed in horse races. Life was good for Isaac Cody and his family.[53]

On September 18, 1854, a settlers' meeting was being held at Rively's store. Isaac was riding by when he was called to make a speech.[54] At first, he declined, but the crowd insisted, so he stood on top of a large box and spoke. He told them he was against slavery in Kansas. He had no problem with slavery existing where it was currently in place but said, "I shall always oppose its further extension."[55]

The crowd turned ugly, shouting him down as men tried to drag him off the box. When Isaac continued to speak, Charles Dunn stabbed him with a Bowie knife twice in the chest. Before Dunn could do more damage, cooler heads restrained him. Dunn was an employee of Elijah Cody.[56]

Isaac was carried inside Rively's store. They discovered one of his lungs was punctured. It was agreed Isaac should be taken to his brother's home in Weston where he could receive better treatment. A message was sent to Mary, who arrived with a wagon and driver. They drove Isaac to Elijah's house where he was cared for over the next three weeks. When Elijah learned of Dunn's attack on Isaac, he fired Dunn.[57]

Isaac never fully recovered. His daughter Julia wrote, "[He] was never strong from that day, just able to get around; had to ride as he could not walk any distance."[58]

Cody's 1879 autobiography would make no mention of him being at Rively's store when his father was stabbed. Julia wrote Willie was at home when it happened, vowing to kill the bad man when he grew up. In later writings, his sister Helen said Willie was at the store when their father was attacked, and an embellished version of that appeared in revised editions of Cody's autobiography.[59]

The September 28, 1854 edition of Liberty, Missouri's *Democratic Platform* stated, "A Mr. Cody, a noisy abolitionist, living near Salt Creek, in Kansas Territory, was severely stabbed, while in a dispute about a claim with Mr. Dunn, on Monday week last. Cody is severely hurt, but not enough it is feared to cause his death. The settlers on Salt Creek regret that his wound is not more dangerous, and all sustain Mr. Dunn in the course he took."[60]

The Cody family's troubles did not end with Isaac's stabbing. Proslavery thieves drove off Isaac's horse herd including Prince. Isaac and his farm laborers had made several hundred tons of hay to supply Fort Leavenworth at $15 per ton; vandals set fire to the haystacks.[61]

Undaunted, Isaac joined four other men to establish the town of Grasshopper Falls, today known as Valley Falls, thirty miles west of the Cody homestead. The five men organized a company and staked their claims on December 25, 1854. By the spring of 1855, they had built a sawmill and a gristmill, and six families had settled there.[62]

Isaac hired Miss Jennie Lyons to teach school in the original cabin on the Cody property. Twelve children, mostly from the Cody family, attended the school. Two Kickapoo boys were pupils and became good friends with Willie. The school lasted only three months. Salt Creek Valley Squatters Association members paid Miss Lyons a visit and told her they would not allow an abolitionist to have a school. They said the next time they returned they would burn down the school no matter if the students were inside or not. Miss Lyons resigned.[63]

On May 10, 1855, the last of the Cody children, Charles Whitney Cody, was born. Unfortunately, he would die at age nine on October 10, 1864.[64]

Politics continued to heat up in Kansas. Isaac continued to advocate the free-soil position while many of his neighbors joined the proslavery militia called the Kickapoo Rangers.[65]

The free-soil residents of Kansas had had enough with the proslavery territorial government. In October 1855, they held a convention in Topeka, drew up a new territorial constitution, and held elections. By January 1856, Kansas had two governments, one proslavery and the other free soil. The federal government continued to recognize the already existing proslavery territorial government and did not recognize the new free-soil government. Both sides made sure they were well armed.[66]

On December 22, 1855, while Abraham Lincoln's friend and free-state editor of Leavenworth's *Kansas Territorial Register*, Mark William Delahay, was at the Topeka convention, Kickapoo Rangers ransacked his office and tossed his press and type into the

Missouri River, ending his newspaper. Later, during the free-soil elections, the Kickapoo Rangers caught free-soil legislative candidate and militia captain Reese Brown and hacked him to death with hatchets.[67]

Isaac Cody was involved in the free-soil convention and was elected to the Topeka legislature, attending the March 4–15, 1856 session. The legislature attempted to meet again that July, but federal troops prevented it.[68]

Isaac's time away from the legislature was spent developing Grasshopper Falls or at his Salt Creek Valley homestead. One evening, when Isaac was home upstairs sick in bed, a proslavery judge named Sharpe rode up to the house on Prince and demanded a meal. As Sharpe sat in a chair awaiting his meal, he sharpened his knife, asking where Isaac was. Mary Cody replied that her husband was at Grasshopper Falls and from there would travel to Topeka. Sharpe declared he would kill Isaac. Mary sent the children upstairs to Isaac's bedroom. Isaac quietly told Willie to get his gun and Julia to take an ax. If Sharpe came up the stairs, Willie was to shoot him, and Julia was to whack him with the ax. Fortunately, when Sharpe finished his meal, he left, stealing Isaac's saddlebags. Julia claimed the next day that Prince had come racing into the yard, and that he must have slipped his halter and come home. Willie was ecstatic his pony was back.[69]

There were many Cody family stories about close calls with proslavery gangs.[70] One night, Isaac had to disguise himself in Mary's clothes, leave the house, and hide in the cornfield while proslavery horsemen surrounded their home and searched for him. Another time, Isaac was at Grasshopper Falls. One of the hired hands at the homestead told Mary he learned proslavery men planned to ride to Grasshopper Falls and murder Isaac. Mary told Willie to go warn his father. Mounted on Prince, Willie came upon the proslavery men camped at Stranger Creek. They recognized him as Isaac's son and several gave chase. Prince outdistanced the pursuers and Willie had plenty of time to warn his father. They left for Fort Leavenworth that night, arriving without incident. Isaac left for Ohio to recruit immigrants, and Willie rode home with two men. Along the way, unknown assailants shot at them.[71]

Isaac spent more time away from home working on establishing and promoting Grasshopper Falls while his family managed the Salt Creek Valley farm. After finishing his chores, Willie and his two Kickapoo friends practiced their marksmanship shooting at targets.[72]

During the winter of 1857, Isaac was back east recruiting settlers for Grasshopper Falls. Many families stopped and camped at the Cody farm on their way to the new town. In March, Isaac returned home. Scarlet fever and measles broke out among the visitors and four children died. Isaac was assisting the immigrants during a rainstorm when he caught a severe cold that developed into pneumonia. On March 10, 1857, Isaac died; the family was devastated. They believed his death was the result of the knife wound he had received three years earlier.[73]

Isaac's older brother Joseph arrived from Cleveland to manage the Grasshopper Falls property for the family. Mary dismissed the farmhands to cut costs, rented the farm, and went to court over a $1,000 debt the family had already paid. She won the case.[74] Writing later about his father's death, Cody said, "This sad event left my mother and the family in poor circumstances, and I determined to follow the plains for a livelihood for them and for myself."[75]

Now eleven years old and being the oldest male in the family, Willie wanted to be called Bill. The family wouldn't do that but started calling him Billy.[76]

Billy found a job driving an ox team to Leavenworth and back for fifty cents a day. However, he really wanted to work for the freighting firm Russell & Majors. The next time he and his mother were in its Leavenworth store, he had her ask Alexander Majors if they had a job for him. After Majors conferred with William Russell, they gave Billy a job as express boy delivering messages from their store in Leavenworth to the telegraph station at Fort Leavenworth and back, a one-way distance of three miles. He occasionally carried messages back and forth between nearby bull trains. As well as being paid $25 per month, he was provided meals, a room to sleep in, and a mule to ride.[77]

All of Billy's pay went to his mother. Majors later wrote, "One of the strongest characteristics of Buffalo Bill, to my mind, was his love for his mother—a mother most worthy the devotion of such a son. His love and devotion to his sisters has also been marked throughout his lifetime."[78]

Billy worked as an express boy for two months before becoming bored with it. One of Russell & Majors's wagon masters, John Willis, told Billy he could assist in caring for his oxen resting between trips to the western forts and back. Billy asked Majors and Russell if he could change jobs, and they agreed. The oxen's pasturage was eight miles from the Cody homestead, so Billy was able to visit his mother and siblings frequently. The job was temporary and when it was over, he returned home.[79]

Early in the summer of 1857, school began again in the cabin on the Cody property. Mary Cody discovered one of her boarders had been a teacher, so she hired him at $2 per pupil per month. She found fifteen to eighteen students, including eleven-year-old Billy and the rest of her children, to attend the school.[80]

Billy was infatuated with fellow student Mary Hyatt. One way a boy showed interest in a girl was to build a playhouse or arbor for her. During the morning recess, Billy built a playhouse for Mary, but an older boy, Stephen Gobel, tore it down. The two boys fought, and Stephen beat Billy. The teacher heard about the fight and whipped them both. Billy rebuilt the playhouse for Mary during the afternoon recess. Stephen again destroyed it as he teased Billy. The next morning Billy began to rebuild the playhouse when Stephen knocked it over. The boys fought. Stephen had Billy pinned to the ground and was beating him. Billy whipped out a boot knife and cut Stephen on the thigh. As Stephen shouted he was killed, the teacher and other children ran toward the boys. Billy raced away to John Willis's bull train camp. After Billy told Willis his story, Willis said he could hide out with him until things died down.[81]

That afternoon, Stephen's father and a constable, along with Stephen and his older brother, arrived at the bull train camp. Billy saw them coming and hid in a wagon. The constable and the Gobels wanted to search the wagons for Billy, but Willis stopped them, asking the constable if he had a warrant for Billy's arrest. He did not. Willis tried to convince them it was nothing more than a little playful spat. The Gobels and constable gave up and left.[82]

Willis took Billy home and suggested to Mary that Billy go with him to Fort Kearny and back, which would take forty days. Willis said by the time they returned, the excitement over Billy stabbing Stephen Gobel should have died down. Mary reluctantly agreed and packed clothes and a quilt for Billy. He kissed his mother and sisters goodbye and headed west with the bull train.[83]

Located in Pawnee territory along the Platte River in central Nebraska, Fort Kearny was a major way station on the Oregon Trail. Thousands of travelers passed through Fort Kearny on their way to Oregon, California, and Utah. As travelers approached the fort, the first thing they saw in the distance was the fort's American flag flying from a very tall flagpole.[84]

Billy enjoyed the bull train experience, and on at least one occasion, Willis took him along on a buffalo hunt.[85] The trip was uneventful except for one mishap. The bull train was approaching a herd of roughly five hundred buffalo grazing between the road and the river. A party returning from California approached the herd from the opposite direction and raced into it, stampeding the buffalo into Willis's bull train. Some frightened oxen tried to run away. Others became entangled in their wagon chains. All were wild, and Billy joined with the men to calm the oxen and return order. Later in life, Willis wrote a letter to Cody saying, "of course you recolect [sic] the time the Buffalo run through the train and stampeded the teams and you stoped [sic] the stampede."[86]

Tensions escalated between the federal government in Washington, DC, and members of the Church of Jesus Christ of Latter-Day Saints, called Mormons, who lived in Utah Territory. In March 1857, newly elected President James Buchanan replaced the territorial governor, Brigham Young, with a non-Mormon, Alfred Cummings, as well as appointing other non-Mormons to territorial government positions. Young, also the president of the Mormon Church, refused to step down. Buchanan ordered 2,500 troops under the command of Colonel Albert Sidney Johnston to escort the officials to Salt Lake City, Utah, and ensure they took their positions.[87]

Mid-July, the Army began sending units from Fort Leavenworth to its western forts along the Oregon and Mormon Trail. On September 17, 1857, Johnston along with six companies of the Second Dragoons began escorting Governor Cummings and other territorial officials to Salt Lake City. However, Brigham Young had no intention of surrendering his position. He called up the Utah militia instructing them to do everything they could to harass the US Army; however, he said, "take no life."[88]

The freighting firm, now Russell, Majors & Waddell, continued to have the contract to supply the US Army including not only hauling the supplies but procuring them as well. This was the Army's largest military operation since the Mexican War. Russell, Majors & Waddell put hundreds of wagons and ox teams into hauling the supplies, and it still wasn't enough so additional companies were hired to help.[89]

Russell, Majors & Waddell also had the contract to provide beef for the army. Two of its employees, Frank and Bill McCarthy, were in charge of taking one of the cattle herds west to follow the Army along the Oregon Mormon Trail. When Billy returned from Fort Kearny, he must have gone straight to Alexander Majors asking to be hired for the cattle drive.[90]

Majors was reluctant, but when Billy reminded him he could ride as good as any man, he won over Majors. Majors hired Billy at $40 a month plus food and would pay the money direct to Billy's mother.[91]

Majors gave Billy a Bible and had him sign the oath all the firm's employees signed:

*We, the undersigned wagon-masters, assistants, teamsters and
all other employees of the firm Russell, Majors & Waddell, do
hereby sign that we will not swear, drink whisky, play cards or
be cruel to dumb beasts in any way, shape or form.*[92]

The cattle drive proceeded without incident until they reached
Plum Creek on the South Platte River, thirty-six miles west of
Fort Kearny. They stopped at noon to allow the cattle to drink and
graze under the watch of two herders while the remainder of the
outfit rested.[93]

Shots rang out. The herders were killed as Indians swooped
in, stampeding the herd. Bill McCarthy ordered everyone to run
to the Platte River and hunker down behind its bank. The Indians let up their attack and concentrated their attention on the
herd. McCarthy led the men downriver toward Fort Kearny. They
walked and waded along the riverbed, not wanting to climb up
on the bank and expose themselves. At times the water was waist
high on young Billy. They did not stop their journey, continuing
through the moonlit night. Billy, struggling along as he carried an
old Mississippi Yaeger muzzleloader, fell behind the men.[94]

Cody later recounted that as he looked ahead, he saw an
Indian on top of a thirty-five-foot bank preparing to fire down
on the men. He aimed his Yaeger and fired, hitting the Indian
who fell dead into the river. The men were impressed with Billy's
marksmanship, but they needed to press on in case more Indians
were in the area.[95]

It was daybreak when they reached Fort Kearny. Soldiers were
sent to recover the cattle and bring back the bodies of the slain
herders. They found no cattle. An eastbound bull train took the
herders and Billy back to Leavenworth.[96]

Russell, Majors & Waddell needed every experienced hand
they could get to haul supplies west to the Army's staging area for
its advance on Salt Lake City. That staging area was Fort Bridger
in Wyoming. Russell, Majors & Waddell wagon master Lew
Simpson must have heard Billy was a good hand, and Billy must

have heard Simpson wanted him. William Russell asked Mary Cody if eleven-year-old Billy could sign on to Simpson's bull train to Fort Bridger. Mary had heard Simpson was a hard man, and it seemed he killed a man on every trip west. Russell assured Mary the rumors were exaggerated; Simpson was one of his best men. Mary met with Simpson and Russell and after getting Simpson to promise he would protect Billy, Mary consented to let him go. Billy's job would be to help care for the horse herd.[97]

It was most likely late summer 1857 when Simpson's twenty-five freight wagons, each pulled by a team of six oxen, headed west on the Oregon Mormon Trail. One of the teamsters was James Hickok.[98]

CHAPTER 2

THE UTAH WAR (1857–1860)

In the fall of 1857, both twenty-year-old James Hickok and eleven-year-old Billy Cody were working for Russell, Majors & Waddell on a bull train headed for Fort Bridger along the Oregon Mormon Trail. The bull train consisted of twenty-five freight wagons each pulled by six oxen. They were hauling supplies for the US Army that was preparing to march on Salt Lake City. There had been little trouble on the trail, and they had no idea that there might be danger.

As Cody later recounted, one of the teamsters had been bullying him. At dinner one day, Billy was sitting with others around the campfire. The bully told Billy to do something for him, but he was slow in reacting. The man slapped Billy with the back of his hand, knocking him off an ox yoke on which he sat. Billy jumped to his feet, grabbed a kettle of boiling coffee, and threw it at the bully's face, scalding him. As the man charged Billy, James Hickok stepped between them and knocked the man to the ground. The bully said to Hickok what right he thought he had to get involved. "It's my business to protect that boy, or anybody else, from being unmercifully abused, kicked, and cuffed," Hickok replied. "And if you ever again lay a hand on that boy—little Billy there—I'll give you such a pounding that you won't get over it for a month of Sundays." Cody later said, "From that time forward Wild Bill was my protector and intimate friend."[1]

On October 5, 1857, Lew Simpson's wagon train was traveling along Big Sandy Creek heading westward toward the Green River when it stopped for a noon rest near present-day Farson, Wyoming. Believing they were in no danger, Simpson and his men were taken by surprise by twenty-four armed members of the Utah militia, known as the Mormon Nauvoo Legion, led by Major Lot Smith.[2]

Smith told Simpson they planned to burn the wagons and everything in them. "Well you have got the advantage of me," Simpson said. "I guess you will have to burn them."

"There is your guns," Smith challenged, "stacked at the head of the corral, you can take them and we will try for it."

Simpson didn't believe the wagons were worth dying over. Instead of fighting, he asked Smith to let them keep one wagon and team of oxen along with clothing, food, blankets, and guns. Smith agreed but would not allow them to keep their guns and told them to start marching east back the way they had come. The Mormon militiamen took what they wanted from the wagons, set them on fire, and left, herding the livestock with them.[3]

As Simpson's men trekked back along the thousand miles of trail to Leavenworth, they were able to trade with a few other travelers for guns. Fortunately, the Indians left them alone. A month later, they arrived at Leavenworth.[4]

James Hickok returned to Monticello, Kansas, where he filed a claim for 160 acres of land. He began improving it for farmland and built a cabin. Elections were held for Monticello township offices, and on March 22, 1858, James was elected one of four township constables. Based on letters he sent to his family, he was doing well at farming and supplemented his food supply by hunting. On occasion, he acted in his capacity of constable, mentioning in one letter that he had been on official business and in another that he received a summons about twenty-five horses stolen by two men—one with the last name of Scroggins and the other called Black Bob.[5]

James's mother, Polly, became concerned about her son. She must have heard reports about James's drinking and gambling. On August 14, 1858, he wrote to one of his brothers that their mother had mentioned her concern. Not the greatest speller, he wrote, "I have not drunk a pint of liquar in a year and have not played for a sent [cent] in twice that time[,] the first time I go to Lawrence I will send you my likeness and you can see whether it looks like a whisky face or not."[6]

James's love life blossomed. John Owens had married a Shawnee woman named Patinuxa. They had one child—a beautiful, intelligent daughter named Mary Jane. James and Mary Jane became infatuated with each other.[7] James raved to the homefolks about Mary Jane's cooking, saying her biscuits beat his mother's. In an August 23 letter home, he mentioned how Mary Jane was always combing and curling his hair and she had cut a lock for them.[8]

While James was away from his cabin, proslavery men burned it to the ground. He rebuilt the cabin, and while called away pursuing his constable duties, proslavery men set fire to it again. The Hickok family became concerned about James and sent Lorenzo to check on him. He arrived at James's homestead soon after the second fire. James must have realized after his cabin was burned down again that the future was bleak in Johnson County. The two brothers left for Leavenworth at the end of 1858. As for Mary Jane Owens, James never mentioned her again.[9]

The Hickok brothers found jobs in Leavenworth. Lorenzo worked as a teamster, and James got a job again with Russell, Majors & Waddell hauling freight.[10]

During the summer of 1859, James and Lorenzo were home in Illinois, helping on the family farm. Charles Gross remembered working with James harvesting wheat. He said James was a good strong worker. He was also good at games: pitching horseshoes, running footraces, jumping, and wrestling. By autumn 1859 through the winter of 1860, James was back in Leavenworth, occasionally boarding with the Codys in their hotel they called the Big House.[11]

In 1858, gold had been discovered along the Front Range of the Rocky Mountains in what is present-day Colorado. In the spring of 1859, prospectors found bonanza loads in the Clear Creek area. Small settlements such as Denver boomed as prospectors and business interests rushed in to make their fortunes.[12] With the influx of people into the mining camps, old trails were expanded into wagon roads, and new roads were developed to bring in people and goods.

In February 1859, Russell, Majors & Waddell was in rough financial shape. It had lost half a million dollars during the Utah War when the Mormons stole their cattle herd and burned their wagons and freight intended for the US Army. The federal government had yet to compensate the company. To make matters worse, the firm owed a million dollars to creditors. This did not stop William Russell from organizing a new stagecoach company to transport passengers between Leavenworth and Denver. He placed an order for fifty-two Concord stagecoaches and began planning the establishment of relay stations along the routes to change out draft animals. At some locations, meals and lodgings would be provided to travelers. His investors soon included Alexander Majors and William Waddell. The new company became closely tied with Russell, Majors & Waddell and was named the Leavenworth & Pike's Peak Express Company. Most folks called it the Overland Stage Company.[13]

During the end of 1859 and into 1860, James continued to work for Russell, Majors & Waddell hauling freight to western forts and towns as far away as Santa Fe, New Mexico Territory where he might have met Kit Carson. In addition, he began driving stagecoaches for the Overland Stage Company.[14]

It was probably in November 1857 when Billy Cody, returning from his western trip, approached the family homestead and whistled. The old family dog Turk bounded out to greet him, followed by his mother and three sisters overjoyed at his return. However, they did not allow him in the house until his matted, bug-infested hair was cut. He then stripped off his dirty clothes and took a bath outside. After putting on clean clothes, he was allowed in the house where he was given a good home-cooked meal.[15]

Billy spent the winter of 1857–1858 attending school, but his heart wasn't in it. He later wrote, "My mother was anxious about my education. But the master of the frontier school wore out several armfuls of switches in a vain effort to interest me in the 'three R's.'"[16]

In the spring of 1858, the US Army was preparing to continue its march on Salt Lake City. General William Harney would be leading reinforcements to Utah and additional supplies were needed. Russell, Majors & Waddell still held the Army's supply contract. Harney wanted eight months of supplies stockpiled at Fort Laramie. That meant three thousand tons of supplies would need to be hauled. Russell, Majors & Waddell hired four thousand men and acquired thousands of wagons and teams of oxen and mules.[17]

Billy was eager to head west again, and wagon master Lew Simpson hired him on as part of his bull train. This time, Billy had a horse to ride part of the time, and he also took a turn at bullwhacking. Cody later said that wagon masters Lew Simpson and Tom Stewart entered into a little friendly competition. Simpson believed a proper team of young, healthy oxen could beat a team of mules over the long haul, and Stewart accepted the challenge. Simpson's oxen train left a week before Stewart's mule train. The goal was to see whose train would reach the north fork of the Platte River first. Stewart said he'd catch Simpson in a few days.[18]

Billy was happy to be back on the plains. Simpson's handpicked oxen were making about twenty-five miles a day. On average oxen usually covered about fifteen miles a day. After Simpson's bull train had traveled 150 miles, one of his men looked behind and shouted, "Here come the mules!"[19]

Stewart's muleskinners were happy and excited as they passed the bullwhackers and their lumbering oxen, leaving them in their dust. However, three hundred miles later, Simpson's train came upon Stewart's, which was having a hard time crossing the Platte River. The mules were weakening while the oxen were maintaining their strength. The oxen crossed the river with less effort, but the mules soon overtook them again.[20]

The oxen continued to pull at their steady pace as the mules began to weaken. The oxen overtook and passed the mules, reaching the north fork of the Platte River first.[21]

Arriving at Fort Laramie, they unloaded their freight. Simpson was told his teams and wagons were needed to haul supplies to Fort Walbach being constructed eighty miles to the south. The wagon beds were removed and stockpiled at the fort so building material could be hauled to the building site. Billy was left behind at Fort Laramie to guard the wagon boxes.[22]

Fort Laramie was a wonderful place for a twelve-year-old boy. Not only was it bustling with soldiers and teamsters preparing for action in Utah, but it was a major stop for emigrants on the Oregon Mormon Trail and a gathering point for Indian tribes. Billy saw thousands of Lakotas, Northern Cheyennes, and Northern Arapahos camped nearby. Trappers and traders arrived at the fort. Billy claimed he saw Kit Carson, Jim Bridger, and other legendary trappers and traders. He might have seen Jim Bridger, but Kit Carson was in New Mexico. It's possible some old duffer passed himself off as Carson to the impressionable boy.[23]

Billy saw the Indians talk with each other and the frontiersmen using sign language. He was fascinated with it and put in the time and effort to learn it, more so than he did while in school. The wagon boxes Billy guarded were natural attractions to Indian children, who wanted to play in them. Billy made friends with them as they played, and they taught Billy their games and "a fair working knowledge" of the Lakota language.[24]

President Buchanan had sent Colonel Thomas Kane to negotiate with Brigham Young. Kane was sympathetic to the Mormons and traveled back and forth between the US troops at Fort Bridger and Young at Salt Lake City. Eventually both the newly appointed governor Alfred Cumming and Brigham Young came to an agreement that Young and the Mormons would be pardoned and US troops would not attack if the Mormons accepted Cumming as governor and allowed the establishment of a US military post forty miles southwest of Salt Lake City. The agreement was formalized, and on June 26, 1858, Colonel Johnston and his troops peacefully marched into Salt Lake City, effectively ending the Utah War.[25]

Cody's various accounts of his return to Leavenworth are jumbled and exaggerated with confusing dates. This is how it may have occurred. In January 1859, Lew Simpson supervised the return of three bull trains to Leavenworth, and Billy accompanied one of them. The trains were spaced well apart on their return along the Platte River. One morning, Simpson was with the middle bull train and planned to ride forward to check on the lead train. He took George Woods and Billy with him. They were out on the exposed prairie when Lakota warriors raced toward them. With nowhere to make a stand, Simpson had the three of them dismount, stand their mules in a triangle formation, and shoot them in the head. They lay down behind the mules' carcasses and held off the warriors until the second bull train reached them.[26]

As the bull trains came within a few days' travel of Leavenworth, Simpson sent two men and Billy ahead with the record books that included each man's time worked. He wanted to have their pay waiting for them when they reached Leavenworth. Before they left, he told them to travel only at night and to hide during the day.[27]

One night, a blizzard set in and the threesome took shelter in a deep ravine. Either being chased by a war party for two hours, or, more mundane, spotting Indian ponies farther down the ravine, the two men and boy led their mounts up to the head of the ravine that ended in a cave-like hollow. They entered and upon striking a match, they discovered they were surrounded by eight to ten human skeletons. They quickly got out of there, not caring about the blizzard or the Indians. In one account, Cody said the bones were Indians, and in another account, he said they were "murdered emigrants."[28]

Billy reached Leavenworth in February 1859, without further incident, received his pay, and had a joyful reunion with his mother, sisters, and little brother.[29] Billy's joy turned to sorrow when he learned his beloved, older, half-sister Martha had died in November 1858. She had married John Crane on February 7, 1858. After their marriage, Martha discovered John was a bigamist. The Codys believed she died of grief.[30]

Mary Cody sent Billy back to school, his teacher being Valentine Divinny. Billy lasted two and a half months, later writing, "the longest period of schooling that I ever received at any one time in my life."[31]

In the spring of 1859, the Rocky Mountain Gold Rush was in full swing. Billy, along with other residents in the Leavenworth area, caught gold fever. Mary allowed him to join a party heading to the goldfields. They traveled across the plains and prospected for gold at Black Hawk on North Clear Creek. After two months of fruitless digging, they decided to head home.[32]

Billy and his friends built a raft and floated down the South Platte. After several days on the river, they wrecked, losing their supplies near the Overland Stage Company's newly established Julesburg way station.[33]

Cody later claimed the station agent, George Chrisman, hired him to be a Pony Express rider. However, that could not have been the case since the Pony Express did not yet exist. Possibly Chrisman hired him to act as a messenger between way stations and company wagon trains. Cody said he rode for Chrisman for two months before receiving a letter saying his mother was sick and he needed to come home.[34]

A bull train was heading to Auraria, just west of Denver. The wagon master knew Billy and hired him on with the promise that after they delivered their freight to Auraria, he could return with them to Leavenworth. This happened without incident.[35]

During the summer of 1859, Mary Cody sold forty acres and used the money to have a hotel built along the road on the Cody property. Julia, now sixteen years old, quit school and helped her mother run the hotel. Mary's medical bills and hotel expenses were depleting the Cody family funds.[36]

On August 26, 1859, Mary Cody wrote a letter to an Iowa friend Laurel Summers. Mary updated Laurel on her situation and provided news on her family writing:

> *Willie is one of the smartest and best of boys, he has always been a great comfort to me, and I hope he is to be distinguished yet. He is decidedly the brightest of the family.*[37]

By the fall of 1859, the Codys had moved into their new hotel they called the Big House and provided room and board to guests who included some of Billy's acquaintances: Lew Simpson, John Willis, and James Hickok. The Cody women were impressed with James. According to Julia, James liked her so much that he asked her to marry him. She consulted with Billy who told her Hickok was his best friend, but he would never settle down and "trying to housebreak him would be harder than saddling a grizzly bear." Julia turned down James's offer.[38]

Twenty-three-year-old family friend and veteran trapper, Dave Harrington, invited Billy to go with him to trap for furs along the Republican River to the west. Mary Cody, who seems to have always allowed Billy to go on any trip where he could make money, gave her permission. Sister Julia not only carried on flirtations with James Hickok, but also Dave Harrington. Nothing came of this relationship either.[39]

Harrington and Billy bought a wagon, a yoke of oxen, supplies, and traps. They headed west on the Smoky Hill Trail until they reached the small settlement of Junction City. From there they turned northwest taking the Overland Stage Company's new wagon road, the Leavenworth & Pike's Peak Route, that roughly followed the Republican River. They slowly worked their way upriver trapping and hunting for furs.[40]

When they reached where Prairie Dog Creek enters the Republican River, one of their oxen slipped on ice, dislocating a hip, and Harrington had to shoot him.[41] They found plenty of beavers in the area and decided to establish their camp there, building a dugout to live in and setting their traps.[42]

One day they spotted a herd of elk. Trying to sneak close to the animals to get a shot, Billy was maneuvering around a sharp bluff along a creek when he slipped, fell, and broke his leg just above the ankle. Harrington laughed when Billy said to shoot him just as he had shot the ox. He carried Billy back to the dugout where he set the break.[43]

Billy and Harrington discussed their situation. They decided Harrington would return to the nearest settlement about 125 miles away to rent a yoke of oxen and return to their dugout. They would load their furs and pelts into the wagon along with all their supplies and then return to Leavenworth where Billy could get better care for his leg. Dave figured it would take him about twenty days to make the round trip. He gathered a supply of firewood to last Billy while he was gone. There was snow on the ground so he could melt that for drinking water. They had plenty of meat and other food supplies so Billy would not starve. Harrington immediately started out on foot.[44]

Billy kept track of the days that seemed to drag. On the twelfth day things picked up. Billy was asleep when he felt a hand on his shoulder. Opening his eyes, he saw a painted Indian warrior standing over him. The man spoke to Billy in a mixture of Lakota and English, asking what he was doing there and how many others were with him. As they spoke, more warriors entered the dugout. There were others outside, but the space was not large enough for all of them. An older Lakota entered and Billy recognized him. He thought he was the chief Rain-in-the-Face.[45]

However, the man could not have been Rain-in-the-Face, who was born about 1851. At this time, he would have been only eight years old.[46] Rain-in-the-Face was a Hunkpapa Lakota. The Hunkpapas were the northernmost Lakotas and did not usually range that far south.[47]

The older man, whoever he was, was the leader of the war party. He knew Billy from his time at Fort Laramie. Billy had played with his children and spent time in his lodge. Billy explained he had broken his leg and his partner had left to get a yoke of oxen to take him away. Billy asked if they were going to kill him. The leader said that was what some of the younger men wanted to do. After the leader conferred with the warriors, they decided to let Billy live since he was still a boy.[48]

The warriors remained the rest of the day, cooking and eating his food. They fed Billy and stayed the night. Leaving early the next morning, they took his weapons, some food, and a few cooking utensils. However, they left the beaver pelts and furs as well as Harrington and Billy's traps.[49]

During the following days, a blizzard raged, and prowling wolves made the nights uncomfortable. Billy had a difficult time getting to the firewood pile, and he was running low on food. By day twenty, the day of Harrington's estimated return, there was no sign of him.[50]

On day twenty-nine, Billy heard Dave Harrington's voice as he brought his oxen up Prairie Dog Creek. Billy was never so happy to see anyone in his whole life. Harrington had been caught in the blizzard for three days. The oxen had wandered away, but he was able to find them. They had to break through deep snow to reach Billy.[51]

Dave loaded the wagon with three hundred beaver pelts along with other furs, their traps, and equipment, and then made Billy comfortable in the wagon bed. It took them eight days to reach a settler's cabin on the Republican River where they rested two days. From there, they continued to the homestead where Harrington had rented the oxen. The owner allowed them to continue to use the oxen to take their wagon to Junction City, sending his son along to bring the oxen home.[52]

At Junction City, they sold their pelts, furs, wagon, traps, and equipment. They caught a ride to Fort Leavenworth with a government mule train, arriving there in March of 1860. Billy was now able to get around on crutches, but it would be several months before he was completely healed.[53]

When they arrived home, Mary Cody was so appreciative of Dave Harrington's efforts to rescue her "darling boy" she insisted he stay with them. Tragedy struck in April when Harrington went to a tree farm to pick up trees for the Codys. On his way home, he developed pneumonia. Mary sent for the physician, but all the best efforts were for naught. A week after coming down with pneumonia, Dave Harrington was dead. The Cody household was stunned with grief.[54]

CHAPTER 3
PONY EXPRESS
(APRIL 3, 1860–JUNE 1, 1861)

The associated firms Russell, Majors & Waddell and the Leavenworth & Pike's Peak Express Company, popularly known as Overland Stage Company, continued to operate but were having financial problems. The federal government had not paid Russell, Majors & Waddell for their losses during the Utah War, and the Overland Stage Company was bankrupt. One of its creditors was Russell, Majors & Waddell, which it owed $190,000. If Russell, Majors & Waddell allowed the Overland Stage Company to go bankrupt, it would drag the freighting firm down with it. On October 28, 1859, Russell, Majors & Waddell entered a contract to take over all assets and liabilities of the Overland Stage Company and form a new company named the Central Overland California & Pikes Peak Express Company (COC&PP Express Company) that would haul freight, transport passengers, and carry the US mail. The COC&PP Express Company would be closely tied to the still existing Russell, Majors & Waddell.[1]

The new company concentrated on developing its stagecoach line on the Oregon Mormon Trail where at Julesburg it turned off on the Overland Trail following the South Platte River southwest and upriver to Denver. The COC&PP Express Company continued to build way stations and relay posts between

Leavenworth and Denver so they averaged twelve miles between stops where fresh mules were hitched to the coaches. Twenty-five of the larger stations were home stations for the drivers, and they were also where passengers could lodge and receive meals. In addition, the COC&PP Express Company established a stagecoach line following the Oregon Mormon Trail to Fort Bridger and on to Salt Lake City. It was then successful in winning the US government contract to carry the mail to Salt Lake City.[2]

In January 1860, William Russell was on the East Coast acquiring new loans to pay off creditors when he hit on a new idea to make money. On January 27, 1860, he telegrammed his son John who was at Leavenworth, "Have determined to establish a Pony Express to Sacramento, California, commencing 3rd of April. Time ten days." The route between the two terminuses—St. Joseph, Missouri, and Sacramento—was 1,966 miles.[3]

The COC&PP Express Company went to work buying five hundred swift, sturdy horses. The company ordered saddles and mochillas, saddle covers with locked pockets, to carry the mail. It hired two hundred additional station employees and eighty top-notch, young riders who were supposed to be around eighteen years old and weigh no more than 120 pounds. Workmen and building materials were sent out along the line to build additional relay stations where horses and riders could be switched out that were to be ten to fifteen miles apart. In the end, there were 153 way stations and relay posts along the 1,966-mile route.[4]

Business prospects were improving for Russell, Majors & Waddell and for COC&PP Express Company in the spring of 1860. On April 3, the first riders took off with their mail from St. Joseph and Sacramento, and the Pony Express was in business. On April 11, Russell, Majors & Waddell received the positive news it had won the government bid to provide the freighting for the army in New Mexico Territory. Then on May 11, COC&PP Express Company learned the federal government had awarded it the mail service monopoly over the central route from Salt Lake City to

Placerville, California. With this award, the company invested in providing passenger service as well.[5]

Both James Hickok and Billy Cody probably visited Julesburg in present-day Colorado and may have met one of COC&PP Express Company's more notorious employees, Jack Slade. Julesburg, along the South Platte River, was one of the main stops for COC&PP Express Company's stagecoaches and Pony Express riders. Julesburg consisted of the stagecoach way station, trading post, blacksmith shop, and a couple of cabins. It was named after Jules Beni, who owned the trading post and ran COC&PP Express Company's way station. He was a rough character who was rumored to have killed a couple of men. Lots of the company's livestock and equipment were turning up missing. Beni and his gang were prime suspects.[6]

Ben Ficklin, superintendent of the company's line to Salt Lake City, appointed Jack Slade as superintendent for Division 2, the stretch of line from Fort Kearny to Horseshoe Creek Station in present-day Wyoming. Julesburg was in Slade's division, and Ficklin told him his first duty was to end the theft of company property.[7]

Establishing his headquarters at Julesburg, one of Slade's first acts was to fire Beni and force him to return stolen livestock and equipment. Angry that his criminal operations had been disrupted, Beni ambushed Slade, firing a blast from a double-barreled shotgun at him. Slade survived and was sent to St. Louis to recuperate.[8]

When Ficklin heard what had happened to Slade, he gathered some employees and caught the next stage to Julesburg. They dragged Beni out of his trading post, hanged him, and then drove away. One of Beni's friends cut him down and discovered he was still alive. As soon as he could ride, Beni and his gang headed west to the South Pass in Wyoming where they continued to prey upon the COC&PP Express Company.[9]

After healing, Slade formed a posse and went after Beni. They caught up with him west of South Pass at Pacific Springs. Beni tried to get away, but Slade shot him out of the saddle. Beni was still alive as Slade tied him to a post and used him as a target, filling him full of holes. Slade cut off both Beni's ears. One ear he nailed to a post, and it was said the other ear he kept as a watch fob.[10]

Slade ran an efficient, no-nonsense operation and it was said there were other hard cases Slade put in the ground. His reputation was legendary. Slade would later die on March 10, 1864, in Virginia City, Montana Territory. Drunk, Slade became belligerent in a saloon. The clientele, having had enough of him, dragged him outside and hanged him from a beam.[11]

Throughout the spring and summer of 1860, James Hickok continued to divide his time between Russell, Majors & Waddell working as a teamster and Central Overland California & Pikes Peak Express Company working as a stagecoach driver. In September 1860, James was driving a stagecoach when he may have met Jack Slade at Plante's Station on the Oregon Trail.[12]

William F. Cody's involvement with the Pony Express is one of the more controversial aspects of his life. Many of his adventures read like dime novel exploits. He doesn't help his case when his stories change with the different versions of his autobiographies and writings. Some historians believe Cody did not ride for the Pony Express, but he claimed he did. Other historians believe he did ride for the Pony Express but added to and embellished stories. I am one of those people who believe the latter. There were contemporary people who said he did ride for the Pony Express, and no contemporary acquaintances who said he didn't. If the COC&PP Express Company kept a record of Pony Express riders, it has not been found. Company partner Alexander Majors listed some of the riders in his book *Seventy Years on the Frontier* and said of Cody, "Among the most noted and daring riders of the

Billy Cody riding for the Pony Express

Pony Express was Hon. William F. Cody, better known as Buffalo Bill. . . ."[13]

Some historians believe Cody did not ride for the Pony Express because of the stated hiring requirements that the riders had to be at least eighteen years old and weigh no more than 120 pounds. In 1860 when the Pony Express began operation, Cody was fourteen years old. However, Majors knew the Cody family and their situation, and Cody had been working for the firm for three years.[14]

I believe Majors made an exception for Cody and hired him as a substitute rider, in case a rider was unable to perform his duty. The following is what I *think* might have happened.

During the summer of 1860, fourteen-year-old Billy Cody met Lew Simpson in Leavenworth. Simpson was taking a wagon train from Atchison, Kansas, to Fort Laramie and hired Billy to go along. Billy went home to tell his mother and then traveled north to Atchison where he met William Russell. Billy wanted to work as a Pony Express rider. Even though Billy was underage, Russell wrote a letter to Jack Slade, who was at Horseshoe Station, to allow Billy to work as a Pony Express rider.[15]

For Billy Cody, it wasn't about seeking fame but purely

financial. The COC&PP Express Company wanted the best riders and was willing to pay to get them. Pony Express riders were paid up to $125 a month plus room and board. The pay was five times more than they could earn elsewhere.[16]

After reaching Fort Laramie, Billy continued along the Oregon Mormon Trail until he reached Slade's headquarters at Horseshoe Station. After reading Russell's letter, Slade took Billy on as a rider. His route was between Red Buttes and Three Crossings Stations in Wyoming, a one-way distance of about seventy-six miles.[17]

Cody claimed that one time when he reached Three Crossings Station, he was asked to continue riding the next route of eighty-six miles to Rocky Ridge as the rider was not available and there was no replacement. Cody completed the second route, then returned with eastbound mail to Three Crossings, and then on to Red Buttes where he had started for one of the longest rides in the short history of the Pony Express.[18]

Cody claimed Indians fired at and chased him. He said they attacked him about a mile west of Horse Creek Station and when he reached the next station (possibly Sweetwater Bridge), the stock tender had been killed and the horses stolen. From there, he continued to race his horse twelve miles to Plante's station, which made it a twenty-four-mile ride on the same horse. Other than Cody's account, there is no record of this.[19]

In September 1860, Cody said Indians attacked a stagecoach between Three Crossings and Split Rock Stations then stole a herd of Pony Express horses. A posse of forty riders, stage drivers, and stock tenders elected James Hickok as their leader, and Billy Cody tagged along. The posse tracked the raiders north to their encampment on the Powder River. They waited until night and then stampeded the Indian herd, recovering all their animals as well as a hundred Indian ponies. Upon their return, they held a drunken spree at Sweetwater Bridge Station. Jack Slade arrived to participate in the celebration only to get into an argument with a stagecoach driver, which ended with Slade shooting and killing the man.[20]

Billy Cody stayed on at Horseshoe Station through the winter of 1860–1861. He only occasionally rode for the Pony Express; mostly he cared for the livestock. From time to time, he would leave on a hunt.[21]

Cody claimed one time while out hunting he came upon a dugout with eight men in it, two of whom had been teamsters Simpson had discharged because he suspected they had robbed and killed a rancher. Believing they were an outlaw gang, Billy knocked one on the head with his revolver, shot and killed another, before racing away on his horse. When he got back to the station, he told Slade who organized a twenty-man posse. When they reached the dugout, the outlaws were gone, leaving behind a freshly dug grave. There are no other accounts of this story.[22]

Cody also claimed once or maybe twice, he was accosted by bandits, but he was always able to get the upper hand. In one case, he whirled his pony around, striking the man and then raced off. In the other case he overpowered the robber, tied him up, and took him along.[23]

In another story, a three-year-old girl was playing with a doll at a stage stop when a bull buffalo charged her. Billy shot and killed the buffalo fifteen yards before it reached her. In a different version of the story, a girl named Mamie Perkins was walking to a river to fetch a pail of water when a charging buffalo bull bore down on her. Billy shot and killed the bull a dozen feet before it reached Mamie.[24]

Maybe all Cody's Pony Express stories took place, maybe some of them happened, maybe none of them did. Take your pick.

During the fall of 1860, James Hickok switched from driving the COC&PP Express Company's stagecoaches and was back working as a teamster for Russell, Majors & Waddell, driving freight wagons from Independence, Missouri, to Santa Fe, New Mexico.[25] James also must have worked off and on from 1858 through 1861 with Jones and Cartwright, another freighting firm associated with Russell, Majors & Waddell.[26] During this time, James was severely injured—so severely he had to stop driving wagons and stagecoaches.

J. W. Buel, in his book *Heroes of the Plains*, related the story that James was driving a freight wagon through the mountains on the approach to Santa Fe.[27] He was two miles ahead of a wagon driven by Matt Farley, when he came upon a large cinnamon bear and her two cubs standing in the road.[28]

The bears appeared to have no inclination of leaving the road. Armed with two single-shot pistols and a Bowie knife, James climbed down from the wagon and approached the bears, possibly to shoo them away.[29]

Instead of fleeing, the mother bear's first instinct was to protect her cubs and she charged James. He fired one pistol at the bear's forehead, which probably did nothing more than aggravate her more. He fired the second pistol hitting her left front leg. He was able to pull out his Bowie knife just as the bear reached him. She clawed and bit James as he repeatedly stabbed her. In the end, he killed the bear; however, he was severely mauled with facial lacerations, a torn shoulder, a crushed left elbow, and his chest raked by the bear's claws.[30]

Matt Farley arrived on the scene and hauled James to Santa Fe where a surgeon, Doctor Sam Jones, attended to Hickok's wounds. James remained in Santa Fe until his wounds healed sufficiently that he could return to work.[31] Other than Buel's story, there are no other accounts of this bear attack.

CHAPTER 4

INCIDENT AT ROCK CREEK STATION
(MAY 1861–JULY 1861)

Rock Creek Station, one of the stops for the Overland Stage Company's[1] stagecoaches and its Pony Express, would become a significant milestone in James Hickok's life. His fight there with the "M'Kandlas gang" would later propel him into the national limelight. Located in Jefferson County in southeastern Nebraska, Rock Creek Station straddled the Oregon Trail as it crossed Rock Creek, a tributary to the Little Blue River.[2]

Rock Creek divided the station into the West Ranch and the East Ranch with a toll bridge over the creek connecting the two. In April 1861, David McCanles sold the West Ranch to David Wolfe and Fredrick Hagenstein to be paid in full one year from the date of purchase. He kept the title as security. That same month McCanles sold the East Ranch to the Overland Stage Company, which paid one-third the price up front with the rest of the purchase price to be paid in two monthly payments. He also kept that title as security.[3]

David Colbert McCanles was born in Iredell County, North Carolina, on November 30, 1828. He was a child when his family moved to Watauga County, North Carolina, in the 1830s. He received a good education and had a zest for life. As a grown man, McCanles stood six feet tall with a heavy build. He liked to talk;

people considered him a good orator. He enjoyed playing practical jokes, was competitive, and always considered himself right. Overbearing and intolerant, he would take matters into his own hands, dealing out his own punishment to those he believed were wrong. McCanles liked to gamble, race, wrestle, and fight bare-knuckled. In 1848, he married Mary Green, and over the years they would have six children. In 1852, McCanles ran for Watauga County sheriff in a hotly contested race and won.[4]

The McCanles family lived next door to Phillip and Phoebe Shull, who had thirteen children, one of whom was Sarah, born on October 3, 1833. Sarah, who was independent, attractive, intelligent, and educated, became pregnant and bore a daughter out of wedlock on May 4, 1856. The community vilified Sarah and suspected McCanles was the father. Unfortunately, Sarah's baby died on July 2, 1857.[5]

In January 1859, David McCanles sold his property to his brother and then on February 9, he and Sarah ran off together, absconding with Watauga County's tax money. Their plan was to make their fortune in Colorado's latest gold rush. As they traveled along the Oregon Trail in eastern Nebraska Territory, they encountered returning, disgruntled prospectors who told them it wasn't worth the trip.[6]

The pair reached the way station on the west side of Rock Creek in March 1859. Believing the way station could be a profitable business, McCanles bought the station on the west side and the property on the east side of the creek. He made improvements, constructing a toll bridge across the creek, and on the east side, he built a second house and a barn. Digging a well, he expanded the water supply.[7]

The East Ranch would later be used by the Overland Stage and Pony Express while the West Ranch was used by freighters and travelers. The toll bridge brought in a steady revenue. Depending on the wagon outfit, the toll ranged from 10 cents to $1.50. McCanles paid Sarah to manage his financial records and act as housekeeper at the West Ranch.[8]

David McCanles wrote to his brother James telling him to come to Nebraska Territory and while he was at it, to bring along David's wife and children. On September 20, 1859, James arrived with his family and David's family along with a nephew, James Woods. The brothers and their families lived together at the East Ranch house, while Sarah continued to work for McCanles and live in the West Ranch house. David McCanles's wife Mary was enraged when she found Sarah there and that David continued to see her.[9]

Business boomed, and McCanles had plenty of money, employing twenty men. He expanded his holdings, developing a ranch three miles southwest of Rock Creek Station, where he moved his family.[10] In the fall of 1860, James McCanles and his family left, moving fifty miles to the east where they bought three farms.[11]

The citizens of Jefferson County grew to respect David McCanles. He established the first school and paid the teacher out of his own pocket (of course, his children attended). He was popular at social gatherings and dances, playing the fiddle or banjo while singing. Being a good orator, he enthralled audiences with his positions on current affairs. Some people later claimed McCanles was a Confederate sympathizer and led a gang of border ruffians, but McCanles was a staunch Republican and local leaders selected him to speak against secession at Jefferson County's 1861 Fourth of July celebration.[12]

McCanles loved practical jokes. One Sunday, a preacher traveling through on the Oregon Trail was giving a sermon at a local ranch house. Unbeknownst to the preacher, David switched his water glass with one filled with clear moonshine. The preacher took a good healthy drink and began coughing and gagging. The congregation exploded in laughter. When the preacher recovered his breath, he appreciated the joke and parted on friendly terms with David.[13]

David McCanles had a mean streak. There are many stories about his abusive nature. Here are a few.

In the spring of 1860, a band of Indians camped near the station. Some of McCanles's items went missing. One morning, Mary McCanles cooked a pan of biscuits and placed them on the windowsill to cool. As an Indian reached in the window to snatch one, David drove a knife into his hand.[14]

One day, McCanles had to leave the station and left his employee, Harry Goff, in charge. Goff started drinking and passed out. When McCanles returned, he found Goff asleep in a drunken stupor. He poured powder over Goff's beard and lit it on fire. Other employees grabbed Goff and threw him into a water trough. Goff threatened to shoot McCanles, who ordered his men to tie Goff to the back of an unbroken horse. The horse bucked and ran until it was tired. Goff was unrepentant so McCanles threatened to give him the "third degree"—forcing a man to climb a honey locust tree covered with thorns. Goff calmed down and the punishment was not inflicted.[15]

In another instance, McCanles stopped at a neighbor's ranch and found Mike Conley visiting there. McCanles did not like Conley and fired a shot into the fireplace behind Conley. Conley jumped out a window and ran off. McCanles claimed it was the best joke he had played since coming to Nebraska.[16]

During a disagreement with John Shumway, who was running another station for the Overland Stage Company, McCanles kicked Shumway under the chin. The next day, McCanles attacked Shumway again, hitting him in the face with a two-pound weight, breaking his nose. McCanles then forced Shumway to sign over to him his store, cattle, and hay.[17]

The Overland Stage Company was expanding its operations with the addition of the Pony Express. It contracted with McCanles to use the East Ranch as a relay station. McCanles made additional improvements to the East Ranch for the Pony Express including a bunkhouse and a twelve-foot-wide lean-to on the south side of the house. At some point during the first months of 1861, the Overland Stage Company sent Horace Wellman to manage the station. Wellman moved into the East Ranch house with his common-law wife, Jane. Overland Stage Company employee James "Doc" Brink worked as stock tender, and in March 1861, James Hickok arrived and worked as Brink's assistant.[18]

Hickok was still recovering from his injuries received that winter. His left arm was useless, and he walked with a limp. The Overland Stage Company sent him to Rock Creek Station to do light duties until he recovered. He lived in a nearby dugout and didn't associate much with the other men.[19]

McCanles picked on James. He took advantage of his injured condition, grabbing him and throwing him to the ground. Some claimed McCanles called James "Dutch Bill" and "Duck Bill" due to his thin protruding lips.[20]

Others claimed James gambled at cards with the employees, winning many times. McCanles roughed him up and told him if he continued to gamble, he would force him to leave the station. James did not talk back to McCanles, biding his time.[21]

There is a third possibility that might have generated animosity between McCanles and Hickok—Sarah Shull. Sarah had moved out of the West Ranch house and was living in a dugout a few miles from the station near McCanles's ranch, but she was still working at the station assisting Jane Wellman. James and Sarah enjoyed each other's company. McCanles saw them together and told Hickok to stay away from her, but James disregarded his threats.[22]

In later years, Sarah told Jessie Williams, "Hickok had steel-blue eyes that were beautiful and gentle but could change in a second and look dangerous. You had better watch his eyes; he wasn't one to run from a fight. I came close to having an affair with Hickok."[23]

The Overland Stage Company was in financial trouble. In June, McCanles arrived at the Rock Creek Station to collect his monthly payment. Wellman told him Ben Ficklin, the superintendent located in Brownville, Nebraska, had not sent the money. McCanles came to the station several times during the month expecting to receive his money only to be put off by Wellman. On

July 1, the next payment was due. Wellman again told McCanles he had not received any money from Ficklin to pay him.[24]

McCanles was furious, demanding he be paid in cash or equivalent goods, otherwise the Overland Stage Company needed to return the station to him. He demanded Wellman travel the hundred miles to Brownville and return with his money. Wellman finally agreed to do so and left the next day. McCanles's twelve-year-old son Monroe went along with Wellman to pick up supplies for McCanles.[25] While Wellman was gone, he placed Hickok in charge and at Wellman's request, Hickok moved from his dugout into the East Ranch house with Jane Wellman.[26]

The more McCanles thought about the Overland Stage Company's nonpayment, the angrier he became. Several times, he went to the East Ranch and told Jane to get out, but she refused.[27] Jane told McCanles that when Horace came home "he would settle" with him "for his impudence."[28]

McCanles believed Jane's father, Joseph Holmes, had stolen property from him. On July 5, McCanles caught Holmes and brought him to the Rock Creek Station. McCanles tied a rope around Holmes and hauled him to the roof of the barn where he dropped Holmes over the side to the ground, hauled him back up onto the roof, and dropped him again. McCanles did this a number of times. Jane as well as Hickok must have witnessed it all.[29]

Horace Wellman and Monroe McCanles returned to Rock Creek Station on July 11. Monroe found his father at a nearby ranch and told him Wellman was not able to get cash or supplies for payment. That was the last straw; McCanles would evict the Overland Stage Company people.[30]

Late on the afternoon of July 12, David McCanles rode into the East Rock Creek Station with Monroe, his nephew James Woods, and an employee, James Gordon, whose bloodhound tagged along. Dismounting at the barn, Woods and Gordon remained there while David and Monroe walked to the house. Inside were Horace and Jane Wellman, Sarah Shull, Sarah Kelsey, and James Hickok.[31]

Was David McCanles unarmed as he approached the house or did he carry Monroe's boy-sized, double-barreled shotgun? Monroe did not say, but later in life, he did record what he saw which follows.[32]

McCanles went to the kitchen door, asking for Horace. Jane appeared at the door, and McCanles asked her if Horace was in the house. She replied that he was.

"Tell him to come out," McCanles said.

"What do you want with him?" Jane asked.

"I want to settle with him," he answered.

"He'll not come out," she replied.

"Send him out or I'll come in and drag him out," he said.

Hickok stepped to the door and stood beside Jane. McCanles looked him in the face saying, "Jim, haven't we been friends all the time?"

"Yes," Hickok replied.

"Are we friends now?" McCanles asked.

"Yes."

"Will you hand me a drink of water?" McCanles asked.

Hickok turned to the water bucket and brought a dipper of water, handing it to McCanles who took a drink then gave it back to Hickok.

As McCanles was handing the dipper to Hickok, Monroe noticed his father must have seen something threatening take place inside. David moved quickly from the kitchen door to the front door, about ten feet to the north. Stepping onto the front step, he said, "Now, Jim, if you have anything against me, come out and fight me fair."

A rifle shot cracked from inside and McCanles fell flat on his back. He raised himself almost to a sitting position, looked at Monroe, and fell back dead.[33]

Monroe did not see who the shooter was as the shot came from behind a calico curtain hanging inside the house as a partition. Monroe did know a rifle had been used to kill his father. In

Incident at Rock Creek

fact, the rifle belonged to his father, who had lent it to Wellman for his protection.[34]

Sarah Shull later said she did not see who shot McCanles as she was standing on the other side of the curtain partition from the shooter. The two Sarahs were ordered to enter the root cellar on the north side of the house and stay there. The roof of the cellar was constructed of split logs.[35]

Hearing the shot, James Woods and James Gordon came running unarmed to the house. Hickok appeared at the door with a Colt Navy revolver and fired two shots at Woods, severely wounding him. Woods ran to the north side of the house where he collapsed.[36]

Gordon turned and ran. Hickok ran after him and fired two shots, wounding him.[37]

Horace Wellman came outside with a hoe and ran after Woods. He caught Woods overtop of the root cellar, smashing in his head with the hoe. Woods's blood flowed between the split logs down into the root cellar and onto Sarah Shull's head, matting her hair. She later said it was the most horrifying experience of her life.[38]

After killing Woods, Wellman came running back around the house, striking at Monroe with the hoe and yelling, "Let's kill them all!" Monroe dodged the hoe and ran for his life. He outran Wellman to a ravine south of the house and stopped. Jane stood in the doorway clapping her hands yelling, "Kill him! Kill him! Kill him!"[39]

The wounded Gordon was hiding down the creek. Doc Brink and a stage driver, George Hulbert, joined Hickok in the hunt for Gordon, putting Gordon's own bloodhound on his trail. The dog found Gordon downstream and either attacked him or was attempting to play with him as Gordon tried to fend him off with a stick. The men killed Gordon with a shotgun blast.[40]

Returning to the station, Brink, Hulbert, and Hickock met Joe Baker, Sarah Kelsey's stepfather. Hickok accused Baker of being a McCanles friend and cocked his revolver. Sarah Kelsey threw her arms around her stepfather, pleading for his life. Hickok relented but said, "Well, you got to take that anyway," as he beat Baker on the head with the barrel of his revolver.[41]

Monroe ran three miles home to tell his mother the horrible news. A hired hand drove her and the children to Rock Creek

Station to see for themselves. She sent word to David's brother James, who rode through the night to Beatrice, Nebraska Territory, to swear out a murder complaint before Justice of the Peace T. M. Coulter. James McCanles organized a posse, which arrested Hickok, Wellman, and Brink and took them to Beatrice for a preliminary murder hearing.[42]

The morning after the shootings, Frank Thomas and Jasper Helvey went to the station and saw the bodies of David McCanles, James Woods, and James Gordon lying in the positions in which they had fallen. Thomas and Helvey saw no weapons on or near the bodies.[43]

On July 15, 16, and 18, 1861, a hearing was held in front of Justice of the Peace Coulter. In the end, Coulter found the charges of murder against Hickok and the others not sustained and allowed the three men to go free. He bought their argument it was a case of self-defense. Coulter was also concerned the county had insufficient funds to pay for the upkeep of the prisoners while they awaited trial. All the accused were employees of the Overland Stage Company, the most influential corporation west of the Missouri River, and the courtroom was packed with its employees. It's interesting to note Coulter was arrested in 1864 for embezzlement but escaped before coming to trial. Sarah Shull eventually made her way to Denver. The Wellmans and Doc Brink disappeared from the scene, as did James Hickok, who headed to Leavenworth.[44]

No one really knew who shot David McCanles—Hickok or Wellman. But Hickok never denied it. Years later Colonel George Ward Nichols wrote what Hickock said about the Rock Creek Station fight, "I don't like to talk about that M'Kandles [*sic*] affair. ...It gives me a queer shiver whenever I think of it, and sometimes I dream about it, and wake up in a cold sweat."[45]

CHAPTER 5

CIVIL WAR (1861–1865)

After Abraham Lincoln was elected president on November 6, 1860, the anger and frustration between the states ruptured the nation as thirteen states eventually left the Union and formed the Confederate States of America. On April 12, 1861, Confederate forces bombarded Union-held Fort Sumter, in Charleston Harbor, South Carolina, leading to open warfare.

Even though there were many proslavery residents in Kansas Territory, enough antislavery settlers had entered that it joined the Union as a free state on January 29, 1861. The neighboring state of Missouri was a different story. With its governor and state government leaning toward the Confederacy, only the use of federal troops kept it in the Union.

Fort Leavenworth was in a precarious position. Located in the heart of eastern Kansas and western Missouri proslavery sympathizers, the fort was undermanned until Union general William Harney ordered western outposts to send reinforcements. On April 20, 1861, approximately forty-five miles to the east of Fort Leavenworth, proslavery sympathizers raided the federal arsenal at Liberty, Missouri, seizing all the ordnance. By June, small skirmishes were erupting between Union and Confederate troops outside Kansas City, Missouri.[1]

At the same time Fort Leavenworth was becoming a staging area for the Union army and a training center for western recruits, the countryside was in turmoil as Union-sympathizing paramilitary groups from Kansas called jayhawkers raided Missouri farms and businesses and Confederate-sympathizing Missouri bushwhackers raided Kansas farms and businesses. Many of these bands were criminals acting under the guise of patriotism for their cause. Patrols were sent from Fort Leavenworth to arrest culprits, no matter their political persuasion. To add to the mix, a large Pawnee war party was spotted in Marshall County, Kansas, sparking frontier settlers' concerns that Indian tribes saw the whites' conflict as an opportune time to inflict their own mayhem.[2]

What were James Hickok and Billy Cody doing during the Civil War? There are some confirmed hard facts, some stories that appear to be true although there were few witnesses to collaborate, and other stories that are outright fables. The following is a best effort to determine what might have taken place.

After the incident at Rock Creek Station in July 1861, James Hickok traveled to Fort Leavenworth where the Union army hired him as a civilian scout. He was sent to southwest Missouri where he joined General Nathaniel Lyon's fifty-four-hundred-man army that was slowly retreating north from a combined Confederate and Missouri state militia force of eleven thousand troops.[3]

Lyon stopped his men outside Springfield, Missouri. On August 8, 1861, the Confederates encamped at Wilson's Creek, ten miles southwest of Springfield. They started to advance on August 9 but decided to return to camp due to threatening rain clouds. That night, General Lyon marched his troops toward the Confederates. He believed if he gave them a surprise pounding it might stall their advance.[4]

Lyon split his troops sending Colonel Franz Sigel leading a contingent of infantry, cavalry, and artillery to attack the Confederate camp from the rear while he positioned the main force to attack the enemy head on. At dawn on August 10, Sigel opened the attack, firing his artillery into the Confederate camp.[5]

After the initial surprise, the Confederates counterattacked Sigel routing his troops. The battle surged back and forth between the Confederates and Lyon's men. During the action, Lyon was wounded three times and had a horse shot out from under him. He found a new mount, rallied his men, driving into the Confederates until a bullet smashed into his heart. The demoralized Union troops broke and fled toward Springfield. From Springfield the army continued retreating until it reached Rolla, Missouri, approximately 110 miles to the northeast. This was the second significant Confederate victory, the first being the Battle of Bull Run outside Washington, DC, on July 21. The Union army's retreat to Rolla left southwest Missouri under the control of the secessionists.[6]

James Hickok had been acting as a scout for the Union troops the day of the battle. At the beginning of the onslaught, he was out ahead of the Union position as a skirmisher. Firing and advancing, the skirmishers worked their way close to the Confederate lines. Without warning, a hidden Confederate artillery battery opened fire in front of them. James later told his brother Horace the artillery's opening salvo was a frightening experience.[7]

Hickok retreated with the Union troops to Rolla. From there he returned to Leavenworth. The freighting firm Jones & Cartwright had sold the Union army one hundred teams of six yoke oxen. The Army hired Hickok as wagon master, paying him $100 per month. His job was to make sure the bull trains, loaded with supplies, reached the troops in Rolla. Hickok hired his young friend Billy Cody as his assistant.[8]

Receiving word his mother Mary was ill, fifteen-year-old Billy Cody had quit his Pony Express job at Horseshoe Station and traveled east arriving at Leavenworth about June 1, 1861. When Billy reached home, it was a bittersweet reunion as his mother's condition had not improved.[9]

After the Confederate attack on Fort Sumter, President Lincoln had called for volunteers to join the Union army. The Cody family had always been staunch Unionists, and Billy was ready to enlist. However, Mary made him promise he would not enlist while she lived. She needed his help managing the farm and hotel.[10]

Jayhawkers were conducting guerrilla operations into Missouri. One jayhawker outfit was based out of Leavenworth and led by a man named Chandler. Chandler's objective was simple: Missourians had been raiding Kansas homesteads stealing horses, and he proposed he and his band would do the same to Missourians.[11]

Billy joined Chandler's twenty-five-member band. He reasoned his mother had made him promise not to enlist in the Union army, but she never said he couldn't join a jayhawker outfit. He believed all Missourians were secessionists. They had tormented his family and taken its livestock, and now it was only right he take their horses.[12]

Chandler spent several days scouting for the best horses around Westport, Missouri. One evening, he rendezvoused with his men, one of whom was Billy Cody, outside Westport and gave them instructions as to which farms to hit. The men spread out on their raids, returning to their rendezvous location the next night. Almost every man had at least two horses and they drove their stolen herd back to Kansas. Some of the men took the stolen horses to their homes while others took them to Leavenworth, presumably to sell. Cody never mentioned what he did with his stolen horses.[13]

Billy continued to ride with Chandler's Jayhawkers sporadically during the summer of 1861, raiding Missouri farms for horses. There were several running fights with the horse owners, but nothing came of it. The federal government assigned detectives to determine who the horse-thieves were, and some of Chandler's men were arrested. Mary Cody learned about her son's horse-thieving ways and made him stop, saying "it was neither honorable nor right."[14]

On October 7, 1861, Union general John Charles Frémont led thirty-eight thousand men out of St. Louis southwest toward Springfield. The Confederate troops began withdrawing into the southwestern corner of Missouri.[15]

It must have been after the Union army reoccupied Springfield when Billy Cody ran into James Hickok in Leavenworth, and Hickok hired him as his assistant to take a hundred-wagon bull train to Rolla, Missouri.[16] The bull train reached Rolla without incident. From there, they took a shipment to Springfield and then returned to Rolla where they found pasturage for the oxen and a place to park the wagons. James had his bullwhackers care for and guard the animals, wagons, and equipment while he and Billy took a side trip to St. Louis.[17]

Everyone in Rolla was talking about the fall St. Louis horse races. James bought a fast-running horse and he believed with Billy as his jockey, it was a winning combination. They traveled to St. Louis and entered a race. In addition to betting all their money, they bet Hickok's horse against $250. They lost.[18]

Penniless, they went to army headquarters where Hickok borrowed money from a friend. He bought Billy a one-way ticket on a Missouri River steamboat to Leavenworth.[19]

When Billy arrived home, he found his mother was so ill that his sister Julia was running the hotel and farm. The family decided it would be best if Billy continued to seek employment elsewhere to earn additional money for the family. The Army hired him to carry dispatches to Fort Larned on the Santa Fe Trail in central Kansas. During the winter of 1861 to 1862, Billy worked with George Long buying horses for the Union army.[20]

After sending Billy Cody back to Leavenworth, James Hickok returned to Rolla where he and his bullwhackers took the bull train back to Leavenworth for more supplies. After loading the freight into the wagons, Hickok led a fifty-wagon bull train heading to Sedalia, Missouri. Nearing the town of Pleasant Hill, secessionists captured the bull train. Hickok managed to escape and rode to Kansas City where he reported the bull train's capture to Colonel Charles Jennison, commander of the newly formed Kansas Seventh Cavalry soon to become known as Jennison's Jayhawkers.[21]

Jennison sent troops with Hickok, who pursued the secessionists and recovered the bull train. A heavy guard escorted the train to Sedalia where additional supplies were loaded onto the wagons. From there, Hickok led the train to Springfield, then southeast to Batesville, Arkansas, with a return to Rolla.[22]

During this time, James Hickok was given the moniker that stuck with him for the rest of his life—Wild Bill. There are several versions of how he got the name. Many people had been using the name "Bill" for James's first name ever since he arrived in Kansas.

One version was associated with the secessionists' capture of his bull train. The story went that he was in Independence, Missouri, waiting for the Kansas Seventh Cavalry to arrive to pursue the bull train attackers. As Hickok wandered around town, he came upon a large, angry crowd standing in the street outside a saloon. He learned that a bartender had tried to break up a fight inside the saloon. The bartender fired a shot, wounding one of the fighters. Now an alcohol-fueled mob of the wounded man's friends was out for the bartender's blood.

Hickok positioned himself in front of the saloon door, and as the mob rushed the door, he drew both his pistols and shouted for the mob to halt. No one listened to him, so he fired two shots over their heads. That got their attention. Hickok told them to leave, then added the threat he would shoot the first man who tried to make a move toward the door. The mob, still angry, dispersed.

That evening, Independence citizens were holding a meeting to form a vigilance committee to support law and order. Hickok was standing at the edge of the crowd when someone spotted him. Many people had heard how he stood down the mob. They started shouting his name. A woman yelled, "Good for you, Wild Bill!" and the name stuck.[23]

In a variation of this story, James Hickok was with his brother Lorenzo, also known as Bill. Lorenzo was wagon master for a bull train hauling freight from Rolla to Springfield. Entering a small town along the way, they came upon a mob that was going to hang a youth who they believed was a horse-thief. Lorenzo stopped the hanging. A woman shouted out, "My God ain't he wild." By the time the bull train reached Springfield, the name Wild Bill was transferred to and stuck with James, not Lorenzo.[24]

Another story recalls that in the summer of 1862 people living in Rolla wanted to differentiate between the two Hickok brothers, so they called James Wild Bill and Lorenzo Tame Bill.[25] This would make sense if James already had the name Wild Bill from the Independence incident.

During the winter of 1861–1862, Hickok pastured the bull train's oxen near Otterville, twelve miles east of Sedalia, Missouri.[26] The army had been paying him $100 per month, but by January 1, 1862, officials believed they were paying him too much and reduced his pay to $60 per month.[27]

The Union forces in southwest Missouri were led by General Samuel Curtis, a West Point graduate and Mexican War veteran who had replaced General John Charles Frémont. During the winter of 1862, Union troops had pushed the secessionist forces out of southwest Missouri, and by March, Curtis was leading a twelve-thousand-man army after them. One of Curtis's men was Wild Bill Hickok, who was working as a civilian scout.[28]

The secessionist forces totaled between sixteen thousand and seventeen thousand men comprised of Confederate troops, Missouri state militia, and three regiments of Indian allies from the Five Civilized Nations of Indian Territory. They were not moving away from the Union troops, but toward them. General Earl Van Dorn, veteran of the Mexican War and Indian fights, led the secessionist troops believing they could retake Springfield, then march on St. Louis.[29]

On March 5, Curtis's scouts, including Hickok, rode in to report the Confederates were on the march toward them. Curtis's troops had been marching in separate formations, and now he ordered them to join together. By March 6, Curtis's four divisions had come together. The men were ordered to dig entrenchments facing south along Sugar Creek with Pea Ridge to their backs and the Elkhorn Tavern on the Wire Road to the rear on their left.[30]

Van Dorn did not want to attack Curtis's army head on. On the night of March 6, he had his men circle to the west of the Union troops, then cross to Pea Ridge and Elkhorn Tavern in the Union rear. Hickok and the other scouts detected Van Dorn's movements and reported what they found to Curtis. The scouts' warning gave him time to reposition his troops to meet the Confederate attack from the rear.[31]

The Confederates attacked on the morning of March 7. The battle raged back and forth. Hickok acted as a mounted scout and courier. It was said he wore out three horses during the battle and had another shot out from under him.[32]

Commanding the Confederate right wing was General Ben McCulloch, one of the leaders at the Battle of Wilson's Creek. McCulloch was killed, as well as his second in command, while his third ranking officer was captured, all within the span of an hour. Some claimed Hickok was the shooter, but that was not the case. McCulloch was killed by Peter Pelican with the Thirty-Sixth Illinois Infantry.[33]

The battle resumed the next morning. The Confederates were cut off from their ammunition supply and were running low.[34]

Hickok may have joined sharpshooters on a ridge shooting into a Confederate position. The shooters cheered when one of their bullets hit an officer. Hickok may have joined with Colonel John Phelps's regiment during the fighting. This is plausible as Phelps formed a six-month regiment from men living in the Springfield area. Hickok would have had plenty of opportunities to meet Phelps and men of his unit. The regiment was in the thick of the fighting at Elk Horn Tavern and took many casualties.[35]

The Union artillery knocked out the Confederate artillery. Franz Sigel, now a general, led a seven-thousand-man infantry charge that routed the Confederates and gave the Union a complete victory. Hundreds were killed, many missing, and well over a thousand men were wounded on both sides.[36]

On March 26, Wild Bill Hickok was appointed chief wagon master and paid $100 per month. Then on June 30, he was transferred from Captain S. L. Brown, assistant quartermaster in Sedalia to Lieutenant S. C. Peck, acting assistant quartermaster in Rolla. By September 20, 1862, the quartermaster records indicated he had been removed, but no records have been found as to whether he was dismissed or transferred.[37]

During the spring and summer of 1862, sixteen-year-old Billy Cody acted as a guide and scout for the Ninth Kansas Volunteer Cavalry Regiment. On March 27, 1862, the state of Kansas organized the Ninth Kansas by consolidating a hodgepodge of smaller units at Fort Leavenworth. Five companies were detached and sent west to garrison forts and patrol the Santa Fe Trail. Cody said the troops he was with patrolled through Kiowa and Comanche country along the trail between Forts Lyon and Larned. They had several run-ins with Indians but nothing of importance.[38]

That fall, Billy Cody returned home. His sister Julia was concerned about the management of the hotel and farm. Their mother was not getting better, and Billy had not been around to help, earning money elsewhere. Julia believed she needed to get married and proposed potential spouse candidates to Billy for his thoughts. He didn't like any of them until Julia mentioned Al Goodman, who lived on a farm across the road from them. Billy thought Al would be the right person. Julia proposed to Al with the condition he would care for the younger Cody children. Al accepted and they married on December 22, 1862.[39]

In the winter of 1862–1863, when not in school, Billy rode with the Red Legged Scouts. Captain William Tough (also spelled Tuff, Tuft, and Tufft) led the scouts, a loose-knit militia not attached to any particular organization. The only semblance of a uniform they had were sheepskin leggings dyed red. The Red Legged Scouts were pretty much thugs, no better than the bushwhackers they chased.[40]

They operated mostly in Arkansas and southwestern Missouri. When not contending with bushwhackers, they carried

Army dispatches between Union forts. Most of the scouts must have been young boys full of themselves. One of them mentioned by Cody was Pony Express rider Johnny Fry.[41] "Whenever we were in Leavenworth we had a very festive time," Cody wrote. "We usually attended all the balls in full force, and 'ran things' to suit ourselves."[42]

During the summer of 1863, Billy was hired to be wagon master of a small bull train outfit hauling freight to Denver. When he reached his destination in September, a letter from Julia was waiting for him. Their mother Mary was very ill; he hurried home. Knowing death was near, Mary sent for her lawyer and put all her affairs in order. Julia's husband Al was named custodian of the younger children and administrator of the estate. Mary gave instructions to each of her children. Billy was holding her hand when she told him to take special care of his seven-year-old brother Charley. Mary Cody died November 22, 1863. Cody later wrote, "Thus passed away a loving and affectionate mother and a noble, brave, good and loyal woman."[43]

With the death of his mother, Billy had no direction, no guidance in life—a ship without a rudder. He later wrote, "going to Leavenworth I entered upon a dissolute and reckless life—to my shame be it said—and associated with gamblers, drunkards, and bad characters generally." After two months of reckless living, Cody was, in his words "becoming a very 'hard case.'"[44]

In February 1864, the Kansas Seventh Cavalry was at Fort Leavenworth for a thirty-day furlough. Also known as Jennison's Jayhawkers, they were the same outfit that had rescued James Hickok's bull train back in 1861. One of their objectives was to find recruits for the regiment.[45]

A number of Cody's friends, neighbors, and companions from the Red Legged Scouts had enlisted in the Kansas Seventh Cavalry and wanted him to join. Cody later wrote, "I had no idea of doing anything of the kind; but one day, after having been under the influence of bad whisky, I awoke to find myself a soldier in the Seventh Kansas. I did not remember how or when I had enlisted, but I saw I was in for it, and that it would not do for me to endeavor to back out."[46]

After being dropped from the quartermaster rolls on September 20, 1862, no official government mention of Wild Bill Hickok has been found until March 10, 1864, when he was paid for services rendered as special police.[47] Brother Lorenzo, who was a Union wagon master, mentioned in a July 16, 1863 letter to the family "I left J. B. at Rolla." What was Hickok doing during that year and a half? There are plenty of stories. They can be summed up by Hickok himself who Colonel George Ward Nichols quoted as saying, "I hardly know where to begin. Pretty near all these stories are true."[48] So with that, let's look at these stories, realizing any and all of them might not be exactly true.

Hickok may have scouted for the Eighth Missouri Militia. In 1867, Henry Stanley stated Hickok said he was a member of the Eighth Missouri. However, his name was not listed on the Eighth's roster. F. A. Carpenter, the historian for the Seventeenth Illinois Volunteer Cavalry, wrote Hickok scouted for them when they battled Price in the fall of 1864, and he saved members of the regiment from being captured. It's recorded he was attached to General Samuel Curtis's staff as a scout and spy.[49]

None of Wild Bill Hickok's contemporaries disputed he served the Union cause during the Civil War. In fact, on January 31, 1868, after the publication of Colonel George Ward Nichols's embellished article on Hickok in the February 1867 issue of *Harper's New Monthly Magazine*, the *Springfield Patriot* editor criticized Nichols's portrayal of Hickok. However, the *Patriot's* editor praised Hickok writing, "No finer physique, no greater strength, no more personal courage, no steadier nerves, no superior skill with a pistol, no better horsemanship than his, could any man of the million Federal soldiers of the war, boast of; and few did better or more loyal service as a soldier throughout the war."[50]

The unidentified author of *The History of Greene County, Missouri* recognized Hickok's service to the Union cause but had a different opinion of him writing, "Hickok had been in the Federal service in Southwest Missouri and Northern Arkansas, as a scout for the army of the frontier, and in the performance of his duties had grown to be well acquainted with danger, and being by nature a ruffian he soon became a desperado—a drunken, swaggering fellow, who delighted when 'on a spree' to frighten nervous men and timid women."[51]

Since no one has discovered any official record of Wild Bill Hickok's actions for a year and a half, it makes sense he could have been acting as a civilian spy and scout with the Eighth Missouri State Militia. One of the militia's roles was to provide scouts and spies to reconnoiter Confederate-held territory.[52]

According to J. W. Buel, soon after the Battle of Pea Ridge, General Samuel Curtis assigned Hickok to work as a spy behind Confederate lines to learn of General Stirling Price's plans and report back to Curtis.[53] It's interesting to note on March 26, 1862, less than two weeks after the battle, Hickok was appointed chief wagon master with an increase in pay from $60 to $100 per month.[54] Could this have been cover for his work as a spy?

Buel wrote while Hickok acted as a spy behind Confederate lines, he assumed the name Bill Barnes. People had given Lorenzo Hickok the nickname Billy Barnes and "Bill" had transferred to James when he first traveled to Kansas. The Union army gave Hickok a good horse. He rode west into Kansas, then south through Indian Territory; turning east, he rode to Little Rock, Arkansas. There, he enlisted with a Confederate unit of mounted rangers that joined the command of General Price.[55]

Buel continued that Hickok became an orderly on Price's staff. Toward the end of September 1862, the Confederates were positioned along the Elk River in southwest Missouri with Union troops on the opposite side of the river. Price entrusted Hickok with dispatches meant for General Jo Shelby. On October 25, Hickok decided it was time to report to Curtis. As he raced his horse from the Confederate lines toward the Union troops, the Confederates shot at him but missed. He reported to Curtis the Confederate troop strength and gave him the dispatches. When Price realized the Union army knew his plans, he withdrew his troops to Arkansas. Colonel George Ward Nichols told the same story, but with different details.[56]

There are four additional stories of Hickok scouting and spying behind enemy lines, then racing his horse from the Confederate lines to the Union position as secessionist troops fired at him. Probably at least one of these stories was true, giving rise to the others.[57]

Another story has it that John Kelso, a captain in the Eighth Missouri Militia, led Hickok and three other men on a spy mission into Arkansas behind Confederate lines. After completing their mission, Kelso and his men were trying to find the Union lines when they came near a cabin. A Black man told them four Confederate soldiers were inside the cabin holding two women against their will. Hickok drew his revolvers and got the drop on all four men. One of the women, Susannah Moore, assisted Hickok and the other spies, giving them directions on how to reach the Union lines. There is no information on Susannah Moore, but her last name might have actually been Pruitt and she might have adopted her stepfather's last name of Moore. Susannah and Hickok must have hit it off as her name reoccurs in accounts of Hickok's later adventures.[58]

Buel claimed that in 1863, General Samuel Curtis again sent Wild Bill Hickok on a spy mission to learn the plans of Confederate generals Earl Van Dorn and Sterling Price. Hickok made his way behind enemy lines and enlisted as a private with the Confederate army near Pine Bluff, Arkansas. As the Confederates marched toward Curtis's troops, a Confederate corporal recognized Hickok. He was arrested, tried as a spy, and found guilty. Sentenced to be shot the next morning, the Confederates bound his hands behind his back and placed him in a log cabin with an armed guard outside the door. During the night, he rummaged through the cabin and found a knife which he used to cut his bounds. The guard had become drowsy and Hickok overpowered him, slitting his throat. Donning the guard's uniform and taking his weapon, Hickok made his way to the Union lines where he reported his observations to General Curtis.[59]

In the fall of 1863, Hickok acquired his famous horse Black Nell. The story goes Hickok was between Rolla and Springfield when he had a gun battle with three secessionists and killed them all. Black Nell belonged to one of the dead men. The US government sold the mare at auction where Hickok acquired her, paying $225. She was an intelligent horse, and Hickok taught her many tricks. Nichols and Buel told extraordinary tales about her and claimed she was supposed to have saved Hickok's life on several occasions. She was Hickok's favorite horse. When she died in 1869 in Kansas City, he buried her and visited her grave when in the area.[60]

The *Springfield Patriot* editor went to the other extreme, printing in the January 31, 1867 edition that Black Nell was not a mare but a "black stallion blind in the right eye and a 'goer.'" The article went on to say Black Nell would have been incapable of doing any of the tricks or feats Nichols claimed.[61]

Another unflattering account of Hickok and Black Nell is found in *The History of Greene County, Missouri*, which stated, "a favorite diversion of his was to ride his horse on sidewalks and into saloons, hotels, stores, and other public places, and make the animal lie down and perform other tricks, to the infinite delight, no doubt, of the proprietors, none of whom, unfortunately, had grit enough to blow the bully's head off."[62]

In March 1864, Wild Bill Hickok emerged again in official records of the Office of the Provost Marshal General in the section "Scouts, Guides, and Spies, 1861–65." He was to be paid $20 for services rendered as Special Police under the direction of Lieutenant N. H. Burns at Springfield from March 1 through 10. Then again, he was to be paid for the rest of the month for his services as Special Police. This was all approved by Brigadier General John

Sanborn with the District of Southwest Missouri Headquarters based in Springfield. Then as happens in all bureaucracies, the payments to Hickok were denied by a Colonel Sanderson "for the reason that no authority was issued by the Pro Mar Genl of Dept of the Mo, for the employment of this man." However, the Springfield District Headquarters listed Hickok employed as a detective. On April 3, 1864, Brigadier General Sanborn issued Special Order No. 89 that Hickok be enrolled as a scout for Headquarters under the direction of Captain Richard Bentley Owen and he would "be furnished a horse, and equipments while on duty as Scout" and "His compensation will be $5 per day."[63]

In September 1864, General Price, leading twelve thousand Confederate troops, invaded eastern Missouri from Arkansas. The plan was to march to St. Louis and raid the Union army warehouses, turn west, and capture Missouri's capital, Jefferson City. Continuing their march westward to Kansas, they were to turn south through Indian Territory, acquiring recruits, horses, and supplies along the way. Wild Bill Hickok was back to spying on Price's army, having joined them as they passed through Dardanelle, Arkansas, on September 2.[64]

After being pummeled by Union troops on September 27 at the Battle of Pilot Knob, south of St. Louis, the Confederate army marched westward along the southern bank of the Missouri River. The Union and Confederate armies clashed throughout the month of October until the Confederates marched south back into Arkansas.[65]

The story goes during Price's westward movement, Wild Bill Hickok, disguised as a Texan officer with General John Marmaduke's command, rode up to a farmhouse and asked the woman of the house for something to eat for which he would pay her. As he sat down at the table for a meal of milk and bread, he heard another person at the door who was also welcomed in to eat. That person was none other than Billy Cody.[66]

Will Cody (let's start calling him Will since he's in the army now) enlisted in the Kansas Seventh Cavalry at Fort Laramie on February 19, 1864, was mustered into service on February 24, 1864, and assigned to Company H commanded by Captain Charles Wall. Army records show he was from Leavenworth, Kansas, and eighteen years old. His eyes and hair were brown, and he stood five feet ten inches tall. His occupation was listed as teamster.[67]

On March 12, 1864, the regiment left Fort Leavenworth under the command of Colonel Thomas Herrick, traveling to St. Louis, then to Memphis, Tennessee, arriving there on June 6. The regiment was assigned to protect work gangs on the Memphis and Charleston Railroad.[68]

The major Confederate force in the area was General Nathan Bedford Forrest's cavalry, which was constantly on the attack. One of Forrest's many sayings was, "War means fighting, and fighting means killing."[69]

Forrest had been striking Union troops raiding into Tennessee and Kentucky. On April 12, 1864, his men had captured Union-held Fort Pillow north of Memphis along the Mississippi River in Tennessee. Approximately half of the garrison of 580 men were Black troops. Forrest's troops assaulted the fort. There were reports his men slaughtered Black troops trying to surrender. Up to 49 percent of the Union troops were killed, and 64 percent of those, possibly as many as 190 of them, were Black. In contrast, Forrest lost fourteen men killed.[70]

On June 10, Union general Samuel Sturgis fought Forrest's troops at Brice's Cross Roads, Mississippi, and was soundly defeated. For two days, Forrest's troops harried the Union soldiers as they retreated toward Memphis. Units of the Seventh Kansas arrived in time to help cover the retreat of Sturgis's troops.[71]

Union general Andrew Smith reorganized the defeated troops. The Seventh Kansas was placed in a cavalry corps led by General Benjamin Grierson. In early July, Smith's forces began to consolidate and march east toward Forrest's troops. The Seventh

Kansas, acting as the advance guard, fought an hour's skirmish with Confederate troops near Ripley, Mississippi.[72]

On July 8, 1864, the Seventh Kansas was the advance guard and fought Colonel Robert "Black Bob" McCulloch's troops at Pontotoc, Mississippi, until Black Bob withdrew. The next day, as the army marched toward Tupelo, Mississippi, the Seventh Kansas saw action against Confederate troops as it acted as the rearguard. On July 14, Smith's and Forrest's forces clashed in the Battle of Tupelo. The Seventh Kansas saw minor action protecting Smith's right. The battle was a defeat for Forrest, who withdrew from the field.[73]

On July 15 and 16, the Seventh Kansas skirmished with Confederate troops. Then from July 17 to 19, the regiment escorted the wounded back to LaGrange, Tennessee, east of Memphis. For the rest of July and all of August, the Seventh Kansas saw plenty of action against Confederate troops in northern Mississippi.[74]

Will Cody said concerning the Seventh Kansas time in Mississippi, "This kind of fighting was all new to me.... I soon became a non-commissioned officer, and was put on detached service as a scout." However, the record shows Cody was mustered out as a private, so if he did become a noncommissioned officer, it was only a temporary change in rank.[75]

On September 6, 1864, the Seventh Kansas was ordered to return to Missouri to help repel the advance of Confederate general Sterling Price and his subordinate generals Jo Shelby and John Marmaduke. The Seventh missed the battle of Pilot Knob but saw action from there on until Price led his army south at the end of October.[76]

Will Cody said he continued working as a scout during the campaign against Price's army. He related that one day he had ridden far ahead of the Seventh Kansas and stopped at a farmhouse. The woman of the house invited him in. He was startled to see Wild Bill Hickok sitting at a table eating bread and drinking milk. He sat down to eat too, and after Hickok paid the woman of the house, they went outside.[77]

When Will Cody told Hickok about his mother's death, Hickok was surprised and grieved. Cody later wrote, "He thought a great deal of her, for she had treated him almost as one of her own children." Hickok told Cody he planned to continue to spy on Price's troops. On parting, he gave Cody verbal information about the Confederate army's position and troop strength as well as a packet of letters to give to General John McNeil, commander of the Second Brigade to which the Seventh Kansas was attached.[78]

A few days later, Will Cody rode with the advance guard ahead of the Union column. He dropped out to obtain water from a farmhouse. The only people there were the woman of the house and her two daughters. They were frightened of Will since he was a Yankee. He assured them he meant them no harm. After realizing he meant what he said, they fixed him lunch. Will knew their concerns were justified about the possibility of troops ransacking their house, so he stayed with them and stood outside telling any troops that approached that the commanding officer had placed him there to guard the house and no one was to enter. He continued to guard the house until the column and rearguard passed. The mother and daughters insisted he stay for a dinner they prepared for him.[79]

As Will finished his meal, three men with leveled, double-barreled shotguns entered the room. The mother explained the situation to the men, who turned out to be her husband and two sons. The husband thanked Cody and shook his hand but told him he had better rejoin the Union column before bushwhackers cut him off. Will quickly caught up with the Union troops and was happy he had done a good deed, even if the family were Confederate sympathizers.[80]

On October 23, Will Cody's Seventh Kansas was in the thick of the battle of Westport, outside Kansas City. When considering the number of men involved, it was the largest battle of the war in Missouri. The fighting seesawed back and forth during the day, with Price's Confederates attacking General Curtis's troops first. Union major general Alfred Pleasonton brought his troops into Price's rear forcing him to retreat.[81]

On October 25, Union troops were pursuing the Confederate army as it retreated southwest into Kansas. General Marmaduke was leading the rearguard at Mine Creek when he was shot in the arm and thrown from his horse. Union private James Dunlavy captured the general and marched him to General Curtis's headquarters.[82]

Cody's last autobiography claimed he was with a small advance party that captured General Marmaduke. Cody asked him if there was anything he could do for him. Marmaduke replied he had had nothing to eat. Cody brought him food from his saddlebag. He also obtained a bottle of whiskey from a friend and gave it to the general. Cody claimed he was in charge of taking Marmaduke to Fort Leavenworth and along the way, they became friends.[83]

However, in Cody's first autobiography he made no mention of Marmaduke. After the Battle of Mine Creek, he remained with the Seventh Kansas pursuing Price's troops reaching the area near Fort Scott, Kansas. There, he saw two riders dash from the Confederate lines toward the Union lines as Confederate troops shot at them. As Cody's regiment advanced to meet the riders, the Confederates shot one of them out of the saddle, but the other rider made it to their position. Cody recognized the rider. It was Wild Bill Hickok wearing a Confederate uniform. Hickok reported to generals Pleasanton and McNeil on Price's troop strength and plans.[84] Hickok's ride may have been just after the battle of Newtonia, Missouri, on October 28. The *Leavenworth Daily Conservative* stated in its February 1, 1867 edition, "He [Hickok] came into Gen. [James] Blunt's camp on the morning after the battle of Newtonia, having previously been with Price, and having spent several months in the [Confederate] camps in Arkansas."[85]

Will Cody could not have escorted General Marmaduke to Fort Leavenworth and fought with the Seventh Kansas at the same time. It's possible Cody met Marmaduke after his capture, but there is no record he was detailed to guard and escort Marmaduke to Fort Leavenworth.

Union General Curtis continued to follow Price and his Confederate army to Webbers Falls twenty miles into Indian Territory.

Price's men had crossed the Arkansas River and burned all the available boats, so Curtis ended his pursuit there on November 8 and returned to Missouri. Cody said after Hickok's return to the Union lines, the two of them scouted together until Curtis ended the chase of Price's army. The Seventh Kansas went to Springfield, Missouri, where Will and Wild Bill spent two weeks "having a jolly good time."[86]

Will Cody's regiment was sent to St. Louis, and then on December 11, 1864, it was ordered south to De Soto, Missouri. On January 23, 1865, Cody was on detached duty at an army hospital at Pilot Knob. On February 19, he was reassigned as an orderly at the Army's St. Louis Headquarters. His duties included working with the Freedman's Relief Society to assist homeless and impoverished former slaves as well as most likely carrying dispatches throughout the military district. This work was briefly interrupted on April 5 when he received a furlough to Weston, Missouri, and from there visited family and friends at Leavenworth.[87]

By May 1, 1865, Will Cody was back in St. Louis. His friend Will McDonald invited him along to visit the home of his aunt and uncle, the Fredericis. There they found McDonald's cousin Louisa asleep in a chair by the fire. Deciding to play a practical joke on her, the two Wills jerked the chair out from under her. Louisa reached around to slap her cousin's face only to hit Cody in the mouth. You might say they hit it off. He began spending his free time with her and later wrote, "Her lovely face, her gentle disposition and her graceful manners won my admiration and love." Louisa said about Cody on first meeting him, "And he was handsome, about the most handsome man I had ever seen! . . . Clean shaven, the ruddiness of health glowing in his cheeks; graceful, lithe, smooth in his movements and in the modulations of his speech, he was quite the most wonderful man I had ever known, and I almost bit my tongue to keep from telling him so." Will and Louisa began seeing each other and soon fell in love.[88]

Wild Bill's race for the Union lines

The whereabouts of Wild Bill Hickok were murky after the Confederates retreated across the Arkansas River. Some sources claimed he joined the Red Legs Scouts and others said he was a member of the Buckskin Scouts, but there is no definitive record of him with either of those groups. It's possible he may have ridden with one or the other or both groups a time or two, never actually joining either. Whatever the case, he most likely continued scouting and spying.[89]

J. W. Buel, in his *Heroes of the Plains*, told a fictitious tale. On January 22, 1865, outside Lawrence, Kansas, Wild Bill was to have fought a traitorous Sioux chief named Conquering Bear in single combat using only knives. After a lengthy struggle, Conquering Bear inflicted a severe knife wound on Hickok's left arm that "struck to the bone near the shoulder point and stripped the flesh half way to his elbow." Hickok ended the combat by slashing Conquering Bear's jugular vein. A young Sioux named Indian Joe was there and bound Hickok's wounds. Hickok took Indian Joe with him to Kansas City where his old friend Doctor Joshua Thorne treated his wounds.[90]

Buel's story has major problems. There was no Sioux chief named Conquering Bear alive at the time of this incident. There is no other record of this fight. There is no record of Indian Joe. No one else mentions Hickok with a severe wound which would have taken a long time to heal. Chalk this story up as a tall tale unless someone finds reliable evidence.

On February 10, 1865, Wild Bill Hickok was in Cassville, Missouri, where he wrote a letter to Brigadier General John Sanborn at his Springfield, Missouri headquarters, reporting on Confederate troop strength at Camp Walker and Spavinaw in Indian Territory. On February 11, Sanborn replied, "You may go to Yellville [Arkansas] or the White River in the vicinity of Yellville and learn what [Colonel Archibald] Dobbin[s] intends to do with his command now on Crowley's Ridge, and from there come to this place." There is no record of what Hickok found concerning Dobbins and his cavalry regiment.[91]

On April 9, 1865, William Darnell's wagon train was approaching Fort Zarah, Kansas, when a heavily armed Wild Bill Hickok raced by on "a dandy horse" shouting, "Lee's surrendered! Lee's surrendered!" There is no record of what Hickok's duties were at the time.[92]

On June 9, 1865, Hickok was back in Springfield, Missouri, when Headquarters District Southwest Missouri issued Special Order No. 142 dropping men from the roll of scouts, including J. B. Hickok.[93]

On October 14, 1890, Brevet-Major-General John Sanborn stated in an address "The Campaign in Missouri in September and October 1864":

Detachments from my command reconnoitered the position and movements of the enemy daily and nightly. My principal scout was William Hickok, "Wild Bill," the real hero of many exploits, and, according to the dime novels, the imaginary hero of many more. Bill was a fine scout and detective.

He entered the Rebel camps, was arrested as a spy, and even taken before General Price; but his inordinate nerve and great self-possession not only saved him, but made him an orderly on Price's staff. He eventually escaped, and returned to me with valuable information during the battle of Newtonia.[94]

CHAPTER 6

INCIDENT AT SPRINGFIELD (JULY 1865–JANUARY 1866)

Twenty-eight-year-old Wild Bill Hickok remained in Springfield, Missouri, when on June 10, 1865, the Union army dropped him from its roll of scouts. On July 20, Hickok was involved in a card game with a so-called friend, Davis Tutt. The two began to argue. The game ended with their quarrel unresolved. The next day they shot at each other in the public square. There was and remains lots of speculation as to what happened between Tutt and Hickok.

In 1883, the author of *History of Greene County* gave his unflattering opinion of Hickok and Tutt. "Hickok," the author wrote, "being by nature a ruffian he soon became a desperado—a drunken, swaggering fellow." The author turned to Tutt: "A man after Wild Bill's heart ... David Tutt, an ex-Confederate soldier ... was a ruffian and a crack pistol shot. He was said to have 'gotten in his work,' not only on Federal soldiers, but on citizens who had crossed his path against his protest. Both Tutt and Hickok were gamblers, and good ones, although the ex-Confederate was the more proficient of the two. The two men were boon companions for a time; the one touch of ruffianism make them both akin. They walked the streets together, they drank together, they gambled together—and in the latter pastime Tutt effectively 'cleaned out' Bill."[1]

Davis K. Tutt, also known as David, was from Yellville, Arkansas. At the time of his feud with Hickok he was twenty-six years old. Davis served as a private in the Twenty-Seventh Regiment of Arkansas Infantry. He was handy with a gun, and there were unconfirmed reports he was a Confederate spy. Some said he betrayed Hickok during the war. In Colonel George Ward Nichols's later story about Wild Bill Hickok, his character "Captain Honesty" would claim, "Bill had killed Dave Tutt's mate, and, atween one thing and another, there war an onusual hard feeling atwixt 'em."[2]

By 1864, Tutt had abandoned the Confederate army for the Union army, working for Richard Owen, chief quartermaster for the District of South-West Missouri in Springfield. Hickok also worked for Owen, and the two of them were friends.[3]

Hickok and Tutt may have first met in Yellville. In 1863, while acting as a Union scout, Hickok lived in a Yellville boardinghouse owned by a Mrs. Estes who said Hickok was "as nice a man at her home as she ever had about her house." J. P. Botkin, a Union scout, later claimed Hickok had an affair with Tutt's sister, who bore him a son out of wedlock. Tutt was furious, swearing revenge on Hickok. Toward the war's end, Lewis Tutt, Davis's Black half-brother, brought Davis's mother, sister, and younger brothers to Springfield where they joined Davis.[4]

Some people claimed Susannah Moore, who allegedly had assisted Hickok in his escape through Confederate lines back in 1862, was now living in Springfield, and she and Hickok were lovers. For whatever reason, the two of them had an argument and broke up. Tutt then made advances toward Susannah. Hickok, in kind, began seeing Tutt's sister, and her mother was not pleased. Tutt told Hickok to stay away from his sister and they quarreled.[5]

Davis Tutt had gambling problems in Springfield. In December 1864, he was charged with illegal gambling and resisting arrest. His court trial was set for July 20, 1865. The judge fined him $100 plus court costs. He could not pay the fine and was thrown in jail. Thomas Martin, one of Hickok's fellow scouts, vouched for Tutt and he was released.[6]

Later that same evening, Tutt and Hickok sat down to a game of cards in Hickok's upper room at the Lyon House also known as the Old Southern Hotel. Hickok pulled out his pocket watch and sat it on the table as they played cards. W. S. Riggs, who was in the room, said a dispute began between Tutt and Hickok when Tutt claimed Hickok owed him $35. Hickok said he owed him $25. He had already paid him $10 at Oak Hall, a clothing store.[7]

Tutt grabbed Hickok's pocket watch saying he was keeping it until Hickok paid up. Hickok invited Tutt to go downstairs with him to get his pocketbook and look in it at his account to check the amount, but Tutt left with Hickok's watch. As Tutt left the room, he told Riggs if Hickok wanted his watch, he would have to pay him not $35 but now $45.[8]

John Orr was in the room and witnessed the affair. Later, most likely the next day, Hickok saw Orr and said "to tell Tutt to bring his watch back in one hour and he would receive the $25 and if he did not return the watch something else would be done." Tutt did not return the watch.[9]

Sources say Hickok's pocket watch was a Waltham gold hunter case repeater, meaning it could be set to chime—a valuable watch.[10]

About 5:00 p.m. the next day, July 21, Eli Armstrong, who was friends with both Hickok and Tutt, saw them sitting with John Orr on the Lyon House porch. Armstrong walked up to the men asking, "Boys, what's up?"

"Nothing much," Hickok responded, telling him there was only a little dispute between Tutt and him over some money and Tutt had grabbed his watch off a table at the Lyon House claiming Hickok owed him $45. Hickok said he only owed Tutt $25.

"Boys, if that is all that is between you, I think I can settle it," Armstrong said. He took Tutt aside telling him he should accept $35 from Hickok and negotiate the additional $10 later. Tutt said he would take it rather than have a fight. Armstrong took Hickok aside and told him what he had worked out with Tutt. Hickok remained firm, saying he would pay $25 and the additional $10 if his memorandum book showed he owed Tutt $35.

Tutt then said he would take nothing less than $45. Pulling out Hickok's watch, he held it up saying, "When you pay the $45, you can get this."

Hickok replied he would rather have a fight with any man on earth than Tutt. "For you have accommodated me more than any man in town for I have borrowed money from you time and again, and we have never had any dispute before in our settlement."

Tutt said he knew that, and he did not want any difficulty himself.

"Boys, that settles it then," Armstrong said.

"Let us all go in and get a drink," Hickok said.

They entered the Lyon House's barroom. As they drank, Tutt said nothing. After finishing his drink, he left—taking Hickok's watch with him. When Armstrong finished his drink, he left Hickok and Orr in the barroom and walked across the square to the courthouse where he sat down in the doorway.[11]

Wild Bill Hickok left the Lyon House and walked north about a block's length to the southeast corner of Springfield's public square and sat down near Robertson and Manson's store. News of Tutt and Hickok's dispute traveled rapidly. A crowd gathered around Hickok.[12]

Oliver Scott walked up to Hickok who said "the Tutts were all going for him." Hickok told Scott about his dispute with Tutt, after which Scott sat down beside him. A. L. Budlong walked up to them, and Hickok told him what he had just told Scott. Hickok then told them to get away from there. Scott and Budlong moved away and sat down in front of May's Store. Before sitting down, Budlong had entered Hursh's store announcing, "There was a difficulty," and Thomas Hudson left with him. Scott heard Hickok talking with F. E. Scholten. He heard Hickok say Tutt should not cross the square with his watch.[13]

It was about 6:00 p.m.; F. E. Scholten had been heading to a supplier when he saw the crowd gathered at the square's corner. It appeared to him Hickok and Orr "were about to get in some difficulty." Hickok "was accusing Orr of being a friend of David

Tutt and told Mr. Orr he had better leave that corner." Orr told Hickok "the street belonged to him as much as any other person and he did not wish to have any difficulty with him." Scholten asked Hickok what the problem was. After Hickok repeated the debt and watch story to Scholten, Davis Tutt's brother, John, "stepped up at the time and stated to Haycock [*sic*] he was sorry there was a difficulty between Haycock & David Tutt & if he (Haycock) would come down David Tutt would settle it with them[,] from that Haycock started toward Crenshaw's store with wit. [Scholten] [They] got opposite McClure's store. Saw Tutt coming from Low and Morrel's Saloon near the Court House[,] after Tutt passed the Court House some thirty paces[,] Haycock hallowed [*sic*] at him & said ['] David you can not come any further [*sic*] and pack my watch['.] from that Tutt put his hand to his side [and] Haycock drew his revolver[.]" Scholten turned around and got about ten to fifteen paces away when he heard the report of a pistol.[14]

Eli Armstrong had been sitting in the courthouse doorway when he saw Tutt walk north from the public square to McDaniel's livery stable. Tutt returned a few minutes later and walked south about ten paces from the courthouse.[15]

Hickok and Tutt, displaying Hickok's watch, walked toward each other and were about seventy-five yards apart, kitty-corner between Hickok's original position and the courthouse, when Hickok called out to Tutt.[16]

Armstrong heard Hickok say, "David you cannot cross this square and jerck [*sic*] my watch." Tutt did not reply but placed his hand on the butt of his revolver. Armstrong said they both fired but he could not tell who fired first.[17]

Tutt had taken a dueling stance with his right-side facing Hickok and reached for his revolver. Hickok saw Tutt's movement and pulled his gun. They both fired. Witnesses said the two shots were so close they sounded as one.[18]

Lorenza Lee said she "looked down for a moment only and as I again raised my eyes saw the flash and smoke of two revolvers."[19]

The Wild Bill and Davis Tutt incident in Springfield, Missouri

Tutt's shot missed Hickok. Hickok's shot hit Tutt in the right side of the chest. Tutt held his chest wound as he ran to the courthouse. Armstrong heard him say, "Boys I am killed." Tutt circled one of the courthouse's columns and fell dead on the sidewalk.[20]

Scholten said to Hickok, "That is rather hard." Hickok replied, "it was too late now & he was not sorry."[21]

Colonel Albert Barnitz, the military commander of the post of Springfield, witnessed the shooting. He had Hickok immediately arrested and handed over to the civilian authorities. That night, Barnitz wrote in his journal:

> *[Hickok] is a noted scout, desperado, and gambler, as was also the man he killed. Both have been in the habit of appearing on the street with two revolvers strapped on their belts—both have been intimate for years and have been gambling together today. The ill will seems to have originated at the gambling table—"Tut" appropriating a watch which belonged to "Wild Bill" and refusing to give it up until a debt of $35 which he*

alleged was due him from "Wild Bill" was paid. "Wild Bill"
desired him thereupon to distinctly understand that he ("Tut")
couldn't walk the streets wearing his ("Wild Bill's") watch, but
the admonition was not heeded. Both fired simultaneously, as
it appeared to me, at the distance of about 100 paces. "Tut"
was shot directly through the chest, he was the son and support
of a widow lady of this place.[22]

Coroner J. F. Brown convened a six-man jury that night. Doctor Edwin Ebert examined Tutt's body stating "that a bullet had entered on the right side between the 5th and 7th rib and passed out on the left between the 5th and 7th rib. . . . From his sudden death I am led to believe that some of the large blood vessels were wounded." The next day, July 22, after hearing eight witnesses give their written testimony, the coroner's jury reached its verdict, "That Davis K. Tutt came to his death by a pistol shot and that the jury further find that the said violence causing said death was committed by a certain James B. Hickock [*sic*]. . . ."[23]

That same day, bail was set at $2,000. Hickok's friend and former boss, Captain Richard Owen, Isaac Hoff, and John Jenkins posted bail for him. Hickok had been charged with murder, but on July 24, the charge was changed to manslaughter.[24]

Owen was the Army's quartermaster in Springfield. He had served as a quartermaster throughout the war, and at times, Hickok had served under him. During the Civil War, the quartermaster was responsible for spying, scouting, and police activities. Owen was well-liked by the Springfield community, and Hickok and he were friends.[25]

Saturday evening, July 22, Barnitz wrote in his journal, "'Wild Bill' has been released on bail. Public sympathy seems to be about equally divided between him and his victim."[26]

Hickok's defense lawyer was Colonel John Phelps. Phelps had organized a six-month regiment named after him that had fought at Pea Ridge. Hickok may have joined with him during that fight. Captain Richard Owen had also served under Phelps as his quartermaster. In July 1862, President Abraham Lincoln had appointed Phelps as the military governor of Arkansas. In 1864, he resigned and returned to his law practice in Springfield.[27]

The state's attorney was Colonel Robert Fyan. The judge was C. B. M'Afee, who had been the Union commander at Springfield at the end of the war.[28]

The trial opened on August 3; Hickok pled not guilty to manslaughter. Thirty witnesses testified including Richard Owen and Hickok's scouting companion Thomas Martin. Of those witnesses who saw the actual shooting, all testified Tutt had fired first, and his revolver was exhibited to show one chamber was empty. Unfortunately, the recorded testimonies of the witnesses are missing.[29]

On August 15, Judge M'Afee gave the jurors their instructions that covered sixteen detailed statements when considering Hickok's innocence or guilt. These instructions had been prepared by Fyan, the prosecuting attorney. Judge M'Afee gave those instructions to the jury as well as his own.[30] M'Afee's instructions were lengthy ending with:

> *That when danger is threatened and impending a man is not compelled to stand with his arms folded until it is too late to offer successful resistance & if the jury believe from the evidence that Tutt was a fighting character & a dangerous man & that Deft was aware such was his character & that Tutt at the time he was shot by the Deft was advancing on him with a drawn pistol & that Tutt had previously made threats of personal injury to Deft & that Deft had been informed of such threats & that Deft shot Tutt to prevent the threatened impending injury & that at the time the Deft shot Tutt the Deft had reasonable cause to apprehend Tutt intended to do Deft great personal injury & that the danger to Deft was imminent & of such design being accomplished the jury will acquit.*
>
> *That if the jury from the evidence have reasonable doubts of the guilt of the Deft they will acquit.*[31]

The jury's deliberations took ten minutes before returning with its verdict, "We the Jury find the Deft not guilty in manner and form charged."[32]

Not all Springfield residents were happy with the verdict. Springfield's *Missouri Weekly Patriot* editorialized in its August 10, 1865 edition, "The citizens of this city were shocked and terrified at the idea that a man could arm himself and take a position at a corner of the public square, in the centre of the city, and await the approach of his victim for an hour or two, and then willingly engage in conflict which resulted in his instant death ... the Court instructed the jury ... that he [Hickok] was not entitled to an acquittal on the ground of self-defense unless he was anxious to avoid the fight, and used all reasonable means to do so; but the jury seems to have thought differently."[33]

Wild Bill Hickok moved on from the shooting of Davis Tutt. He ran for the office of Springfield's marshal. The election was held September 13, 1865. Out of a slate of five candidates, Charles Moss won with 107 votes; Hickok came in second with 63 votes.[34]

That same day, Hickok met Colonel George Ward Nichols, who would later write of Hickok's exploits. Nichols was in Springfield accompanying General Thomas Church Haskell Smith, the inspector general of the District of South-West Missouri. Originally from Maine, Nichols was raised in Boston, Massachusetts, and was the same age as Hickok. He was on the staff of the New York *Evening Post* before joining the Union army as a captain in 1862. Nichols served as an aide to Major General John C. Frémont, and then in 1864, he joined the staff of Major General William Tecumseh Sherman with whom he became friends. He was on Sherman's Georgia and Carolinas campaigns and wrote bestselling accounts of them. By March 13, 1865, he had been promoted to lieutenant colonel for meritorious service.[35]

Realizing Hickok might make a great story, Nichols took notes of his impressions and their conversations as well as obtained Hickok's photograph before leaving town.[36]

On January 26, 1866, Springfield policeman John Orr shot and killed James Coleman. Coleman and his brother Samuel along with a friend named Bingham rode into town from the country and went on a drinking spree. When they had their fill of fun, they prepared to ride out of town. Bingham disturbed the peace, whooping and hollering. As the police started to arrest him, the Coleman brothers came to his rescue. Wild Bill Hickok witnessed the fight and testified at the coroner's jury that as the police tried to subdue Bingham, "the two Colemans wanted to stop the police and have a talk with the police, from that they got to jarring worse and worse until the[y] commenced shooting; the first I saw of the shooting I saw John Orr jerk his pistol and put it up against the man [James Coleman] and shot. . . ." The fight continued and Hickok told how Orr also shot Samuel Coleman. Hickok and others carried James Coleman into a drug store.[37]

People living in the countryside were incensed. They believed they were held to a higher standard than townspeople. After meeting with irate citizens from the countryside, city leaders fired the entire police force. Orr was arrested and released on bail. He fled and was never brought to trial.[38]

Soon after this incident, Wild Bill Hickok received a message from Captain Richard Owen, who was now assistant post quartermaster at Fort Riley, Kansas. He had a job for Hickok. There was nothing to hold Hickok in Springfield. Davis Tutt's sister had left town, and there was no mention of the elusive Susannah Moore. Hickok headed west.[39]

CHAPTER 7

SCOUTS (JULY 1865–AUGUST 1867)

As the Civil War was winding down, Will Cody continued on special duty as an orderly at the Army's St. Louis Headquarters, assisting former slaves through the Freedman's Relief Society, and carrying dispatches throughout the military district.[1] Cody continued to court Louisa Frederici, and they fell in love.[2]

On September 13, 1865, Private Will Cody received orders to return to Fort Leavenworth to rejoin the Seventh Kansas, where on September 29 they were mustered out of service. That October, Will returned to St. Louis for a brief visit to ask Louisa if she would marry him. She said yes, and they planned to marry in the near future. Cody said, "When I bade her goodbye, I was one of the happiest of men."[3]

Returning to Leavenworth, Cody drove a string of horses to Fort Kearny where he met Bill Trotter, an old friend who was the division stage agent for the Overland Stage Company then owned by Ben Holladay. Trotter hired Cody to drive a stagecoach between Fort Kearny and Plum Creek Station to the west on the Oregon Trail.[4]

Most likely Cody was dressed in the attire Holladay wanted his drivers to wear—broad-brimmed sombreros, velvet-trimmed corduroy pants, and boots with high heels. Each driver was given a nine-foot rawhide whip with a silver-decorated handle.[5]

Cody drove the stagecoach until February 1866 when he resigned to return to Louisa in St. Louis. On March 6, they were married in Louisa's parents' house. Attending were Louisa's friends and soldiers who had served with Will in the army.[6]

An hour after the wedding ceremony, Louisa's parents escorted them to the riverfront where they bid Will and Louisa "a fond farewell and a God-speed" as the newlyweds boarded a riverboat bound for Leavenworth.[7]

When the riverboat pilot, a Frederici family friend, learned Louisa and Will had just married, he gathered the passengers in the main cabin where he introduced the newlyweds. Black crewmembers, belonging to the boat's orchestra, played the "Wedding March" and other tunes to celebrate the Codys' wedding.[8] Some passengers recognized Will and shunned the Codys because they said Will was a Kansas jayhawker and "one of Jennison's house burners."[9]

One night, the boat stopped alongside the riverbank to take on firewood for the steam engine. The Black workers were singing as they brought the wood onboard. Will and Louisa stood on deck listening to their songs when shots were fired on shore. Mounted bushwhackers attacked the workers, who quickly returned to the boat. As the boat gathered steam and pulled away from the riverbank, Will claimed the bushwhackers' leader shouted, "Where is the black abolition jayhawker?" while another shouted, "Show him to us and we'll shoot him!" Cody believed there were bushwhackers aboard who had wired ahead to friends to let them know he was onboard and planned to capture and murder him.[10]

When the steamboat stopped in Kansas City, Will did his own telegraphing ahead to Leavenworth so when their riverboat pulled up to Leavenworth's wharf that evening, sixty family and friends as well as a brass band were there to welcome the newlyweds. A carriage awaited them, and they were driven to Will's sister Eliza's house where a reception was held. Sister Julia gave Louisa the family stamp of approval telling Will, "We all love sister Lou."[11]

The Cody family's old home and hotel in Salt Creek Valley was now owned by Doctor J. J. Crook, who had been the Kansas

Seventh Cavalry surgeon. Crook rented the entire hotel to Will Cody, who lived in it with Louisa and his sister Helen, while renting out the rest of the rooms. He named it the Golden Rule House.[12]

Helen said, "Now, Will radiated hospitality, and his reputation as a lover of his fellowman got so widely abroad that travelers without money and without price would go miles out of their way to put up at his tavern. Socially he was an irreproachable landlord; financially his shortcomings were deplorable."[13]

In September 1866, Cody had enough of running a hotel and became restless. Settling his hotel accounts and finding a house for Louisa and Helen, he headed west to make his fortune—alone. He planned to get a job with the construction of the Union Pacific Railroad, Eastern Division, at Salina, Kansas, the railhead at that time.[14]

During midwinter 1866, Wild Bill Hickok arrived at Fort Riley, Kansas. His friend Captain Richard Owen, who was the fort's assistant quartermaster, had sent him a message that he had a job for him.[15]

The Army had built Fort Riley in 1853 to protect travelers on the Santa Fe Trail. The fort's location was in the Flint Hills at the confluence of the Smoky Hill and Republican Rivers, approximately 116 miles west of Fort Leavenworth. The Army believed the fort did not need walls. Its parade ground was rimmed by buildings including headquarters, six-double houses for officer quarters, six two-story barracks, five stables, chapel, post office, and sutler's store, all constructed using native limestone.[16]

Fort Riley was a rough and tumble place. On January 24, 1866, before Owen and Hickok's arrival, a 2:00 a.m. fire destroyed the commissary building where the quartermaster had storerooms. First estimates were a million dollars in property was destroyed. Later Fort Riley's Board of Officers determined the value to be $33,366.64. Rumor had it an officer started the fire to balance his books. The board stated, "that the fire originated in the south side of the building in a room used by the Quartermaster for storage of clothing, camp and garrison equipage."[17]

The Army sent Captain Richard Owen to Fort Riley to make things more efficient and restore order. Owen, in turn, believed Hickok was just the man to help him do that and sent him a message to come join him. George Hance had been a friend of Wild Bill and his brother Lorenzo Hickok since 1862 when they were teamsters together in Rolla, Missouri. Hance was currently working as a wagon master for Owen out of Fort Riley. He later wrote that Owen and Major General Langdon Easton, chief quartermaster based at Fort Leavenworth, recommended Hickok be appointed a deputy US marshal, although no official records have been found. At the time, Thomas Osborne was the US marshal for Kansas. It would not be until 1896 that the US Marshals Service would keep records of appointments and pay regular salaries. In 1866, deputy marshals might be identified by letters of authorization and would usually be paid fees for services rendered as well as travel expenses. Deputy marshals were authorized to be concerned with federal offenses and government property. It would make sense to empower Hickok with the deputy marshal authority if he was to track down missing government property, which is exactly what he was hired to do.[18]

On March 11, 1866, Owens contracted with Wild Bill Hickok to track down missing public property and paid him $125 per month. Hickok's brother Lorenzo was also working out of Fort Riley for the quartermaster department as a wagon master. He had been there since October 1865 and would continue until December 1866.[19]

Hance said one day he met Wild Bill returning to Fort Riley from a three-week trip through the Council Grove and Little Arkansas River country to the south. Singlehanded, Hickok had recovered nine mules and captured three deserters. One of the deserters, a large man, rode alongside Hickok. Hance wrote, "I asked Wild Bill if he was not afraid to take such chances, as that big man could reach and draw one of the six-shooters, and then they would be on equal terms. He replied he could easily draw the other and shoot every one of them dead before they could fire a shot."[20]

From April to September 1866, Wild Bill Hickok was listed as a "guide" and paid $75 per month. Lorenzo later wrote Wild Bill worked as a government scout while at Fort Riley. He may have also assisted Owen in keeping the peace at the fort, but no official records or newspaper accounts have been found to verify that.[21]

When Hickok first arrived at Fort Riley, he became friends with Dr. William Finlaw and his family. Finlaw was with the Fifth US Volunteer Infantry and acting surgeon at the fort. In April 1866, Finlaw was transferred to Fort McPherson in Nebraska Territory, but left his family behind at Fort Riley to join him later.[22]

General William Tecumseh Sherman, whose scorched earth policies during the Civil War helped defeat the Confederacy, was appointed commander of the Army's Division of the Missouri that took in most of the territory north of Texas between the Mississippi River and the Rocky Mountains. Sherman was interested in seeing the progress of the railroad lines being built across the plains.[23]

In early May 1866, Sherman and his escort traveled the Union Pacific Railroad, Eastern Division, from Kansas City to its western terminus near Topeka east of Fort Riley. They proceeded by horse the rest of the way to Fort Riley. From there, they planned to travel by horseback and wagon north to Fort Kearny, then travel east to Omaha, and on to St. Paul, Minnesota. Sherman asked Owen for a reliable scout to take them north, and Owen suggested Wild Bill Hickok. Sherman and Hickok agreed he would guide the party as far as Fort Kearny. Dr. Finlaw's family joined Sherman's party as well.[24]

Stopping at Marysville, Kansas, seventy miles north of Fort Riley, Wild Bill Hickok and the Finlaw's little daughter enjoyed themselves along the Big Blue River, catching enough frogs to make a meal of them.[25]

From Marysville, Sherman's party traveled northwest to Rock Creek where they camped near Rock Creek Station, the site of

Hickok's deadly encounter with David McCanles and his men. Frank Helvey, who had been in the area at the time of the incident, was at the station when Sherman and Hickok rode in to warn the station employees not to sell the soldiers whiskey. When they arrived at Fort Kearny, Sherman headed east, and Hickok remained at the fort.[26]

This is a good place to tell a Will Cody story that most likely didn't happen. Years after the fact, Cody claimed he acted as a guide for General Sherman in 1865–1866 and had a letter from Sherman to prove it.

According to Cody, beginning in September 1865, he was one of General Sherman's guides during a tour of forts traveling from Fort Riley to Fort Kearny. Along the way, they detoured west to Council Springs at the confluence of the Arkansas and Little Arkansas Rivers where the Kiowas, Comanches, and other plains tribes were meeting with Indian agent Colonel Jesse Leavenworth and a federal peace commission. As they journeyed toward Council Springs, Cody believed the chief scout, Dick Curtis, was taking them too far west. Cody mentioned this to an officer who took Cody to Sherman and Curtis. Curtis conceded he might be wrong, and they corrected course. Cody was right. After the peace commissioners and tribal representatives signed what became known as the Little Arkansas Treaty on October 18, 1865, Cody guided Sherman and his party to Fort Kearny and on to Fort Leavenworth.[27]

Years later in 1887, when Cody's *Buffalo Bill's Wild West* was exhibiting in London, England, Cody wrote to General Sherman asking for a testimonial. Sherman wrote back that Cody "had guided me honestly and faithfully, in 1865–66, from Fort Riley to Kearny in Kansas and Nebraska."[28]

In Cody's first autobiography, *The Life of Hon. William F. Cody, Known as Buffalo Bill*, published in 1879, he does not mention guiding General Sherman's party. Then after Sherman's 1887 testimonial, Cody tells the story of guiding the general from Fort Riley to Fort Kearny in his later autobiographies. Other than Cody's story no other record has been found documenting Cody guiding Sherman from Fort Riley to Fort Kearny in 1865.[29]

Sherman was interested in the railroads heading west. Late September 1865, he traveled from St. Louis to Omaha where he inspected the progress of the Union Pacific railroad and rode the rails to its terminus fifteen miles to the west on the railroad's first locomotive *Major General Sherman*. Sherman was impressed with the ongoing construction and stated how important it was to the unity of the nation to connect the East and West Coasts by rail.[30]

Sherman returned to Omaha and boarded the riverboat *Majors* that headed downriver, making stops at every town along the way including Leavenworth where he was forced to make a speech, finally arriving at Wyandotte, Kansas, outside Kansas City, the eastern terminus of the Union Pacific Railroad, Eastern Division. The railroad's chief contractor met Sherman there and together they traveled by rail in a private car to ten miles west of Lawrence to the western terminus where Sherman witnessed the crews laying track at an average of one mile per day. From there, he returned to St. Louis.[31]

The record shows Sherman did not travel any farther west than the terminuses of the two railroads and did not attend the Little Arkansas Treaty council. Most likely, by 1887, more than twenty years after the fact, Sherman confused Buffalo Bill with Wild Bill and the years 1865 and 1866. Cody did not correct the mistake but used it.

Back at Fort Kearny, Nebraska, in June 1866, Wild Bill Hickok and General Sherman had parted ways. General James Pope and his party had arrived at the fort. Pope was traveling westward along the Oregon Trail and planned to proceed to Denver, head south to Santa Fe, and return east by way of the Santa Fe Trail. Hickok signed on as Pope's guide. James Meline, who was part of Pope's party, described Hickok in his book *Two Thousand Miles on Horseback*, in the chapter "Letter IV, Nebraska. Fort Kearny, Nebraska Territory, June 11, 1866":

> By the way I forgot to tell you about our guide—the most strik-
> ing object in camp. Six feet, lithe, active, sinewy, daring rider,
> dead shot with pistol and rifle, long locks, fine features and
> mustache, buckskin leggings, red shirt, broad brim hat, two
> pistols in belt, rifle in hand—he is a picture. Has lived since he
> was eleven on the prairies; when a boy, rode Pony Express on
> the California route, and during the war was scout and spy.
> He goes by the name of Wild Bill, and tells wonderful stories
> of his horsemanship, fighting, and hair breadth escapes. We do
> not, however, feel under any obligation to believe them all.[32]

Wild Bill must have been pulling their legs a bit. Meline's book does not mention Hickok after this (Meline hardly mentioned any of the party by name). Meline wrote after touring Colorado and New Mexico they traveled east along the Santa Fe Trail and reached Fort Riley the first week of September 1866, where they would have left Hickok and taken a carriage to Wamego, Kansas, the passenger terminus for the advancing railroad line.[33]

Hickok resumed his duties at Fort Riley, tracking down horse-thieves, recovering stolen horses, and stopping illegal timber cutting. That fall, Dr. William Finlaw was reassigned to Fort Riley, and Hickok, leading ten men, escorted Finlaw's wife, her mother, and their children from Marysville to Fort Riley. When they camped for the night, he assured them they had nothing to fear from Indians; he would sleep close to their ambulance.[34]

On July 28, 1866, Congress had authorized the formation of four additional cavalry regiments, one of which was the Seventh Cavalry. The US Army selected Fort Riley as the organizational location for the Seventh and recruitment began in August.[35]

On October 16, Civil War hero Lieutenant Colonel George Armstrong Custer along with his wife Elizabeth, known as

Libbie, arrived at Fort Riley. Custer reported for duty on November 1 and assumed immediate command of the Seventh. However, it was temporary; he left on November 9 for Washington, DC, to take a mandatory exam all officers in new regiments were required to take. He did not return to Fort Riley until December 16. By then the Seventh Cavalry's commander Colonel Andrew Smith had arrived and taken command. There is no information as to when George and Libbie first met Wild Bill Hickok, but they did.[36]

Two developments took place during the fall of 1866 that affected Fort Riley and Hickok. Starting in Kansas City, the Union Pacific Railroad, Eastern Division, which would later change its name to Kansas Pacific Railroad, had laid its tracks as far west as nearby Junction City, and had constructed a spur line from Lawrence to Leavenworth. The rate of travel in eastern Kansas had been greatly increased.[37]

The second development was more personal. Hickok's good friend, Captain Richard Owen, was mustered out of service November 3, 1866, and returned to Springfield, Missouri. It's possible his health was failing. The 1870 Census would list him as an invalid, and he would die July 17, 1872.[38]

Sometime during late fall 1866, Will Cody stopped in Junction City on his way to Saline, Kansas, and ran into Wild Bill Hickok. Cody was heading west with the hope of getting a railroad construction job. Hickok, who was basing his activities out of Fort Ellsworth (later Fort Harker), told Cody the Army needed scouts. They traveled westward to Ellsworth, where the Army hired Cody as a scout.[39]

Hickok continued his scouting and deputy US marshal law enforcement activities. Thieves were stealing large numbers of horses from Fort Riley. In early January 1867, Hickok chose a small number of scouts and led them into the Solomon River Valley and then down the Republican River, pursuing horse-thieves. Hickok and his posse returned later that month with over two hundred horses and mules, but no thieves. Hickok reported some of the thieves had fought back, but they would not be troubling the region anymore.[40]

January continued to be a busy month. Hickok and his good friend and scouting partner, Jack Harvey, arrested two men for possessing stolen mules. He led a posse west of Fort Riley and north of the railroad construction where he arrested John Hobbs and twenty-eight workmen, who were on federal land illegally felling trees to cut into railroad ties. Hickok and his men escorted their prisoners to Topeka. Later that summer, a federal court acquitted the tree cutters as Hickok and his deputies could not testify against them as they were out scouting for the Army.[41]

In January 1867, copies of the February edition of the widely read *Harper's New Monthly Magazine* began to be distributed nationwide. With its release, Wild Bill Hickok's life would never be the same.[42]

Colonel George Ward Nichols wrote *Harper's* lead article, "Wild Bill." This was the same Colonel George Ward Nichols who had visited Springfield, Missouri, and had met Hickok on September 13, 1865. Nichols and Hickok likely had a good talk over a few drinks.

The Bostonian Nichols opened his article with four long paragraphs insulting the citizens of Springfield, calling them "strange, half-civilized people. . . . Men and Women dressed in queer costumes." After describing the men's filthy clothing, he continued his attack, "These men . . . were lazily occupied doing nothing . . . their highest ambition to let their hair and beards grow." Into this scene of "a Rip Van Winkel sleep," Wild Bill, riding his horse Black Nell, dashed across the town square and came to a stop in front of Nichols and the people with him including his new acquaintance, "Captain Honesty." Hickok dismounted and Captain Honesty said to Nichols, "This yere is Wild Bill, Colonel." Then to Hickok he said, "How are yer, Bill? This yere is Colonel N—, who wants ter know yer."[43]

Throughout the story, Nichols called Hickok either "William Hitchcock" or "Wild Bill." Nichols said about Hickok, "As I looked at him I thought his the handsomest *physique* I had ever seen." Nichols spent a long paragraph describing Hickok. He portrayed Hickok speaking the same made-up, backwoods jargon as Captain Honesty, "I allers shot well; but I come ter be perfect in the mountains by shootin at a dime for a mark, at best a half dollar a shot. And then until the war I never drank liquor nor smoked."[44]

Nichols backtracked to before Hickok's arrival having Captain Honesty relate "in his own words" the Hickok-Tutt fight including statements and conversations by the participants in the same made-up jargon. After finishing the account of the fight and Hickok's acquittal, Nichols had Captain Honesty say the following, "*The fact is thar was an undercurrent of a woman in that fight.*"[45]

After spending time with Nichols and Honesty, Hickok left to visit the widow of a "mate" of his who had been killed during the war as the two of them made a dash from the Confederate lines to the Union lines.[46]

A Union cavalry lieutenant, who was sitting at their table, told that tale using proper grammar. Confederate riders were chasing Hickok on Black Nell and his mate on another horse when they reached a long deep ditch, twenty feet wide. They had to either cross it or surrender. They chose to jump it. "Bill's companion never reached the ditch," the lieutenant recounted. "He and his horse must have been shot at the same time, for they went down together and did not rise again." The lieutenant continued, "Bill . . . spoke to Black Nell . . . who knew as well as her master that there was life and death in that twenty feet of ditch, and that she must jump it; and at it she went with a big rush. I never saw a more magnificent sight. Bill gave the mare her head, and turning in his saddle fired twice killing both of his [closest] pursuers, who were within a few lengths of him. They were out of their saddles like stones, just as Black Nell flew into the air and landed safely on our side of the ditch."[47]

Later that afternoon, Wild Bill came to visit Nichols at his hotel. He raced Black Nell up to the hotel porch, waved his arm, and she "instantly stopped and dropped to the ground as if a cannon-ball had knocked life out of her." Hickok let her lie there and walked up to the porch where he talked to the small crowd. He claimed she would do anything for him. "Won't you Nelly?" Still lying on the ground, Nell winked her eye.[48]

Hickok bet the crowd drinks Black Nell would walk up the steps into the barroom, climb up on top of the billiard table, and lay down on it. Hickok whistled. Black Nell rose and walked up to him, then as he walked up the steps into the barroom, she followed. He got her to climb up onto the billiard table, and Hickok allowed some of the onlookers to sit on her.[49]

After Hickok had her get down from the table, he "sprang upon her back, dashed through the high wide doorway, and at a single bound cleared the flight of steps and landed in the middle of the street." Hickok dismounted, snapped his whip, and she raced off to her stable.[50]

Nichols and Hickok conversed in Nichols's room. Hickok told how time and time again Black Nell had saved his life during the war. Nichols switched topics to the gunfight with Tutt. "Do you regret killing Tutt? You surely do not like to kill men?"

"As ter killing men," he replied, "I never thought much about it. The most of the men I have killed it was one or t' other of us, and at sich times you don't stop to think; and what's the use after it's over?" Hickok claimed he did not want to kill Tutt, but Tutt "tried to degrade me, and I couldn't stand that, you know, for I am a fighting man, you know."

Hickok said, "And there was a cause of quarrel between us which people round here don't know about. One of us had to die; and the secret died with him."

Later in the conversation, Nichols asked, "The people about here tell me you are a quiet, civil man. How is it you get into these fights?"

"'D—d if I can tell,' he replied, with a puzzled look which at once gave place to a proud, defiant expression as he continued— 'but you know a man must defend his honor.'"[51]

After Nichols got Hickok to talk about some of his spy activities and one of his races from the Confederate lines to the Union lines, he asked him to tell the story of the Rock Creek Station fight with the M'Kandlas (McCanles) Gang. Nichols wrote, "I had heard the story as it came from an officer of the regular army who, an hour after the affair, saw Bill and the ten dead men—some killed with bullets, others hacked and slashed to death with a knife."[52]

Nichols wrote a disclaimer, "As I write out the details of this terrible tale from notes which I took as the words fell from the scouts lips, I am conscious of its extreme improbability." Nichols equated Hickok's strength and daring to "the powers of a Sampson and Hercules combined." At the end of his lengthy disclaimer paragraph he wrote, "Be the story true or not, in part, or in whole, I believed then every word Wild Bill uttered, and I believe it today."[53]

Hickok began with, "I don't like to talk about that M'Kandlas affair. It gives me a queer shiver whenever I think of it, and sometimes I dream about it, and wake up in a cold sweat."[54]

Even though Hickok didn't like to talk about the "M'Kandlas affair," he went to great lengths to tell the tale. Hickok had gotten the best of M'Kandlas in a shooting match and then a wrestling match. M'Kandlas, who headed a gang of ten border ruffians, swore revenge. Hickok had stopped to visit a Mrs. Waltman at her cabin when M'Kandlas and his gang discovered he was there. They surrounded the cabin. M'Kandlas entered, gun leveled, but Hickok's rifle shot went through his heart and he fell dead outside. The remaining nine men rushed the cabin. Hickok shot four dead. Two more fired shotguns at him. He shot one and knocked the other out. Three of them pushed him onto a bed and grappled with him. One hit him on the chest with a rifle stock. Blood gushed from his nose and mouth. Hickok said, "Then I got ugly." He found a knife and fought with that "striking and slashing until I knew that every one was dead."[55]

Nichols asked Hickok if he had ever been afraid and Hickok replied he was at Wilson's Creek when he was under artillery fire.

Nichols said he would like to see Hickok shoot. Hickok obliged Nichols by going to a window and pointed to the letter O in a sign over fifty yards across the way. He shot six bullets and they all hit the sign within the O. As Hickok reloaded his pistol, he said, "Whenever you get into a row be sure and not shoot too quick. Take time. I've known many a feller slip up for shootin' in a hurry."[56]

When it was time for Nichols to ride out of town, Hickok approached him to say goodbye. Nichols asked if he could write an account of his adventures, and Hickok gave him his permission, but said he hadn't seen his mother back in Illinois who was "old and feeble" and he didn't want her to think he was "a cut-throat and vagabond." He wanted her to know he "fought for the Union like a true man." Nichols ended his piece with:

[William Hitchcock—called Wild Bill, the Scout of the Plains—shall have his wish. I have told his story precisely as it was told to me, confirmed in all important points by many witnesses; and I have no doubt of its truth.—G. W. N.][57]

When citizens of Springfield received their February copies of *Harper's* and read Nichols's story "some were indignant" while "the great majority are convulsed with laughter." The editor of Springfield's *Missouri Weekly Patriot* critiqued the story in the January 31, 1867 edition in an article titled "'Wild Bill,' *Harper's Monthly* and 'Colonel' G. W. Nichols."[58]

The editor wrote, "A good many of our people—those especially who frequent the bar rooms and lager-beer saloons, will remember the author of the article when we mention one 'Colonel' G. W. Nichols, who was here a few days in the summer of 1865, splurging around among our 'strange, half-civilized people,' seriously endangering the supply of lager and corn whisky, and putting on more airs than a spotted stud-horse in the ring of a county fair. *He's the author!*"

The editor corrected Wild Bill's name. It was James B. Hickok not William Hitchcock. The editor praised Hickok: "No finer physique, no greater strength, no more personal courage, no steadier nerves, no superior skill with a pistol, no better horsemanship than his, could any man of the millions Federal soldiers of the war, boast of; and few did better or more loyal service as a soldier throughout the war." However, the editor disputed Nichols's claim Wild Bill had killed several hundred rebels. The editor later stated in the article, "Except his [Hickok's] 'Mate' Tom Martin, (who swore yesterday that Nichols' pathetic description of his untimely murder in 1863, in that article, was not true,) Bill was the best scout, by far, in the Southwest."

The article went on to dispel the Black Nell myth stating the mare was actually a stallion, blind in one eye and hard to handle. The horse never dropped to the ground as if hit by a cannonball nor winked. As for Black Nell entering the barroom and climbing on top of a billiard table, that never happened and "if Bill had, (as the 'Colonel' describes on his own veracity,) mounted her in Ike Hoff's saloon and 'with one bound, lit in the middle of the street' he would have got a severe fall in the door-way of the bar-room, *sure.*" The editor went on to say he measured the length of the bound and it would have been forty-nine feet. The article stated Hickok did kill McKandlas and two other men, not eleven.

The article turned to Captain Honesty, who historian and researcher Joseph Rosa believed was Hickok's friend Captain Richard Owen,[59] "We must add the remark that so far as we are capable of judging, 'Captain Honesty' (who can forget more than Nichols ever knew, and scarcely miss it,) speaks very intelligible, good English. He was at least considered so capable and reliable an A. Q. M. [Assistant Quartermaster] as to be retained by the War Department for more than a year after the war had closed, and his regiment mustered out, to administer and settle the Government affairs in one of the most important posts in the country."[60]

The *Patriot* article concluded, "In reading the romantic and pathetic parts of the article, 'the undercurrent about a woman' in his quarrel and fatal fight with Dave Tutts [*sic*]; and his remarks with 'quivering lips and tearful eyes' about his old mother in

Illinois, we tried to fancy Bill's familiar face while listening to the passage being read. We could almost hear his certain remark, 'O! hell! what a d—n fool that Nichols is.' We agree with 'Wild Bill' on that point."[61]

Nichols must have been drinking in Springfield's saloons when he ran into Hickok and Owen, who must have had a good time trying to outdo each other, telling the eastern dude their tall tales. Remember, Hickok's own family said he had a vivid imagination, enjoying a good practical joke and pulling someone's leg.[62] Then when Nichols had time to write his story, he embellished it, adding in their poor language skills and trashing the town of Springfield.

Several newspapers in Kansas condemned the story and Hickok always denied Nichols's version of his stories.[63] It didn't matter: Nichols's story spread across the country and Wild Bill Hickok became known nationwide as a fighting man—a cold-blooded killer of men.

DeWitt's Ten Cent publication saw the popularity of Nichols's "Wild Bill" story and in July 1867 published *Wild Bill the Indian Slayer*, which used as its front cover the illustration of the M'Kandlas fight from *Harper's*. The entire story was fiction. Several months later, *DeWitt's Ten Cent* would publish another piece of fiction, *Wild Bill's First Trail.* These dime novels drew even more attention to Hickok.[64]

Of course, he didn't get paid anything for the use of his name. Meanwhile, as newspapers attacked Nichols's portrayal of Hickok, he couldn't bask in the limelight but had to earn a living.

Hickok continued with his deputy US marshal duties when called upon, but that was not full-time work. On January 1, 1867, Captain G. W. Bradley, Fort Riley's acting quartermaster, signed Hickok to be a scout for the Seventh Cavalry. This also was not a full-time job. He lived in Junction City where he gambled while waiting for the next deputy US marshal law enforcement action or Army scouting mission. During the winter, he left for western Nebraska to hunt for hides and trap for furs. He might have also done some trading for hides and furs as well. While there, he also gambled with the officers and men at the newly established Fort Sidney.[65]

On February 13, Leavenworth's *Daily Bulletin* announced Hickok had arrived in town with "trains loaded with furs, peltries, and buffalo robes. Wild Bill brings his wife along, and is resting at the Brevoort. The value of the furs and robes he brings with him is said to exceed $20,000."[66] The February 19, 1867 issue of the *Leavenworth Daily Conservative* confirmed his arrival reporting "'Wild Bill'.—This somewhat noted individual was in the city yesterday having recently arrived from [Fort] Riley with a lot of furs and skins."[67]

By March 2, Hickok stopped by the *Weekly Free Press* office in Atchison, Kansas. The newspaper reported Hickok was in town for a few days on personal business and he "is in good health and fine spirits, and enjoys himself in the very best manner." The paper expounded on his good service during the Civil War then continued, "although he is as fierce as a lion when aroused on the side of right, yet ordinarily he is gentle as a lamb. If we are the judge of human nature, 'Wild Bill' has a heart as big as an ox, and would scorn to do a mean act."[68]

Who was Hickok's "wife" mentioned in the *Daily Bulletin*? Is it possible it was Indian Annie? Not much is known about her. In 1867, Hickok lived with her in the settlement near Fort Ellsworth when he used it as his base for deputy US marshal and scouting activities. After his work was done at Ellsworth, there is no evidence he had any more contact with her. People always referred to Indian Annie as Mrs. Wild Bill Hickok.[69]

Another possibility for Wild Bill's "wife" was eighteen-year-old Mary Logan, who J. W. Buel said was of mixed Indian and white ancestry. Her brother was Indian Joe, who was with Hickok when he allegedly killed Sioux leader Conquering Bear. Buel said Mary Logan, Indian Joe, and Hickok all lived together in a cabin on the Niobrara River in Nebraska during the fall of 1865. Mary fell madly in love with Hickok. Buel is noted for getting his dates and locations wrong and making up stories or passing along Hickok's leg-pulling tales. If there is a kernel of truth to the Mary Logan and Wild Bill story, it would fit with his hunting and trapping expedition to Nebraska sometime in the early winter of 1866–1867.[70]

It's not known exactly when, but Lieutenant Colonel George Custer and his wife Libbie became acquainted with Wild Bill Hickok. Custer became good friends with Hickok and would write about him for *The Galaxy* magazine in 1872, later published in book form as *My Life on the Plains* in 1874. After a lengthy description of Hickok's physical attributes and clothing, Custer ended the description, "and you have Wild Bill, then as now the most famous scout on the Plains." Here is a small portion of Custer's glowing description of Wild Bill: "Whether on foot or on horseback, he was one of the most perfect types of physical manhood I ever saw. Of his courage there could be no question; it had been brought to the test on too many occasions to admit of a doubt. His skill in the use of the rifle and pistol was unerring; while his deportment was . . . entirely free from all bluster or bravado. He seldom spoke of himself unless requested to do so. His conversation, strange to say, never bordered either on the vulgar or blasphemous. His influence among the frontiersmen was unbounded, his word was law; and many are the personal quarrels and disturbances which he has checked among his comrades by his simple announcement that 'This has gone far enough,' if need be followed by the ominous warning that when persisted in or renewed the quarreler 'must settle it with me.' Wild Bill is anything but a quarrelsome man; yet no one but himself can enumerate the many conflicts in which he has been engaged, and which have almost invariably resulted in the death of his adversary."[71]

Not to be outdone by her husband, Libbie Custer would write a book titled *Following the Guidon* that would be published in 1890. She spent over five pages describing in glowing terms Wild Bill and his actions. Here is a sampling of her adoration of Hickok: "He was really a very modest man and very free from swagger and bravado. . . . Physically, he was a delight to look upon. Tall, lithe, and free in every motion, he rode and walked as if every muscle was perfection, and the careless swing of his body as he moved seemed perfectly in keeping with the man, the country, and the time in which he lived. I do not recall anything finer in the way of physical perfection than Wild Bill when he swung himself lightly from his saddle, and with graceful, swaying steps, squarely set shoulders and well poised head, approached our tent for orders."[72]

Libbie continued on for several pages describing Hickok as mild mannered. He reminded her of a thoroughbred.[73]

In 1867, the federal government was conducting an active war with the Lakotas and other tribes in Nebraska, Dakota Territory, and what would become Wyoming Territory. To the south of that fighting, officials believed Indian tribes needed to be relocated out of a swath of the Great Plains with the Platte River being the northern boundary and the Arkansas River being the southern boundary. This would allow companies to construct railroads and build towns, and settlers to establish farms and pursue commerce—in peace.[74]

To accomplish a portion of this mission, Major General William T. Sherman, commander of the Military Division of the Missouri, assigned General Winfield Scott Hancock, commander of the Department of the Missouri, a subdivision of the Division, to remove the tribes from between the Smoky Hill and Arkansas Rivers. Hancock was a Civil War hero and through his decisions and actions, more than any other man, saved the Union army at the Battle of Gettysburg. Sherman's orders stated Hancock was "to confer with them [the Indian tribes] to ascertain if they want to fight, in which case he will indulge them."[75]

Hancock assembled a force of fourteen hundred men, seven companies of the Thirty-Seventh Infantry, a battery of the Fourth Artillery, and six companies of the Seventh Cavalry led by Custer. Also included was a mix of Delaware Indians and white scouts including Wild Bill Hickok.[76]

General Hancock, accompanied by the infantry and artillery, arrived by rail the last week of March 1867, joining the Seventh Cavalry at Fort Riley. From there, they marched west on March 26, toward Fort Larned where Hancock hoped to meet with the leaders of a large combined Indian village. The weather had been wet and would continue to be—flooding streams and saturating the ground, making marching and hauling supplies difficult. Equally bad for the troops were camping conditions and just trying to stay warm and dry.[77]

Hancock's column stopped at Fort Harker on its march to Fort Larned. Accompanying the troops were Theodore Davis, an artist for *Harper's Weekly*,[78] and Henry Stanley, special correspondent for the *Weekly Missouri Democrat*. Stanley would later become a world-famous reporter and would be sent to Africa to find a noted physician and missionary, and when Stanley tracked him down, he greeted him by saying, "Doctor Livingstone, I presume?"[79]

Davis. who wrote about Hickok, did not have a high opinion of him; but then his writing sounds sour for just about everything. For instance: "I was seated on the ground wrapped in a blanket for warmth, and just by the opening of the tent to catch enough of the waning light to finish a drawing over which I was shivering—and then my especial aversion, 'Wild Bill' sauntered up. Seeing that he was not welcome, the Scouts [*sic*] stay was short and starting off remarked with some irony, 'Ther's another dodgasted sardine of a newspaper cuss bunken [*sic*] in the sutlers [*sic*] shack what wants my wind, I see you dont! [*sic*].'" Davis went into great detail describing Hickok's clothing and cleanliness. He sounded almost envious.[80]

The "newspaper cuss" Hickok referred to was Henry Stanley, who Davis did not have a high opinion of either. Davis wrote, one morning Stanley awoke to find a deserter had stolen some of his equipment and a saddle blanket. When Hickok learned about the theft, he put together a posse to go after the deserter and recover Stanley's property. They followed the deserter's trail for ten to twelve miles to a cabin where the man was hiding. Hickok went to the door, asked to come in, and was let in. He arrested the deserter and recovered Stanley's items. Davis tagged along with the posse and after witnessing Hickok in action thought better of him and the tales he told.[81]

Leaving Fort Harker on April 3, Hancock's column continued its march southwest toward Fort Larned.[82]

Henry Stanley was impressed with Hickok from the start. In his April 4 dispatch to the *Weekly Missouri Democrat*, printed in the April 16, 1867 edition, Stanley described Hickok: "James Butler Hickok commonly called 'Wild Bill' is one of the finest examples of that peculiar class now extant, known as Frontiersmen, ranger, hunter and Indian scout." Stanley went to great lengths to describe Hickok's almost perfect physical appearance including a "herculean chest." When describing Hickok's eyes, he said, "bluish-grey eyes, with a calm, benignant look, yet seemingly possessing some mysterious latent power. . . ."

As to Hickok's character and speech, Stanley wrote, "He is brave, there can be no doubt; that fact is impressed on you at once before he utters a syllable. He is neither as coarse and illiterate as *Harper's Monthly* portrays him. . . ."

Stanley wrote, "The following *verbatim* dialogue took place between us: 'I say, Bill, or Mr. Hickok, how many white men have you killed to your certain knowledge?' After a little deliberation, he replied, 'I would be willing to take my oath on the Bible tomorrow that I have killed over a hundred, a long way off.'"

Hickok, the leg-puller, had found another gullible reporter. "What made you kill all those men?" Stanley asked. "Did you kill them without cause or provocation?"

"No! by Heaven!" Hickok replied. "I never killed one man without good cause."

Stanley asked Hickok to tell about the first man he had killed. Hickok said he was twenty-eight years old at the time (he was almost thirty years old when he was talking to Stanley, so he would have had to kill a hundred men in two years). Hickok said the man was a gambler and counterfeiter who deserved killing.

Hickok was in a Leavenworth hotel room and had some money on him. Five men entered his room bent on killing him and taking his money. Well-armed, Hickok lay on his bed pretending he was asleep. Hickok said just as one man's "knife touched my breast; I sprang aside and buried mine in his heart, and then used my revolvers on the others right and left. Only one was wounded, besides the one killed." Hickok raced to the fort and, returning with soldiers, captured the rest of the fifteen-member gang. "We searched the cellar and found eleven bodies buried there—men who were murdered by those villains," Hickok said and ended his tale by saying "That was the first man I killed, and I never was sorry for that yet."[83]

On April 7, Hancock's column arrived at Fort Larned on the Santa Fe Trail at the confluence of the Arkansas River and Pawnee Creek. The fort was at the southern end of the Southern Cheyenne and Arapaho buffalo hunting range. Tribes had wintered in the area and the local Indian agents had sent messages to them requesting they meet with Hancock when he arrived. A large, combined village of Cheyennes, Arapahos, Kiowas, and Lakotas was along Pawnee Creek about thirty-five miles upstream of the fort.[84]

On April 9, freezing temperatures and a snowstorm hit, dumping eight inches of snow. The conference was set for April 10 but was postponed until the next day due to the amount of snow, but that did not happen because the Indians were out on a buffalo hunt. On April 12, a delegation of twelve Indian chiefs arrived at the fort and met with Hancock and Indian agents.[85]

Hancock told them the railroad would be crossing from east to west through the Smoky Hill County. He spoke of peace. However, if the tribes attacked whites, there would be war. Hancock had his men fire the artillery for the tribal leaders' benefit. They named him Old Man of the Thunder. Hancock announced he was disappointed more chiefs had not attended the meeting, and he planned to march his troops to their village and hold a council meeting there.[86]

Edward Wynkoop, agent for the Cheyennes, told Hancock that was not a good idea. The Indians were concerned about the presence of Hancock's troops. They well remembered an army attack on Black Kettle's Cheyenne village on Sand Creek, in Colorado Territory.[87]

Back on November 29, 1864, Colonel John Chivington, leading seven hundred troops of the Colorado Territory cavalry, had attacked a combined Cheyenne and Arapaho village under the leadership of Black Kettle. The village located on Sand Creek had been peaceful. Most of the men were away on a buffalo hunt. Learning they were about to be attacked, Black Kettle hoisted an American flag and under it a white flag to show they were peaceful, but Chivington disregarded the flags and ordered the attack. An estimated two hundred Cheyenne and Arapaho people were murdered, most of them women and children. Soldiers mutilated their victims, cutting off body parts for grisly trophies.[88]

Hancock did not listen to Wynkoop. On the morning of April 13, 1867, he marched his column twenty-three miles upstream toward the Indian village and established camp. White Horse, representing the Cheyennes, and Pawnee Killer, representing the Lakotas, rode into Hancock's camp and agreed the chiefs would meet with him the next day.[89]

When no one appeared for the meeting on April 14, Hancock ordered his men to break camp and march toward the Indian village. The column advanced several miles and halted when they came upon a line of three hundred mounted warriors arrayed along the top of a ridge ready to prevent Hancock's further march on their village. Roman Nose, a Cheyenne leader, who had not attended the meetings and who Hancock had insisted on meeting, held a white truce flag.[90]

Alone, Wynkoop rode to the waiting warriors and assured them the army meant them no harm; Hancock only wanted to hold a council. Roman Nose and several chiefs rode with Wynkoop midpoint between the two sides where they talked with Hancock.[91]

"Do you want peace or war?" Hancock asked.

"We do not want war," Roman Nose said. "If we did, we would not come so close to your big guns."[92]

The tribal leaders agreed to allow Hancock to continue his advance to a location near the village where his troops would camp. After establishing camp about a half mile from the village, Roman Nose and the other tribal leaders arrived and met with Hancock and told him all the women and children had fled. Hancock insisted they had to come back to the village, and after negotiations, the tribal leaders told Hancock the women and children would be returning. About 9:30 p.m., Edward Guerrier, who was of mixed Cheyenne and white ancestry and one of Hancock's interpreters, informed Hancock that not only were the women and children not returning, but the men were now leaving.[93]

Hancock ordered Custer to immediately take the Seventh Cavalry and surround the village. When the soldiers heard nothing but barking dogs, Custer, Guerrier, and a few others crept into the village to find it empty except for two people, an old Lakota man unable to travel, and a ten-year-old girl of mixed race who had been raped by a few young Indian men lingering around the village after the people had left. Both the man and girl were sent back to the fort and cared for.[94]

Early morning on April 15, Hancock sent Custer to follow the fleeing Indians. His command consisted of four companies of the Seventh Cavalry and a number of Delaware and white scouts including Wild Bill Hickok.[95]

Custer's command followed the large Indian trail until it split into a hundred smaller trails fanning out to the north. Custer decided to follow the central trails heading toward the Smoky Hill River.[96]

At 4:00 a.m. on April 16, Custer and his men mounted their horses and continued following the central trails north. Custer was eager to do a little hunting. Riding ahead of the column with only his dogs and the chief bugler, Custer came upon a herd of antelope and gave chase. His horse outdistanced the bugler who returned to the column. Custer was out of sight of his men when he came upon a large buffalo and chased after it. Getting close to the animal, he drew his pistol to shoot. The buffalo veered toward the horse. Custer was holding the horse's reins in his left hand and pistol in his right. Reaching for the reins with his right hand to help control the horse, his finger pressed the trigger. The pistol fired into his horse's head, killing it. Custer estimated his walk back to the column was three to four miles.[97]

Wild Bill Hickok later told Captain Henry Lindsay of the Eighteenth Kansas that while scouting for General Hancock it was more dangerous during twenty-four hours than it was during a week's scouting during the Civil War. He would ride through the night and hide during the day. While he was out scouting to the north ahead of Custer's command, he was hiding in a grove of trees at the head of a ravine when six warriors rode in. He shot at them, climbed on his horse, and raced away, claiming he killed three of them.[98]

He had ridden south about a mile when he came upon a small band of Indians traveling north toward the Smoky Hill River. They were between him and Custer's command. Using a ravine, Hickok almost sneaked past them, but when he reached an exposed area, he was spotted by two separate groups of mounted warriors who gave chase. Seeing his horse easily outdistanced their horses, he eased up until they were within shooting range. He claimed he killed three of them, and then raced off to rejoin Custer.[99]

Custer's men rested their animals the afternoon of April 16, from 2:00 to 7:00 p.m., and then continued following the Indian trails through the night. They arrived at the Smoky Hill River at 4:00 a.m. on April 17, where they rested.[100]

Once they reached the Smoky Hill Road, they rode east toward Fort Hays. On April 18, they came upon the still-smoking ruins of Lookout Station, a mail station fifteen miles west of Fort Hays. They found the mutilated and partially burned bodies of three men. From there they proceeded on to Fort Hays. They had ridden approximately 150 miles in four days.[101]

Custer sent a message to Hancock concerning his movements and the Lookout Station murders. In reprisal for that attack, Hancock ordered the destruction of the Indian village, burning everything. The items were inventoried before being destroyed—251 tepees, 962 buffalo robes, food, 436 saddles, hundreds of containers called parfleches, lariats, mats, cooking pots and utensils, and personal items. The destruction of their property enraged the Indians, who were now prone to attack whites even as the military and civilians thought they had been taught a lesson.[102]

Hancock marched toward Fort Hays, reaching Custer at that location on May 3, 1867. The major effort of Hancock's military expedition against the Indian tribes was starting to wind down. The May 4, 1867 edition of Junction City's *Union* stated Jack Harvey, Hickok's scouting partner, had returned and, "We are now looking for Wild Bill and when he appears we will conclude the Indian war is over." One of Hickok's duties was to act as a courier. He must have been sent east with a message when on May 11, the *Union* reported, "Wild Bill came in from the west the other day. He reports all quiet at the front. . . . Hancock will be in in a day or so. Custar [*sic*] will be the only notable left behind."[103]

After being resupplied, Custer's immediate commander, Colonel Andrew Smith, ordered him to lead six companies of the Seventh Cavalry to Fort McPherson on the Platte River in Nebraska, a distance of 225 miles. Custer's orders included, "The object of the expedition is to hunt out and chastise the Cheyennes and that portion of the Sioux who are their allies, between the Smoky Hill and the Platte."[104]

On June 1, Custer's command, consisting of 350 men and twenty wagons hauling supplies, left Fort Hays heading north. Hickok accompanied them as one of the scouts. Their only sighting of Indians was just after crossing the Republican River, when they came upon a hundred mounted warriors who raced off as soon as they saw the troops advancing.[105]

Custer and his command arrived at Fort McPherson on June 10. There, Custer received orders to head to Fort Sedgwick,

Colorado, and led his troops westward on June 17.[106] At this point, Hickok most likely separated from Custer's command and returned to Kansas. Army records for May and June show Hickok "scouting with the 7th Cavly [*sic*] in the field."[107]

Hickok continued carrying dispatches between forts and troops in the field as well as scouting. There are plenty of tales of Hickok's close calls and fights with Indians. It was hard even at that time to decipher what was true and what might be a real leg-puller. For instance, Leavenworth's *Daily Conservative* published a report from "Our Special Correspondent" in its July 10, 1867 edition stating another newspaper, the *Commercial*, reported on July 2, 1867, four men had been killed and scalped eight miles west of Fort Harker. Troops guided by Wild Bill Hickok were sent after the perpetrators. The next day they returned to the fort with five Indian prisoners and had killed eight others. However, the *Daily Conservative*'s special correspondent reported they did not find any Indians to kill and capture.[108]

Captain Augustus Armes commanded Company F of the recently formed Tenth US Cavalry, which went on the scout to find the warriors causing the depravations. The Tenth US Cavalry was made up of Black enlisted men and white officers. Colonel Andrew Smith ordered Armes to take every man he could spare. They left at 4:00 a.m. on July 2, and each man carried one hundred rounds of ammunition and two days' rations. Armes's scouts were a man named Wentworth and Wild Bill Hickok. After they found the warriors' trail, they followed it until it was too dark to ride farther. They remained in the field searching for Indians, returning to Camp Grierson on July 4. Armes made no mention of finding any Indians. He can be excused for that since on his return Colonel Smith informed Armes his brother had died in camp that afternoon from cholera. In the next two days, twelve of Armes's men came down with cholera.[109]

On the morning of July 9, 1867, Colonel Smith ordered Armes to "take thirty men and scout up the Smoky Hill River to Wilson Creek to capture and punish a war party of Indians reported to be depredating in that vicinity." That evening as Armes and his men were camped west of Fort Ellsworth, near Bunker Hill, Kansas, he wrote, "Wild Bill, my guide, reports fresh signs of Indians this evening." The next day, with Hickok acting as scout, Armes and his men rode through the tributaries fifteen miles south of the Smoky Hill River looking for signs of Indians. Finding nothing, they returned to camp at 6:00 p.m. that evening. Armes reported his findings to Smith's satisfaction.[110]

By July 31, 1867, Wild Bill Hickok's work with the cavalry temporarily ended, but his adventures did not.[111]

What had Will Cody been doing since the fall of 1866? Cody said the winter of 1866–1867, he scouted for the Army between Fort Harker and Fort Fletcher, near present-day Hays, Kansas.[112]

Scouting didn't begin as a full-time job for Cody. On December 16, Louisa gave birth to a daughter. She sent a telegram to Will who raced back as fast as horses and trains could travel. When he reached Louisa and his daughter in Leavenworth, it was a joyous occasion. Louisa wanted to name their daughter Arta and he agreed. There is no information how long Cody stayed with his family. Louisa later said, "But the West called again, and he went away, not, however, before his education in the care and culture of infants had been somewhat bettered."[113]

Henry Northrop said Cody stayed with him the winter of 1867 in a dugout along Mulberry Creek in Saline County. During that time, Cody helped a former Leavenworth neighbor, Arthur Larkin, haul supplies to his new store in the emerging town of Ellsworth near Fort Harker; and he most likely began hunting buffalo, providing meat for railroad workers.[114]

Cody said when General Winfield Scott Hancock's column advanced to Fort Larned in the spring of 1867, he guided Lieutenant Colonel George Custer and a ten-man escort from Fort Fletcher to Fort Larned, cross-country, a distance of sixty-five miles in one day.[115]

The problem with Cody's story is it doesn't fit known facts. If the story did happen when it was supposed to have occurred, it would have had to have been as part of Hancock's column advancing to Fort Larned, not as an independent trip by Custer from Fort Fletcher to Fort Larned. It's doubtful, but maybe Cody's story happened at a different time and location. Other than Cody's account there is no known supporting information. With that said, here is Cody's story.

The morning Custer and his ten-man escort were to set out from Fort Fletcher to Fort Larned, Will Cody arrived on a mouse-colored mule. Custer and his men were mounted on good horses. Custer was dubious about the ability of Cody's mule to stay ahead of the horses, and for the first fifteen miles south, Cody's mule had a hard time staying ahead until they reached the Smoky Hill River. Custer constantly criticized Cody saying the mule was no good and he should have brought a horse. From that point on, Cody's mule kept up a steady pace while the horses began to tire and fall behind. Custer had to admit Cody's mule performed better than he had expected. Cody guided Custer and his men to Fort Larned by 4:00 p.m. that same day. Custer thanked Cody for bringing him cross-country and told him if there was ever a time he was not employed, he would find him a job.[116]

Cody was at Fort Fletcher when it was flooded and abandoned in the spring of 1867. The fort was moved several hundred yards to the northeast, and Cody continued his scouting activities from there. In November 1866, the fort would be renamed Fort Hays.[117]

On August 1, 1867, Captain Armes in command of the Tenth Cavalry's Company F was in camp at Fort Hays when he received a report at 2:00 p.m. that Indians were near. By 3:00 p.m., Armes was leading forty-four mounted men toward Campbell's Camp thirteen miles west along the Union Pacific Railroad, Eastern Division tracks. Will Cody said he rode with them as a scout. When Armes and his command reached the camp, they found Indians had killed and scalped seven railroad workers and driven off livestock. He was told the warriors had ridden up the north branch of Big Creek. Armes and his men rode upstream eighteen miles but could not follow the Indians' trail in the dark. They returned to Campbell's Camp and Armes sent six men back to Fort Hays requesting an additional thirty men and one piece of artillery.[118]

The morning of August 2, the reinforcements failed to arrive. After several hours, Armes decided not to wait any longer. Leaving four sick men behind, he and thirty-four men rode fifteen miles to the Saline River, which they reached August 3 at 8:00 a.m. They followed the Saline twelve miles upriver when they were attacked by about seventy-five warriors.[119]

Armes saw what he thought was a buffalo herd approaching, only to realize it was more warriors. As he began an orderly withdraw back toward Fort Hays, the warriors surrounded them. Some warriors dashed through his lines. Sergeant Christy was placing his men when he was shot in the head and killed. Another sergeant and two corporals had their horses shot out from under them. Three horses were wounded. The Indians stayed with them for fifteen miles. Armes estimated the Indians fired two thousand rounds. A rifle bullet hit Armes in the hip. He was unable to walk or stand, so his men helped him onto his horse. During the fight, six of Armes's men came down with cholera and had to be strapped to their horses. In his report, Armes mentioned two guides, Mr. Becker and Mr. Brink; there was no mention of Mr. Cody. Armes estimated they were attacked by between 350 and 400 Indians.[120]

Will Cody's remembrance of the fight was flawed. He said a cannon was taken along, captured by the Indians, and had to be left behind. However, twenty-five mounted infantrymen with a howitzer arrived at Campbell's Camp a half hour too late to accompany Armes. They did follow Armes's trail, had their own separate fight firing three shells at a party of fifty Indians, and then returned to Fort Hays—with the howitzer. Cody said several men were killed, but Armes reported only the death of Sergeant

Christy. Armes's thigh wound would soon heal and he would be back in the saddle leading his troops.[121]

General Winfield Scott Hancock's treatment of the Indians enraged them. They indiscriminately killed whites, ran off livestock, and destroyed property, bringing travel along the Smoky Hill Road to a standstill. Superintendent of Indian Affairs Thomas Murphy wrote, "General Hancock's expedition, I regret to say, has resulted in no good, but on the contrary, has been productive of much evil."[122]

CHAPTER 8

BUFFALO (AUGUST 1867–MAY 1868)

With the arrival of the Union Pacific Railroad, Eastern Division's tracks[1] in August 1867, the new town of Ellsworth, Kansas, boomed to a population of two thousand. With incorporation, the townspeople held an election for city officials on August 10. Wild Bill Hickok ran for marshal but failed to win the election. However, he continued in his deputy US marshal duties.[2]

As construction crews continued to lay railroad tracks west from Ellsworth to Fort Hays (the former Fort Fletcher), Hickok arrested five woodcutters on Paradise Creek illegally felling timber on federal land. He took his five prisoners to the Fossil Creek Station, boarded the eastbound train to Topeka, and turned them over to the federal court.[3]

On October 21, the editor of the Manhattan, Kansas, *Independent* was riding the train from that town to Leavenworth. Also riding the rails were Wild Bill Hickok, his fellow scout, Jack Harvey, and "some dozen of their companions." Not impressed, the editor wrote, "All the party were more or less affected by frequent potations from their bottles, and Wild Bill himself was tipsy enough to be quite belligerent." After commenting on Wild Bill and his companions supposed lifestyle, he wrote, "At a word any of the gang draws his pistol and blazes away as freely as if all mankind were Arkansas Rebels, and had a bounty offered for their scalps."[4]

Hickok ran for public office again, this time for Ellsworth County sheriff along with four other candidates including incumbent Captain E. W. Kingsbury. The election was to be held on November 5, 1867. Hickok heard one candidate, M. R. Lane, had made a remark that could hurt Hickok's chances to win. Hickok confronted Lane about the remark in a public setting. Lane denied it. Neither man would back down until friends intervened and diffused the situation.[5]

Wild Bill Hickok performed an election day stunt. Mounted on a good horse and dressed in buckskin, he raced a westbound train from Fort Harker to Ellsworth, a distance roughly four miles. Hickok won. Even though he ran his horse on a straight course while the train had to follow the tracks with curves and gradients, everyone was impressed with his horsemanship.[6]

Hickok received 156 votes; however, Kingsbury won the election by a narrow margin. After losing the election, Hickok traveled west to the new railroad town of Hays City near Fort Hays where he would continue his deputy US marshal duties.[7] The founding of Hays City was also the end of one of William Frederick Cody's great dreams.

After participating with the Tenth Cavalry in what became known as the Battle of the Saline River on August 3, 1867, Will Cody carried Army dispatches from Fort Hays east to Fort Harker. After delivering the messages, he stopped in at nearby Ellsworth where he met Bill Rose, a Union Pacific, Eastern Division contractor, who was doing grading work for the railroad near Fort Hays. Indians had stolen Rose's livestock, and he was in town buying more animals.[8]

Rose told Cody he planned to establish a town a mile west of Fort Hays on the west bank of Big Creek where the railroad was to cross. Cody was enthusiastic about Rose's town and said he thought it was "a big thing." Rose asked Cody if he wanted to be his partner and Cody jumped at the opportunity. They planned to open a store and saloon in their town and bought building material and supplies. After purchasing the land, they hired a railroad surveyor to lay out streets and lots. Rose and Cody named their town Rome.[9]

To entice people to Rome, they gave away lots to anyone who promised to build on them. However, the two partners kept the valuable corner lots to sell for $50 apiece. Within a month, Rome mushroomed to two hundred houses, several stores and saloons, and a good hotel. Cody later wrote, "Rose and I already considered ourselves millionaires, and thought we 'had the world by the tail.'"[10]

One day, Doctor William Webb, an agent for the Union Pacific, Eastern Division, arrived in Rome to look over the town. One of Webb's duties was to select townsites before the railroad tracks were laid. When Cody and Rose talked with Webb, they believed he was enthusiastic about Rome. Cody later said, "I thought I was going to sell him quite a number of lots from the way he was looking over the town." When Webb learned Cody was riding out on a buffalo hunt, he asked to go along. Cody said after Webb killed his first buffalo, he "was so delighted and seemed so happy over the killing a buffalo that I thought I would sell him a block when I got back that night."[11]

The next morning as Cody prepared to ride out on another buffalo hunt, Webb approached Rose and him, offering each of them one-twelfth interest in their own town. Webb explained it was his job to locate townsites for the railroad. Rose said Rome was the only suitable townsite in the immediate vicinity, and Cody and he had saved the railroad lots of money by establishing the town. Webb responded that selling land and town lots was one way the railroad funded itself. If they did not accept his offer, he would probably start a town nearby. Cody responded they were not going to accept his offer and he could go start his own town. Cody later said, "I thought he had gone daft and I rode off and left him."[12]

Cody and Rose traveled to Leavenworth to get their families. By the time they returned to Rome, Webb had started his new town on August 23, 1867. It was about a mile to the east of Rome and Webb had named it Hays City. Webb told Roman residents the Union Pacific, Eastern Division was designating Hays City as the railroad stop and would be locating its roundhouse and machine shops there. With Webb's assurance Hays City would become a business center, Roman citizens tore down their buildings and relocated to Hays City.[13]

Will and Louisa took their daughter Arta and joined the other Romans moving to Hays, where they rented a room at the Perry Hotel. Hays was a rough and tumble town, but Louisa said her life there with Will Cody was a happy time "full of brightness and enjoyable incident."[14]

Even though the railroad defeated Cody's plans for a steady income generated by his town, he did not give up, continuing to work, hunting buffalo to sell the meat to railroad contractors and townsfolk; scouting and acting as a courier for the Army; and working with Rose on their contract with Schumacher, Miller & Company to grade five miles for the railroad tracks west of Big Creek and right through Rome. Cody and Rose still had hopes people would realize Rome was a better place to live and do business than Hays, but that never materialized.[15]

As Cody and Rose came to know Dr. William Webb, they grew to like him even though he had cost them their fortunes. Webb must have felt a little bad he had caused the fall of Rome and gave Cody and Rose each two lots in Hays.[16]

Cody took Doc Webb along on buffalo hunts. Webb later wrote in 1872, "Cody is sparse and wiry in figure, admirably versed in plain lore, and altogether the best guide I ever saw. The mysterious plain is a book that he knows by heart. . . . He led us over its surface on starless nights, when the shadow of the blackness above hid our horses and the earth, and through many a time with no trail to follow and on the very mid-ocean of the expanse, he never made a failure. . . . We award him the credit of being a good scout and most excellent guide; but the fact that he can slaughter buffalo is by no means remarkable, since the American bison is dangerous game to only amateurs."[17] The tone of Webb's last sentence appears tinged with sour grapes.

On one hunt, Cody and Webb were ten miles from Hays when they saw a party of thirteen Indians about two miles distant riding to cut them off from town. Cody mounted on his swift, buffalo-hunting horse Brigham and Webb mounted on a fleet thoroughbred bay raced their horses three miles toward Hays, getting between the warriors and town. They were about three-fourths mile from the Indians when they stopped. Waving their hats, they fired a few long-distance shots at their pursuers who were now speeding closer. Cody and Webb turned their horses and continued to race toward Hays. Firing a few parting shots at Cody and Webb, the warriors turned their horses toward the Saline River.[18]

Cody said his horse Brigham was "the fleetest steed I ever owned. On several subsequent occasions he saved my life, and he was the horse that I rode when I killed sixty-nine buffaloes in one day." Cody had bought Brigham from a Ute Indian from Utah, and since Brigham Young was the most influential man in Utah, Cody named the horse after Young. Doc Webb said Brigham was a tough, roan pony and Cody was very fond of him. Brigham was nothing to look at; he had no visible attributes to impress anyone, but he could run with the buffalo and Cody said, "Old Brigham knows as well as I what I am doing, and sometimes a great deal better."[19]

Will Cody acquired a newly improved needle gun which Cody had obtained from the Army. The gun was a .50-caliber Springfield model 1866 rifle converted to breech loading. Needle guns were a new innovative technology. The firing pin resembled a needle. When the gun was fired, the needle passed through the paper cartridge and struck a percussion cap at the bullet's base, firing the bullet. Cody loved the gun and named it Lucretia Borgia (Lucrezia Borgia) after a famous Italian Renaissance woman, beautiful but deadly, portrayed in a popular nineteenth-century play by French playwright Victor Hugo. That's exactly what Cody thought of his rifle—beautiful but deadly—and had "Lucretia Borgia" etched into the rifle's lock plate.[20]

Will Cody and Bill Rose continued their contractual work to grade five miles for the railroad tracks west of Big Creek. One day, Cody had Brigham harnessed to a scraper when one of the workers called to him that a small buffalo herd was coming over the hill. No buffalo had been seen for days and their meat supply was running low. Cody decided to go on a hunt and told one of the workmen to hitch a team of horses to a wagon and follow him. Since he had left his saddle back at camp, a mile away, Cody removed the harness from Brigham and gripping Lucretia Borgia, rode Brigham bareback using what he had on hand, a bridle with blinders.[21]

As Cody rode toward the herd of eleven buffalo, he saw five officers riding from Fort Hays toward him and the herd. When they caught up to Cody, he saw they were a captain and four lieutenants, newly arrived at Fort Hays. Not knowing anything about Cody, they told him they were out to hunt the buffalo. Appraising the looks of him and his workhorse, the officers believed he was "a green hand at hunting."[22]

The captain, George Wallace Graham, said, "Do you plan to catch those buffaloes on that Gothic steed?"

"I hope so, by pushing on the reins hard enough," Cody replied. The officers didn't believe Cody and his old workhorse could catch up with the buffalo. Graham told Cody, they were out for a pleasure hunt and only wanted the tongues and tenderloins and they would give him the rest. Cody thanked Graham and said he would follow along.[23]

The buffalo were about a mile away as the officers raced after them. Cody saw the herd was making its way toward water and nothing would deter the animals. He saw he could intercept the herd as the officers chased from behind. Cody reached the herd first. He pulled the bridle with blinders from Brigham's head. The horse knew exactly what to do and raced alongside the nearest buffalo, close enough Lucretia Borgia's muzzle was inches from the animal. Cody shot, and as that buffalo went down, Brigham was racing to the next and Cody shot again. The duo repeated the process again and again until all eleven buffalo were killed using twelve shots. The officers were disappointed they did not get a chance to shoot, but that was offset by seeing Cody and Brigham's performance.[24]

When they rode up to Cody, he introduced himself. One lieutenant, John Milton Thompson, remembered Cody had been a scout at Fort Harker. Cody gave the tongues and tenderloins to the officers and loaded his wagon with the hindquarters to take back to camp.[25]

That night, Indians raided Cody and Rose's camp stealing five to six teams of workhorses, severely limiting the amount of work their men could do. Cody rode to Fort Hays and requested the Army attempt to recover the stolen livestock. The commander assigned Captain Graham and Lieutenant Myron Amick, who had been at the buffalo hunt the day before, to take one hundred troopers of the Black Tenth Cavalry to track down the warriors and recover the stolen animals. Within the hour, they were on the thieves' trail. Cody went along as scout and guide.[26]

They followed the raiders' trail to the Saline River and then on to the Solomon River. While Graham and the troops waited, Cody scouted ahead and discovered the Indians' camp along the river. Returning to the Tenth Cavalry contingent, Cody reported his findings to Graham and suggested they attack the camp later that night. Graham agreed. Before they could fully get into position, one of the troopers fired his gun. The Indians jumped to their horses and were off before Graham's men could do anything. They followed the Indians' trail the next day, but as there was little chance of catching the thieves and they only had rations for one day, Graham made the decision to return to Fort Hays, empty-handed.[27]

The Union Pacific Railroad, Eastern Division contracted with the Goddard Brothers to feed twelve hundred men employed working on the railroad. With that many men, it was important and economical to provide them fresh buffalo meat. The herds were moving farther from the railroad construction, and it was becoming more dangerous as Indians were prone to attack hunters. The Goddard Brothers were hiring professional hunters to bring in fresh buffalo meat.[28]

They had heard of Will Cody's buffalo hunting exploits and hired him to hunt for them. Cody left Bill Rose to finish their grading project. The Goddard Brothers paid Cody $500 per month to bring in meat cuts from twelve buffalo per day—the hindquarters and hump from each animal. One man, driving a wagon, went with Cody to help butcher and haul back the meat.[29]

Cody brought back the best buffalo heads giving them to the Union Pacific Railroad, Eastern Division. A taxidermist preserved the heads, and they were distributed to the railroad's offices and depots, hotels, and government buildings, becoming symbols for the railroad.[30]

Each day, Cody rode between five to ten miles from the railroad camps to find buffalo. It was dangerous work. Indians watched for white hunters. Cody claimed, "During my engagement as hunter for the company—a period of less than eighteen months—I killed 4,280 buffaloes; and I had many exciting adventures with the Indians, as well as hair-breath escapes."[31]

There is controversy with Cody's statement. His work with the Goddard Brothers would end in May 1868. He most likely started working for them in October 1867. Historian Don Russell, in his analysis of the information, believed "eighteen months" was a mistake and that it should have been "eight months," which fits the timeline from October 1867 to May 1868. As to the number of buffalo Cody killed, again there is controversy. Russell calculated if Cody killed twelve buffalo per day over the course of eight months, the number would have been 2,928.[32] The number was probably even less than this since Cody was not out hunting constantly every day, bringing in buffalo meat.[33]

As Will Cody fulfilled his buffalo meat quota, the railroad workers gave him the nickname Buffalo Bill. Louisa said on one

Buffalo Bill acquiring his name

occasion Cody took her along to the railroad work camp at the
end of the line. He left her in the care of the commissary steward
while he rode out to hunt buffalo. Louisa overheard the cook refer
to Cody as Buffalo Bill. It was the first time she had heard the
nickname. The cook told her one of the workers had come up with
a little poem:

> Buffalo Bill, Buffalo Bill,
> Never missed and never will;
> Always aims and shoots to kill,
> And the comp'ny pays his buffalo bill![34]

The poem made the rounds. Cody said about his nickname,
"It stuck to me ever since, and I have never been ashamed of it.[35]

One of the first written mentions of Cody as Buffalo Bill
was in the November 26, 1867 edition of the *Leavenworth Daily
Conservative*, which reported a buffalo hunting excursion made
up of nine gentlemen. The Union Pacific Railroad, Eastern Division provided them a special car to travel from Leavenworth to

Hays. At Lawrence, they were joined by four additional gentle-men from Ohio. They rode out on their hunt the morning of Friday, November 24, accompanied by army officers including Captain George Graham and "Buffalo Bill and other scouts." The hunters had killed five buffalo when the hunt ended abruptly for the day when H. L. Newman, the elected leader of the hunting party, was injured. "While riding full speed across the prairie, his horse stepped into a gopher hole, and fell, dismounting Mr. New-man, who had a severe gash cut in his forehead, and remained insensible for twelve hours afterwards." Judge R. G. Corwin from Dayton, Ohio, had strayed from the hunting party and could not be found.

The next day, Saturday, they went out again and managed to kill seven buffalo. Then the newspaper reporter stated, "Much anxiety was created on Saturday night by the non-arrival of Judge Corwin." Sunday morning two search parties set out to find Cor-win. Lieutenant William Kennedy led a contingent of the Tenth Cavalry, and Buffalo Bill with a party of fifteen citizens made up the second group. "After a long ride [Buffalo Bill and his] party found the lost man about five miles from the fort, nearly starved and almost exhausted."[36]

Louisa Cody said her time at Hays was full of sunshine and enjoyment, even though she was under nervous strain from the hardships of living in a raucous, frontier town such as Hays. Will instructed Louisa not to leave the hotel without an escort when he was away hunting or scouting, so she would sit by her hotel win-dow and watch the hustle and bustle in the streets. If he could, Will planned his hunting trips so he was usually back in the evening.[37]

On occasion, Will saddled Brigham with a sidesaddle and gave him to Louisa to ride. On free days, they rode out onto the prairie where Cody set up targets and taught Louisa to shoot a revolver. After she mastered it to his approval, he had her shoot at targets from Brigham's back as the horse galloped past them. Cody placed Arta on Louisa's lap as she sat on Brigham and had her gal-lop by the targets, shooting at them. He wanted her prepared in case someone tried to attack her. When Will had completed Louisa's training, he said, "I'll feel easier now when I'm away." Louisa later wrote, "And I must admit, I felt a great deal more comfortable myself."[38]

Even though most of the women of Hays were "painted, bedizened persons who leered from the doorways of the dance halls," Louisa found a few "good women" to associate with, participating in sewing bees and attending the weekly dance in the Hotel Perry's lobby.[39]

It must have been early November 1867, before one such dance, when Will told Louisa his old friend Wild Bill Hickok would be at the dance and had requested a dance with her. She was upset she would have to dance with a cold-blooded killer, but after she met Wild Bill, her opinion changed. Louisa found him courteous, pleasant, and mild-mannered. She danced with him more than once.[40]

Saturday horse races were a regular pastime for Hays residents. A valley had been selected outside town and a course marked off at a mile long. Cody was a regular participant and Louisa went with him. One of the women's jobs was to watch the horizon for Indians while the men concentrated on the race. Before one particular race, Will asked Louisa to secretly make him a jockey uniform—skin-tight pants, cowhide boots, a red flannel shirt, and a long-billed cap. The day of the race, Cody rode to the crowded racetrack with his uniform concealed under a linen duster. When he took off the duster revealing his uniform, it was the talk of the town.[41]

Wild Bill walked up to Cody and quietly said, "I don't guess I'll race my horse today."

"What's the matter?" Cody asked.

"That's a good horse," Wild Bill said as he turned away. "I'm not going to risk him going blind from looking at bright lights."

That was the beginning of good-natured joking at Cody's expense. Finally, "the Major" who was in charge of the race announced, "We'd better be holding our races. Some of the men have reported Indians in the vicinity and," he looked at Cody as he continued, "if anything can draw them here this afternoon, it's that prairie fire that Bill's wearing."[42]

Louisa and other women took positions a few hundred yards from the track to scan the hills for any sign of Indians as the races proceeded.[43]

Cody had bet everything on winning his race, including Brigham and Lucretia Borgia. The race began, and by the halfway mark, Cody and Brigham were in fourth place. One of the women beside Louisa spied several mounted figures on the far hills. The two women raced to the crowd shouting, "Indians!" The race was disrupted, and the men raced after the Indians who rode away. Later, Cody explained to Louisa he was about to win the race. He had been holding Brigham back and was going to turn him loose on the home stretch.[44]

Louisa was homesick for St. Louis. She reasoned maybe a buggy would help. Wanting to please her, Will ordered one from Kansas City and had it delivered to Hays City. Louisa was extremely happy when it arrived. Later that day, she insisted they take it for a drive out into the country to view the sunset. Cody was hesitant but caved in and hitched Brigham to the buggy, something Brigham was not used to, having only been harnessed a few times in his life.[45]

They were some distance from Hays when a band of Indians came upon them. Cody turned Brigham toward Hays, gave the reins to Louisa, then pulled his pistol. As they raced toward town, some of Cody's friends were riding toward them. Cody had asked them to ride out and check on them if they were not back by nightfall. The Indians gave up the chase and rode away, as Cody took the reins and Louisa fainted.[46]

Louisa's account of the Indian chase was melodramatic, but she was shaken. Ever since her arrival at Hays, real and imagined threatening incidents had happened to her. Louisa claimed it began when Will left her and baby Arta alone in a tent while he went out hunting. Even though Cody had asked for soldiers to guard Louisa's tent, she still felt in danger. A fight broke out among nearby soldiers. Louisa said she emerged from the tent with a gun saying, "Get back there. I've got a gun and I know how to use it. Get back there!" A soldier struck her, knocking the gun from her hand. An old man coming to her assistance was beaten. A detachment arrived and chased away the brawlers. When Cody returned from his hunt, he found Louisa "collapsed from the strain, hysterical, and nerve-wrecked."[47]

She never really got over her fright. After the failed horse race, she wrote, "my health began to once more fail and my nerves to become frayed and raw." The buggy ride incident was the last straw. Will conferred with a doctor who said Louisa needed to go to St. Louis to recover. She cried when hearing the news. A week after the incident, Will accompanied Louisa and Arta by rail to St. Louis where he left them with her parents. He made her promise not to come west until she recovered. Cody returned to Hays where he continued to hunt buffalo to feed the railroad workers, and when called upon scout and deliver dispatches for the Army.[48]

By November 1867, Wild Bill Hickok was working out of Hays City as a deputy US marshal and scout for the Army carrying dispatches between army posts. Hickok went to Paradise Creek halfway between Hays and Ellsworth where he arrested five woodcutters illegally felling trees on government land. He hauled them to Topeka to await trial in federal court. Adolph Roenigk described Hickok as he stepped off the train at the Fossil Creek Station to go after the culprits: "He wore a broad brimmed hat and a brand new buckskin suit with fringes on his elbow sleeves and trouser legs. A pair of six-shooters strapped to his sides, he made the appearance of just such a picture as one could see on the cover of a dime novel."[49]

Frank Root, editor of the Atchison, Kansas, *Daily Free Press*, traveled to Hays City and wrote in the January 6, 1868 issue about meeting Wild Bill Hickok, "He is in the employ of the

Government as a detective and is probably better acquainted with the plains than any other man living, of his age."[50]

On February 20, 1868, J. Parks, special correspondent for the *Kansas State Journal*, wrote about Hays City. He talked about meeting Wild Bill Hickok. After extolling his virtues and excellent scouting record during the Civil War and on the frontier, Parks wrote, "Reports say Bill is a blustering desperado. I found the report false. I was introduced to him, and received with a hearty shake of the hand, such as does the heart good; none of your touching of two fingers, or a gentle pressure of thumb and finger, but a grasping of the whole hand, a regular squeeze, and good o'd western shake of the arm. Quiet and gentlemanly in his conduct and appearance; he is well respected by all who are really acquainted with him. . . . He is not quarrelsome as has been represented, but as far as I can learn, peacefully inclined. A true friend to his friends, but a bold enemy to his enemies. He is now devoting himself to business and is doing well."[51]

On March 13, Wild Bill Hickok lost his good friend and scouting partner, Jack Harvey, who died of tuberculosis at Ellsworth. It's not known if Hickok visited Harvey before he died. The March 17 issue of *Leavenworth Daily Conservative* stated, "No man in the army did his duty more faithfully and willingly than Captain Jack Harvey, and few as effectively. Brave, cool in the hour of danger, and one of the best shots on the western border, Jack was always ready for a bold ride or a fight with the enemy. He was as generous and true-hearted as he was brave, and no man hereabouts had more friends." The Burlingame, Kansas, *Chronicle*'s March 28, 1868 issue related, "For several years past, he was the companion and partner of Wild Bill."[52]

Buffalo Bill Cody continued to hunt throughout the winter. The January 11, 1868 issue of the *Leavenworth Daily Commercial* repeated a news item from the January 9th issue of the *Hays City Advance*: "Bill Cody and 'Brigham' started on a hunt Saturday afternoon and came in Tuesday. The result was nineteen buffalo. Bill brought in over four thousand pounds of meat, which he sold for seven cents per pound, making about $100 per day for his time out."[53]

In early February, J. Parks spent nearly two weeks on a hunting expedition led by Buffalo Bill Cody. There were ten members in the party, and by the time they had been out ten days, longer than they had said they would be out, Hays residents started to become concerned. The February 14, 1868 issue of the *Kansas Daily Tribune* stated, "Fears are expressed that they have been captured or killed by the Indians, who have shown decided symptoms of hostility of late. Some efforts are being made toward organizing a party to go in search of them." They did return unharmed and Parks wrote three installments of his buffalo hunting experiences for his newspaper.[54]

Parks described the frigid conditions and the hunting. He witnessed a mishap that happened to Cody and Brigham. Cody and a scout named Crockett were chasing a bull buffalo:

Brigham, who understood his business as well as his master, with outstretched neck and flashing eyes, taking advantage of short cuts and uneven ground steadily gained on his victim and soon brought his master along side. Cody firmly seated upon his back dashed along with his eyes steadily fixed upon his game, the long fringe of his buckskin coat fluttering in the wind, which was howling across the prairie with bitter blasts, and when near enough, cooly [sic] raised his long rifle and sent a lump of lead through the lungs of the monster. At this reception the buffalo turned and charged on Brigham, who, was always on the alert, sprang to one side, but unfortunately jumped upon what appeared to be a small patch of snow upon the level ground, but which, in reality, proved to be a drift covering a small ravine. Plunging into this, before he could extract himself and rider, the enemy struck him, sending master and horse floundering in the snow. Cody could easily have made his escape while the buffalo's attention was directed to the horse, but unmindful of his own danger struck the ugly brute across the head with his gun. At this stage of the game, when the buffalo had a decided advantage in the fight, his career was suddenly terminated by a ball from Crockett's rifle.[55]

Each day after Cody had led the hunters to buffalo, they returned to camp where the cook prepared a buffalo dinner. Parks wrote "The ponies were generally busy at night looking out for number 1. Brigham was as sharp in finding good quarters as he was after buffalo. He would stand by the fire like a man, and was always ready to eat anything which came in his way."[56]

Parks explained there were two ways to hunt buffalo: the first was the chase, where the hunter rode close to the buffalo and shot, and the second was "still hunting," where a hunter started out on foot downwind of a herd and worked his way through gullies and uneven ground to get close enough to the herd that he could shoot the animals.[57]

Riding north, the hunting party "reached a bluffy country, where buffalo were to be seen in every direction, in heards [*sic*] of dozens, fifties, hundreds, and thousands which proved to be very wild." The weather grew colder. Snow was fifteen feet deep in some ravines. One extremely cold night, Parks wrote, "The wind whistled through the tree tops, and rushed, shrieking, over the prairie. Our horses hovered over the camp fire until the hair was burned from their legs and sides. We were compelled to cover them with our blankets to keep them from freezing."[58]

On the morning following the extremely cold night, Cody led a party on foot in "still hunting." It was so cold they ended the hunt after killing six buffalo. Parks wrote, "Everyone of our party had his eyes or fingers frozen."[59]

On another day, several hunters fired at a large buffalo herd. The animals ran in the direction of the rest of the party. Parks wrote, "with a thundering tread which shook the earth, a large herd came rushing toward us. Brigham became surrounded by and entangled among two herds as they came together, and was forced to keep with them for a long distance, while Cody was fixing his rifle, which by some accident had got out of order. Being obliged to pull off his gloves, his fingers were soon so benumbed with the cold, that it was some time before he was able to do any execution. Brigham appeared to understand the case, and held his position in the herd until his master having succeeded in getting his gun all right again, opened fire. . . . On came the multitude toward us with Cody in their midst, now dealing death among them, causing them to scatter and fall like leaves in Autumn."[60]

The hunters had many adventures before returning to Hays. Parks estimated they killed seventy buffalo, loading two wagons with hams, tenderloins, and tongues. Hays townsfolk had become concerned about the hunting party's safety as they were gone longer than planned and "numbers of Indians had been seen in the vicinity, and several sensational stories started."[61]

After cleaning up, the hunting party went to Field's restaurant to eat. Parks wrote Brigham "followed his master into the room, and around the table, eating whatever was given to him, and making himself as much at home, in store, restaurant and hall, as upon the prairie, and in the camp of the hunter."[62]

Wild Bill Hickok checked into the Massasoit House, Atchison, Kansas's premier hotel on March 12, 1868.[63] There was no indication why he was there or what direction he was heading. Over a week later, he again checked into the Massasoit House, Saturday morning, March 21, 1868, with no information on why or what direction.[64]

Deputy US marshal Wild Bill Hickok didn't stay long in Atchison. He traveled back to Hays where with the assistance of "W. F. Cody Government detective," they captured eleven members of a gang of robbers headquartered on the Solomon River and jailed them in the Fort Hays guardhouse. A former major of the Seventh Kansas by the name of Smith was the gang's leader. They were "charged with stealing and secreting government property, and desertion from the army." On March 28, 1868, Hickok requested Captain Sam Ovenshine, Fort Hays's commander, assign a corporal and five men to help take the prisoners to Topeka. Hickok wrote, "I would respectfully call your attention to the number and character of these prisoners and the feeling in their behalf in this community which renders a guard of U.S. soldiers absolutely necessary." Ovenshine issued Special Order No. 51, detaching Sergeant William Alloways and five privates to assist Hickok and Cody in delivering the prisoners to Topeka. Arriving in Topeka on March 30, the prisoners were jailed to await trial.[65] After Hickok's delivery of the thieves, records of his activities are scanty for the next few months.

Through May 1868, Buffalo Bill Cody continued hunting buffalo for the Goddard Brothers and claimed he had many encounters with Indians.[66]

One story Cody related happened in the spring of 1868. He was riding Brigham headed toward the Smoky Hill River and was twenty miles from the Union Pacific Railroad, Eastern Division's end of tracks camp, when he saw about twenty warriors a half mile away. Spotting Cody, they gave chase as he raced back toward camp. Mile after mile, the warriors followed. Some of their horses began to tire and became strung out behind except for one warrior riding a spotted horse. The man occasionally fired his rifle at Cody. The spotted horse closed the distance to Brigham by eighty yards. Cody stopped, aimed Lucretia Borgia, and shot the spotted horse. Whipping Brigham around, he raced ahead of the other warriors who had closed the distance. Several warriors fired their rifles at him and from time to time, he stopped and shot back. He hit one horse's leg, removing that warrior from the chase. Roughly eight warriors were close enough to do Cody harm as Brigham raced to within several miles of the railroad camp.[67]

Soldiers at an outpost saw Cody being chased by Indians and gave the alarm. Tenth Cavalry troopers and railroad workers sprang to action to help Cody, some racing on foot, others on horseback. The warriors turned their horses and raced away in the direction from which they had come. Captain Nicholas Nolan, commanding Company A, Tenth Cavalry, prepared to pursue the warriors and invited Cody along. He was given a fresh mount, and they chased after the warriors; the pursuers now became the pursued. Cody claimed they killed eight warriors.[68]

Cody wrote in his autobiography about his second major Indian encounter while hunting buffalo along the Saline River. A butcher named Scotty was along to help with the buffalo carcasses and drove a wagon pulled by two mules to haul the meat. Cody was not riding Brigham, but "a most excellent horse belonging to the railroad company." After he killed fifteen buffalo, they loaded the meat into the wagon and were returning to the railroad camp. They were roughly eight miles from their destination when about thirty warriors intercepted them. The two men quickly unhitched the mules and tied them and Cody's horse to the wagon. They unloaded the meat to build a breastwork under the wagon, then hunkered down with their ammunition box, four revolvers, and Cody's Lucretia Borgia.[69]

The warriors charged. Cody and Scotty fired, knocking a few off their horses. The warriors raced their horses circling the wagon and killed Cody's horse and Scotty's mules.[70]

Cody had a prearrangement with the Army that if the pickets saw smoke coming from the buffalo range where he was hunting it meant he was under attack and needed help. During a lull in the action, Cody set fire to the prairie downwind of the wagon. The grass fire quickly spread sending black smoke billowing into the air. The warriors dismounted and shot at Cody and Scotty from behind a knoll.[71]

An hour after Cody had set the prairie on fire, the cavalry arrived and the warriors rode away. Cody claimed they killed five warriors. He said the buffalo meat "was found to be all right, except that it had a few bullets and arrows sticking in it."[72]

Cody's hunting for the Goddard Brothers ended in May 1868 when the railroad tracks reached the end of the line at Sheridan, Kansas, a few miles short of Fort Wallace to the west. The Union Pacific Railroad, Eastern Division was now calling itself the Kansas Pacific Railroad to lessen confusion between itself and the Union Pacific Railroad. Even though the Union Pacific had won the federal government rights to link up with the eastbound Central Pacific Railroad for a transcontinental line, the Kansas Pacific had plans to eventually complete its line westward to Denver, Colorado, and hoped to extend its own transcontinental route to Santa Fe, New Mexico, then through Arizona to California.[73]

Shortly after the completion of the tracks to Sheridan, Cody had a buffalo hunting contest with William "Medicine Bill" Comstock.

Medicine Bill Comstock was an Army scout who had been based out of Fort Wallace since 1866; he was also considered a friend of the Cheyennes and acted as an interpreter with them. He had been Lieutenant Colonel George Custer's guide during the 1867 campaign.

Describing young Comstock, Custer wrote, "No Indian knew the country more thoroughly than did Comstock. . . . He knew the dress and peculiarities of every Indian tribe, and spoke the languages of many of them. Perfect in horsemanship, fearless in manner, a splendid hunter, and a gentleman by instinct, as modest and unassuming as he was brave, he was an interesting as well as valuable companion on a march."[74]

In January 1868, Comstock had shot and killed a contractor in a dispute over a debt at Fort Wallace's sutler store. Comstock was taken to Hays City where he said before Justice of the Peace Marcellus E. Joyce that he was guilty. Joyce responded, "Ye are a damned fool for tellin' it. I discharge ye for want of evidence."[75]

Comstock had a reputation for being a successful buffalo hunter. The officers of Fort Wallace backed Comstock in a match against Cody and his supporters among the officers of Fort Hays. Each side wagered $500. The two men agreed to hunt for eight hours from 8:00 a.m. to 4:00 p.m. Whoever shot the most buffalo would be declared the winner.[76]

The hunt became well advertised and the Kansas Pacific ran a special train out to Sheridan, carrying about one hundred men and women; many of them were from St. Louis including Louisa and little Arta. Cody said the site for the contest was about twenty miles east of Sheridan. George Allaman, a scout and meat hunter, and Pete Ziegler, an early day rancher, both said the contest was held one and a half miles west of Monument, Kansas, then up a draw to the northwest of the railroad tracks. Charles Tauscher, a railroad section boss, later found hand-blown beer bottles and champagne bottles at the site.[77]

The day of the contest, the excursionists on horseback and riding in wagons followed the hunters out to the buffalo range, staying well out of sight so as not to spook the herds. Each hunter had a referee follow behind to tally the number of animals killed. Buffalo Bill was mounted on Brigham, and his weapon of choice was Lucretia Borgia. Medicine Bill was using a Henry rifle, which he would be able to fire more rapidly than Cody.[78]

The two hunters raced into a buffalo herd, splitting it in two. Medicine Bill went after the herd to the left, and Buffalo Bill took the herd to the right. Cody claimed that morning he killed thirty-eight buffalo and Comstock killed twenty-three. The two hunters took a break with their audience. As champagne was being served, a small buffalo herd headed toward them. Both hunters took off after the herd with Cody killing eighteen and Comstock killing fourteen.[79]

After lunch and more champagne, the two hunters found another herd about three miles from their lunch spot and shot more animals. Cody claimed he killed a grand total of sixty-nine buffalo and Comstock killed forty-six buffalo. Comstock and his backers realized he would not be able to catch up to Cody's number and conceded the match. Buffalo Bill Cody was proclaimed champion buffalo hunter of the plains.[80] Unfortunately for Medicine Bill Comstock, he would be killed later in August.[81]

With Cody's buffalo hunting for the railroad ending and prospects of scouting for the Army increasing, he felt he should sell Brigham since he did not want to wear him out scouting nor did he have a place to keep him. Friends convinced Cody to raffle off Brigham. There were ten chances at $30 apiece. Ike Bonham won Brigham and took him to Wyandotte, Kansas. Brigham was later bought by a Mr. Wilcox from Memphis, Tennessee, and years later Cody would visit Brigham.[82]

Buffalo Bill Cody's commercial buffalo hunting career was closing, but his scouting career was about to take off.

CHAPTER 9

SCOUTING FOR THE ARMY (MAY 1868–JULY 1870)

Back in the fall of 1867, a US Indian Peace Commission that included General William Tecumseh Sherman had met with Comanche, Kiowa, Cheyenne, Arapaho, and Plains Apache leaders at Medicine Lodge Creek about seventy miles south of Fort Larned, Kansas. Black Kettle, chief of the Southern Cheyennes whose village had been attacked by Colonel John Chivington's troops back on November 29, 1864, and Tall Bull, leader of the Cheyenne Dog Soldier Society, were there. The commission proposed what would be called the Medicine Lodge Creek Treaty. Even though Kiowa leader Satanta and others spoke against the treaty, many leaders signed it.[1]

The tribes were supposed to vacate lands north of the Arkansas River. In exchange for supplies and goods, they were to live on reservations set aside for them in western Indian Territory, modern-day western Oklahoma, where the government would provide cattle and teach them to farm. All tribes were allowed to hunt buffalo south of the Arkansas River. The Cheyennes understood they could continue to hunt north of the river as long as buffalo remained there, but the government changed that provision without their knowledge.[2]

Most tribal leaders did not understand the ramifications of the treaty. Before signing it, the Cheyenne leader Buffalo Chief said, "that country between the Arkansas [River] and Platte [River] is ours.... You give us presents and then take our land; that produces war." Captain Albert Barnitz, who was present with the Seventh Cavalry, wrote, "[The Cheyennes] had *no idea that* they are giving up . . . the country north of the Arkansas. The treaty amounts to nothing, and we will certainly have another war sooner or later with the Cheyennes." Congress, preoccupied with impeaching President Andrew Johnson, did nothing until late July 1868 when it appropriated $500,000 to uphold its end of the treaty.[3]

The Cheyenne leader, Roman Nose, had not signed the treaty. He was still angry over Hancock's needless burning of the Indian village back in April 1867. He was leader of the Dog Soldiers, one of six men's societies. The Dog Soldiers were found in every Cheyenne band, but during summer, they came together socializing and sharing common songs, dances, symbols, and dress. Roman Nose, with up to four hundred warriors, remained north of the Arkansas River.[4]

General Philip Sheridan had been appointed commander of the Department of Missouri and arrived at Fort Leavenworth on February 29, 1868,[5] taking command on March 2. Sheridan toured Forts Zarah, Larned, and Dodge, all within his department. Bands of Cheyennes, Kiowas, and Arapahos camped along Pawnee Creek near Fort Larned. He visited the tribal leaders and learned they were upset the government had not lived up to its promises. They had nothing but contempt for the Medicine Lodge Creek Treaty. Sheridan wrote to his wife, "The poor Indians are starving. We kill them if they attempt to hunt and if they keep within the Reservations they starve. . . . Congress makes no provision and of course nothing is done. I wish Congress could be impeached." Sheridan issued Army rations to the tribes, but it was too little, too late. Even though the Army attempted to provide a portion of what had been promised over the next few months, the tribes that had agreed to the treaty were restless, and those who had not signed continued to harass whites. Tall Bull and other leaders began to cross the Arkansas north to the buffalo ranges. In June, a Cheyenne raiding party stole a herd of horses from a Kaw Indian village and robbed several settler homes near Council Grove, Kansas. Indian people were hungry, and the federal government had not lived up to its promises.[6]

After Buffalo Bill Cody's hunting contest with Medicine Bill Comstock and raffling off his buffalo pony Brigham, Cody accepted a scouting position offered by the quartermaster at Fort Larned. Before heading to his new post, Cody took Louisa and Arta to Leavenworth where he found them a comfortable house.[7]

Cheyenne and Arapaho bands began crossing the Arkansas River heading for the buffalo ranges to the north. A large concentration of Comanches and Kiowas were still camped near Fort Larned when Cody arrived.[8]

Fort Larned's commander was Captain Daingerfield Parker of the Third Infantry. Buffalo Bill Cody was selected to act as the personal scout and courier for Colonel William Hazen, who was based out of Larned. General Sheridan created two army districts to oversee the two new reservations in Indian Territory that the treaty had created, and he appointed Hazen as commander of the southern district.[9]

One day during the summer of 1868, fourteen-year-old Bill Tilghman was driving a wagon filled with his sisters, brother, and friends on their way to gather blackberries along the Missouri River.[10] The children were on the main road traveling west of Atchison, Kansas, when they met a tall stranger mounted on a government mule approaching from the west. Tilghman remembered, "he rode with the easy grace of a Plainsman." The man wore a broad-brimmed hat, fringed buckskin jacket, two pistols on his belt, and fine tanned leather boots. Reining in the mule, the man greeted the children, "Good morning boys; and young ladies." He continued by asking, "Did you happen to see a man driving a span of mules to a covered wagon?"

"Yes, sir, we did," Bill answered. "About two miles back."

The man thanked them, lifted his hat, and rode on. Bill Tilghman later read in the newspaper that Deputy US Marshal Wild Bill Hickok had recovered a stolen wagon and team of mules as well as captured the thief. Young Tilghman and the children had met Wild Bill Hickok. From that time on, Wild Bill was his hero. Tilghman later became a noted lawman himself.[11]

Possibly after Wild Bill Hickok's return to Hays City from capturing the thief, a nineteen-year-old youth named Harry Young, originally from New York, arrived in Hays City with $40. After spending the night in one of the dance halls, his entire fortune had dwindled to $1.50. Hickok had observed how Young had been taken advantage of during the night and had pity on him. He introduced himself and gave Young advice on spending his money. Hickok asked Young what he was doing in Hays. Young answered he was looking for a job. Hickok asked if he could drive a six-mule team, to which Young said no. Hickok thought he could do it, taught him some useful knots he would need, and then took him to Fort Hays where he convinced the corral boss to give Young a chance and hire him. Over the next few days, Hickok would stop by and give Young pointers on driving mules.[12]

On August 6, 1868, a special train from Topeka arrived at Hays. It was making a trip to Monument, just short of the end of the line at Sherman. On board were Union Pacific, Eastern Division officials and "nearly three hundred sons and daughters of Topeka" accompanied by a brass band and an additional musical and choral ensemble. It must have been prearranged for Wild Bill Hickok to be their Hays City host. Most likely it was J. F. Cummings, the editor of the *Topeka Leader*, who wrote, "The first man we saw 'Wild Bill.' He was ready, waiting to give welcome to the excursionists. Gentle William said he had brought two hundred of the nastiest, meanest Cheyennes to Hays that we might get a sight at the red men who did most of the murdering and scalping during the troubles of the last two years." These Cheyennes were peaceful and content as Cummings noted their leader "Old Black Kettle passed two [*sic*] and fro around the town as if the whole belonged to him."[13] Hickok must have been on good terms with Black Kettle to convince him to bring his band to Hays City.

The excursionists stayed in town for the night. There were not enough rooms for them all and many slept outside. Some visited the saloons and others tried to keep warm around bonfires of buffalo chips. Justice of the Peace Marcellus Joyce, who had one of the nicer houses, offered beds at his home for the women of the tour. Hickok led those who accepted the offer to Joyce's home. At 5:00 a.m., the tourists left on their train for Monument.[14]

However peaceful Black Kettle's Cheyenne band might have been, the smoldering trouble between the whites and Indian tribes was about flare up into a raging prairie fire.

During August, Cheyenne bands north of the Arkansas River gathered on the Arikaree branch of the Republican River. Roman Nose, Tall Bull, and White Horse, the three men leading three hundred warriors and their families, were there. Some Arapahos and Pawnee Killer's Lakotas joined them. A two-hundred-man Cheyenne war party, including a few Arapahos and Sioux, planned an attack on the Pawnees. However, when they reached white settlements along the Saline and Solomon Rivers, they attacked them instead. From August 10 through the 12, they rampaged through the countryside, killing fifteen men and raping five women.[15]

Captain Frederick Benteen with a Seventh Cavalry troop arrived in the Saline Valley as the war party was attacking the home of a Mr. Schermerhorn. Settlers had gathered there for common defense. Benteen's men charged the warriors, who left off the attack and rode away.[16]

Earlier that summer, General Sheridan appointed three scouts, Medicine Bill Comstock, Abner "Sharp" Grover, and Dick Parr, as his mediators to work with the tribes to keep the peace and to report back on the tribes' activities. Sheridan put the three scouts under the direction of Lieutenant Frederick Beecher with the Third Infantry. Comstock and Grover were friends with the Cheyenne chief Turkey Leg. It was believed warriors from Turkey Leg's village had taken part in the raids on Saline and Solomon River settlements. Beecher sent Comstock and Grover from Fort Wallace to find Turkey Leg to hear the Cheyenne side of the story and ask Turkey Leg to end the attacks. On August 16, they found Turkey Leg's village on the Solomon River about twenty-five miles northeast of the Union Pacific's Monument Station. At first, the Cheyennes were friendly but then drove the two men from camp. They were about two miles away when seven warriors rode up, acting friendly. When Comstock and Glover relaxed their guard, the warriors shot them. Comstock was killed instantly. Wounded, Glover fought them off and eventually made it back to Fort Wallace.[17]

General Sheridan was determined to stop the Indian attacks on settlements and to protect the railroad. He planned to give it his undivided attention and transferred his headquarters from Fort Leavenworth to Fort Hays.[18]

He requested more troops, supplies, and equipment. He was sent seven companies of the Fifth Cavalry which arrived at Fort Hays, and the state of Kansas was raising a volunteer regiment at his request. Sheridan ordered his assistant inspector general, Major George "Sandy" Forsyth, to form an elite unit of forty-seven scouts and three officers—Forsyth was in command, Lieutenant Frederick Beecher, second in command, and Doctor J. H. Mooers was surgeon. Forsyth recruited thirty scouts at Fort Harker and the rest at Fort Hays by August 20.[19] Neither Wild Bill Hickok nor Buffalo Bill Cody joined.

About the same time that the Cheyenne war party had attacked the Saline and Solomon River settlements, Kiowa and Comanche warriors raided along the Arkansas and Cimarron Rivers. Sheridan believed the Kiowa warriors were under the direction of Satanta.[20]

Buffalo Bill Cody recounted that one August morning, Colonel Hazen planned to travel along the Santa Fe Trail to Fort Zarah thirty miles away and then continue on to Fort Harker. Cody, riding a mule, and an escort of twenty men accompanied Hazen. Arriving at Zarah about noon, Hazen proceeded on without the escort and Cody. The escort would return to Larned the next day, but Cody did not want to wait and started back to Larned, alone. Halfway there, forty young Kiowa warriors surrounded him. They acted friendly and wanted to shake his hand. When he did so, they seized him, disarmed him, and whipped him and his mule toward Satanta's village. When they reached the village, the people were breaking camp. The young men took Cody to Satanta and other principal chiefs and warriors. Cody believed they meant to do him harm.[21]

He thought he would try to lie his way out of his fix. He told Satanta and the others he was out looking for a cattle herd expected for the tribes' use. Satanta said he believed him and apologized for the way the young men had acted and made them give back Cody's weapons. Satanta let Cody go, asking him to bring the cattle to the village, which Cody said he would do.[22]

Once Cody was out of sight of the village, he raced his mule toward Fort Larned. It was evening and a dozen warriors chased after him. He came upon an Army detail and Denver Jim, "a well-known scout," who were recovering seven to eight bodies of herders and woodchoppers killed by Indians. They ambushed the warriors following Cody, killing two and scalping them.[23]

Cody and the others returned to the fort where he learned that earlier in the day, Satanta and about eight hundred warriors had ridden circles around the fort, occasionally firing into it as the rest of the people in the village packed preparing to move away.[24]

No other sources confirm Cody's story. Maybe warriors intercepted Cody and took him to Satanta's village where the Kiowa leader asked him about the expected beef herd and then let him go—not as exciting as being chased by Indians then turning the tables on them.

A storm was brewing the night Cody returned to the fort. He reported to Captain Parker, who was meeting with the scouts. Parker had important dispatches he needed taken to General Sheridan. The other scouts did not want to do it. They claimed they did not know the country well enough to ride through it during a stormy night with the added possibility of running into Indians who were camping along Walnut Creek on the route to Fort Hays. Parker asked Cody to deliver the dispatches, but Cody was tired from his ride and ordeal with the Kiowas. He finally gave in and agreed to go as long as they gave him the best horse at the post.[25]

Cody ate a meal, filled his canteen with brandy, put his saddle and tack on the best horse, and by 10:00 p.m., he began the sixty-five-mile ride north to Fort Hays. He had only ridden several miles when the horse stepped in a prairie dog hole and threw him. Fortunately, the horse couldn't run off. Cody had tied one end of his rawhide lariat to the bridle and the other end wrapped around his waist.[26]

Twenty-five miles north of Fort Larned he came upon the rough breaks along Walnut Creek. Cody could hardly see five feet in front of him and let the horse pick his way down through the draws. When they reached a meadow along the creek, Cody realized they were in the middle of an Indian horse herd. The horses spooked, racing wildly in all directions as a dog barked. Alerted, the herders mounted their horses and raced in Cody's direction. Hoping his horse wouldn't step in a hole, Cody urged him to run. They soon left their pursuers behind.[27]

Cody reached Fort Hays by early morning and reported directly to General Sheridan. Sheridan quickly read the dispatches and questioned Cody about the Comanches and Kiowas at Fort Larned and his ride to Fort Hays. Cody asked that someone take care of the horse, and Sheridan had an orderly ensure it would be done. Sheridan thanked Cody and offered him breakfast. Cody declined saying he was headed to Hays City to visit friends. Sheridan told him to come back later, and he promised to return in a few hours.[28]

Cody visited the Perry House where he enjoyed "refreshments" with friends and then took a two-hour nap. Returning to Fort Hays, a group of scouts told him Sheridan needed dispatches carried to Fort Dodge ninety-five miles to the southwest. Indians had killed several dispatch riders between the two forts, and no one wanted to do it even though the Army offered a reward of several hundred dollars.[29]

Cody reported to Sheridan who told him about the orders he needed carried to Fort Dodge. Those orders were based on information Cody had brought. The scout Dick Parr walked in reporting to Sheridan that no one would take the dispatches to Fort Dodge.[30]

"It was impossible to get one of the various 'Petes,' 'Jacks,' or 'Jims' hanging around Hays City to take my communication," Sheridan wrote. "Cody learning of the straight [*sic*] I was in, manfully came to the rescue and proposed to make the trip to Dodge."[31]

Cody returned to Hays City to get some rest but instead had "a time with the boys." About 5:00 p.m., he set out for Fort Dodge, riding a fine horse Sheridan had selected for him.[32]

Cody followed the Fort Hays to Fort Dodge Road through the night. Just before daylight, he reached Saw-log Crossing on the Pawnee Fork where a contingent of Black cavalry was stationed. He slept for an hour, ate a meal, exchanged his horse for a fresh mount, and completed the last twenty-five miles to Fort Dodge by midmorning.[33]

The Fort Dodge commander had dispatches for Fort Larned, Cody's home post. The Fort Dodge scouts were hesitant to leave the fort as the Indians were becoming more dangerous. Cody agreed to take the dispatches since that was the direction he had to head anyway and would leave at nightfall. Fellow scout, Johnny Austin, invited Cody to his house to sleep during the day.[34]

There were no fresh horses available, so Cody was given a

government mule. He left under cover of darkness traveling east but south of the Santa Fe Trail, hoping to avoid Indians. Reaching Coon Creek, roughly thirty miles from Fort Dodge, Cody dismounted and led the mule to the creek where they both drank. Cody held the reins in one hand while using his hat for a water dipper. Catching Cody off guard, the mule jerked the reins out of his hand and headed down Coon Creek toward the Santa Fe Trail. Once the mule reached the trail, he started trotting toward Fort Larned. Cody ran after him, but the mule would never let him catch up. It was thirty-five miles to Larned. They made good time. Cody was so angry not only at the mule but at himself for failing to tie the mule to himself with his rawhide lariat. He cursed the mule who always stayed just ahead of him. Fortunately, no Indians discovered them.[35]

At daybreak, they reached the rise of a hill and Cody could see they were about four miles from Fort Larned. When they were within a half-mile of the fort, Cody's anger overwhelmed him. Raising his rifle to his shoulder, he shot and killed the mule. Soldiers rushed from the fort to Cody's position. When he explained what had happened, they believed Cody was justified in shooting the mule.[36]

After delivering the dispatches to Captain Parker, Cody slept for several hours. General Hazen returned that day and had dispatches to be delivered to General Sheridan at Fort Hays. Hazen's information was the Indian villages were moving to the south. Again, other scouts were hesitant to leave the fort, but when Cody learned about the dispatches, he volunteered to deliver them. He left at dark that same night arriving at Sheridan's headquarters the next morning. Cody estimated he had traveled 355 miles in fifty-eight hours of riding and walking.[37]

Sheridan said of Cody's feat, "such an exhibition of endurance and courage was more than enough to convince me that his services would be extremely valuable in the campaign, so I retained him at Fort Hays till the battalion of the Fifth Cavalry arrived, and then made him chief of scouts for that regiment."[38]

Buffalo Bill and the Army mule

Meanwhile, on August 18, 1868, Wild Bill Hickok was hired at Fort Hays as a guide for Captain G. H. Graham with the Tenth Cavalry for an expedition north to the Republican River. They would return on August 31 and Hickok would be paid $43.43 for thirteen days of service.[39]

Buffalo Bill Cody was not lazing around. He was assigned to scout once again for Captain Augustus Armes, commanding Company F of the Tenth Cavalry. On August 24, 1868, they rode out of Fort Hays. Along the way, they ran into Captain Frederick Benteen and his Seventh Cavalry troopers returning to Fort Harker after patrolling of the Saline Valley. Armes wrote in his diary that day, "Bill Cody (Buffalo Bill), one of our scouts and one of the best shots on the plains, keeps us well supplied with plenty of buffalo and deer. He gets $60 per month and a splendid mule to ride, and is one of the most contented and happy men I ever met." By August 27, Armes and his men had returned to Fort Hays.[40]

Wild Bill scouting for the Tenth Cavalry

September 2, 1868, the Tenth Cavalry's Company F was patrolling south to Walnut Creek. Armes wrote, "We started out at seven o'clock this morning with Wild Bill [Hickok] as our scout, and while resting a few moments and allowing the horses to graze he came rushing in with fifteen of his scouts to inform me that a fresh Indian trail had been discovered." He wrote on September 4 that they determined the trail had been made by a burial party that had placed a war chief's body wrapped in a buffalo robe in a walnut tree.[41]

While waiting for the Fifth Cavalry to arrive in Kansas, Buffalo Bill Cody worked at any job available. He returned to Fort Larned where from September 9th through the 14th, he was paid as a laborer at $30 per month resacking forage. On September 15, Cody's status was changed to scout and his pay was increased to $75 per month.[42]

General Sheridan instructed Major Sandy Forsyth to ride west to Fort Wallace with his fifty scouts and officers to search for hostile Indians. Forsyth and his men reached Wallace on September 5, 1868. That same day, they learned a war party attacked freight wagons near the end of the tracks town of Sheridan, killing two teamsters. As Forsyth and his men tracked the raiders' trail to the northwest, it grew larger and larger, indicating bands of warriors were coming together. On September 16, the scouts were camped along the Arickaree Fork of the Republican River in Colorado when they were attacked by a combined force of Lakotas, Arapahos, and Cheyennes under the leadership of Pawnee Killer, Bull Bear, Tall Bull, and Roman Nose.[43]

Forsyth's men made a stand on a river island. All their horses were killed as hundreds of warriors surrounded them. Lieutenant

Beecher, Doctor Mooers, and five scouts were killed while Forsyth and eighteen others were wounded. Roman Nose and thirty warriors died in the fighting. Two scouts sneaked past the Indians and walked eighty-five miles to Fort Wallace where they reported the scouts' situation. A Tenth Cavalry detachment rode to the rescue, arriving at the scene of what would be called the Battle of Beecher's Island on September 25.[44]

On September 19, 1868, General Sherman had written, "I now regard the Cheyennes and Arapahos at war, and that it will be impossible for our troops to discriminate between the well-disposed and the warlike parts of those bands, unless an absolute separation be made." Sheridan instructed Colonel William Hazen to inform the tribes they were to go to Fort Cobb in Indian Territory, which would act as their agency and where they would receive food and supplies. The government gave General William Sherman the responsibility of distributing the tribes' $500,000 of supplies appropriated by Congress. Those Indians who did not comply would be considered hostile.[45]

Sheridan needed an officer who could defeat the Indian tribes. He needed Lieutenant Colonel George Custer. Custer was absent due to being court-martialed. In July 1867, he took actions resulting in two major charges being brought against him: "Absence without leave from his command" and "Conduct to the prejudice of good order and military discipline," which listed a number of additional charges. Custer was found guilty and sentenced "To be suspended from rank and command for one year, and forfeit his pay for the same time."[46]

By September, Custer had two months to serve out his sentence, but Sheridan's plea to General Sherman for Custer worked, and on October 4, Custer arrived at Fort Hays. Sheridan told Custer he wanted him to lead the Seventh Cavalry in a winter campaign against the hostile tribes. Sheridan gave him free rein to do whatever needed to be done to defeat the tribes. On October 10, Custer arrived at the Seventh Cavalry camp thirty miles southeast of Fort Dodge.[47]

On October 3, the day before Custer's arrival at Fort Hays, seven companies of the Fifth Cavalry, commanded by Major William Royall, stopped on their way west. Buffalo Bill Cody joined them there as their scout. The Fifth Cavalry left Fort Hays, proceeding west several miles then north toward the South Fork of the Solomon River. They were to patrol westward toward Beaver Creek in the northwestern corner of Kansas, searching for hostile Indians. During the first leg of their journey, they chased a small band of warriors who eluded them, and Cody hunted buffalo to supplement the men's food supply.[48]

Late one afternoon, they established camp along the South Fork of the Solomon River. Cody related that Major Royall asked him to kill some buffalo for the men. Cody asked Royall to send along wagons to haul back the meat. Royall refused telling Cody to first kill the buffalo then he would send wagons. Cody rode out and killed six buffalo, then rode back to camp and asked Royall to send out the wagons.[49]

The next afternoon as camp was being set up, Royall again asked Cody to hunt some buffalo. This time, Cody did not ask for a wagon. He found a small buffalo herd and chased seven of them toward the encampment. Cody shot them right at the camp. Royall was angry and asked Cody why he had shot the buffalo at camp and not out on the prairie. Cody responded, "I didn't care about asking for any wagons this time Colonel [brevet rank]; so I thought I would make the buffaloes furnish their own transportation."[50]

The Fifth Cavalry reached Beaver Creek on October 14. Royall established his encampment there and sent out patrols to find Tall Bull's Cheyenne Dog Soldiers. However, it was Cheyenne warriors who found Royall's encampment first. Cody was out on patrol when the Cheyennes attacked, killing two men and running off twenty-six horses.[51]

When the patrols returned to camp, Royall set out after the warriors, but failing to catch them and running low on provisions, they turned south to resupply at the railroad, reaching Buffalo Tank Station about halfway between Fort Hays and Fort Wallace.[52]

On October 22, Major Eugene Carr arrived and took command of the Fifth Cavalry. Carr, a West Point graduate, had served with the Mounted Rifles and seen combat with Plains Tribes from 1852 to 1860. He was in the thick of the fighting during the Civil War, rising to the rank of major general and winning the Congressional Medal of Honor. Carr was one of those people who inspired confidence.[53]

Carr thought Cody was another "one of those confounded scouts posing"; but soon realized, "His splendid physique, nonchalant manner, promptness to act and superb horsemanship disarmed, as regarded him, my prejudices." Carr wrote, "He was a wonderful shot from horseback, killing game, even antelopes running, which was an extraordinary feat in those days, had eyes as good as a field glass and was the best white trailer I ever saw."[54]

Carr led the Fifth Cavalry back to Beaver Creek where they located Tall Bull's Dog Soldiers. Carr's troops had running fights with them for five days but were never able to defeat them. Cody participated in several fights. In one case, he was scouting ahead of the troops when his horse was shot out from under him. Several Indians were charging him when the advanced guard arrived and the warriors rode away. By October 31, Tall Bull's people were gone, and Carr took his troops to Fort Wallace to resupply and wait for orders.[55]

Cody took small parties on buffalo hunts. One day, about fifty warriors attacked Cody's party. The hunters were able to hold off the warriors. Several horses were hit, and one hunter wounded. Cody said after they killed four warriors, the rest rode off. Cody and his companions finished the hunt and returned to Fort Wallace with plenty of fresh meat.[56]

During the fall of 1868, Wild Bill Hickok was an Army courier and scout. He most likely remained with the four companies of the Tenth Cavalry which were ordered to Fort Dodge, reaching that post on September 14. They were there for a little over a month and then ordered to Fort Lyon, Colorado, and placed under the command of Captain William Penrose.[57]

General Sheridan believed the situation in the Department of the Missouri was dire. He reported from August 3 to October 24, 1868, Indians had killed 110 civilians; raped thirteen women; stolen over a thousand head of livestock; and destroyed farms, depots, and other buildings. Eighteen of Sheridan's soldiers had been killed and forty-five wounded.[58]

General William T. Sherman gave his approval for General Sheridan's harsh winter campaign against those hostile tribes who had not moved to Fort Cobb. Many of these tribes were thought to be located along the Red River south of the Antelope Hills in Indian Territory. Three columns of troops would converge on the Indian villages. One was to head straight east from Fort Bascom, New Mexico, another would march southeast from Fort Lyon, Colorado, and the third would move straight south from Fort Dodge, Kansas.[59]

Major Andrew Evans commanded the column that left Fort Bascom on November 18. It was made up of six companies of the Third Cavalry, two companies of the Thirty-Seventh Infantry, and four mountain howitzers. Evans's mission was to march east along the South Canadian River searching for Indian encampments for as long as his supplies lasted.[60]

Captain William Penrose, with four companies of the Tenth Cavalry, one company of the Seventh Cavalry, and Wild Bill Hickok as scout, had been ordered to Fort Lyon. They left the fort for the North Canadian River to the southeast on November 13.[61]

With Buffalo Bill Cody as scout, Major Carr's five companies of the Fifth Cavalry were ordered to leave Fort Wallace for Fort Lyon. Taking along additional supplies for Penrose's men, Carr was to rendezvous with Penrose's troops on the North Canadian River. From there, they were to proceed toward the Antelope Hills as long as they received supplies from Colorado. Sheridan did not expect the two western columns to see much fighting, but he hoped they would block tribes trying to flee west.[62]

The main force headed south from Fort Dodge. Sheridan joined them on November 21 at a new post named Camp Supply being constructed on the North Canadian River in Indian Territory and manned by five infantry companies. From Camp Supply, Lieutenant Colonel George Custer led eleven companies of the Seventh Cavalry on November 23. Sheridan's orders to Custer were, "To proceed south in the direction of the Antelope Hills, thence towards the Washita River, the supposed seat of the hostile tribes; to destroy their villages and ponies; to kill or hang all warriors, and bring back all women and children."[63]

Captain Penrose, with Wild Bill Hickok as one of his scouts, led his troops from Fort Lyon without forage for the horses and mules. Captain Augustus Armes believed not taking forage was a mistake. Armes did not have any confidence in the success of the mission writing, "I left all my private property with the Post Quartermaster and sent my father $360, retaining fifty for personal expenses. As the chances are that we may never return alive, I have made my preparations accordingly."[64]

Armes was right about the forage. It was a brutal march. On November 15, a heavy snowstorm hit. There was no fuel available to even make coffee. The horses and mules had nothing to eat and twenty-five of them had to be shot. November 17, fourteen horses had to be shot in the morning, although at the evening's camp there was plenty of forage and wood for fires. Each day they lost more and more horses. They were hit by blizzarding snow and bitter cold temperatures. Indians had severely wounded Private Brown, and on the night of November 27, they stole sixty mules. On November 30, Private Brown died. On December 1, they reached a location with plenty of grass, wood, and water. Penrose decided to allow the men a day of rest while he went buffalo hunting with the scouts most likely including Hickok. They killed four buffalo and brought back the meat for the men.[65]

Years later, Private James Massey with the Tenth Cavalry said, "The weather was so very cold that our horses froze to death on the picket line. . . . We run short of rations, was without anything to eat except quarter rations for some three or four days."[66]

Meanwhile, Custer led the Seventh Cavalry south to the Washita River where his Osage scouts discovered a fifty-lodge Indian village. Custer positioned his troops, surrounding the sleeping, unsuspecting people. Early on the morning of November 27, 1868, Custer ordered the attack as the band played the tune "Garry Owen" and the troops gave a cheer. It turned out it was Black Kettle's Cheyenne village. These were the same people Colonel John Chivington's Colorado troops had attacked back on November 29, 1864. These were the same people Wild Bill Hickok had introduced to the Topeka tourists in Hays City back on August 6.[67]

The initial attack was over in ten minutes and the village captured. Black Kettle and his wife were among the 103 Cheyenne people killed. The troops captured fifty-three women and children. They burned the lodges, food, and possessions, and shot over eight hundred ponies and mules in the corrals. However, the remaining Cheyenne warriors were turning the tables, surrounding the troops and fighting back. Warriors from other villages were arriving, adding to their number. Custer decided to extract his troops, but Major Joel Elliott, leading the sergeant major and sixteen troopers, had been last seen galloping after Indians fleeing downriver. Custer sent a detachment to look for them, but they were not seen.[68]

Custer left the village, abandoning Elliott and his men to their fate.[69] On December 2, Custer and his men returned to Camp Supply in a triumphant pageant reviewed by Sheridan and the rest of the troops. In the lead were the Osage scouts, followed by the white scouts, the captive Cheyenne women and children, the band playing "Garry Owen," Custer's sharpshooters, then Custer himself, followed by eleven companies of the Seventh Cavalry.[70]

Major Eugene Carr's Fifth Cavalry, with Buffalo Bill Cody as chief of scouts, had been ordered from Fort Wallace to Fort Lyon, arriving there on November 29, 1868. On December 2, Carr led seven companies of the Fifth Cavalry from Fort Lyon southeast toward the North Canadian River where he was to rendezvous with Captain William Penrose and the Tenth Cavalry. Carr ensured his troops were well supplied and took additional supplies to reprovision Penrose. The supply train included seventy-five wagons pulled by teams of six mules each, ambulances, and pack mules. He also took over two hundred head of cattle for food for the men of both commands. Sergeant Luke Cahill, in command of Carr's headquarters guard, said Cody "helped to bed the cattle and did many valuable things that were very useful for the camp."[71]

They had been following Penrose's trail for three days when a blizzard struck, and Carr halted the column. The high winds blew over some of the wagons and blew down tents. Sergeant Cahill said the temperature dropped to −30. Four men on picket duty died, while others were so badly frozen they were sent back to Fort Lyon. Much of the cattle drifted away, and thirty-six horses and mules died.[72]

As the falling snow wiped out the trail, Carr sent Cody and four scouts to find Penrose's camp. After riding twenty-five miles, they found an abandoned Tenth Cavalry camp along a Cimarron River tributary. Leaving the other scouts there, Cody rode back to Carr's camp, arriving there at 11:00 p.m. The Fifth Cavalry broke camp the next morning. The snowfall was so heavy that in places the men had to shovel through drifts so the wagons could pass.[73]

Reaching the Cimarron River, they followed the east bank downriver as the terrain along the west bank was too rough to take the wagons. At day's end, they reached a tableland in the Raton foothills, needing to descend steep bluffs to the valley below. The grade concerned the teamsters, but Cody believed the wagons could make it down. He helped tie chains to the wagon wheels, rough locking them, so they would not turn, helping to slow the wagons' rates of descent and not overrun the mules. The wagons all made it safely to the bottom.[74]

In the following days, Carr's column continued in a southeasterly direction following Penrose's trail toward the Canadian

River. The nighttime temperatures remained below 0. Cody was out ahead of the column when he heard someone call his name. A trooper from the Tenth Cavalry had spotted him and Cody recognized the man. It turned out there were three more troopers with him who said they had become lost from Penrose's column. They were hungry and said Penrose's men were out of rations and starving. When Cody asked them where Penrose was, they couldn't tell him, being lost themselves.[75]

Upon learning the condition of Penrose's troops, Carr sent ahead fifty pack-mules carrying provisions escorted by Captain William Brown leading two companies of cavalry and Cody as their guide. Three days later, a week before Christmas, they found Penrose's camp on Palo Duro Creek. Penrose's men had been on quarter rations and were famished.[76]

When Cody rode into camp one of the first people he saw was Wild Bill Hickok. Cody said, "That night we had a jolly reunion around the camp-fires."[77]

When Carr reached Penrose's camp, he took command. Penrose's men were in a bad situation; not only were they low on provisions, but they had lost two hundred horses and mules. Penrose had sent his Seventh Cavalry company back to Fort Lyon for more supplies but had heard nothing from them. All the men in both groups had been suffering from the cold. Carr sent his wagons back to Fort Lyon for more supplies as he reconnoitered both branches of the Canadian River. On December 28, he encamped on the South Canadian twelve miles upriver from Major Andrew Evans's supply camp.[78]

Hickok and Cody learned that a bull train with supplies for Evans's camp was due to arrive soon from New Mexico. They were also informed the bull train was hauling a load of beer. Hickok and Cody intercepted the wagon carrying the beer and convinced the Mexican owners to stop at Carr's camp instead of continuing on to Evans's camp. The Mexicans did a lively business selling the beer in pint cups to the soldiers. Cody said as the weather was very cold, the men stuck heated picket pins into their cups to warm the beer. He later wrote, "The result was one of the biggest beer jol-lifications I ever had the misfortune to attend."[79]

On January 1, 1869, General Sheridan met with Cheyenne and Arapaho leaders who agreed to come to Fort Cobb, but they were concerned soldiers would fire upon them. Sheridan sent mes-sages to Carr and Evans to cease operations against Indians head-ing to Fort Cobb.[80]

During this time, Cody carried dispatches to Fort Cobb and back, and Hickok did the same. The scouts must have been get-ting restless in camp. Cody tells of a fight that broke out between American scouts and fifteen Mexican scouts who were with Pen-rose's command. Cody said alcohol was involved. When Carr heard about the ruckus, he called for Hickok and Cody to hear what had happened. He concluded both sides were to blame.[81]

Men were becoming sick; some were developing signs of scurvy. Carr wanted fresh meat and sent Cody on a buffalo hunt with a detail of twenty wagons and drivers escorted by twenty infantrymen commanded by Sergeant Luke Cahill. After a four-day journey, Cody located a herd. He had the men and wagons remain hidden while he stampeded the buffalo into a snow-choked ravine where the animals bogged down in snow almost twenty feet deep. Cody shot all fifty-five of them, never having to use more than one shot on each animal. The men wrapped chains and ropes around the carcasses and used the mules to pull them out. It took the rest of the day and into the night to finish butchering. They sent back some wagons loaded with meat and Cody continued his hunt the next day, killing forty-one buffalo and exhausting his two hunting ponies. He hurt his right arm and shoulder so bad it was a mass of black and blue, and he needed assistance to put on his coat. A couple of days later, Cody was healed enough, and his ponies rested that he shot enough buffalo to load all the wagons.[82]

Cody and his detail were four miles from camp with their wagonloads of buffalo meat when Major Carr, Captain Penrose, Wild Bill, and a large group of mounted men and officers rode out to meet them. Sergeant Cahill later wrote, "General [brevet rank]

Carr and General [brevet rank] Penrose took every mother's son of us by the hand and thanked each of us for the splendid work that we had done in behalf of the troops. General Carr excused every man from doing night guard for one month and also said that he would like to give each of us double pay if he had the power to do so. Buffalo Bill came in for his share of the glory. He was wined and dined by the officers and was at once declared the Lion of the command."[83]

Even with supplemental buffalo meat, Carr's men were running low on supplies. He marched his troops back to Fort Lyon, arriving there on February 19. They did not have any major confrontations with Indians, but they had kept any bands in Indian Territory from escaping to the west.[84] Not all Cheyenne bands had made peace; it was still dangerous on the prairie.

Wild Bill Hickok continued riding as a courier when called upon. Toward the end of February 1869, he carried dispatches from Fort Lyon to Fort Wallace. The ride was uneventful. Since he had seen no signs of Indians, he was careless on his return to Lyon. Coming upon a buffalo herd, he shot one, taking the hump and tongue. At noon, he stopped at a creek to water his horse. It was as good a place as any to eat, so he built a fire near the stream's cutbank, cooked his buffalo meat, and ate his fill.[85]

Hickok was about to mount his horse when seven Cheyenne riders appeared on top of the cutbank. They charged. He shot four of them before they reached him. Hickok's horse was rearing as he tried to control it, holding onto the bridle bit. A fifth man lunged at him with a lance ripping a deep gash in his right hip. As he shot that man, a sixth thrust a lance toward him. Hickok's horse swiveled between him and the warrior. The man stabbed killing Hickok's horse instead of Hickok, who shot that man. As the seventh warrior was riding away, Hickok shot him out of the saddle.[86]

Seven Cheyenne warriors were dead. Hickok washed and bandaged his wound. He caught and mounted the horse belonging to the man who had stabbed him and taking the lance, continued his ride to Fort Lyon. Somewhere along the trail, the horse got away from him. He continued on foot using the lance as a staff. The next morning, a detail of woodchoppers came upon Hickok and took him to Fort Lyon where the surgeon cared for his wound. Was Hickok's story embellished? No one knows, but he did have a nasty gash in his right thigh, and he did have a Cheyenne lance. Hickok gave Buffalo Bill Cody the lance and Cody still owned it in June 1914.[87] Hickok never scouted again for the Army.

While Hickok was recuperating at Fort Lyon, a letter arrived from his sister Lydia. His mother was ill and wanted to see him. His journey took him to Fort Wallace, then to Sherman where he caught the train. In early spring, he arrived in Troy Grove, Illinois, and had a tearful reunion with his mother. He brought gifts for family members, and everyone had an enjoyable time reminiscing and catching up on each other's lives. His hip wound was not healing well, and Doctor Edward Thomas operated. Hickok refused to take chloroform and didn't flinch when Thomas pealed back the flesh and scraped the bone.[88]

In the meantime, Major Eugene Carr gave Buffalo Bill Cody a month off to visit his family in St. Louis. Since the distance from Fort Lyon to Fort Wallace and the railhead of Sheridan was 140 miles, Carr and the quartermaster gave Cody permission to use his government horse to ride and a government mule to haul his belongings. He was told to leave the animals at the Fort Wallace corral. Instead of doing what he was told, he left the animals with a friend named Perry who kept a hotel in Sheridan.[89]

Cody caught an eastbound train. After spending a pleasant twenty days with Louisa and Arta in St. Louis, Cody returned to Sheridan. While he was gone, the quartermaster's agent for Fort Wallace reported to the commander that Cody had sold the government horse and mule to Perry. He had the animals confiscated and threatened to have Perry arrested for illegally buying government property. Perry tried to explain the situation to the Fort Wallace officers, but they wouldn't listen. Cody was furious. The quartermaster's agent office was in Sheridan. Cody tracked down the agent and gave him "just such a thrashing as his contemptable lie deserved."[90]

Cody tried to explain to the Fort Wallace commander what had happened, but he wouldn't listen to Cody and ordered him to leave the fort. Still furious, Cody returned to Sheridan where he saw the quartermaster's agent again and beat him a second time. The commander had Cody arrested. Cody wrote a telegram to send to General Sheridan. The commander intercepted it and tore it up. After some reflection, the commander had a change of heart and allowed Cody to take the horse and mule and return to Fort Lyon.[91]

Reaching Lyon two days later, Carr put Cody to work as a government detective. During the past two weeks, thieves had been stealing horses and mules, including Carr's horse and Lieutenant W. C. Forbush's racing mule. Bill Green and other scouts had tracked the thieves to the vicinity of the original Fort Lyon. There the scouts lost the trail.[92]

Cody left Fort Lyon taking a posse of Bill Green, Jack Farley, and Long Doc, as well as a pack mule hauling eight to ten days' provisions. They rode to where the thieves' trail disappeared. Cody discovered where the stolen animals had been held. There were many false trails leading from the hiding spot. Cody and the posse members rode out five miles from the thieves' hideout and then rode a circuit, discovering the tracks of twelve horses and mules. As they followed the trail, it was plain the thieves were headed to Denver. The number of hoofprints increased the closer they rode to Denver, and they eventually lost the trail. Cody believed the thieves would sell the animals at Denver's regularly held Saturday auction. Through a little sleuthing, Cody and his posse nabbed one thief named Williams and later his partner Bill Bevins;[93] both had been civilian packers working for the Army. Cody and his posse recovered all the missing livestock, tied each prisoner on top of a mule, and began the long journey back to Fort Lyon.[94]

They made it as far as Cherry Creek about seventeen miles out of Denver. It was April, and the night was cold and stormy with snow falling. They built a fire, and everyone sat around it trying to stay warm. Williams and Bevins had been cooperative and had not tried to escape. Cody had them remove their shoes. With plenty of cacti growing in the area, it would be hard to run through that in stocking feet. The posse members took turns standing guard.[95]

About 3:00 a.m., Farley was on guard duty, sitting by the fire. As he turned to face it with his back to the prisoners, Williams kicked him into the fire as he and Bevins made a dash to escape. Bevins grabbed his shoes and disappeared into the night as Cody and Green shot at him. Williams was slower than Bevins, and Cody whacked him down with his pistol. As Cody and Green pursued Bevins, they discovered he had lost a shoe. They heard him running through the brush but knew it was next to impossible to find him in the dark.[96]

The next morning, Cody and Green followed Bevins's footprints in the snow leading toward the South Platte River. Sharp stones and prickly pears covering the ground took a toll on his shoeless foot—blood spots appeared in the snow. After twelve miles, they spotted Bevins two miles ahead and raced to catch him. Cody got within one hundred yards shouting to Bevins to stop or he'd shoot. Bevins surrendered. When Cody and Green saw Bevins's bleeding foot, they felt sorry for him. Cody gave Bevins his Bowie knife to pry the cactus spines out of his foot, and then Cody and Green took turns allowing Bevins to ride a horse.[97]

They rejoined the others and continued eastward. Finding a deserted cabin on the Arkansas River, they planned to spend the night there. It was storming outside. Bevins's foot had swollen, so there was no chance he would escape. For some reason, they did not bind Williams. During Long Doc's watch, Williams asked if he would let him "step to the door for a moment." Long Doc granted his request. Believing he could handle the situation, Long Doc did not wake the others. As Williams stood in the doorway, he jumped to the right and raced away. Long Doc fired at him, but he was gone. They took turns guarding the horses and mules through the night. Cody said that was the last he ever saw or heard of Williams.[98]

Cody and his posse returned to Fort Lyons with their prisoner and the recovered horses and mules. Carr was highly complimentary, even though they lost a prisoner. Cody turned Bevins over to civilian authorities; however, he never stood trial. He was confined in a log jail but escaped from it.[99]

Wild Bill Hickok was home with his family for three weeks. Neighbors and boyhood friends visited him including James Wylie, the boy he had rescued from drowning. Wylie and others asked Hickok to show them his shooting ability. They were amazed at his speed and accuracy. Young boys would follow him around town and listen to him tell tales of the West.[100]

By May 1869, Hickok had returned to Hays City and resumed his deputy US marshal duties. He traveled to Fort Wallace where on May 16, the Army turned over to his custody two thieves who had stolen mules. Hickok escorted them as well as two witnesses to Topeka where the thieves would stand trial.[101]

In mid-July, newspapers were carrying the story that "Wild Bill" had been shot and killed in Pueblo, Colorado. Apparently, there was a person in Colorado going by that name. The stories varied as to how and where "Wild Bill" was killed, but by September, the *Topeka Daily Commonwealth* reported, "We have the best reason for believing that the great original 'still lives.'"[102]

Many excursionists who detrained at Hays City wanted to meet Wild Bill Hickok. The Junction City *Weekly Union* reported in July a party of excursionists that included Richard Browne, Esq., a prominent member of the New York bar, and his family and Charles Alioth from Lausanne, Switzerland, stopped in Hays City on their way to Sheridan. "At Hays City, the excursionists had the pleasure of meeting 'Wild Bill,' of *Harper's Magazine* notoriety."[103]

In the spring of 1869, the Seventh Cavalry encamped two

miles east of Fort Hays, and by May, Libbie Custer joined George there.[104] Libbie wrote about one excursion whose members were eastern acquaintances of the Custers:

> *They begged to see Wild Bill. They sent the brakeman into the little street to ask him to come in, and they gave flowers to any bystander whom they saw, requesting that they be given to the renowned scout. But the more he was pursued with messages the more he retired from sight, hiding in the back room of one of the drinking-saloons opposite. He was really a very modest man and very free from swagger and bravado. Finally, General [brevet rank] Custer, persuaded by pretty girls, whom no one ever can resist, returned with the hero of the hour, for Wild Bill and General Custer were fast friends, having faced danger together many times.*
>
> *Bill's face was confused at the words of praise with which General Custer introduced him, and his fearless eyes were cast down in chagrin at the torture of being gazed at by the crowd. He went through the enforced introduction for General Custer's sake, but it was a relief when the engine whistle sounded that released him.*[105]

After Cheyenne and Arapaho leaders had met with General Sheridan and agreed to go to Fort Cobb on January 1, 1869, most Cheyenne and Arapaho bands remained peaceful except those Dog Soldiers led by Tall Bull, White Horse, and Bull Bear. The Dog Soldiers moved farther north joining with Sioux and Northern Cheyenne bands. In the spring of 1869, Tall Bull's Dog Soldiers returned to the Republican River area threatening the railroad and white settlers.[106]

Carr's Fifth Cavalry was being transferred from Fort Lyon to Fort McPherson on the Platte River in western Nebraska to counter the Dog Soldiers' threat, and Carr was taking Buffalo Bill Cody with them. The seven companies of the Fifth Cavalry rode out of Fort Lyon on May 1 to Fort Wallace. While camped at the fort, Cody and Captain William Brown drove a wagon to the town of Sheridan, where instead of buying provisions for their mess, they bought a large supply of liquor, which they later traded for food with other messes making a profit for their mess.[107]

On the afternoon of May 13, Carr's battalion was setting up camp north of Fort Wallace on Beaver Creek when Cody reported a large Indian trail. Carr sent Lieutenant Edward Ward and twelve troopers with Cody to follow the trail. Five miles downstream, Ward and Cody peered over a hilltop and saw an Indian village three miles farther downstream at Elephant Rock. Ward wrote a message to Carr and gave it to a trooper to take back as fast as he could. The patrol was slowly falling back when they heard shots. The messenger came racing back pursued by up to five Indians. After Ward's men drove off the Indians, Cody volunteered to take the message.[108]

He reached camp and reported the message to Carr. Carr left two companies to guard camp while he led the rest of the men toward the village, picking up Ward's patrol along the way. It was 3:00 p.m. when the troops attacked the village numbering an estimated five hundred warriors. The fighting was intense. Lieutenant C. A. Schenofsky's Company B was cut off from the rest of the command and had to be rescued. Three of the four troopers killed during the fight were from Company B. The Army estimated thirty Indians were killed or wounded. After nightfall, the village headed north toward the Republican River.[109]

Carr's troops followed the village's trail for three days. On May 16, Cody was guiding a forty-man detachment commanded by Lieutenants John Babcock and William Volkmar. They were on Spring Creek north of the Republican River and three miles in advance of the main column when around noon, two hundred warriors surrounded and attacked them.[110]

The officers ordered the troopers to dismount and form a skirmish circle with the horses and designated horse holders inside the circle. The troopers slowly retreated toward the main column, which was advancing toward them. Cody's career almost ended in this fight. A bullet blew off his hat and plowed a gash along the top of his skull. The regimental history stated he "was distinguished for coolness and bravery" during the fight.[111]

As the main column approached the advanced detachment, Carr later wrote what he saw: "A figure with apparently a red cap rose slowly up the hill. For an instant it puzzled me, as it wore the buckskin and had long hair, but on seeing the horse I recognized it as Cody's 'Powder Face'[112] and saw that it was Buffalo Bill without his broad brimmed sombrero. On closer inspection I saw his head was swathed in a bloody handkerchief, which served not only as a temporary bandage, but as a chapeau—his hat having been shot off, the bullet plowing his scalp badly for about five inches. It had ridged along the bone, and he was bleeding profusely—a very 'close call,' but a lucky one."[113]

As the column advanced, the warriors continued to put up a defensive fight the rest of the day until they recrossed to the south side of the Republican River, abandoning many items in their haste to outrun the troops.[114]

With supplies running low, Carr ended the chase at the end of the day. The nearest depot was at Fort Kearny fifty miles away. Even though he was wounded, Cody said he was the best man to make the ride and left that night, reaching Kearny the next morning with Carr's request for supplies. After being resupplied, the Fifth Cavalry arrived at Fort McPherson on May 20.[115]

The Fifth Cavalry had been reassigned from the Department of Missouri to the Department of the Platte with its headquarters in Omaha, Nebraska. In his official report to headquarters, Carr stated, "Our Scout William Cody, who has been with the Detachment since last September, displayed great skill in following it [the Indians' trail] and also deserves great credit for his fighting in both engagements, his marksmanship being very conspicuous. He deserves honorable mention for this and other services and I hope to be able to retain him as long as I am engaged in this duty." In a separate letter to headquarters, Carr requested "to pay my scout

William Cody, $100 extra for extraordinary good services as trailer and fighter in my late pursuit of hostile Indians." The request went up the chain of command to the secretary of war, who approved it. Cody was then appointed chief scout and guide for the Republican River expedition.[116]

Unknown to the Fifth Cavalry, on May 30, Tall Bull's Cheyenne Dog Soldiers struck the settlers along the Solomon River. They captured twenty-four-year-old Susanna Alderdice, who was pregnant, along with her infant daughter Alice. In Susanna's presence, the warriors killed two of her sons and presumed they had killed her third son, Willis, but he survived with horrific wounds. Several days later, the warriors strangled baby Alice. Tall Bull's warriors also captured twenty-three-year-old Maria Weichel after killing her husband. Maria, who was pregnant, was a German and had been in the United States less than a month.[117]

With Buffalo Bill Cody as the expedition's chief scout and guide, the Fifth Cavalry prepared to go after the Cheyenne bands in the Republican River territory. Accompanying eight companies of the Fifth was a battalion of three companies of Pawnee Scouts commanded by Major Frank North with his brother Captain Luther "Lute" North in command of Company A.[118]

The Fifth Cavalry and Pawnee Scouts left Fort McPherson on June 9, 1869, heading to the Republican River. It was about 5:00 p.m. on June 15. They had been encamped on the Republican River at the mouth of the Beaver River several days waiting for Lute North's new Pawnee company to join them. Soldiers had taken the mules to water when about fifty Sioux warriors attacked and attempted to stampede the animals. Only Cody and the Pawnee Scouts, who all mounted their horses bareback, were able to give chase to the raiders. Cody said they raced after the warriors fifteen miles, killing several of them.[119]

One of the Pawnees' horses, a large buckskin, impressed Cody with his speed. All the horses were government owned, but Cody wanted to ride this particular horse and asked Major North if he had any objections to Cody trading with the Pawnee rider for the horse. North had no objection. After Cody offered his government-issued horse and stacked on additional presents, the Pawnee Scout agreed to the trade. Cody was pleased, naming the horse Buckskin Joe.[120]

It was possibly on June 23 that Cody wanted to demonstrate to the Pawnees his buffalo hunting skills. The Pawnees had come upon a buffalo herd and killed thirty-two of them. North noted in his diary, "killed lots of Buffalo had lots of ribs." Cody had learned Buckskin Joe was an excellent buffalo horse. As the Pawnees were butchering the buffalo they had killed, a second herd approached. Cody, astride Buckskin Joe, galloped into the herd and killed thirty-six animals. The Pawnees were impressed.[121]

For twenty days, Carr's command scouted along the Beaver and Prairie Dog Rivers occasionally having running fights with small bands of warriors.[122]

After the Solomon River raid, Tall Bull led his Dog Soldier Cheyennes west into northeastern Colorado and set up camp at Summit Springs. From there, they planned to head to the Powder River country in Wyoming.[123]

On July 5, fifty Pawnee Scouts had a fight with Cheyenne warriors; and on July 8, four troopers of Company M fought thirteen warriors, killing three. Cody was not involved in either fight. However, he probably was involved in driving off raiders trying to stampede the horses and mules at the main camp on the night of July 8.[124]

It was about this time, Carr's men learned Tall Bull's Cheyenne Dog Soldiers had captured two white women. It was also apparent the Cheyennes were heading toward the Powder River country.[125]

Carr pushed his men to follow the trail as rapidly as possible. On July 10, they reached a camp that Tall Bull's people had vacated the day before. Carr decided to make a push to circle around and get ahead of the Cheyennes. He left his supply wagons behind with a guard and selected the ablest men to go on the attack: 244 officers and troopers, fifty Pawnee Scouts, and Buffalo Bill Cody.

They set out at 2:00 a.m. on July 11.[126]

The column approached the South Platte River from the south. Royall led a squadron ahead to the river to determine the direction the Cheyennes were traveling and upon his return, he reported he believed they were heading upriver to the southwest. Cody and five to six Pawnee Scouts had ridden upriver and found Tall Bull's village and large pony herd about six miles away south of the South Platte at Summit Springs.[127]

An unnamed officer later reported to the *New York Herald*, "the chief scout, Mr. William Cody, came dashing up hatless, reporting he had come upon their camp about eight miles to the left and near the Platte River."[128]

Cody conferred with Carr about the lay of the land and how to approach the village. Carr decided to head northwest, circle to the west, and then ride south to position the troops between the South Platte River and the village. They would advance on the village from the north. As the troops rode to their positions, they remained out of sight behind ridges or in ravines. By 1:30 p.m., the troops were in position and still out of sight. The ground in front of them was a level plain stretching about twelve hundred yards to the village. They could see the people were preparing to move the village and there were horses in camp to load with belongings.[129]

Carr split his men into three groups. He sent Company H, led by Captain Leicester Walker, to his left, and Company A, led by Captain George Price, to his right. Their mission was to circle behind the village and capture the pony herd to the south. Carr with the rest of the troops, Cody, and the Pawnee Scouts would charge into the village center. The bugler would signal the advance. Carr waited until everyone was in position.[130]

A windstorm was blowing so fierce that when Carr told the bugler to signal the advance only those closest to him could hear it, but the others saw his motion of bringing the bugle to his lips and charged. At the same time, a Cheyenne boy herding the ponies saw the troops advance and was racing his white pony to the camp shouting to warn the people, but the wind was so strong, they failed to hear him.[131]

The Cheyenne people saw the riders bearing down on them and scattered in every direction. Those who had horses jumped on them while those on foot ran to the nearby hills. [132]

Carr's men gave a cheer as they hit the village. The Pawnee Scouts were everywhere. Carr's troops shot at anything that moved. The attack was over quickly. The boy who had tried to warn the village was killed as well as his white horse.[133]

However, the conflict was not over. Tall Bull and nineteen warriors fought back from a ravine in the high bluffs south and east of the village. Cody saw a warrior encouraging the Dog Soldiers as he dashed back and forth on a large bay horse. Cody wanted that horse and maneuvered to within thirty yards of the warrior, close enough to shoot him without hurting the horse. He shot knocking the warrior off the horse. He later learned the warrior was Tall Bull. Cody claimed the horse and named it after its previous owner.[134]

Lute North first told historian George Bird Grinnell in 1889 that his brother Frank killed Tall Bull, but in each retelling over the years, the details of North's story changed. Frank North never mentioned killing Tall Bull in his diary.[135]

It was general knowledge among the men of the Fifth Cavalry that Cody killed Tall Bull. No one said otherwise. Years later, Carr wrote, "As he [Cody] advanced he saw a chief on a horse charging about, and haranguing his men. He and his party laid for him and, as he came near, Buffalo Bill shot him off his horse and got the horse. . . . When he came into camp 'Mrs. Tall Bull' said that was her husband's horse. So that left no doubt that Buffalo Bill killed the chief." Besides Cody and North, there may have been others who actually killed Tall Bull including a Pawnee Scout, Lieutenant George Mason, and Sergeant Daniel McGrath.[136]

At the end of the fight, a severe hail and thunderstorm hit. Lightning struck a horse being ridden by a trooper. The horse was killed, but the man was uninjured.[137]

Major Carr appointed three officers and a recorder to count

casualties and captured property. They reported fifty-two Cheyennes killed[138] and seventeen women and children captured. None of Carr's men were seriously injured.[139]

It was not good for Susanna Alderdice and Maria Weichel, the two white women captives. A warrior had fired a pistol into Maria's back. As the bullet passed through her body, it hit a rib, and stopped in her left breast. She would survive and recover at Fort Sedgwick.[140] Susanna was not so fortunate. She was found dead, shot above the eye and her skull crushed.[141]

Carr's troops captured 274 horses and 144 mules, which were distributed among the officers, Pawnee Scouts, and troopers. Cody acquired the horse he named Tall Bull as well as a pony he named Powder Face. Carr ordered the men to burn the eighty-five lodges with all their furnishings, as well as an estimated ten thousand pounds of dried meat, and one thousand buffalo robes. It took 160 fires to destroy all the property. Later, it was claimed the Fifth Cavalry's attack on Tall Bull's village was the end of major warfare with Indians in Kansas and Nebraska.[142] Whether that claim was accurate or not, there was still much for the Fifth Cavalry to do.

The troops rode to Fort Sedgwick near Julesburg, Colorado, where they rested and prepared for their next assignments. It wasn't long until the Army needed Cody's services. Major Carr received a telegram that a war party had raided the Union Pacific Railroad's O'Fallon's Station, killing several men and running off livestock. Two companies commanded by Captain William Brown would be pursuing them. Carr ordered Cody to take the next train east to Fort McPherson and act as Brown's guide. Cody took the train that night and was ready to ride with Brown and his men the morning of July 24.[143]

Brown informed Cody that a civilian guest was riding with them, the popular writer Ned Buntline. At the time, Buntline was considered one of the country's top novelists. Buntline, whose real name was Edward Zane Carroll Judson, was returning to the East from California on the Union Pacific Railroad after spending a year traveling throughout California, Nevada, and Utah giving lectures on the evils of drinking while seen occasionally imbibing himself.[144]

The squadron rode west to O'Fallon's Station, having to swim their horses in several places as they crossed the South Platte River. Reaching O'Fallon's Station at 11:00 a.m., the men followed the raiders' trail north to the North Platte River. It appeared to be a small raiding party and since the trail was two days old, Brown decided to end the pursuit and return to Fort McPherson. Cody, accompanied by Buntline, headed west, returning to Fort Sedgwick. During the short scout, Buntline peppered Cody with questions. When they reached the fort, Cody introduced Buntline to those officers Buntline didn't already know. Buntline wanted to go on another scout, but that never happened. While Buntline was at the fort, Cody gave him Powder Face to ride. It's not certain how long Buntline remained at Fort Sedgwick, but he arrived in Omaha on August 10.[145] It's also not certain if Buntline told Cody he planned to write about him.

One of the soldiers' and Pawnee Scouts' pastimes was horseracing. After receiving their pay, everyone—officers, soldiers, and Pawnee Scouts who had acquired horses from Tall Bull's camp—wanted to test their running ability. Lieutenant George Mason owned a racing horse he wanted to ride against Cody and Tall Bull. Cody accepted the challenge with a $100 bet. Officers and the post trader made so many side bets with Cody that all his money was tied up. A half-mile course was laid out and rules agreed upon. The two riders brought their horses up to the starting line. When they were ready, the judge shouted, "Go!" Cody knew Tall Bull was a fast runner and could easily beat Mason's horse, so he held him in check so as not to reveal his true speed. As Cody predicted, Tall Bull easily won the race.[146]

For several days, the Pawnees held races against each other's horses until they determined which was the best racer. They wanted to race that horse against Cody's Tall Bull, and Cody agreed. The Pawnees pooled some of their money and put up $300, and Cody matched them. Of course, he took side bets again. This race was a mile in length. Cody on Tall Bull beat the Pawnee rider and his horse with no problem. Cody was ahead almost $700. Cody's problem now was no one would race against Tall Bull.[147]

Captain Lute North and Cody agreed to race North's pony against Cody's pony, Powder Face. North selected a Pawnee boy to ride his pony and Cody found a small white boy to ride Powder Face. The Pawnees wanted to make big bets again. Cody was dubious about Powder Face's ability and limited his bets. This race was for four hundred yards. As Cody led Powder Face toward the track, he acted up and tossed the boy to the ground. Cody tried to control Powder Face as he danced around. The boy was not certain he could remain on Powder Face's back. They brought the ponies up to the line, and the judge shouted, "Go!" The ponies jumped forward. Powder Face's rider was left sitting in the dust, but Powder Face flew on, winning the race—riderless. No one would race against Cody's critters after that.[148]

Major Carr had left the fort on emergency leave, and Major William Royall was in command of the Fifth Cavalry in his absence. Major Frank North was also gone at this time. On August 2, with Buffalo Bill Cody as guide, Royall led seven companies of the Fifth Cavalry and the Pawnee Scouts south from Fort Sedgwick. The plan was to search for hostile bands of Indians along Frenchman's Fork to the Republican River.[149]

They didn't have far to go. Ten miles south of the fort, they ran into Pawnee Killer's Lakota band who turned and raced toward Frenchman's Fork with Royall's men in hot pursuit. Once the Lakotas reached Frenchman's Fork, they turned heading straight north crossing the South Platte River, and Royall and his men continued to follow.[150]

Royall's troops reached the Union Pacific Railroad lines on August 6 where Major Frank North rejoined his Pawnee Scouts. The next day, Major North paid off his brother Lute and sent him home. After the fight at Summit Springs, Lute had had a confrontation with Major Carr and did not think much of the officers of the Fifth Cavalry.[151]

The troops and scouts continued their pursuit into Nebraska's vast Sand Hills. It was rough on the horses for both the Lakotas and their pursuers. Royall later reported they found forty-two abandoned horses, and he had to kill seventeen of his animals that couldn't go on. Many horses were so bad off they had to be led. By the time they reached the Niobrara River in northern Nebraska, they were running low on provisions. On August 12, Royall abandoned the chase and returned to Fort McPherson, arriving there on August 22.[152]

Back in July, the Fifth Cavalry had established Fort McPherson as its regimental headquarters commanded by Colonel William Emory and with Lieutenant Colonel Thomas Duncan second in command. When Cody returned to the fort with Royall's men after chasing Pawnee Killer, Emory assured Cody of regular employment. He told Cody he would have a log house built for him and he could bring his family to live at the fort. Louisa and Arta were currently living in St. Louis.[153]

Cody sent for his wife and daughter and met them in Omaha. From there, they traveled together the rest of the way by rail to Fort McPherson, arriving there in late August before their house was completed. The post trader, William Reed, allowed them to stay in his building until their home was completed. It was nothing fancy. The logs were chinked with mud and the inside walls lined with old army tents. An army stove served double duty for heating and cooking. Louisa wrote of Cody's appearance, "Where his close-cropped hair had been were long, flowing curls now. A mustache weaved its way outward from his upper lip, while a small goatee showed black and spot-like on his chin."[154]

Cody found plenty of game within an easy ride from the fort—deer, antelope, and elk herds abounded. He continued to race his horses. On September 9, Frank North recorded in his diary, "I made a horse race with Cody and got beat." Cody didn't win all the time. Lieutenant Edward Doherty won $20 from him.[155]

On September 15, Lieutenant Colonel Thomas Duncan led five companies of the Fifth Cavalry, two companies of the Second Cavalry, Major North and the Pawnee Scouts, and Cody as guide.[156] Their mission was to search for and attack any hostile Lakota and Cheyenne bands in the Republican River country.[157] Another scout John Y. Nelson went along. He and Cody became good friends, although Cody later said of Nelson, "a good fellow though as a liar he has few equals and no superior."[158]

The first day, Duncan's men marched south a short distance from the fort. That night, Cody and Captain William Brown returned to the fort and went on a drinking spree at the sutler's store. The next day, the men remained in camp, and Duncan wanted to hold a shooting match against Cody. Cody wrote later, "I did not feel like shooting anything except myself." Then he realized he had left his rifle back at the sutler's store. Brown was amused at Cody's predicament but sent a man back to the store to retrieve Cody's rifle, while Nelson let Cody borrow his. Duncan and Cody fired away at the target with Duncan winning the match.[159]

They hunted buffalo along the way. Major North wrote in his diary on September 23, "the Gen. [Duncan] Cody and I killed 13 Buffalo our men killed lots."[160]

After crossing the Republican River, they reached Prairie Dog Creek on September 26. Cody and North were out ahead of the command scouting for a campsite and killing a few buffalo for meat when they were attacked by up to ten Indians. North wrote, "[they] gave us a lively chase you bet." Cody and North raced back toward Lieutenant William Volkmar's pioneer troops about a mile and a half ahead of the main column.[161]

Volkmar and his men gave chase. Cody rode along while North signaled to his Pawnee Scouts farther behind to come on and they raced forward at a gallop. They chased after the warriors who were actually decoying them away from the village. A lone warrior raced to the village and the people were on the move before the troops realized their mistake. They charged after the fleeing Indians until nightfall. One warrior was killed, and no one in Duncan's command was injured.[162]

Duncan's column continued to chase after the Lakota band.

On October 2, they came upon an old woman who either was lost or had been left behind. John Nelson and the woman recognized each other. She was a relative of his Lakota wife. She told him the Lakota band they were chasing was led by Pawnee Killer, Whistler, and Little Bull. The Lakotas turned north and crossed the Platte River. Duncan ended the chase as they were getting low on provisions and returned to Fort McPherson on October 28, 1869, where most of the Fifth Cavalry's companies would be garrisoned for the winter. Cody was discharged as scout on October 31, 1869. However, that same day he was hired as chief herder at the same salary of $75 per month.[163]

Ned Buntline had been busy writing, and on December 7, 1869, *Street & Smith's New York Weekly* published the first installment of his serial story *Buffalo Bill, the King of the Border Men*, which ran from December 1869 into March 1870. The story took place during the Civil War, not the era of the Western Frontier. Buffalo Bill and his sidekick Wild Bill Hickok fought villains such as Jack M'Kandlas, a Missouri bushwhacker who had murdered Buffalo Bill's father. Buffalo Bill not only avenged his father but had to rescue his fictional sister Lottie who was kidnapped by a M'Kandlas gang member. The story raced from one adventure to the next. The reading public was enthralled and by the end of the series, they wanted more. The real Buffalo Bill Cody appreciated what Buntline had done and liked the story.[164]

Louisa described Christmas at the fort. Besides Arta there were only two other little children. The soldiers wanted to hold a real Christmas for the children and pooled their money to buy presents for the three little girls and other festive items. They selected Cody to be the messenger to Santa Claus. He was sent to Cheyenne with a long list of items to buy. The soldiers rode out to find pine trees to cut down and set them up in the fort's assembly hall. The women made popcorn strings and Christmas ornaments and decorated the trees and hall, as well as making Christmas treats. Christmas Day everyone gathered in the hall and Santa Claus handed out presents to the children, songs were sung, and speeches made.[165]

During the winter months of 1870, Cody did lots of hunting and guided two hunting parties for Englishmen. A Mr. Flynn led one party of Englishmen; the other was for Arthur Boyd Houghton, a popular London artist and illustrator.[166]

Cody continued to race Tall Bull and Powder Face, although the horse and pony were so good, it was hard to find those who would put up their animals against them. Cody had seen a circus bareback rider mount and dismount as the horse raced around a track. He practiced doing this with Tall Bull, and said he could do it eight times on a one-mile track. He performed this stunt during a race against a Second Cavalry horse; Cody didn't mention if he won or not.[167]

It was early in the morning on June 7, 1870, when Lakota raiders stole horses from ranchers along the North Platte and from Fort McPherson's herd including Cody's pony Powder Face. The first company ready for the chase was the Fifth Cavalry's Company I commanded by Second Lieutenant Earl Thomas. Thomas had fought in the Civil War, but this was his first time dealing with Indians. Buffalo Bill Cody went with them mounted on Buckskin Joe; he wanted Powder Face back. Colonel William Emory told Thomas, "Follow Cody and be off quick," saying other troops would be coming after them shortly.[168]

They left the fort at 8:00 a.m. without provisions, following the raiders' trail and galloping the horses when the terrain permitted. It was raining, and at times, it was hard to find the trail. By dark, they had covered sixty miles. Cody believed the horsethieves would be camping at Red Willow Creek. While Thomas and his men waited, Cody scouted ahead and found a horse herd on the opposite side of the creek. He returned to Thomas and led the men into position where they could surprise the raiders.[169]

The next morning at 5:00 a.m., it was light enough Cody and the troops could see the Lakota camp in the creek bottom about one hundred yards away. Thomas gave the order and they charged into the camp. The warriors quickly mounted horses and began to flee. Cody said two warriors had mounted one horse and started to ride out; when they were thirty feet away, he fired a shot killing them both. The troops recovered thirty-three horses and mules. However, Powder Face was not among them. The last Cody saw of Powder Face, he was racing away with a warrior mounted on his back.[170]

Company I returned to Fort McPherson on June 8, at 7:00 p.m., riding 120 miles in two days. Major Eugene Carr wrote in General Order No. 7, "Lieutenant Thomas especially commends scout Cody for the manner in which he followed the trail, particularly at night, during a storm of rain, and for gallant conduct in the fight."[171]

July 1, 1870, the Army rehired Cody as a scout at $100 per month. Even though the Red Willow Creek fight was the only action with Indians in 1870, Cody was still very active hunting to provide fresh meat for the fort and guiding hunting expeditions.[172]

CHAPTER 10
HAYS CITY
(MAY 1869–JULY 17, 1870)

Hays City, Kansas, was a raucous town where buffalo hunters sold their meat and hides, and railroad workers labored in the Kansas Pacific rail yards and roundhouse. The Army had a large warehouse where supplies arrived by rail then shipped by bull train out to forts. It was the county seat and with Fort Hays nearby, there were government workers, contractors, and soldiers in town. Immigrants and excursionists stopped while passing through. A large service industry developed including dry goods, grocery, and clothing stores; barbershops; restaurants; and hotels as well as saloons, gambling houses, and brothels.[1]

"There is a row of saloons on the Kansas Pacific Railway called Hays City," a journalist for Junction City's *Weekly Union* wrote. "Having visited the place, we should call it the Sodom of the plains. . . . Only a faint glimmering of its wickedness has been put on record." The writer listened to witnesses who told him of "acts of fiendish inhumanity too black to relate. It has been the rendezvous of thieves and robbers, of murderers and accomplished villains."[2]

Hays City was in Ellis County. The county's first sheriff was Thomas Gannon, elected on December 5, 1867. Gannon took his job seriously, but by April 1868, he vanished. He was scheduled to testify in a criminal case; people believed he was murdered to keep him quiet. On April 14, 1868, a district judge appointed Hays City drugstore owner J. V. Macintosh acting sheriff; and then on November 3, 1868, Isaac Thayer was elected sheriff.[3]

In January 1869, Kansas governor James Harvey heard that Hays City had been placed under martial law. Lieutenant Colonel Anderson Nelson, commander of Fort Hays, responded to the governor he had not placed the town under martial law, but he had taken actions. Three to four hundred government teamsters were in town and had become rowdy, firing their revolvers in "a bawdy dancehall." Citizens asked Nelson to do something. He sent a patrol to town, making fifty arrests, most in the dance hall. Nelson informed the governor, three Black soldiers being held in Hays City's jail were taken out and hanged "by the inhabitants of that town."[4]

In May, there was a fight between Black soldiers and Hays City residents, and Sheriff Thayer left town—for good.[5] The county was without a sheriff.

After visiting his family in Illinois, Wild Bill Hickok had returned to Hays City by May 1869, resuming his deputy US marshal duties. He might have also been employed by Ellis County. An undated document stated the county was to pay him $122.50 for one month and nineteen days for "services as a policeman," although this could have been for any time period he resided in Hays City.[6]

Some Hays City citizens formed a vigilance committee to keep a semblance of law and order. In late July, the committee targeted two "ruffians" they wanted gone: a saloonkeeper, Joseph Weiss, who had spent time in the penitentiary at Leavenworth, and a Fort Hays teamster and courier, Samuel Strawhun.[7]

The vigilance committee selected one of its members, postal clerk Alonzo Webster,[8] to serve notice upon Weiss and Strawhun to get out of town. The two ruffians were furious and threatened to kill Webster. On Friday, July 30, at 3:00 p.m., they entered the post office where they "abused, slapped, and finally drew a revolver upon Webster." However, Webster fired his pistol into Weiss's bowels, mortally wounding him. Strawhun fired a shot at Webster and fled the scene. Strawhun soon returned with Weiss's friends ready to take revenge. When they entered the post office, they saw Wild Bill Hickok sitting on the counter. Hickok told them Webster had done the right thing and he was ready to take up the fight. Strawhun and Weiss's friends backed down and left. A coroner's jury exonerated Webster from all blame.[9]

In August 1869, a special election was held to elect a sheriff to finish the term, and to elect a justice of the peace. Wild Bill Hickok ran for sheriff and won, and Marcellus Joyce won justice of the peace. No official record of the actual date of the election has been found, but by August 18, 1869, Hickok was performing his duties as sheriff. At the time, the end of the track town of Sheridan was under the jurisdiction of Ellis County. A correspondent for Leavenworth's *Times and Conservative* wrote, "The greatest need of Sheridan is a magistrate. If Wild Bill arrests an offender there is a log jail to receive him, but no justice to try the case." Hickok's sheriff position was short term until the regular election could be held November 2.[10]

Hickok began wearing a Prince Albert frock coat. He continued to wear two revolvers and a Bowie knife as well as carry a shotgun.[11]

On August 21, Hickok arrested two Black troopers from the Tenth Cavalry's Company C who had deserted their post in Indian Territory during the winter and had been living in Sheridan. Hickok turned them over to the Fort Hays commander.[12]

The following night of August 22, Bill Mulvey[13] led a number of "intoxicated roughs or 'wolves'" in shooting up the town. Mulvey was quarrelsome with everyone he met; fortunately, he missed those he shot at. When Hickok learned of the ruckus, he found Mulvey, revolver in hand, and tried to persuade him to disarm. When Mulvey refused, Hickok distracted him, drew his revolver, and shot him. Mulvey died soon afterward. One report said Hickok's bullet hit Mulvey behind the right ear, while another report said the bullet went through Mulvey's neck and lung.[14]

J. W. Buel in his book *Heroes of the Plains* told of Hickok's confrontation with Mulvey. Hickok tracked down Mulvey,

> *who had a pistol in each hand and was still yelling like a tribe of victorious Comanches. Approaching him in a quiet manner Wild Bill said, "Stranger, I shall have to arrest you for disorderly conduct; come with me."*
>
> *Raising his two pistols in Bill's face Mulvey replied: "Well, now stranger, suppose you come with me, I hold the winning hand."*
>
> *"That's so," responded Bill, "I can't beat that pair."*
>
> *"No, I guess you can't, and since you are so fresh it will be a good thing for me to hang you up till you dry. March!" was the command given by Mulvey.*
>
> *Before Bill turned he backed off two or three steps and raising his hand as if to warn Mulvey against an attack about to be made on him from the rear said: "Don't hit him boys, he's only in fun."*
>
> *The strategy was perfectly successful, for Mulvey immediately turned about expecting to confront a new adversary, but this act was the last of his career, for Wild Bill secured the drop in an instant and shot Mulvey in the head, killing him.*[15]

True or false, Buel's account was the stuff of legends. Hickok's diversion would be used later by many writers.[16]

Hickok was serious about maintaining law and order. He posted anti-firearm notices, although there were those who failed to obey. He was kind and considerate to children, and a posse of them followed him as he made his rounds each day.[17]

Public opinion was mixed about Sheriff Wild Bill Hickok. Those in favor of law and order believed he was doing a good job. Those who believed he was restricting their freedoms or overstepping his authority had a negative opinion.[18]

J. C. Bascom, who worked for the railroad, later wrote that he and Jim Curry, saloonkeeper and gunfighter, walked into Tommy

Drum's saloon. Curry and Hickok were feuding over a woman named Ida May. Curry saw Hickok playing cards. His back was to the door, and he did not see Curry walk up behind him. Putting his six-shooter's muzzle against Hickok's head, Curry said, "Now you son of a gun, I've got you."

Not batting an eye, Hickok said, "Jim you would not murder a man without giving him a show."

"I will give you the same show you would give me, you long-haired tough."

Tommy Drum, the saloon owner, appeared more excited than Hickok and Curry. As he jumped around and cussed, he promised to provide a bottle of champagne if they ended the feud. The tension broke and everyone laughed. Curry and Hickok shook hands, and everyone drank compliments of Tommy Drum.[19] This incident might have emphasized to Hickok to sit with his back to the wall.

Wild Bill Hickok had more to learn about being cautious. Making his nighttime rounds through town, someone shot at him several times from out of the dark. He avoided standing in front of bright lights, entering dark alleys, and using sidewalks. He walked in the middle of the street, his eyes constantly roving, looking for signs of trouble. He never allowed anyone to get too close, especially from behind. When he entered an overly raucous saloon or other house of entertainment, he would push his way through the crowd to the bar, turn his back to it, say his piece, and then leave. When he spoke, he spoke quietly, but people usually listened.[20]

Sergeant John Ryan was stationed with the Seventh Cavalry at Fort Hays and had known Wild Bill Hickok since Hancock's 1867 campaign. He wrote about Hickok, "I have seen him sitting on different occasions in front of Tom Drum's saloon reading a newspaper, his eyes evidently cast on that paper. All the time he took in every detail of the people who passed him and had his eye open all the time. He was the only man according to my estimation who was able to hold his own among the tough element in that city."[21]

Sunday night, September 26, 1869, Sam Strawhun was again causing mayhem. He and up to eighteen cronies were on a drinking spree and after vigilance committee members. Strawhun and friends mobbed John Bitter's saloon about 11:30 p.m., intent on wrecking the place. The men demanded beer "in a frantic manner." New glasses were constantly being filled. Bitter saw Strawhun and his friends were taking beer glasses outside, leaving them in a vacant lot, then returning. "The noise was fearful, all the men crying at the top of their voices, beer! beer! and using the most obscene language."[22] They threw beer on each other and made threats such as "I shall kill someone to-night just for luck," and "Someone will have to go up to-night."

Bitter sent a message to Hickok asking for help. It was about 1:00 a.m. when he arrived on scene with his assistant Peter Lanihan. Bitter asked Hickok if he would retrieve his missing beer glasses. Hickok said that he would. As Hickok returned with both hands full of glasses, Strawhun proclaimed he would shoot anyone who interfered with his fun. As Hickok set the glasses on the counter, Strawhun grabbed one, raising it to hit Hickok. Hickok pulled his revolver and shot Strawhun in the head, killing him.[23]

Justice of the Peace Marcellus Joyce held an inquest at 9:00 a.m. The *Lawrence Daily Tribune* reported, "The evidence in one or two instances was very contradictory. The jury returned a verdict to the effect that Samuel Stringham [*sic*] came to his death from a pistol wound at the hands of J. B. Hickock, and that the shooting of said Stringham was justifiable."[24]

Desperados weren't the only ones who contested Hickok's authority as the duly elected sheriff of Ellis County. Government officials did too. On October 3, Hickok and his assistant Pete Lanihan arrived at Fort Hays with a warrant for the arrest of Bob Conners. Conners had murdered a drover outside of Pond City near Fort Wallace and had been captured and placed in the Fort Hays guardhouse. Hickok was going to take Conners to Pond City, the county seat for the new county of Wallace. Major George Gibson, commander of Fort Hays, refused to turn over Conners to Hickok because even though the warrant was signed by John Whiteford, the Pond City justice of the peace, it did not have a seal on it. Gibson asked to see Hickok's sheriff commission from the governor. When Hickok said he did not have one, Gibson refused to turn Conners over to him. That same day, Gibson wrote to Governor James Harvey about the matter. Harvey responded to Gibson on October 5, "Your refusal to deliver Conners on the demand of Mr. J. B. Hickok meets with my full approval. That person has no legal authority whatever to act as Sheriff of Ellis county, nor under the circumstances through which the vacancy occurred can any Sheriff be chosen until the regular election in November next." Even though the governor didn't recognize Hickok's authority, the Ellis County commissioners and residents did.[25]

On the night of October 8, about 11:30 p.m., a Fort Hays mason boss named Cole and a German wagon driver named Allmeyer got into an argument over Cole unscrewing bolts from Allmeyer's wagon parked opposite the depot. Cole pulled his revolver and fired twice; one bullet hit Allmeyer in the right chest. As Cole ran away, Allmeyer pulled his pistol and shot at him three times but missed. Allmeyer was carried into Tommy Drum's saloon and then taken to the Commercial Hotel for treatment. After Allmeyer had left Drum's, Cole walked in looking for his hat, saying it had been shot off his head. The crowd recognized Cole as the shooter and tried to capture him. He started to draw his revolver when one of the patrons shot him in the right chest. The crowd found a rope and secured it around Cole's neck. They were ready to drag him out and hang him when Hickok arrived and prevented the hanging. Both Cole and Allmeyer eventually recovered, and through the efforts of a Catholic priest, they reconciled.[26]

On November 2 elections were held for Ellis County offices. Most people in the county belonged to the Democratic Party. Hickok ran as an Independent against his assistant Pete Lanihan, who was a Democrat. Lanihan won with 114 votes to Hickok's 89 votes. Hickok would serve out his term to December 31, 1869.[27]

The rest of Hickok's service as Ellis County's sheriff was relatively peaceful. The *Topeka Daily Commonwealth* reported on December 9, "Hays City under the guardian care of 'Wild Bill' is quiet and doing well."[28] That same newspaper recorded one of his final acts as sheriff, "Jas. B. Hickok, *alias* Wild Bill sent a whole buffalo to McMeekin [*sic*] yesterday from Hays City. Mac serves up buffalo roasts and steak today with the usual etceteras."[29] H. D. McMeeken and his son were the proprietors of the popular Topeka House near the courthouse, opposite the state government buildings.[30]

Wild Bill Hickok left Hays City January 1, 1870. There were two legends with no evidence that before he left Hays City, he was in a fight with soldiers from the Seventh Cavalry. William Connelley wrote that Tom Custer, brother to George Custer, sought revenge on Hickok for clamping down on his reckless behavior including racing his horse down the street as he yelled and shot his revolver, and riding a horse into a saloon, then after unsuccessfully trying to get the horse to climb on top of a billiard table, shot it. Hickok arrested Tom Custer, and the judge levied a heavy fine. Custer was out for revenge. He found two to three men who attacked Hickok for him, and Hickok killed them. J. W. Buel told another story: Hickok got into a bar fight with a Seventh Cavalry sergeant and fourteen soldiers. When it was over, he had been shot seven times and left three of them dead and three wounded. Both tall tales are probably based on an incident that would happen later in July 1870.[31]

Wild Bill Hickok arrived in Topeka to visit his friend Captain Henry Lindsay, who had been with the Eighteenth Kansas Battalion Cavalry. They likely met during the Civil War and knew each other while Hickok scouted for the Army. Lindsay, now a deputy sheriff, owned a livery and a sales stable. Hickok enjoyed leaning on the fences and talking about horses and the latest news with visitors and exploring Topeka's saloons with Lindsay. Hickok was still a deputy US marshal, and would visit the sheriff's office and make the rounds with Topeka's marshal.[32]

Hickok got into a little trouble while in Topeka. The *Daily Commonwealth* reported in its February 8, 1870 issue, "Wild Bill was up before Judge Holmes yesterday and fined $5 for striking straight out from the shoulder and consequently hitting a man."[33]

Later that month, Hickok left Topeka helping Lindsay drive a herd of horses and mules to Kansas City.[34] From there, Hickok traveled to Warrensburg, Missouri, where he visited his old comrade J. W. McLellan during the week of February 24.[35] He was in Jefferson City the last week of March. The *Jefferson Democrat* reported he created quite a stir when he visited the Missouri House of Representatives and met many old friends who were now members of the house.[36]

The April 29, 1870 issue of Topeka's *Daily Commonwealth* stated, "Wild Bill is in the city again."[37] He must have stayed long enough to receive his next assignment as a deputy US marshal. On May 2, 1870, he arrived in Junction City to serve a subpoena to two witnesses for the defense in a case of larceny and misappropriation of US property. For the next few weeks, Hickok remained around Topeka, gambling and giving shooting exhibitions.[38]

Colonel Lewis Granger claimed Wild Bill Hickok joined his circus in 1870. Granger organized the circus in Des Moines, Iowa, traveling south through Nebraska and Kansas where he would have picked up Hickok. Granger took his circus into Indian Territory where they gave two performances at Fort Gibson then traveled to Sherman, Texas, and gave two performances. Hickok left the circus there. Granger did not mention what Hickok did, but it was probably demonstrating his marksmanship. Granger gave no reason why Hickok left.[39]

By mid-July 1870, Wild Bill Hickok was in Hays City where he ran into trouble. Newspaper accounts were sketchy and old-timer reminiscences became distorted over the years. Sergeant John Ryan with Company M of the Seventh Cavalry had one of the best plausible accounts which will be followed here for the most part.

On the night of July 17, Privates Jerry Lonergan and John Kile,[40] both of Company M, left camp after tattoo roll call, bound for Hays City. Ryan, who was a friend of Kile's, thought they left without permission. They went to Tommy Drum's saloon, a favorite soldiers' haunt.[41] Upon entering, they saw Wild Bill Hickok talking with Tommy Drum who was behind the bar. Hickok was standing at the bar with his back to the door.[42]

Kile had a record of multiple desertions as well as being court-martialed and convicted for being intoxicated in camp and breaking into the sutler's store, stealing over $600 in goods. Lonergan was a troublemaker. "Lonergan was a big powerful man and was considered one of the pugilists of M troop," Ryan wrote. There had been previous trouble between Lonergan and Hickok, and now Lonergan had Hickok in his sights.[43]

Lonergan walked up behind Hickok, threw both arms around Hickok's neck, and pulled him over backwards to the floor. Lonergan straddled Hickok and held both Hickok's arms out at arm's length. As they struggled, Hickok broke Lonergan's hold on his right arm and jerked his revolver from its holster.[44]

Kile whipped out his pistol, pushed the muzzle into Hickok's ear, cocked the hammer, and pulled the trigger. Misfire![45]

Lonergan grasped Hickok's right wrist, but Hickok was able to cock the revolver's hammer and turn it to fire a bullet into Kile's right wrist. Hickok cocked the hammer a second time and shot. The bullet hit Kile's side, passing almost all the way through his body.[46]

Lonergan was still on top of Hickok holding his wrist down so Hickok could not get a shot. Hickok saw Lonergan's knee and swiveled his revolver enough to fire a bullet into Lonergan's kneecap. In instant pain, Lonergan released his hold and Hickok escaped from underneath him. There must have been lots of other soldiers in the saloon, more than enough to take on Hickok and prevent his leaving through the front door. Ryan wrote Hickok ran to the backroom where he jumped through a window, taking the glass and sash with him.[47]

Lonergan and Kile were taken to the Fort Hays hospital where Kile would die on July 18 and Lonergan would eventually recover.[48] Kile's comrades scoured Hays City looking for Hickok, but he was long gone. Ryan wrote, "The party that went in pursuit of Wild Bill did not find him; if they had probably it would have been the end of him."[49]

The July 22 edition of the *Topeka Daily Commonwealth* said, "On Monday last 'Wild Bill' killed a soldier and seriously wounded another at Hays City. Five soldiers attacked Bill, and two got used up as mentioned above. The sentiment of the community is with 'Bill,' as it is claimed he but acted in self-defense."[50]

Rumors emerged that the soldiers had wounded Hickok. There were several stories as to how Hickok left Hays City and where he went. An arrest order was never issued for him.[51]

Years later, Libbie Custer's recollection of the soldiers' attack on Hickok was similar to John Ryan's. She wrote in *Following the Guidon*, "Some of our men having received, as they considered, a deadly insult to their company, determined to right their wrongs, and planned to assassinate the renowned scout. . . . Three desperate characters, planning to kill Wild Bill . . . attacked [him] from behind as had been planned. His broad back was borne down by a powerful soldier, and his arms seized, but only one was held in the clinching grasp of the assailant. With the free hand the scout drew his pistol from the belt, fired backward without seeing, and his shot, even under these circumstances, was a fatal one."[52]

Writing a series of articles for *The Galaxy* magazine beginning in April 1872, Lieutenant Colonel George Custer described Hickok in glowing terms and then mentioned Hickok killing Kile, "Wild Bill is anything but a quarrelsome man; . . . I have a personal knowledge of at least a half a dozen men whom he has at various times killed, one of these being at the time a member of my command. . . . Yet in all the many affairs of this kind in which Wild Bill has performed a part, and which has come to my knowledge, there is not a single instance in which the verdict of twelve fair-minded men would not be pronounced in his favor."[53]

No matter: Wild Bill Hickok disappeared for a while.

CHAPTER 11

THE CHIEF SCOUT AND THE ABILENE MARSHAL (JULY 1870–DECEMBER 1871)

By October 21, 1870, Wild Bill Hickok was back in Topeka. Information on his whereabouts after he left Hays City on July 17 is sketchy.[1]

Through the winter of 1870–1871, Hickok divided most of his time between Topeka and Junction City gambling and demonstrating his marksmanship. He may have had an interest in Emma Williams, who was in Ellsworth. Williams was a well-known madame who had operated houses of ill repute in Leavenworth and Kansas City. Based on her letters written to the newspapers and actions taken, she must have been educated, financially well off, and had compassion for the less fortunate. J. W. Buel relates the story that a large bully named Bill Thompson[2] was jealous of Hickok's interest in Emma Williams. On February 17, 1871, Hickok was sitting in a restaurant with his back to the door. He had ordered oyster stew and as the waiter was bringing the bowl to him, Hickok saw a look of fright on the man's face. Whirling around he saw Thompson coming at him with a pistol pointed in his direction. Hickok dove to the side as Thompson fired, missing him. Hickok jerked a derringer from his pocket and fired a bullet hitting Thompson in the forehead killing him. Hickok was arrested, but following a preliminary hearing, he was released after it was determined it was justifiable homicide. Other than Buel's recounting of the event, no other documentation of this story has been found.[3]

Hickok was at Fort Harker in early April 1871 when a messenger arrived from Abilene, Kansas, with an offer to possibly be hired as town marshal.[4]

Meanwhile, Buffalo Bill Cody continued to work as an Army scout out of Fort McPherson, Nebraska, through the summer and fall of 1870 and all of 1871, with Louisa and Arta living with him in the house outside the fort. Besides occasionally scouting for the Army, he was hunting buffalo and other game to provide meat for the troops. On occasion, he guided important guests on hunts for buffalo and other game animals.[5]

Cody was associated with a hunt of a different nature—Yale University's first scientific expedition led by Professor Othniel Marsh. Its mission—to discover fossils of extinct animals. General Phil Sheridan provided the expedition with a Fifth Cavalry escort and two Pawnee Scouts as well as Frank North and Cody.[6]

Cody remained with the expedition for part of its trip into Nebraska's Sand Hills, but he was ordered to return to pursue an Indian raiding party. He rode with Marsh long enough for Marsh to explain to him the geologic history of the area. Cody later wrote Marsh "entertained me with several scientific yarns, some of which seemed too complicated and too mysterious to be believed by an ordinary man like myself." Cody showed Marsh how to buffalo hunt. Years later, Marsh wrote about hunting a buffalo "coming alongside, ready to shoot, in the exact manner my first guide Buffalo Bill had taught me." Cody and Marsh remained lifelong friends. When Marsh's expedition retuned at the end of July, they had discovered remains of six species of early horses, two types of rhinoceroses, and other fossils.[7]

On November 26, 1870, Louisa gave birth to the Codys' first son. Buffalo Bill was so enthralled with what Edward Z. C. Judson, aka Ned Buntline, had done for his notoriety that he wanted to name the baby Elmo Judson. Cody's friends convinced him not to name the boy that. Captain William Brown suggested Kit Carson, and the Codys went with that name.[8]

That December, Cody was required to testify at a court-martial at Fort D. A. Russell outside Cheyenne, Wyoming. Louisa gave him a list of furniture and other items to buy while in Cheyenne. Cody spent a good portion of his time with the officers and other witnesses in the case. The court-martial was delayed for a week, so Cody and the others spent their time enjoying Cheyenne's entertainment "from roulette to horse racing." Cody sent for Tall Bull, who he planned to race against a local favorite. But by the time Tall Bull arrived, the court-martial was over and the race called off. Cody had spent all his money including that set aside to buy Louisa's items. Cody sold Tall Bull to a Lieutenant Mason who had always wanted him. Cody said his companions were such a wild bunch that they distracted him from buying Louisa's things. When he returned home, he quickly ordered the items from Omaha, and they arrived a week later to Louisa's delight.[9]

That winter, Cody guided Sir John Watts Garland, who had been coming from Great Britain to America on a regular basis to hunt. Garland had gone to the extent of establishing permanent camps with employees to care for his own horses and dogs. Cody guided Watts on several hunts.[10]

During the spring of 1871, Cody guided the Fifth Cavalry on several scouting expeditions that didn't amount to much. On May 24, he rode with Lieutenant Hayes, the regimental quartermaster, who was leading thirty troopers from four different companies. At Birdwood Creek, Nebraska, they conducted a surprise attack on Lakota raiders, capturing six of them along with sixty horses and mules. The Fifth Cavalry's regimental history stated Cody was "conspicuous for gallant conduct" during the fight.[11]

Colonel William Emory was concerned about crime around the fort caused by civilians not under military jurisdiction. He approached the twenty-five-year-old Buffalo Bill Cody and told him he would be a good candidate for justice of the peace. Cody thanked him, but said, "I don't know any more about law than a government mule does about book-keeping."[12]

Emory went to the county commission and asked it to appoint Cody to the justice of the peace position, and they soon did. Nothing is known of Cody's activities as justice of the peace except for two humorous stories he told.[13]

Cody was new to the office when a man came to him and told him a stranger was riding off with his horse and he wanted a writ of replevin to seize the animal. Cody didn't have any legal forms, so he grabbed his rifle Lucretia Borgia, mounted his horse, and rode with the man to track down the stranger. They found him driving a horse herd away from the fort. Cody confronted him about the claim and said he was taking him along with the horses back to the fort. The stranger said he didn't have time for that. Compromising, Cody told the man to return the horse to its owner and pay a $20 fine and he could leave. The stranger turned over the horse, paid the fine, and went on his way.[14]

Just after Cody received a copy of Nebraska's statutes, a sergeant asked him to perform the marriage ceremony for his bride and him. Right before the ceremony, Cody fortified himself with a little too much alcoholic stimulant. He searched through the laws but couldn't find the marriage ceremony statutes. When it was time for the ceremony, he improvised ending with, "I now pronounce you man and wife, and whomsoever God and Buffalo Bill have joined together let no man put asunder. May you live long and prosper. Amen."[15]

In September 1871, General Phil Sheridan returned to the United States after a year observing the Franco-Prussian War and touring Europe. He headed straight for the West. His good friend and staff surgeon Morris Asch and Sheridan's brother Mike had organized a buffalo hunt for sixteen New York and Chicago businessmen and Washington-based Army officers. General Sheridan was the expedition's host, and he selected Buffalo Bill Cody as their guide.[16]

The editor of the *New York Herald*, James Gordon Bennett, was a member of the hunting party. On September 22, his newspaper reported, "General Sheridan and party arrived at the North Platte River this morning and were conducted to Fort McPherson by General [brevet] Emory, commanding. General Sheridan reviewed the troops consisting of four companies of the Fifth cavalry. The party start across the country tomorrow, guided by the renowned Buffalo Bill and under the escort of Major [brevet] Brown, Company F, Fifth cavalry[.] The party expect to reach Fort Hays in ten days[.]"[17]

A member of the expedition, Henry Davies, who had been a Civil War major general, wrote a book about the hunting party's experiences: *Ten Days on the Plains*. Davies wrote "our expectations about roughing it on the plains were not likely to be realized." There were six wall tents for the guests to sleep in, tents for a mess hall, kitchen, and servants sleeping quarters. They had a hundred-man escort led by Captain Brown. Sixteen wagons carried supplies including one loaded with ice. Three additional wagons carried guns and baggage, and if a dignitary became tired of riding in the saddle, he could ride in a wagon.[18]

Sheridan's guests were introduced to Buffalo Bill the evening before they left on their hunting excursion. Davies was impressed. Instead of being "the typical desperado of the West, bristling with knives and pistols, uncouth in person, and still more disagreeable in manner and address," Davies learned Cody was a justice of the peace and found him to be "a mild, agreeable, well-mannered man, quiet and retiring in disposition, though well informed and always ready to talk well and earnestly upon any subject of interest, and in all respects the reverse of the person we had expected to meet."[19]

The next morning as they prepared to break camp, Davies described the arrival of "Buffalo Bill, riding down from the Fort to our camp, mounted on a snowy white horse. Dressed in a suit of light buckskin, trimmed along the seams with fringes of the same leather, his costume lighted by the crimson shirt under his open coat, a broad sombrero on his head, and carrying his rifle lightly in his hand, as his horse came toward us on an easy gallop, he realized to perfection the bold hunter and gallant sportsman of the plains."[20]

Over the next ten days and two hundred miles to Fort Hays, Cody guided them to buffalo herds and other game animals. The hunters killed over six hundred buffalos, hundreds of elk, antelope, and turkeys, and considered the hunt a success. Reaching Fort Hays on October 1, and before boarding their train to Chicago, Davies wrote "we all shook hands and exchanged a hearty good-bye with Buffalo Bill, to whose skill as a hunter, and experience as a guide, we were so much indebted."[21]

Later that month, Cody guided notable British sportsman, Lord Adair, who would become Windham Thomas Wyndham-Quinn, fourth earl of Dunraven and Mount-Earl. A year later he would start buying property at Estes Park, Colorado, for a sixty-thousand-acre game preserve.[22]

General Sheridan was helping Dunraven with his hunting trip on the plains. Dunraven visited Sheridan's Chicago headquarters where he saw a mounted elk head, a present from Fort McPherson. Dunraven had never seen an elk and was impressed. He wanted one. Sheridan wrote to McPherson's commander, Colonel Emory, requesting he offer Dunraven any assistance he needed and to have Buffalo Bill Cody act as his guide.[23]

Late October 1871, Dunraven and his companion left the train at the station near Fort McPherson. Buffalo Bill and his friend and scout Texas Jack Omohundro galloped their horses to the station platform, dismounted, and introduced themselves. Dunraven described the two men: "I thought I had never seen two finer-looking specimens of humanity, or two more picturesque figures. Both were tall, well-built, active-looking men, with singularly handsome features. Bill was dressed in a pair of corduroys tucked into his high boots, and a blue flannel shirt. He wore a broad-brimmed felt hat or sombrero, and a white handkerchief folded like a little shawl loosely fastened around his neck, to keep off the fierce rays of the afternoon sun . . . he wore his hair in long ringlets over his shoulders in true Western style. As he cantered up, with his flowing locks and broadbrimmed hat, he looked like a picture of a Cavalier of olden times."[24]

Fort McPherson's officers were welcoming. Lord Dunraven and his friend would accompany an Army scouting and hunting expedition to provide meat for the soldiers. The lord and his friend spent several days acquiring what was needed for their hunt as the scouts and soldiers put together provisions, equipment, tents, and wagons, and the officers assigned an escort.[25]

The second day out from the fort, Dunraven was away from the party when he killed an elk. Cody heard the shots and rode up to Dunraven. Cody helped him butcher the carcass, load the meat, and escorted him back to the rest of the party. A few days later, Texas Jack, Cody, Dunraven, and his friend came upon a herd of 120 to 130 elk. They shot three before the rest ran off. For the next several days the party killed enough elk to fill the wagons. Dunraven wrote, "It must not be supposed that an ounce of all that meat was wasted; we hauled every bit of it out to the fort, where the demand of fresh venison exceeded our supply."[26]

This might have been the hunting expedition where Cody played a practical joke on a Mr. McCarthy from Syracuse, New York, who was a relative of Colonel Emory. Cody worked it out with the Pawnee Scouts to pretend they were hostile Indians and charge him and McCarthy when they were away from the camp. Cody said the two of them were along Deer Creek about eight miles from camp. Cody had been talking to McCarthy about Indians and "he had become considerably excited" when the Pawnees appeared on horseback racing toward them, whooping and firing their guns. Cody asked McCarthy if they should stay and fight or make a run for it to camp. Without answering, McCarthy wheeled around his horse and galloped back toward camp, dropping his gun and losing his hat. Cody yelled at him to stop, but he kept on going. Cody picked up McCarthy's things and raced after him trying to get him to stop, but to no avail. McCarthy reached camp and announced hostile Indians had attacked them. Colonel Carr was preparing to send two companies after the Indians. Cody reported to Carr telling him it was just a practical joke the Pawnees played on McCarthy and him, failing to tell Carr it was his idea. Cody said Carr liked a good practical joke and was not too angry. McCarthy didn't find out until later that Cody was behind the joke.[27]

There was no time to rest after the hunting party returned to Fort McPherson. Royal Buck was at the post with a letter from the department commander stating that a detachment accompany Mr. Buck to find and bury his father's body. Buck's father and others had been killed by Pawnee Killer's band on Beaver Creek. Two companies and Cody, as scout, escorted Buck to Beaver Creek. After two days of searching, they found human remains and among the wreckage, they discovered letters Buck recognized were in his father's handwriting. They buried what remains they could find and returned to Fort McPherson.[28]

On November 1, 1871, the Fifth Cavalry received orders to head to Arizona for field service against the Apaches. Headquarters and most of the men left Fort McPherson on November 27. Cody had been with them for over three years and was willing to go along, but General Sheridan sent instructions that Cody was to stay at Fort McPherson and act as scout for the Third Cavalry, which would be taking the Fifth's place. Cody was sad when he saw his friends off at the railroad station.[29]

Abilene, Kansas, was a cowtown. Back in 1867, Illinois cattleman Joseph McCoy saw the small settlement's possibilities as a good location where cattle could be driven up from Texas on the Chisholm Trail and then shipped east to Chicago on the Kansas Pacific Railroad. He asked the railroad to provide him access and it agreed to build a hundred-car switch. McCoy had workers install scales and construct transfer pens and feed yards with a capacity of fifteen hundred head. There was plenty of good rangeland where cattle could graze while waiting to be shipped east. McCoy sent notices to Texas cattlemen informing them of the Abilene facilities. The first of many herds arrived on September 5.[30]

Abilene was a wild town. After spending up to three months on the trail, Texas cowboys were ready to let loose. Racing their horses down the street, cowboys fired their pistols in the air as they whooped and hollered. Local businesses thrived; there were plenty of ways to separate cowboys from their money through liquor, games of chance, and prostitutes.[31]

Many Texans visited Abilene. The *Leavenworth Times and Conservative* correspondent writing under the name Traveler reported on June 25, 1869, "Abilene, 159 miles west of Leavenworth, might be called a Texan town, so much of the Texan being apparent on surface. In the busy season thousands of Texan steers are the principal inhabitants, but at present the Texan drovers take a prominent position."[32]

In September 1869, Abilene was incorporated as a town. A judge appointed several prominent citizens as trustees until an election could be held. They established the position of town marshal on May 2, 1870. An ordinance was passed banning brothels as well as an ordinance banning firearms; but the brothels remained, and the cowboys shot up the posters announcing the firearms ban. The town fathers built a jail, but the cowboys shot it up and then tore it down. It was rebuilt under armed guard.[33]

On June 4, Thomas Smith was appointed chief of police. He was a good law enforcement officer, but on November 2 he and his deputy, James McDonald, attempted to arrest Andrew McConnell for murder. They rode to McConnell's homestead, and when Smith attempted to arrest McConnell, a fight ensued, and Smith was killed.[34]

After Smith's death, Abilene struggled to maintain an adequate police force until the first municipal election was held on April 3, 1871, when cattleman Joseph McCoy was elected mayor.

McCoy's first order of business was to find a marshal who could control the cowboys. His friend and employee Charles Gross recommended Wild Bill Hickok, who he had known back in Illinois. McCoy had heard of Hickok and was impressed with Gross's recommendation. He sent Gross to track down Hickok and bring him to Abilene to meet with him.[35]

Gross found Hickok at Fort Harker and told him about the Abilene marshal position. Hickok was interested enough to agree to listen to Mayor McCoy's offer and took the eastbound train to Abilene with Gross. On April 11, Hickok met with McCoy and Gross and they discussed the position. Hickok wanted to look over the town first and spent the next few days doing so. In 1871, Abilene had 250 residents. Waiting for the cowboys' arrival were 32 saloons, 64 gambling tables, and 130 gamblers. Hickok learned there was friction between Texans who owned gambling houses and saloons and local Kansan businessmen. He let McCoy know he would accept the job, knowing his reputation most likely put a target on his back.[36]

The city council met on April 15, 1871, and unanimously confirmed thirty-four-year-old James Butler Hickok as Abilene's marshal. His salary was set at $150 per month with a bonus of 25 percent of court-imposed fines. Later, he would also be paid 50 cents for every stray dog he shot and killed. The city council allowed Hickok to keep the peace using his own methods; however, the council reserved the right to make policy decisions. Wild Bill Hickok's hiring was big news not only in Abilene but in all of Kansas as well as in Texas and along the Chisholm Trail.[37]

Emporia, Kansas's *Emporia News* reported on May 26, "Wild Bill the loyal scout, who was killed by the Indians in 1869, and lynched by the Ku Klux last fall, and shot dead in a quarrel at Christmas, is marshal of the town of Abilene, Kan."[38]

Hickok's first concern was strengthening the jail before the cattle herds arrived with their cowboys who would be paid off at the end of the trail. With cash in hand, they would be ready for a good time. The year 1870 had proved to be a banner year with three hundred thousand head of cattle shipped from Abilene, and it appeared 1871 would be an even bigger year.[39]

On May 8, 1871, Marshal Hickok assisted in maintaining a quorum for a city council meeting. The city council was made up of five members. There was a dispute between two members who wanted a $200 liquor license for the saloons, two members who wanted a $100 fee, and S. A. Burroughs who wanted a $500 fee. It was a complicated affair, but in the end, the two councilmen who wanted the $100 fee resigned at the meeting and left. The remaining three councilmen voted on the resignation. The two $200 fee councilmen voted to accept the resignations, and Burroughs voted against accepting them and left the meeting. With Burroughs gone, the council didn't have a quorum and could not do business.[40]

The remaining councilmen directed Marshal Hickok to bring back Burroughs to the meeting. Hickok found him and brought him back. Burroughs took off again, and again Hickok was directed to find him and bring him back.[41]

Hickok found Burroughs in his office and explained he needed to return to the council meeting. The *Topeka State Record* May 9, 1871 issue reported what happened next: "[Burroughs] spread his legs and smoked defiantly. He wouldn't go. But the untamed William was not there to argue the question, but to obey orders. He kicked the city father's feet from under him, tossted [*sic*] him lightly on his own shoulders and started off with him as a 'roust-about' does a sack of corn. City father kicked and smoked, but it was 'no go,' he was as helpless as a hog in a gate. 'Wild Bill' entered the council chamber with his load, 'dumped' Mr. Councilman in a chair sat down beside him and looked serenely at the Mayor at [*sic*] if to enquire if there was any further 'toting' to be done. The council then proceeded to order an election for two councilmen to fill the vacancies, and the city government of Abilene was saved, all because 'Wild Bill' is 'some on the lift.'"[42]

Marshal Hickok, carrying out his orders, was quite the sensation not only in Abilene but statewide. The *Topeka Daily*

Wild Bill ensures the Abilene city council has a quorum.

Commonwealth stated, "At McKeekin's is a fine engraving, executed by Topeka's celebrated artist and caricaturist, Prof. [Henry] Worrall, of Wild Bill 'toting' on his shoulder the refractory and absconding councilman of Abilene. Knight has photographed it, and copies can be obtained at the Riverside."[43]

On May 10, 1871, Columbus Carroll arrived at Abilene with sixteen hundred head of beef, the first Texan herd of the year, soon to be followed by many more.[44] By June 1, the rangeland around Abilene was populated with cattle, and the saloons, gambling halls, and houses of prostitution were populated with cowboys. One old-timer estimated Abilene's population swelled to seven thousand. With a large unruly population, Marshal Hickok appointed deputies to assist him. The following men served as deputies: James Gainsford; James McDonald; Thomas Carson, a nephew of Kit Carson; "Brocky Jack" Norton; and Mike Williams.[45]

Hickok and his deputies were determined to enforce the no firearms ordinance. The *Abilene Weekly Chronicle* June 8 issue reported, "Fire Arms—The Chief of Police has posted up printed notices, informing all persons that the ordinance against carrying fire arms or other weapons in Abilene, will be enforced. That's right. There's no bravery in carrying revolvers in a civilized community. . . ."[46]

There were those who flaunted the ordinance. On the morning of June 22, the *Weekly Chronicle* reported two men had a disagreement on First Street: "It seems that hard words passed between them, when one drew his revolver and No. 2 remarked 'you know you have got the advantage of me.' No. 1 then put back his weapon, whereupon No. 2 drew a Derringer and fired at No. 1 who also managed to draw his six-shooter. Each fired two shots; one was hit in the wrist and the other the shoulder. The police [Hickok and/ or one or more deputies] were promptly on hand and arrested the parties in time to prevent one or both being killed."[47] After this gunfight, the city council added more teeth to its anti-gun stance, passing two more ordinances on June 24.

The first stated "That any person who shall carry within the corporate limits of the city of Abilene or the commons, a pistol, revolver, gun, musket, dirk, bowie knife, or other dangerous weapon upon his person either openly or concealed, except to bring the same and forthwith deposit it or them at their house, store room, or residence, shall be fined in a sum not more then [sic] $75. Provided that the provisions of this ordinance shall not apply to the city and county officers while in the discharge of their duty."[48]

The second ordinance stated, "That any persons who shall intentionally discharge any pistol, revolver or gun, within the city of Abilene, in any street, alley, highway, lot, house or other place where the life or limb of any person could be endangered, shall be punished by a fine not less than ten nor more than $300."[49]

Clearly, these ordinances were aimed at the cowboys, and the city council meant business. It wanted Hickok and his men to enforce them.

Many of the saloons, gambling halls, and other forms of entertainment were on Texas Street. Prostitution had been outlawed, and most of the prostitutes had been plying their trade north of town, but they had gradually returned after the death of Marshal Smith and were now conducting business on Texas Street and vicinity. In July, Abilene citizens petitioned the city council to remove the prostitutes. A solution was finally found; they were all moved outside the city limits to the southeast where they were not under the town's jurisdiction. The Texans were fine with it. The red-light district went by many names: Texas Town, Beer Garden, Devil's Addition, and Fisher's Addition since the land was owned by George Fisher.[50]

One of the thousands of young cowboys who rode the Chisholm Trail to Abilene was eighteen-year-old John Wesley Hardin. Hardin arrived with Columbus Carroll's herd in May 1871. Hardin wrote a book about his life published after his death in 1895.[51] In it, he talked about men he had killed and his experiences with Wild Bill Hickok. By the time Hardin reached

Abilene, he claimed he had killed fifteen men. Since many people refer to Hardin's version of events while in Abilene, the following is a brief look at his early life and claims about his interactions with Marshal Wild Bill Hickok.

John Wesley Hardin was born in Bonham, Texas, on May 26, 1853. When he was fifteen years old he shot and killed a Black man named Mage who attacked him after they had a wrestling match. Law enforcement and federal troops were sent to arrest Hardin. He ambushed and killed three pursuing soldiers.[52]

In 1869, Hardin killed a soldier, and then on Christmas Day of that year, he got into a dispute over a card game with an Arkansas desperado he called Jim Bradly. They both shot at each other at close range while on horseback. Hardin won, continuing to shoot bullets into Bradly to ensure he was dead.[53]

In January 1870, Hardin shot and killed a man who he had angered by accidently bumping him and later that month killed another man who tried to rob him. In January 1871, he killed a total of four men who tried to arrest him.[54]

Hardin arrived at his Clements cousins' ranch in Gonzales County, Texas, where they convinced him to join Columbus Carroll's cattle drive to Abilene, Kansas. While rounding up cattle to drive north, cousin Mannen Clements and Hardin stopped at a Mexican camp joining in a card game with several Mexicans. There was a dispute, and a fight ensued between Hardin and three Mexicans ending with "a Mexican with his arm broken, another shot through the lungs and another with a very sore head."[55]

In March 1871, Hardin and cousin Jim Clements helped drive Carroll's herd north. As they passed through Indian Territory, Hardin claimed he killed two Indians. When they crossed into Kansas, there was a dispute with Mexicans driving another cattle herd. Hardin shot killing the Mexican boss and general fighting erupted between the Mexicans and Hardin and the cowboys with him. Hardin said, "In comparing notes after the fight we agreed that I had killed five out of the six dead Mexicans." When Columbus Carroll reached Abilene, he kept Hardin on the payroll to help with the herd until the cattle were shipped east.[56]

Phil Coe and Ben Thompson, gamblers Hardin had known from Texas, had become friends serving together in the Confederate army, or in an alternate version of the story, side-by-side in Mexico. They were now owners of the Bull's Head Saloon and Gambling Hall on Abilene's Texas Street. Coe and Thompson had several run-ins with Marshal Wild Bill Hickok. One point of contention was the Bull's Head's sign. Coe and Thompson had a large bull painted on their building's exterior. Abilene citizens were offended by the male portion of the bull's anatomy. The city council ordered the sign be removed or altered, and Hickok delivered the message to Coe and Thompson. Hardin said Coe didn't care, but Thompson was furious. Hickok found painters who "materially altered the offending bovine."[57]

Thompson told Hardin that Hickok always selected southern men to kill, especially Texans. When Hardin asked Thompson why he didn't kill Hickok, he responded, "I would rather get someone else to do it." When Thompson asked Hardin to kill Hickok, he declined. Hardin wrote, "I had not yet met Bill Heycox, [sic] but really wished for a chance to have a set-to with him just to ply his pluck."[58]

Hardin said, Hickok was in a wine room drinking with George Johnson and other friends of Hardin's when Hardin entered. Hickok had Johnson introduce him to Hardin and they drank several glasses of wine together. Hickok asked about the fight with the Mexicans and showed him a Texas wanted poster for his arrest. He was favorably impressed with Hardin and warned him not to let Ben Thompson influence him. Hardin wrote, "I was charmed with his liberal views, and told him so. We parted friends."[59]

Hardin's tale continued. A few days later, Hardin and other Texans had been drinking and were rowdy as they played ten pins. Hardin had his pistols strapped on when Hickok entered to tell them to quiet down. Hickok told Hardin to remove his pistols.

Hardin said no. They walked out on the street where Hickok pulled out his pistol telling Hardin he was arresting him and to hand over his pistols. A crowd of mostly Texans began to gather.[60]

Hardin wrote, "I said all right and pulled them out of the scabbard, but while he was reaching for them I reversed them and whirled them over on him with the muzzles in his face, springing back at the same time. I told him to put his pistol up, which he did. I cursed him for a long-haired scoundrel that would shoot a boy with his back to him (as I had been told he intended to do to me). He said, 'Little Arkansaw [Hardin's nickname], you have been wrongly informed.' By this time a big crowd had gathered with pistols and arms. They kept urging me to kill him. Down the street a squad of policemen were coming, but Wild Bill motioned them to go back and at the same time asked me not to let the mob shoot him."[61]

Hardin claimed Hickok took him to a private room where Hickok bought him a drink and had a long talk with him. Hardin said, "we came out friends." No one else recorded Hardin's tale of getting the drop on Hickok.[62]

Hardin said that night he and a one-armed Texas cowboy named Pain were eating in a restaurant when several drunks entered saying they hated Texans. Hardin said, "I'm a Texan." The nearest man cursed Hardin and was about to slap him when Hardin pulled his gun. The man pulled his and they both shot. One of Hardin's shots hit Pain in his arm, another passed through Hardin's antagonist's mouth. When it was over the Texan hater was dead. As Hardin left the restaurant, he ran into a policeman and shoved his pistol in his face saying, "Hands up!" Hardin mounted his horse and rode out of town.[63]

The *Kansas City Daily Journal of Commerce* reported on the shooting that there was an attempt to assassinate saloon owner Pat Downey: "Four shots were fired, one ball only taking effect on Downey, passing entirely through his lower jaw. One shot struck a one-armed gentleman by the name of Payne, shattering the bones badly, and fears are entertained that amputation will be found necessary. The assassin escaped in the darkness, and no arrests were made." Cattleman George Steen remembered, "one night a man was drinking at a bar in a saloon and somebody fired in from outside, the bullet striking him in the mouth and instantly killing him." No one knew who the shooter was until Hardin confessed in his book.[64]

Hardin said he rode north to Cottonwood, where he learned a cowman named Billy Coran had been killed by a Mexican, Juan Bideno. The cattle owners wanted Bideno brought to justice. They had Hardin made a deputy sheriff and gave him a warrant for Bideno's arrest. Hardin tracked down Bideno to the town of Bluff where he found him eating in a restaurant. When Hardin told Bideno he was under arrest, Bideno reached for his pistol and Hardin shot him dead. Everyone thought Hardin a hero for killing Bideno. When he returned to Abilene, Hickok continued to let him and his friends wear their pistols in town as he drank with them.[65]

Hardin's tale continued with an intricate escape of his cousin Mannen Clements from jail with the help of Hickok, who had promised Hardin he would do anything for him. Hardin collected on Hickok's promise. At midnight when Hickok released Clements from jail, he had to beat up his own deputy, Tom Carson, in the process.[66]

Hardin wrote, "In those days my life was constantly in danger from secret or hired assassins, and I was always on the lookout." The night of July 7, he and Jim Clements were in their room at the American Hotel when he heard a man unlock the door and enter with a dirk. Hardin fired four bullets into the man, killing him.[67]

Hardin and Clements went out on top of the hotel portico and saw Hickok and four policemen arrive. When they entered the hotel, Hardin and Clements jumped to the ground and ran off. Hardin found a place for Clements to hide, and he borrowed a horse from a cowboy. The police saw him, mounted their horses, and gave chase. Hardin outdistanced them and reached camp where he hid. When Tom Carson and the other deputies arrived, the cook told them Hardin was out with the herd. He gave the deputies something to eat and when their hands were full, Hardin emerged with a rifle and got the drop on them. After disarming the deputies, he forced them to remove their clothes and hoof it back to town. On July 11, 1871, John Wesley Hardin and Jim Clements rode away from Abilene, bound for Texas.[68]

What fraction of Hardin's Abilene stories about Wild Bill Hickok were true? There is no evidence Hickok and Hardin met. Hickok never mentioned meeting Hardin. No one who was in Abilene ever wrote about the two of them meeting; and the newspapers didn't write anything about Hardin and Hickok together. One of the most popular of Hardin's tall tales is when he claimed he reversed his pistols on Hickok, the so-called border roll or road agent's spin. Hardin alleged it happened in plain sight of a large crowd. No one else mentioned it. The newspapers never printed the story. It didn't happen. Hickok would never have allowed Hardin and his cronies to walk the streets of Abilene, armed. It's ludicrous to think Hickok would beat up his own deputy to let Mannen Clements out of jail. It's even more ludicrous that after Hardin killed a man, he would be hired as a deputy sheriff, and Hickok would allow him to continue to wear his revolvers and have drinks with him. Hardin was a bad man and a bad liar.

What is known is Hardin probably did kill two men while he was in Abilene and the surrounding area. One was killed on July 7, 1871, while eating at a restaurant in Sumner City, Kansas, south of Abilene. The other was killed on the night of August 6, in the American House hotel where Hardin said he was staying.[69]

On July 5, a Mexican herder shot and killed a young Texan, William Cohron. The *Abilene Chronicle* July 13, 1871 issue reported two Texans followed the Mexican and killed him in a restaurant. The July 13, 1871 issue of Kansas's *Oxford Times* reported a man was sitting in Sumner City's Southwestern Hotel's dining room drinking coffee when a man calling himself Conway from Cottonwood River walked in and shot the man in the forehead, killing him. Conway said the man was a Mexican who had killed his brother. He handed the hotel owner $5 to clean up the mess and rode out with the "Mexican's" fine horse. No arrest was made.[70] Did Hardin do the shooting?

The August 10, 1871, *Lawrence Daily Journal* reported: "Murdered.—A cattle herder by the name of Condry was shot by a Texas outlaw at Abilene on Sunday night [August 6], and instantly killed. The murderer fled, and at last accounts had not been caught."[71]

The same day, the *Abilene Chronicle* added, "A most fiendish murder was perpetuated at the American House, in this place, on the night of the 6th inst. The murdered man's name was Charles Couger, and that of the murderer Wesley Clemens, *alias* 'Arkansaw.' Couger was a boss cattle herder, and said to be a gentleman; Clemens is from Mississippi. Couger was in his room sitting upon the bed reading the newspaper. Four shots were fired at him through a board partition, one of which struck him in the fleshy part of the left arm, passing through the left rib and entering the heart, cutting a piece of it entirely off, and killing Couger almost instantly. The murderer has escaped, and has thus far eluded his pursuers. If caught he will probably be killed on sight."[72] The August 17 issue of the *Abilene Chronicle* stated the man who killed the Mexican was the same man who killed Charles Couger.[73]

Since Hardin was a wanted man, he did not use his last name but that of his Clements cousins to obscure his identity. The last name of the man Hardin killed was spelled a variety of ways: Couger, Carver, Coredey, Condry, and Conger. The postmaster advertised an unclaimed letter to C. Conger.[74]

The city council believed it needed to impose more controls on rowdy cowboys and those parting them from their cash. On July 19, the council instructed Marshal Hickok "to stop dance houses and the vending of Whiskeys Brandies &c., in McCoy's addition [another name for the red-light district] to the town of Abilene." Then on July 22, the council told Hickok to "close up all dead & Brace Gambling Games and to arrest all Cappers for the aforesaid game." Hickok and his deputies did not win any friends by enforcing the orders.[75]

Ben Thompson and Phil Coe didn't care much for the city council's rules or the way Marshal Hickok enforced them. Bad blood may have originated from Hickok having painters cover up a certain part of their painted bull's male anatomy, or it might have been that Hickok had enforced the city's orders bringing the faro games from out of the dark back room into a much more lighted space where cheating would be harder to do. Thompson had a hot temper and had committed violent acts in the past. However, he was soon out of the picture. In early July, he had returned to Texas to bring back his family, but there was a buggy accident in which his wife lost an arm and Thompson had multiple injuries. On August 2, Coe transferred the Bull's Head license to Tom Sheran, but he remained as a house gambler.[76]

Major W. M. "Buck" Walton, who was Ben Thompson's friend and his attorney who would later defend him in the shooting death of gambler Jack Harris in 1882, wrote a biography of Thompson. It alleged Hickok and the city council were in cahoots with other saloon owners and gamblers. Thompson and Coe "did deem their duty to protect Texans, as far as they could, from the well nigh highway robbery that was practiced on them by the associated Abilene authorities."[77]

With five deputies on duty, Hickok was determined to keep the peace, even if there were an estimated five thousand Texan cowboys ready to whoop it up. Once a day he walked down Texas Street, and at night he did the same at various times. He had deputies constantly patrolling the town. He frequently rode or walked through the "Devil's Addition" red-light district. These actions reduced the amount of violence. When not in his office or walking the streets, Hickok could be found in the Alamo Saloon.[78]

There were Texans who were out to get him. He continued the practices he had learned in Hays City—stay out in the middle of the street, stay off the sidewalk, avoid open doorways and windows, and always sit with back to the wall. John Conkie, Abilene's jailor, wrote, "It was a very common sight . . . to see Wild Bill sitting in a barber's chair getting shaved, with his shotgun in hand and his eyes open."[79]

When Hickok first arrived in Abilene, he stayed at the Drover's Cottage. It was *the* place to stay. A couple of months later he rented a two-story house at the south end of town. Hickok never talked about the women in his life. The mysterious Susannah Moore's name resurfaced that she was living with him, but there is no substantiated evidence. Charles Gross said Hickok had two or three mistresses while in Abilene. However, Gross could not remember their names. He said a woman arrived in Abilene and tried to make amends for a wrong she had done to Hickok. He said it was over, gave her $25, and told her to move along.[80]

On July 31, 1871, the Hippo-Olympiad and Mammoth Circus performed in Abilene. It had arrived on its special train from Salina and would be leaving for its next performance in Topeka on August 1. The widow Agnes Lake owned the circus. Her husband Bill had been shot and killed by a man who had tried to sneak into the circus performance back on August 21, 1869. Hickok and Agnes must have met on the circus's arrival in town. Hickok provided protection for the circus from the rougher element.[81]

An advertisement for the circus on the front page of the August 2, 1871 *Leavenworth Daily Commercial* had an image of a balloon and said, "The only company traveling that gives a free balloon ascension." It advertised "Most Daring and Accomplished Equestriennes, Most Skillful and Graceful Equestrians, Most Intrepid and Thrilling Gymnasts." The circus was a great success, with the August 3 issue of the *Abilene Chronicle* reporting, "The attendance was large at each performance." Agnes was interested in Wild Bill right from the start; they would stay in touch.[82]

On September 2, the city council let go two deputies, James McDonald and James Gainsford, "by reason that their services are no longer needed." That left Tom Carson and "Brocky Jack" Norton on Hickok's force. Then on September 6, 1871, the council passed an ordinance, "That all Dance Houses or places kept for the purpose of public dancing within the corporate limits of the City, be and the same are hereby declared to be public nuisances and it shall be the duty of the Marshal to suppress the same." Violators were to be fined $50 to $100.[83]

The *Abilene Chronicle* proclaimed on September 14, 1871, "Wholesome and magnificent changes have been wrought in the moral *status* of Abilene. For the last ten or twelve days almost every train eastward bound has carried away and relieved this community of vast numbers of sinful humanity. Prostitutes, 'pimps,' gamblers, 'cappers,' and others of like ilk, finding their several nefarious avocations no longer remunerative or appreciated in this neighborhood [have found funds] to procure passage to Newton, Kansas City, or St. Louis, where in all probability most of them will end their miserable lives in dens of shame." The newspaper blasted the city government, "We regret to admit that such characters have been invited here by those in official position, and protected by officers whose sworn duty it is to see that the laws and ordinances are enforced." The article continued about how good it was for Abilene to remove these less than desirable people ending with, "Let the good work go on until the wickedness and sorrow of the old city shall be entirely submerged by the virtue and happiness of the new Abilene. So mote it be."[84]

Was the writer talking about deputies McDonald and Gainsford who were just discharged from the police force, or was he talking about Marshal Hickok? Probably not Hickok. Most of the permanent Abilene residents' reminiscences about him were positive. Theophilus Little, a resident at the time, wrote Hickok "was a great lover of children and tender hearted." Little's nine-year-old son Will had an accident that cut off two fingers. "As Dr. McCollam was dressing his [Will's] hand one day, Wild Bill stepped in.

'Ah,' said he, 'that is too bad, too bad and such a fine manly little fellow too,' patting him on the head."[85]

On another occasion, Little and his family were at an evening school function where the public was invited. Rowdy Texas cowboys were in attendance. Two of them sat in front of Little and his family, laughing and cursing. Little confronted them, forcing them to be silent. After the program was over, Hickok walked up to the Little family and "bowed to Mrs. Little, in most gracious tones, said, 'Mr. Little if you will allow me, I will walk home with you and your family this evening.' I thanked him saying, 'We would deem it an honor but not a necessity.' Said he, 'I think I understand this case better than you do, Mr. Little' and he went to our home with us."[86]

By the first week of October 1871, many cowboys had left as well as those who separated the cowboys from their money. Those Texans still in town went to the Dickinson County Fair for excitement, but stormy weather put a damper on that. On the evening of Thursday, October 5, the Texans began roaming town, looking to make their own entertainment.[87]

One of those Texans was the gambler Phil Coe, who had been co-owner in the Bull's Head Saloon. Coe was a large man standing at six feet four inches and weighing over 220 pounds. People's opinions of him were mixed depending on who was giving it. The few times he visited his family, he was not very sociable. Theophilus Little said Coe was "a red mouthed, bawling 'thug'—'plug' Ugly—a very dangerous beast." Coe owed Little $40. "I asked him to pay and he was very abusive and I was always afraid that he would burn me out."[88]

Besides Hickok's confrontations with Coe over the Bull Head Saloon's obscene sign and the Bull Head's shady faro games, Ben Thompson's friend Buck Walton wrote in his book that Coe and Hickok had clashed over a prostitute named Jesse Hazel.[89] However, there was no mention of her anywhere else. The *Chronicle* later wrote, "It is said that he [Coe] had a spite at Wild Bill and had threatened to kill him—which Bill believed he would do if he gave him the opportunity."[90] The *Junction City Union* reported on October 7, "It is said that the leader of the party had threatened to kill Bill, 'before frost.'"[91]

The mob of Texans was on a drinking spree, hopping from saloon to saloon. Whenever they caught a citizen of Abilene, they would carry him on their shoulders into a saloon where he was compelled to buy them a round of drinks. They found Marshal Hickok and carried him into a saloon. He was a good sport about it and bought them a round but told them they needed to stay within the bounds of the city's rules or he would have to stop them.[92]

Theophilus Little said, "I saw this band of crazy men. They went up and down the street with a wild swish and rush and roar, totally oblivious to anything in their path. It was a drunken mob."[93]

Around 8:00 p.m., Hickok heard the report of a revolver. He went to where the shot had been fired, outside the Alamo Saloon where the Texan mob had gathered. The *Chronicle* said Hickok "knew at once the leading spirits in the crowd, numbering probably fifty men, intended to get up a 'fight.'"[94]

Hickok stood on the Alamo's veranda facing the mob. Many of the Texans in the street were armed, and several had their guns drawn. They were in violation of city ordinances banning the carrying of guns as well as the discharge of guns. Phil Coe, gun in hand, confronted Hickok telling him he had fired at a stray dog.[95]

Coe and Hickok were standing about eight feet apart when Coe pulled a second pistol and fired twice at Hickok; one shot went between Hickok's legs hitting the floorboards behind him. The other bullet punctured a hole in the tail of Hickok's coat. Other shots were fired at Hickok from the crowd. The *Chronicle* reported: "As quick as thought the Marshal drew two revolvers and both men fired almost simultaneously. Several shots were fired, during which Mike Williams, a policeman,[96] came around the corner for the purpose of assisting the Marshal and rushing between him and Coe received two of the shots intended for Coe. The whole affair was the work of an instant. The Marshal surrounded by the crowd, and standing in the light, did not recognize Williams whose death he deeply regrets."[97]

Two of Hickok's bullets hit Coe in the stomach, one exiting out his back. More shots from Hickok, Coe, or others in the crowd hit one or two people, but none were seriously injured. Mike Williams died instantly. Coe died several days later on Sunday evening. Hickok was unhurt. "The fact is Wild Bill's escape is truly marvelous," the *Chronicle* stated. [98]

Theophilus Little said after Hickok fired at Coe, "Whirling on the mob, his two .44 six shooters drawn on them, he calmly said, 'If any of you want the balance of these pills, come and get them.' Not a word was uttered, they were sobered and paralyzed. 'Now every one of you mount his pony and ride for his camp and do it damn quick.' In less than five minutes every man of them was on the west side of Mud Creek."[99]

Hickok saw the second man he had shot was his friend Mike Williams. Horrified and grief-stricken, Hickok picked up Williams's body and carried it into the Alamo where he laid it on top of a billiard table. Angry, Hickok raged through town, kicking everyone out of the saloons and gambling houses and shutting them down until the town was silent.[100]

Mike Williams would later be buried at Kansas City, and Hickok paid for the funeral expenses. Phil Coe's body was shipped back to Texas for burial.[101]

The *Chronicle* stated, "We hope no further disturbances will take place. There is no use in trying to override Wild Bill, the Marshal. His arrangements for policing the city are complete, and attempts to kill police officers or in any way create disturbance, must result in loss of life on the part of violators of the law. We hope that all, strangers as well as citizens, will aid by word and deed in maintaining peace and quietness."[102]

However, Kansas's *Oxford Times* gave a different version of the Coe and Hickok fight summing up saying, "Coe is said to have been a kind and generous hearted man well thought of by all who knew him. He had many friends among the Texans and cattle dealers about Abilene. It is darkly hinted that avengers are on the trail and we will probably soon hear of another tragedy in Abilene." Texas newspapers were not favorable to Hickok. Austin's *Weekly State Journal* October 26, 1871 issue stated, "The gallows and penitentiary are the places to tame such blood thirsty wretches as 'Wild Bill.'"[103]

The *Junction City Weekly Union* summed up Abilene residents' feelings: "The verdict of the citizens seemed to be unanimously in support of the Marshal, who bravely did his duty."[104]

Hickok received threatening letters from Texas. He now carried a shotgun when he made his rounds, but all was quiet in Abilene for the rest of October and into November. Hickok left town for a few days to conduct some business in Topeka. While he was gone, deputy Tom Carson got into trouble shooting and wounding an unarmed bartender. The city council held an emergency meeting on November 27 and voted that Hickok discharge both Carson and Brocky Jack Norton from the police force.[105]

The *Abilene Chronicle*'s November 30, 1871 issue reported a foiled attempt on Hickok's life onboard the train to Topeka. Hickok had received a letter from Austin, Texas, warning that five men were on their way to Abilene and would be paid $11,000 to kill him. They reached town, but Hickok was unable to locate them. When he boarded the train for Topeka, five Texans also boarded. As one of Hickok's friends boarded the train, he overheard the largest Texan who must have been their leader say, "Wild Bill is going on the train." Hickok kept an eye on them after that.

Hickok and his friend entered a car and sat down. The five men entered the same car and took seats right behind him. Hickok stood and took a seat behind them. They stood up and left the car, moving into the forward car.

Hickok wanted to determine if they really were after him, so he and his friend left their car, went to the last car, and took seats toward the back. About ten miles out of Topeka, the five men entered their car. Four of them stood in the aisle while the leader took a seat behind Hickok. A woman who knew Hickok walked by and told him she saw the man behind him was holding a revolver between his overcoat and dress coat.

Hickok kept an eye on them and when the train arrived in Topeka, he and his friend got off. When the Texans reached the door, he asked them where they were going. They replied they were getting off in Topeka. Hickok said, "I am satisfied that you are hounding me, and as I intend to stop in Topeka, you can't stop here." They began to object, but Hickok pulled both his revolvers and pointed them at the Texans to enforce his words. They remained on the train.[106]

The citizens of Abilene had had enough of the cattle trade and the entertainment businesses that went with it and planned to end them, so they would not need their current law enforcement officers. While Mayor Joseph McCoy was out of town, Abilene's city council met and voted to fire Marshal Hickok and his deputies.[107]

"Be it resolved by the Mayor & Council of City of Abilene that J B Hickok be discharged from his official position as City Marshall [sic] for the reason that the City is no longer in need of his services and that the date of his discharge Take place from and after this 13th day of December A D 1871. Also that all of his Deputies be stopped from doing their duty."[108]

James Gauthie, who had called for Hickok's dismissal, was hired in his place at $50 per month, a third of Hickok's salary. Hickok remained in town until the end of December, negotiating with the city council for his last month's salary.[109]

By February 22, 1872, the glory days of cattle drives to Abilene were over. The cattlemen needed to find somewhere else to drive their herds. Roughly 80 percent of Dickinson County citizens, where Abilene was located, signed a petition, "We, the undersigned, members of the Farmers' Protective Association, and officers and citizens of Dickinson county, Kansas, most respectfully request all who have contemplated driving Texas cattle to Abilene the coming Season to seek some other point for shipment, as the inhabitants of Dickinson will no longer submit to the evils of the trade."[110]

Years later, Mayor Joseph McCoy would say, "For my preserver of the Peace, I had 'Wild Bill' Hickok, and he was the squarest man I ever saw. He broke up all unfair gambling, made professional gamblers move their tables into the light, and when they became drunk stopped the game."[111]

CHAPTER 12

LIFE ON THE PLAINS
(JANUARY 1872–NOVEMBER 1872)

T here was no rest for Buffalo Bill Cody at the end of
1871 and into 1872. Grand Duke Alexis, the third son
of Russia's Czar Alexander II, was visiting the United
States and had expressed a desire to go hunting on the prairie.
General Phil Sheridan was in charge of planning and hosting the
twenty-one-year-old duke's prairie hunts. One of the reasons he
had ordered Cody to stay at Fort McPherson was so he could act
as chief guide for the duke and other dignitaries. The duke would
be busy visiting various American cities until January 1872. This
gave Sheridan time to plan the hunt.[1]

Around the first of January, Sheridan's staff members, Major
Sandy Forsyth and Dr. Morris Asch, arrived at Fort McPherson
to make arrangements for the hunt. They met with Cody, who told
them there were plenty of buffalo in the Red Willow Creek area
forty miles south of the fort. Cody guided Forsyth and Asch along
with Lieutenant Edward Hayes, the Fifth Cavalry quartermaster,
out to Red Willow Creek. Hayes had remained to provide logisti-
cal support for the hunt. They selected a pleasant spot on a knoll,
naming it Camp Alexis.[2]

Sheridan wanted the Brulé Lakota chief Spotted Tail and a
hundred men to join in the hunt and perform dances for the duke.

Forsyth and Asch told Cody that Sheridan had asked that he ride to Spotted Tail's village to request his assistance.[3]

Spotted Tail's winter camp was along the Republican River in Nebraska, and Cody believed it was about 150 miles from the fort. It was a two-day journey through the bitter cold. Although Spotted Tail was friendly to the whites, Cody was concerned other individuals might not be so friendly, therefore he remained vigilant.[4]

Late on the second day of riding, he saw Spotted Tail's village in the distance. He was concerned he might be attacked if he rode straight into camp. Leaving his horse behind, he crept closer until he could discern which lodge was Spotted Tail's. Cody waited until dark, threw a blanket over his head to help disguise he was a white man, and rode into camp.[5]

Finding Spotted Tail's lodge, he dismounted and approached the door flap. As Cody opened it, he saw Spotted Tail and announced who he was. Spotted Tail recognized Cody and invited him in. Todd Randall, Spotted Tail's trader and interpreter, was there, and he interpreted for them. Cody explained about the Russian prince and Sheridan's request for Spotted Tail to participate in the hunt and demonstrate Lakota dances. Spotted Tail liked the idea and agreed to it. He invited Cody to stay in his lodge for the night, ordered that Cody's horse be looked after, and had his wife give Cody a meal.[6]

The next morning, Spotted Tail assembled his leaders and explained what was going to happen. He told them Cody was under his protection and they were to treat him as a friend. Spotted Tail then assured Cody no one would follow him after he left the village.[7]

After another two-day ride, he was back at Red Willow Creek. Even though there was deep snow, soldiers were busy leveling the ground and erecting large wall tents with carpet-covered floors and stoves to provide heat. Lieutenant Hayes sent seventy-five of Fort McPherson's best horses to Camp Alexis for the hunting party's use. An abundant supply of food and liquors arrived from Chicago as well as bedding and tent furniture.[8]

Spotted Tail arrived on time with one hundred warriors and their families. Also included in Spotted Tail's party was Chief Whistler and his Cut Off Band of Oglala Lakotas, and Pawnee Killer and his Lakotas.[9]

On the morning of January 13, 1872, a special Union Pacific train arrived at North Platte with Grand Duke Alexis and his party along with General Sheridan and his party, which included Lieutenant Colonel George Custer. All were in high spirits for the buffalo hunt. The *Kansas City Times* correspondent reported, "It was a beautiful day," while the *New York Daily Herald* correspondent worried about falling snow, until the sun broke through the clouds.[10]

The *New York Daily Herald* correspondent wrote about Grand Duke Alexis meeting Buffalo Bill, who was wearing a fringed buckskin suit:

> *General Sheridan beckoned the notorious Bill to approach. He advanced carelessly and yet respectively.*
>
> *"Your highness," said the General, "this is Mr. Cady [sic], otherwise and universally known as 'Buffalo Bill.' Bill this is the Grand Duke."*
>
> *"I am glad to see you," said the hero of the Plains; "you have come out here the General tells me, to shoot some buffalo?"*
>
> *"Yes," answered Alexis, "and I hope to have a good fine time. I have heard of you before, and am glad to meet you here."*
>
> *"Thank you, thank you," said Bill, with a smile as honest and sweet as that of a love sick maiden; "if the weather holds good we will have one of the finest hunts that there ever was on this Continent."*
>
> *At this moment Dr. Chaudrin of the Duke's suite, stepped up to Bill and mentioned a word or two about his rig out.*
>
> *"Do you always dress this way?" asked the Doctor.*
>
> *"No, sir; not much. I have got this suit particularly for this occasion. When Sheridan told me the Duke was coming I*

thought I would throw myself on my clothes. I only put on this rig this morning, and half the people in the settlement have been accusing me of putting on airs;" and then Bill laughed heartily, and so did the Doctor, the Duke and the whole imperial crowd.[11]

At 8:00 a.m., the hunting party climbed into waiting wagons. Duke Alexis and General Sheridan rode in a carriage pulled by four spirited horses. The *Kansas City Times* correspondent reported, "After entering the carriages Buffalo Bill, in a buckskin suit, made his appearance on horseback and was presented to Alexis, and then in the capacity as guide to the hunting camp, led off, followed by the party, Gen. Sheridan and the Grand Duke taking the advance position. They were met at the Platte River, two miles south of this place [North Platte], by an escort of cavalry under the command of Gen. [brevet rank Innis] Palmer, who has charge of all the troops of the expedition."[12]

The hunting party reached Camp Alexis eight hours later without incident, except for the breakdown of a wagon hauling several Russian and American dignitaries including Custer. As they approached camp, the Lakotas gave the grand duke an enthusiastic welcome and he greeted them.[13]

An Army band played "the Russian hymn" as Sheridan assisted the grand duke from the carriage. A banquet was held in two large tents joined together and festooned with flags. The dinner included meats from game found on the prairie as well as a variety of wines. After the banquet, the members sat around a blazing campfire where songs were sung and tales were told. Buffalo Bill regaled his audience with his own hunting stories.[14]

The grand duke questioned Cody about buffalo hunting. How did he hunt buffalo? What kind of a gun or pistol was used? Would he have a good horse? Cody said, "I told him that he was to have my celebrated buffalo horse Buckskin Joe, and when we went into a buffalo herd all he would have to do was to sit on the horse's back and fire away."[15]

Early the next morning, Cody rode out to locate the buffalo herds, returning before 10:00 a.m. to announce he found a herd about fifteen miles distant on the divide between Red Willow and Medicine Creeks. After breakfast the hunting party rode out. The *New York Daily Herald* correspondent wrote, "When the three started off from camp together the Duke, Custer and Bill— all large and powerful and all hardy hunters—they attracted the attention and admiration of every one [*sic*]. Most of the imperial party went along and all the staff officers in camp."[16]

Cody and Custer stayed close to Alexis. According to Cody, Alexis preferred to fire his pistol instead of a rifle. He shot wildly six times at buffalo with no effect. Cody rode up to Alexis and handed him his pistol, which Alexis fired six times again with no effect. Cody again rode up to Alexis and handed him his favorite hunting rifle, Lucretia Borgia. Cody told him to urge Buckskin Joe close to a buffalo. Cody would ride close with him and tell him when to shoot. Alexis raced to within ten feet of a big bull and Cody said, "Now is your time!" He shot and down went the buffalo. Alexis stopped Buckskin Joe, dropped Lucretia Borgia to the ground,[17] and waved his hat to the members of his party.[18]

The Russians were excited. Alexis cut off the buffalo's tail as a trophy. General Sheridan arrived, and champagne bottles were brought out in honor of the grand duke's first buffalo. "'Another bond of union between Russia and America,' said a member of the imperial party, while all joined in congratulations to the Duke," the *New York Daily Herald* correspondent wrote. Four buffalo were killed in all. On their return to camp, the hunting party discovered Spotted Tail and his Lakotas had moved their camp close to Camp Alexis on the opposite side of Red Willow Creek.[19]

On the second day, Cody rode ahead of the hunting party to find buffalo herds. Spotted Tail and his hunters went along with the Russians and Americans but followed behind to allow the grand duke to hunt first. Following Cody's lead, they were fifteen miles from camp when they came upon buffalo. Cody was already at the herd to assist the grand duke, and Custer rode at Alexis's

Buffalo Bill guides Grand Duke Alexis's buffalo hunt.

side. Cody singled out a cow and her young bull for Alexis to kill. The duke raced his horse alongside the cow and fired one shot instantly killing her. Alexis and Custer continued to chase after the young bull. After firing two shots, the grand duke killed him.[20]

General Sheridan and other members of the American and Russian hunting party also killed buffalo. After they were finished, Spotted Tail and his hunters were asked to demonstrate their hunting skills using bows and arrows. The *New York Daily Herald* correspondent wrote, "Spotted Tail and his chosen Sioux, with a wild whoop, charged into the midst of the fleeing herd, and with unerring aim let fly the feathered arrows from their bows. . . . It was difficult to decide which to admire the more—the skill of the Indian in managing his horse or the rapidity and accuracy with which he let fly his feathered darts into the side of the doomed buffalo. In some respects the scene resembled the charge of cavalry upon troops already routed and fleeing in disorder; and the Duke was forcibly reminded of the Cossacks in his native country." The grand duke was amazed to see an eighteen-year-old Lakota hunter shoot an arrow clean through a buffalo. The youth gave the arrow to Alexis who told him to visit him at camp where he would give him a present.[21]

As the hunting party began a leisurely ride back to camp, they met a wagon that had been sent out to provide them lunch and champagne. The buffalo cow the grand duke had killed was a beautiful animal, and he wanted to take the head and hide back to Russia. Sheridan directed Cody to take care of the buffalo hide and head for the duke. Cody also butchered the animal, cutting out choice portions for the duke and his party to eat, and they loaded the entire young bull into a wagon to take back to camp.[22]

After dinner, the grand duke and his party and the American officers were treated to a Lakota war dance. A large bonfire and lanterns lit the dance area. Spotted Tail, his wife, and sixteen-year-old daughter, as well as principal Lakota leaders and their families, were in attendance as drummers established the beat and young warriors danced around the fire recounting their deeds. Cody said "Alexis paid considerable attention" to one of the young women in attendance. Many young officers, including Custer, were enchanted with Spotted Tail's daughter, and some of them gave her presents. A Lieutenant Clark presented two earrings to her. Custer insisted on placing them on her ears, and then kissed her.[23] One wonders what Spotted Tail and his wife thought of that.

After the dance, Spotted Tail and Sheridan talked. Spotted Tail wanted two things. The first was to continue to hunt buffalo below the Platte River to which Sheridan agreed. The second request was to allow more traders to trade with them. At present, the government allowed them only one trader. If there were more, the price of goods would be reduced through competition. Sheridan could not commit to that but said he would look into it. The grand duke gave Spotted Tail and other leaders green-colored blankets and a bag of silver. Sheridan gave them hunting knives and three months provisions to distribute among the people.[24]

The next day, it was time for the hunting party to return to the railroad at North Platte and continue their journey. Cody, leading the party north, was followed again by General Sheridan and Grand Duke Alexis in the open carriage pulled by the four spirited horses.[25]

Toward the end of the trip, Sheridan told the grand duke that Cody had once been a stagecoach driver, and Alexis wanted to see his driving ability. Cody dismounted and exchanged places with the driver. Sheridan encouraged Cody to drive faster, which he did, only to learn there was no break on the wagon as the horses continued running at a fast pace. It was a wild ride to North Fork, but they arrived safely. The grand duke invited Cody into his railroad car where he gave him valuable presents and said if he ever got to Russia, he was to visit him.[26]

When Cody acted as scout for Sheridan and his hunting party back in September 1871, James Gordon Bennett Jr., editor of the *New York Herald*, and some of the other eastern dignitaries had invited him to visit New York City. Sheridan was pleased with Cody's arrangement of the grand duke's buffalo hunt. Before he left, he told Cody he should take Bennett and the other businessmen's offer. Sheridan would see to it Cody received a thirty-day leave of absence with pay and told him who to contact for a railroad pass.[27]

General Edward Ord, commander of the Department of the Platte, told Cody he and General Sheridan wanted him to apply for an army officer's commission and they would support him. Cody thanked him but turned down the offer; he liked his life just the way it was. Ord told Cody if he ever changed his mind, they would support him.[28]

Cody contacted Bennett saying he would like to take him up on his offer and travel to New York City. Bennett sent Cody $500 for expenses, and after he received his railroad passes, he headed east in early February 1872.[29]

Cody stopped in Chicago for a few days and stayed at General Sheridan's house. The general and his brother Mike showed Cody the sights of Chicago. They introduced him to many people, and he was wined and dined. General Sheridan took Cody to a ball in the Chicago suburb of Riverside. He was unaccustomed to being stared at and asked hundreds of questions. He said, "I became so embarrassed that it was more difficult for me to face the throng of beautiful ladies, than it would have been to confront a hundred hostile Indians."[30]

It was time for Cody to leave Chicago. His route was to take him to Buffalo, New York, visit Niagara Falls, continue to Rochester, then to New York City. Fortunately, Cody ran into Professor Henry Ward who lived in Rochester. The year before, Cody assisted Ward in collecting wild animal specimens, and Ward now offered to guide Cody. They spent a day viewing Niagara Falls and a day touring Rochester including dining with the mayor.[31]

When Cody detrained in New York City, J. G. Heckscher met him on the platform. Heckscher had been a member of Sheridan's buffalo hunt. Heckscher escorted Cody to the Union Club where James Bennett, Leonard Jerome, and other buffalo hunt members held a reception for him. They told him while he was in New York he was welcome to stay at the Union Club and use it as his headquarters.[32]

After dinner, Cody wanted to find Ned Buntline, and Heckscher assisted him in tracking down the novelist who was at the Brevoort Place Hotel. Buntline was happy to see Cody, insisting he stay with him. The hotel owners wanted Cody to stay with them. Cody said, "I finally compromised the matter by agreeing to divide my time between the Union Club, the Brevoort House, and Ned Buntline's quarters."[33]

Cody spent the next few days touring New York City. He said he had so many invitations to dinner as well as "different places of amusement and interest" that he "became badly demoralized and confused." He claimed on one day he had accepted six invitations to dine at the same time.[34]

One of those invitations, the most important, was from James Bennett, who planned a dinner in Cody's honor, inviting a large number of friends to attend. Cody claimed, "I forgot all about it, and dined elsewhere." The next day, Leonard Jerome confronted Cody at the Union Club, stating they had waited for him until 9:00 p.m. and there was "considerable disappointment" he did not show for his own reception. Jerome wanted to know what had happened. Cody said, "I apologized as well as I could, by saying that I had been out on a scout and had got lost, and had forgotten all about the dinner; and expressed my regret for the disappointment I had created by my forgetfulness."[35]

However, the *Chicago Tribune*'s February 24, 1872 Saturday edition published a story of what probably happened to Cody. It was submitted by "Our Special Correspondence, New York, February 19," and at the end was the name "Harold." Among the stories concerning the goings on in New York City was a section titled "Buffalo Bill."

This mighty hunter of yours, and prairie guide, has been in the city for a week or two. He has come on to visit his friends, the New York bloods, who, when hunting the bounding buffalo under his leadership, always asked him to "come and see us in the city." He has accepted the invitation, and the only one of all his friends who really "does him honor" is Ned Buntline. To be sure, Jim Bennett did make up a little dinner-party for him, the other night, and invited Larry Jerome and a few others, whom "Buffalo Bill" had taught to shoot; but Bill wasn't there when the guests assembled. The fact is, some of "the boys," learning that a dinner was to come off, took "Buffalo Bill" out to see "the sights." Their idea was to get him drunk, but for a long time, he defeated them by sticking to "whiskey straight." After they had seen him drink a couple of barrels of this they concluded that whiskey wouldn't fetch him; so they introduced him to a few ballet-girls, and they introduced champagne to him. This did the business. Before the third basket was finished "Buffalo Bill" was laid out. Carbonic acid gas, flavored with Jersey cider, was too much for the mighty hunter and so he was carefully put in his little bed, where he "slept till morn." Meantime Jim Bennett, and Larry Jerome, and the other fellows, tired of waiting for the "rip-roaring guide of the pe-raries," ate Delmonico's dinner by themselves and drowned their disappointment in Widow Cliquot [sic].[36]

What might have been going on here? Is it possible Ned Buntline got Cody drunk and maybe even wrote the *Chicago Tribune* story? Buntline was obsessed with Cody and most likely didn't want to share him with anyone. Note above that "Harold" wrote Buntline was the only friend who truly honored Cody.

Buntline and the Bennett family were not on good terms. Bennett's father had been the editor of the *New York Herald* years earlier when Buntline had gotten into some trouble and the *Herald* had covered the story in detail. Buntline retaliated against the Bennett family.

In 1849, Buntline had printed an article referring to Kate Hastings, a high-class prostitute, as an "infamous cast-off mistress" and "strumpet" keeping "a low house of prostitution." Hastings encountered Buntline on the street and told him the next time she saw him she would cowhide him. Five days later, she saw him on the street and whipped him twice on the head. Buntline had her arrested. Bennett's *Herald* covered the story extensively. Buntline swore revenge on the Bennetts telling his assistant Thomas Paterson, "I will rip up the character of the whore of a sister of that cockeyed villain Bennett next week." He did just that, printing a story that Miss Georgina C. Crean, Bennett's sister-in-law, had been seen in various houses of "ill-fame" as a prostitute. Buntline was arrested for libel, but the case became overshadowed when Buntline was arrested on May 11, 1849, on suspicion of starting a riot.[37]

It's quite likely Buntline was "some of 'the boys'" who made sure Cody would never make Bennett's dinner. Buntline could have been the author of the story in the *Chicago Tribune*. He was known to write under various pen names and it's interesting the pen name used for the story was "Harold" and the name of Bennett's newspaper was *Herald*. Cody had no idea what he had stepped into. Bennett forgave Cody, and invited him to more dinner parties.

On the evening of February 15, 1872, Bennett took Cody to the Liederkranz masked ball. The ball was an annual affair held at

New York City's Academy of Music. Cody had brought along his buckskin suit and Bennett convinced him to wear it.[38]

It was a gala affair and all of New York's upper society attended. Two rival orchestras performed and before the stage curtain rose, a variety of tunes were played: polkas, waltzes, galops, and quadrilles. The Liederkranzers were in a festive mood. When the curtain was raised at 11:00 p.m., a procession moved across the stage. The parade was led by several men in Yankee costumes. "After them rambled a cortége of Russian bears, with a huge snowball in tow, out of which emerged a perfect likeness of the Grand Duke Alexis. This proved to be Prince Carnival, and a right merry potentate he was. He was quickly surrounded by bayaderes and bewitching representatives of La Folie and conducted to his throne," the *New York Herald* reported. The parade continued with an elephant followed by a lion, domestic animals, and monkeys.[39]

The *Herald* said, "there were dresses splendid, but fantastical; Masks of all times and nations. . . . and harlequins and clowns with feats gymnastical. . . ." People danced and danced. Cody said he danced and "exhibited some of my backwoods steps." He was the only individual singled out by the *Herald*: "Even the scout of the Plains, Buffalo Bill, came from the land of the buffalo and redskin to see for himself the difference between an Indian pow-wow and a genuine masquerade."[40]

The *Herald* continued, "As the morning hours advance, the scene becomes more brilliant and the enjoyment free and unrestrained is the rule. The Liederkranz ball of '72 is now over, and a more thoroughly enjoyable affair has never been given to any society on the oft-trodden boards of the Academy."[41]

While Cody had been leading the grand duke and his party across the prairie hunting buffalo, his reputation was increasing in the East due to Ned Buntline's *Buffalo Bill, the King of the Border Men*. One of New York City's prominent playwrights, Fred G. Maeder, collaborated with Buntline to adopt his series into a play called *Buffalo Bill*. Maeder hired a well-known melodrama actor, J. B. Studley, to play Buffalo Bill, and the popular Millie Sackett played Kitty

Muldoon, Buffalo Bill's love interest. Performances would be held at the Bowery Theatre, located in an entertainment and working-class neighborhood. Established in 1826, it was one of the largest theaters in America and could hold three thousand people.[42]

Buntline must have informed Cody when he arrived in the city about the play's production. An advertisement in the *New York Daily Herald* on the day of its opening stated, "Wm. F. Cody (Buffalo Bill) . . . has been present at many of the rehearsals."[43]

February 20, 1872, opening night, Buntline and Maeder took Cody to the Bowery Theatre where a box was reserved for them. The theater was filled to capacity "from pit to gallery." The reviewer for the *New York Daily Herald* wrote, "When the real Buffalo Bill was recognized upon his entrance the audience rose *en masse* and greeted him with an ovation such as actors at the more aristocratic theatres never received."[44]

The four-act play was filled with action. The reviewer was impressed: "this soul-stirring melodrama is truly amazing—hair-breath escapes, burning prairies, trappers' last shots, Indian war dances, guerilla raids, &c., follow each other with startling rapidity sufficient to meet the desires of the most ardent lover of the ultra-sensational. There is a peculiarity about Bowery audiences—they detest anything that approaches the sentimental, and only recognize as glorious that which is terrific and terrible."[45]

The reviewer predicted, "of the future success of this drama there cannot be the faintest shadow of a doubt." *Buffalo Bill* ran for four weeks with Studley continuing to play the part of Buffalo Bill and then William Walley succeeded him for two performances until March 20, when *Ten Nights in a Bar-room* began to run.[46]

Cody had been in New York City for about twenty days when General Sheridan arrived, and Cody went to meet with him. Sheridan asked Cody if he was enjoying himself. Cody replied he "had struck the best camp" he had ever seen, then asked for a ten-day extension to his leave of absence. Sheridan said yes, but his services would be needed back at Fort McPherson as an expedition would soon be heading out.[47]

Cody had relatives in West Chester outside Philadelphia, Pennsylvania, who he wanted to visit. When Buntline heard about it, he insisted on going along. They took a train to Philadelphia and then to West Chester where he visited relatives on his mother's side of the family. They wanted him to stay, but he had to return to New York City to finish up with some business. He promised to return and spend time with them, which he later did on his return West.[48]

While in Philadelphia, Buntline took Cody to a play its playwright had invited Cody to see, then Buntline took him to a fraternal order he had organized, the Commandry Degree of the Patriotic Order of Sons of America.[49]

On Saturday, February 24, a reporter for the *Philadelphia Public Record* interviewed Cody about the grand duke's buffalo hunt and was impressed with him, writing, "From the wild cognomen, 'Buffalo Bill,' it has been the impression of many persons that he was a sort of semi-barbarian, or a regular border ruffian. On the contrary Mr. Cody is a fine specimen of a well-bred, bright-minded western pioneer."[50]

By the time Cody was heading west, Buntline was working on a second fictional account titled *Buffalo Bill's Best Shot; or, The Heart of Spotted Tail*, which started in the *New York Weekly* on March 25, 1872. Buntline would follow that with another serial story starting on July 8, titled *Buffalo Bill's Last Victory; or, Dove Eye, the Lodge Queen*.

Meanwhile, back at Fort McPherson, Cody reunited with Louisa and their two children before again heading out to scout for the Army. The Fifth Cavalry, which had been stationed in Arizona, had been replaced by the Third Cavalry with Colonel Joseph Reynolds in command.[51]

On April 24, 1872, an Indian raiding party attacked the Union Pacific Railroad's McPherson Station about five miles to the north of the fort, stealing seven horses.[52]

The next day, after experiencing exasperating delays with their supply wagon and issuing five days' rations, Captain Charles

Meinhold, frontier army and Civil War veteran, and First Lieutenant Joseph Lawson led forty-seven members of the Third Cavalry's Company B after the raiders. Buffalo Bill Cody and Texas Jack Omohundro scouted for the company. For two days, they followed the raiders' trail northwest into the Sand Hills to the South Fork of Nebraska's Loup River where the raiders' trail showed they were scattering.[53]

Meinhold let the men rest and horses graze for two hours. He sent Sergeant John Foley, leading ten men and Cody as scout, upriver on the south side of the Loup. Meinhold later followed with the rest of the company on the north side. Eleven miles upriver, Cody discovered a raider camp and horse herd. He and Foley's men were about a mile in advance of Meinhold and the rest of the command. Cody led Foley's men to within fifty yards of the camp before the raiders spotted them.[54]

Thirteen raiders were in the camp. They put up a fight, firing at the troops and then leaped on their horses. Cody, mounted on Buckskin Joe, jumped an intervening creek and raced toward the raiders. The cavalry horses balked at crossing the creek. Two mounted warriors rode close to Cody and shot at him. He returned fire and saw one man fall from his horse. Cody felt a trickle of wetness on his forehead and, touching it, realized it was blood from a head wound. The second warrior, who was about ten yards away, wheeled his horse around and began to run. Racing alongside the warrior, Cody fired a bullet into his head, killing him. By then, Foley's troops had dismounted and crossed the creek on foot. Meinhold had heard the shots and arrived on scene with the rest of the troops as the raiders fled. Meinhold's troops had killed two warriors who were fleeing from Cody and Foley's attack.[55]

Cody spied six mounted raiders leading two horses racing downstream. They were about two miles away, when Meinhold sent Lieutenant Lawson leading fifteen troopers with Cody to pursue them. At first Lawson's men gained on the raiders. The two lead horses were slowing them down, so they released them and kept well ahead of the troops. After a twelve-mile chase, the cavalry horses gave out and the raiders made their escape. Cody had killed one of the three dead raiders, and the troops recaptured much of the stolen livestock. Cody believed the raiders were Miniconjou Lakotas based on their moccasins and arrows. Three horses were recaptured and restored to their rightful owners.[56]

Captain Meinhold wrote in his report, "Mr. Cody's reputation for bravery and skill as a guide is so well established that I need not say anything else than but he acted in his usual manner." Based on Buffalo Bill Cody's actions recorded in Meinhold's report, he was awarded the Medal of Honor on May 22, 1872. However, in 1916, after a review of the records, Congress removed Cody's award on June 16, 1916 "on the ground that at the time of the act of gallantry he was neither an officer nor an enlisted man, being at that time a civilian." In 1989, that decision was reversed, and the Medal of Honor was restored to Buffalo Bill Cody.[57]

During the summer of 1872, Cody was on several scouts, one of which was for thirty days with Captain Alexander Moore leading a Third Cavalry detachment. Another was with Captain James Curtis who led fifty men of Company I of the Third Cavalry in further pursuit of the Indians who had stolen livestock from McPherson Station back in April. They left Fort McPherson on June 5, following the trail north to Fort Randall on the Missouri River in Dakota Territory. They ran out of rations and for fifteen days lived off game they killed. On July 21, they returned to Fort McPherson, after a march of 496 miles.[58]

August 15, 1872 was a special day for the Cody family. At 3:00 p.m., Buffalo Bill and Louisa welcomed their third child, a girl they named Orra Maude.[59]

That fall, the Earl of Dunraven and three friends were back to hunt. They were escorted by a detachment of the Third Cavalry led by Captain Anson Mills, and Cody was their guide. It was mid-November and after several weeks of hunting, a party of General Sheridan's friends arrived with a letter from him requesting Cody also guide them on a hunting trip. The earl was not quite finished with his hunt. Cody explained the situation to him and got Texas

Jack to guide him for the rest of the hunt. Cody later wrote, "The Earl seemed somewhat offended at this, and I don't think he has ever forgiven me for 'going back on him.' Let that be as it may, he found Texas Jack a splendid hunter and guide, and Jack has been his guide on several hunts since."[60]

It was mid-November when the Chicago hunting party arrived at Fort McPherson. The members were Alexander Sample, Thomas Burton, William Milligan of the firm Heath & Milligan and who was a noted Chicago hunting sportsman, and Elijah P. "George" Greene of New York, the son-in-law of the rifle manufacturer Philo Remington. Milligan was enthusiastic and Cody said he was "boiling over with fun." Milligan was spoiling for a fight with Indians.[61]

A Third Cavalry company commanded by Captain Gerald Russell escorted the hunters. They were encamped along Nebraska's Dismal River. One day, Cody, Sample, and Milligan were five to six miles from camp when they spotted thirty mounted Indians. Milligan was concerned saying they should return to camp. Cody knew the Indians were distant enough they could make it to camp in plenty of time if the Indians decided to come after them, so he decided to have a little fun with Milligan and delayed their return, and Sample played along. Milligan became nervous, saying, "It's all very fine for you fellows to stand here and talk, but I am not doing justice to my family by remaining. Sample, I think we are a couple of old fools to have come out here, and I never would have done so if it had not been for you."[62]

By now the Indians had spotted them, and Cody decided to return to camp. He informed Captain Russell of the Indians, and Russell took the company out to pursue them. Cody, Sample, and Milligan rode along. "Now, Alek, let them come on," Milligan said to Sample. "We may yet go back to Chicago covered with glory." Cody found the Indians' trail and they followed it north, but their purpose was to hunt game, and they soon returned to camp. When the hunt was over, the businessmen invited Cody to visit Chicago and they would take care of him.[63]

Cody guided another party of buffalo hunters from Omaha: Judge Dundy, Colonel Watson Smith, and US District Attorney Neville. Cody was amused by Neville, who wore a stove-pipe hat and a long, swallow-tail coat. He was not much of a rider, holding on to the saddle's pommel while bouncing in his seat. The hunters heard Cody could lasso a buffalo and asked to see it done. He picked out an old bull, lassoed him, and then tied him to a tree. He then captured a few more this way. When the hunt was over, the Omaha hunters left pleased.[64]

The Democrats held a convention in Grand Island, Nebraska, where some of Cody's friends put his name on the ballot to run for a seat in the state legislature, representing the Twenty-Sixth District. Cody believed he didn't stand a chance since he was a Democrat, and his district was heavily Republican. However, he won with a vote of 407 to 363. Since he was an elected legislator, he was entitled to the title "Honorable," which he used the rest of his life.[65]

Throughout the summer and into the fall of 1872, Ned Buntline had been writing Cody asking him to come to Chicago and perform his part in the play *Buffalo Bill*. Cody responded he was not good on stage; it would be a complete failure. Buntline wouldn't take no for an answer. When Cody talked about performing onstage to family and friends, they laughed at the idea.[66]

Buntline tried a different approach, saying why not experiment with acting for a few months? If Cody failed or didn't like it, he could always return to his old job. Louisa wanted to visit her family in St. Louis, so Cody decided to give it a try. He told Colonel Reynolds his plan. Reynolds tried to convince Cody to stay. He had a nice house, and he was making a good living for his family, whereas earning money as an actor was an uncertain venture. However, Cody had set his mind to it and there was no turning back.[67]

Texas Jack Omohundro wanted to go along with Cody. Since Buntline used Texas Jack in one of his stories, Cody thought it would be a good idea for him to come along. The Army paid off

Cody on November 30, and in December, he and his family, along with Texas Jack, boarded an eastbound train for Omaha where Cody parted from Louisa and the children heading to St. Louis, and he and Texas Jack heading to Chicago.[68]

Louisa later wrote about Buffalo Bill and Texas Jack, "Neither of them ever had seen more than a dozen stage plays in their lives. They had no idea how to make an entrance or an exit, they did not know a cue from a footlight, and they believed plays just happened. The fact that they would have to study and memorize parts never entered their heads."[69]

After the Abilene City Council discharged Wild Bill Hickok from his duties as city marshal, he left town by early January 1872 and may have headed to Kansas City. The name Wild Bill was mentioned in two newspapers, but no last name was given. The January 19, 1872 edition of the *Kansas City Times* had a snippet, "Wild Bill distinguished himself in the parquette [*sic*] of the Opera House last night." A popular comedian, Joe Murphy, played to a "fine house," which included impersonations. "Murphy got off some fine local hits, which delighted the people and kept them in a constant state of laughter." There was no mention if Wild Bill was one of his subjects.[70]

The second reference to Wild Bill is in the January 31, 1872 issue of the *Saint Joseph Daily Gazette*. Two Kansas City editors, Charles Whitehead and Frank Grice, were feuding. An intoxicated Whitehead began searching Grice's Kansas City haunts to confront him. "He went to the Walnut Street Theatre, where he had some words with 'Wild Bill,'" then continued on his search until he found Grice who during a scuffle shot Whitehead in the butt with a derringer.[71]

There is another possibility to Hickok's whereabouts. The January 18, 1872 issue of the Saline County, Kansas, *Weekly Journal*, which was no fan of Hickok, said he was in Boston, Massachusetts, where "the credulous New Englanders have an opportunity to interview in person the man who has shot men down in cold blood by the scores and is as big a criminal as walks the earth."[72] There is no other reference to Hickok's appearance in Boston.

By March 1872, Hickok was staying at a boardinghouse in the mining town of Georgetown, Colorado. His good friend Colorado Charlie Utter was the boardinghouse owner. Hickok spent between six to eight weeks in Georgetown playing poker. A. D. McCanles, a relative of the Rock Creek Station David McCanles, wrote about Hickok's stay in Georgetown, "He was very pleasant, and agreeable, and never had any trouble while there." That spring, Hickok returned to Kansas City where he may have stayed with his friend Dr. Joshua Thorne.[73]

J. W. Buel, who would later write about Hickok, said he became good friends with him when he worked as a *Kansas City Journal* reporter. Buel said Kansas City was "bustling with sports and excitements well suited to his [Hickok's] disposition." Buel wrote, "Kansas City was a brisk town in 1872 . . . and was the parent block off which was chipped all the gambling towns along the Kansas Pacific railroad. Games of chance, cards, keno, faro, roulette, dice, cock-mains, dog fighting and kindred means for hazarding money ran day and night." Buel recalled it was a violent time in Kansas City but Hickok was able to remain out of trouble.[74]

Earlier in 1872, Sidney Barnett, a Canadian Niagara Falls promoter and museum owner, began organizing a Fourth of July mock buffalo hunt at Niagara Falls. His initial efforts to obtain buffalo and Pawnees met delays and federal government roadblocks, so he rescheduled the show later in the summer. Most likely in June 1872, Barnett visited Indian Territory obtaining a small number of buffalo and hiring Sac and Fox Indians and Mexican cowboys to put on the buffalo hunt. In Kansas City, Barnett met Wild Bill Hickok, who he hired to manage the show.[75]

The Niagara Falls buffalo hunt performance took place on August 28 and 30, 1872, on an eighty-acre enclosure near the falls on the Canadian side. The attendance was not as high as

Barnett had hoped and reviews were mixed. There were those who enjoyed the show and others who thought it was too tame. Wild Bill Hickok was the master of ceremonies. The Mexican cowboys chased after and roped Texas steers. The Indians raced their horses alongside the four buffalo while shooting blunt arrows at them. Two newspaper accounts reported many of the arrows landed among the spectators.[76]

Things got out of hand. The *New York Herald* reported, "At five o'clock the hunt was abruptly closed on account of a few roughs having broken down the fences and rushing pellmell [*sic*] into the arena where the hunt was being conducted. Fearing that the animals would become unmanageable, and being unable to drive the crowd back, the buffaloes were captured and safely housed."[77]

The *Buffalo Commercial* was not impressed with the performance but was complimentary of Hickok saying, "Mr. HICKOX [*sic*] is a handsome fellow, dressed in buckskin and mounted on an excellent horse. He did all in his power to make the hunt a success, and the poor quality of the entertainment is not to be attributed to him."[78]

The *Niagara Falls Gazette* was pleased saying, "the whole show was such as every person would like to see." Sidney Barnett's expenses exceeded the money he took in and he never recovered from the loss.[79]

Wild Bill Hickok returned to Kansas City. Buel related a story that on September 17, 1872, Hickok and a friend entered the bar and billiard parlor of the upscale St. Nicholas Hotel where they sat at a table near a billiard game. Four intoxicated men recognized Hickok and walked up to his table where one of them insulted Hickok who allegedly said, "See here, young man, I'll lift you with the toe of my boot if you don't get away from here in five seconds." The man pulled back his coat revealing the butt of a pistol and called Hickok "every vile name that a wicked native was capable of uttering." Hickok tried to defuse the situation, which only emboldened the man. Hickok rose from his seat, gripped the man's shoulder, and punched his head. He grabbed one of the man's ears and continued to punch him in the face until he howled for mercy. The man left the room crying followed by his three friends. Hickok apologized to the others in the room, but everyone said he was justified in his actions.[80]

From September 23 through 28, 1872, Kansas City was holding its Industrial Exposition and Agricultural Fair with an attendance of up to sixty thousand people a day, twice the city's population. The exposition exhibited the latest in machinery, fine art, floral displays, contests, and races.[81] There were awards for the best cattle, swine, fruits, grains, and minerals.[82]

Late on Thursday afternoon, September 26, two mounted men stole the cash box from the ticket booth and made off with $978. The robbers were never apprehended, but many believed it was Jesse James and one of the Younger brothers.[83]

The following day, Hickok joined the crowd at the exposition. Topeka's *Daily Commonwealth* reported, "Wild Bill made a big point at the fair grounds. A number of Texans prevailed upon the band to play Dixie, and then the Texans made demonstrations with the flourishing of pistols. Wild Bill stepped forward and stopped the music, and more than fifty pistols were presented at William's head, but he came away unscathed."[84]

For the rest of autumn 1872, Hickok spent most of his time in Topeka.[85] There was a controversy that a Wild Bill and his outfit shot and killed three Oglala Lakota leaders, Whistler, Fat Badger, and Hand Smeller, along Nebraska's Republican River. Whistler had been one of the Lakota leaders who had participated in the Grand Duke Alexis buffalo hunt. The Army was concerned the murders could trigger further violence.[86]

Samuel Gast of Harlan County, Nebraska, was buffalo hunting on December 3, 1872. Gast was looking for water when he came upon the camp of two wolf hunters. The men tried to direct him in a different direction from where he was headed. He didn't follow their directions but rode to where they did not want him to go. After a half-mile, he discovered three Indian bodies later determined to be Whistler and the other two Oglala leaders.[87]

Gast saw one of the men watching him from a high bluff. In his deposition, Gast said he believed one of the men was Jack Ralston who belonged to "Wild Bill's Outfit." Gast went on saying, "a gentleman by the name of E. A. Cress took a rifle from their [the Oglalas'] bodies."[88]

Mortimer Kress lived on Nebraska's Little Blue River in Little Blue Township, and was called "Wild Bill of the Blue" Kress. He had an associate, Jack Ralston, and there were those who believed those two killed the three Oglalas. Luther North believed Newt Moreland killed Whistler and the others, writing, "John Williamson . . . said when he was camped at Plum Creek that Moreland came to his camp. He was riding a spotted pony which was recognized as Whistler's and he told John that he had killed Whistler, Fat Badger, and another Indian."[89]

It was never settled in a court of law who killed the three Oglalas. Hickok was not in the area at the time of the murders; he was living and gambling in eastern Kansas towns. There were many Wild Bills on the frontier, but Wild Bill Hickok was not involved in the murders of the Oglalas.

CHAPTER 13

THE WILD EAST
(NOVEMBER 1872–MARCH 1874)

Buffalo Bill Cody and his family, along with Texas Jack Omohundro, arrived in Omaha on December 4, 1872. The *Omaha Bee*'s December 5 edition recorded, "Hon. W. F. Cody, otherwise known as 'Buffalo Bill,' member elect of the legislature, arrived in the city yesterday from the west. Last evening, he was given an elegant supper at Wurth's restaurant, by the United States officers, whom he took on a buffalo hunt some weeks ago. He is stopping at the Metropolitan Hotel, and as usual, owing to his reputation as a scout and a hunter, is the object of considerable curiosity and admiration."[1]

Cody and Omohundro arrived in Chicago on Thursday, December 12. Cody had sent telegrams to Ned Buntline and William Milligan, and those two met the scouts at the train station. Milligan took them to the Sherman House, one of Chicago's premier hotels where the scouts would be his guests while in the city.[2]

Buntline did not stay long; he was scheduled to give a temperance lecture that evening. As soon as he had received Cody's telegram, he did not waste time in advertising the play. The same day Cody and Texas Jack arrived, the *Chicago Evening Mail*, referring to Nixon's Amphitheatre, stated, "For the next week the bills announce 'the Sioux and Pawnee chiefs,' in Ned Buntline's 'Buffalo Bill.'"[3]

However, the original *Buffalo Bill* was still being produced. The *New York Times* November 10, 1872 edition advertised "Maeder's celebrated drama of *Buffalo Bill*" would play at Wood's Museum.[4] The troupe moved on to Buffalo, New York, where it played at the Academy of Music. The November 19 *Buffalo Commercial Advertiser* gave its "blood and thunder" performance a positive review praising J. B. Studley in his role of Buffalo Bill.[5]

At least one other troupe performed the play. The December 12, 1872 edition of Kansas City's *Wyandott Herald* said, "Lord's Dramatic Troupe will give an entertainment at Dunning's Hall this evening. They present Fred. C. Maeder's drama of Ned Buntlines [*sic*] in the New York Weekly entitled Buffalo Bill. . . . If our exchanges are to be relied on this troupe is one of the best in the country, and the popular drama of 'Buffalo Bill' should be attended by all."[6] Buntline's new production had competition.

Friday, December 13, the day after Cody and Omohundro's arrival in Chicago, they met with Ned Buntline, who took them to meet James Nixon, the manager and owner of Nixon's Parisian Hippodrome and Chicago Amphitheatre. Nixon's Amphitheatre was huge, capable of seating twenty-five hundred people. The building, circular in shape with a canvas top, was lighted by gas and well ventilated. Ten tiers of seats descended to a circular stage in the middle.[7]

Buntline and Nixon had arranged to split production costs. Buntline was providing the play, the actors, and pictorial printing, receiving 60 percent of the profits. Nixon would furnish the building, orchestra, staff, and local printing, receiving 40 percent. Buntline planned that the first performance would be Monday, December 18. Nixon told Buntline he was ready and asked if he had his actors lined up. Buntline said no. Nixon said he would help find actors and asked to see the script. Buntline responded he hadn't written it yet.[8]

"What the deuce do you mean?" Nixon replied. "This is Wednesday [actually Friday] and you propose to open on next Monday night. The idea is ridiculous. Here you are at this late hour without a company and without a drama." Buntline replied he could write the script in a day, find actors, and have them at the theater for practice the next morning. Nixon laughed saying he wanted nothing to do with it. Buntline asked how much to rent the amphitheater for the week and Nixon replied $600. Buntline gave him $300 in advance and Nixon said nothing after that.[9]

Buntline and his two would-be actors returned to the hotel, where Buntline went to his room and started writing. At the end of four hours he was finished, shouting "Hurrah for 'The Scouts of the Plains!' That's the name of the play. The work is done. Hurrah!" He hired clerks who were busy copying the parts for each actor. Buntline told Cody and Texas Jack to memorize their parts for rehearsal to be held at 10:00 a.m. the next day at the amphitheater. "I want to show Nixon that we'll be ready on time," Buntline proclaimed.[10]

Cody later remembered, "I looked at my part and then at Jack; and Jack looked at his part and then at me. Then we looked at each other, and then at Buntline. We did not know what to make of the man." Cody and Texas Jack returned to their room with their lines. Cody thought it would take him six months to learn his part. Texas Jack responded, "It will take me about that length of time to learn the first line." They began studying, then ordered "refreshments." After studying for another hour or two, they gave up after memorizing a few lines.[11]

Buntline came to their room and asked, "Boys, how are you getting along?" Cody told him they weren't any good at studying their lines. Buntline had them recite what they had learned, but he quickly interrupted saying, "Tut! Tut! You're not saying it right. You must stop at the cue." Of course, Cody responded the only cue he knew was found in a billiard room. Cody and Texas Jack wanted out. They wanted to head back to the prairie, but Buntline told them that would not do, and they needed to stick with it, saying, "It may be the turning point in your lives and lead you on to fortune and to fame." They agreed to stick it out for now, but after Buntline left their room, they didn't do any more studying.[12]

The first rehearsal was Saturday morning at 10:00 a.m. However, instead of spending their time learning their lines, Cody and Texas Jack may have been helping the Chicago police. The Saturday December 14 edition of the *Chicago Tribune* related, "The two bears in Lincoln Park are to be attached for debt. Captain Harry Faith claims that Captain Mat. Boardman owes him $122, and that Boardman owns the animals. Justice Scully issued the necessary writ yesterday, but constable Slavin declined to serve it, as his life is not insured. Constable Slavin, after consulting with 'Buffalo Bill' and 'Texas Jack,' who are staying at the Barnes House, consented to capture the bears and bring them before Scully. The three will start for Lincoln Park this morning."[13] Unfortunately, there is no additional information on the capture of the bears.

Cody and Omohundro made it to rehearsal, but Cody said it was hardly a success. The stage manager helped them the best he could during all the rehearsals up until showtime.[14]

The Saturday December 14 edition of the *Chicago Evening Post* mentioned the show: "If you ask me whence these stories, whence these legends and traditions, I will answer that Ned Buntline has found them on the prairies, and mixed them up with an ocean of blood and a firmament of thunder has given them to the world." Further on the writer stated, "Truly in the language of the play bill the performance must be seen, for it cannot be described. Buffalo Bill, Texas Jack, and Cale Durg, the real heroes, will themselves appear, shoulder their rifles, and show how scalps are won."[15]

An advertisement in that day's edition of the *Chicago Tribune* proclaimed Nixon's Amphitheatre would present, "The Real BUFFALO BILL, TEXAS JACK and TEN SIOUX AND PAWNEE CHIEFS in Ned Buntline's great drama 'BUFFALO BILL.'" However, this was false advertising. There were no chiefs; there were no Pawnees and no Sioux. Buntline hired over forty supernumeraries or extras to play Indians. They were all white actors made to look like Indians, wearing tan frocks and flannel on their heads to resemble hair.[16]

The Sunday December 15 edition of the *Chicago Tribune* had an expanded advertisement for "The Scouts of the Prairie! And Red Deviltry as It Is." It promised much—"realistic pictures of LIFE ON THE PLAINS, and accurately depicting those vivid and thrilling scenes so brilliantly described by him [Ned Buntline] in his great Indian Stories. . . ." It listed the main personages: Buffalo Bill, Texas Jack, and Cale Durg. It would later be revealed Cale Durg was played by Buntline. The advertisement continued there would be "Indian Chiefs and Warriors, represented by the real heroes themselves. The management has the great pleasure in announcing the engagement of the great Star Danseuse, Pantomimist, and Actress, MORLACCHI! AS DOVE EYE, THE INDIAN MAIDEN." Mademoiselle Giuseppina Morlacchi was a popular Italian dancer and actress who had introduced America to the French dance, the cancan. The play would have it all from "prairie fires" to "desperate fights." And if this wasn't enough, "NOTICE—Every lady visiting the matinees will be presented with beautiful photographic cartes de visite of Buffalo Bill, Texas Jack, Ned Buntline, and Morlacchi." Now Buntline's troupe would have to produce.[17]

Scouts of the Prairie opened Monday evening, December 16, 1872, at 7:00 p.m. Nixon's Amphitheatre was packed. Texas Jack and Cody were extremely nervous.[18]

The play opened with Ned Buntline on stage, portraying trapper Cale Durg. In his opening monologue he was telling the audience that Indians had stolen his traps. A *Chicago Inter Ocean* reviewer reported what happened next: "Just as Durg had clapped the butt of his rifle on the stage with a terrible thump, a half-tipsy fellow from the upper row stumbles on the stage. Possibly with the best intentions, he pulls a bottle of whisky from his pocket and presents it to Buntline. It was the poor fellow's humble tribute of admiration—his way of throwing a bouquet. There was a moment of breathless suspense, and then the valiant Cale seized the offender by the neck and dashed him into the orchestra, smashing a half dozen footlights as he went." Buntline warned no one was to come on stage or they would receive the same treatment, as a policeman dragged away the "wildly protesting" admirer as the audience applauded.[19]

Continuing his monologue, Cale Durg wondered where his partners could be. That was Cody and Texas Jack's cue to enter on stage. Cody said, "We were rather slow in making our appearance. As we stepped forth we were received with a storm of applause, which we acknowledged with a bow." It would have been intimidating for anyone to step on a stage before a huge crowd that included General Sheridan and Chicago dignitaries.[20]

The *Chicago Inter Ocean* reviewer said, "Mr. William Buffalo came to the front, a tall, handsome-looking fellow, but looking, and evidently feeling, exceedingly ill at ease, and quite at a loss what to do with his hands."[21]

Buntline gave Cody his cue to speak, but Cody couldn't remember his lines. Buntline improvised saying, "Where have you been Bill? What has kept you so long?" Cody saw William Milligan sitting in the audience and said, "I have been out on a hunt with Milligan." It was a hit. The crowd cheered and applauded. Cody related about their hunt and the sighting of the Indian band. He became more comfortable as he told the tale, adding in a bit of humor. This gave Cody confidence to continue through the show ad-libbing instead of reciting his lines. From time to time, the audience broke in with applause.[22]

There was plenty of shooting, fights, romance, and even a long temperance lecture by Cale Durg while he was tied to the stake. There weren't enough "Indians" to die in all the scenes, so they had to be resurrected and brought back on stage to be killed again. Cody said, "Finally, the curtain dropped, the play was ended; and I congratulated Jack and myself on having made such a brilliant and successful *debut*. There was no backing out after that." The three-act play, lasting three hours, was a success; and the first night brought in $2,800. Everyone was happy, including amphitheatre owner James Nixon.[23]

Newspaper reviews were mixed. The *Chicago Evening Post* was typical: "'Scouts of the Prairie,' a realistic, blood-and-thunder, Indian war dance—rifle-banging drama filled Nixon's Amphitheatre with an immense crowd of dime novel students last evening. The effect was all that could be desired. The Indian tribes were decimated. Several white renegades paid the tribute of their crimes. Suffering maidens were rescued from vile danger. Scalps were universally lifted and oceans of gore were shed. 'Buffalo Bill,' 'Texas Jack,' and 'Ned Buntline' were among the celebrities who participated in the slaughter. The exercises will be repeated nightly during the week, by the end of which period everybody will have been slain or rescued."[24]

The *Chicago Evening Mail* proclaimed, "The management at this place [Nixon's Amphitheatre] have made a hit in the presentation of the red-hot sensation 'Scouts of the Prairie,' with real border men, at least as far as the box office is concerned. The large auditorium was packed, and the various sensations were received with uproarious applause," The newspaper was complimentary to Cody and Texas Jack's honest "rendition of their parts."[25]

Some Nebraskans were concerned Cody should not be in Chicago acting on stage but back in Nebraska representing his district in the legislature. The December 21, 1872 edition of the *Leavenworth Daily Commercial* reprinted an article from the *Omaha Republican's* December 18, 1872 edition titled "Buffalo Bill. A Nebraska Legislator Before Chicago Footlights. Humiliating Spectacle for His Constituents." The article opined, "We advise the constituents of this gentleman to send a deputation to him, reminding him that he is now Hon. W. F. Cody, member of the legislature of the State of Nebraska. We fear he is sadly offending against the dignity of the State, and unfitting himself for the grave and important duties of a legislator."[26] Whether a delegation talked to Cody or he decided on his own, on December 28, Iowa's *Sioux City Journal* announced, "Buffalo Bill (W. F. Cody) has resigned his seat in the [Nebraska] Legislature."[27]

After a prosperous week in Chicago, the *Scouts of the Prairie* troupe traveled to St. Louis for six days of performances, where Cody said they did "an immense business." Louisa went to the opening night at DeBar's Opera House, taking along six-year-old Arta. During the performance, Cody rushed on stage and after shooting several Indians, he turned to face the audience. There he saw Louisa with Arta on her lap, sitting in the third row. He walked to the front of the stage, leaned out over the footlights, and waved his arms as he shouted, "Oh, Mamma! I'm a bad actor!" and threw her a kiss. The house roared with laughter, and then learned Louisa was Cody's wife. Someone called to get her onstage so they could see her, and Cody agreed. Louisa and Arta were placed on straight-back chairs and lifted up onstage. Cody was laughing as his daughter and embarrassed wife stood there beside him with the audience loving every minute of it. Louisa said, after that, whenever she went to see his performances she would sit toward the back in the darkest area, but he would always spot her and shout, "Hello Momma. Oh, but I'm a bad actor!"[28]

On December 26, 1872, a more serious event hit the troupe— Ned Buntline was arrested in the Southern Hotel's lobby for skipping bail after being arrested for assault to kill and rioting back in 1852.[29] Buntline had moved to St. Louis in late 1851. He was one of the founders of the American Party, an anti-immigrant organization commonly known as the Know Nothing Party. German immigrants were becoming a political force in St. Louis. There were two Democrat candidates for governor, one proslavery and the other antislavery. The Germans were backing the antislavery candidate. Buntline planned to frame the Germans in a bad light and pull voters to the American Party candidate. April 5, 1852, the polls opened, and things became heated when Buntline poured oil on the fire. Riding a horse into a crowd, Buntline shouted anti-German remarks. The crowd swelled to an estimated five thousand people as Buntline led them toward the German neighborhood. Things got out of hand. Shots were fired. One club-wielding mob member began smashing in the door to a German-owned tavern where one of the shots might have come from. As a door panel caved in, someone inside fired a gun through the hole, killing the man. The mob set that building on fire as well as others owned by Germans. Homes and businesses were looted. When it was over, one man was dead, ten people severely wounded, and twenty-five more slightly wounded. Buntline was arrested as a riot instigator. Two friends put up $1,000 bail for him. Buntline left town; the trial was postponed until January 1853. Buntline failed to appear and his friends forfeited their bonds.[30]

Now, Buntline was taken before a judge, who after hearing the circumstances of the case, set the bonds at $500 for each of the two original cases. Two friends signed the bonds for him, and he was released and scheduled to appear at the January 1873 criminal court.[31]

The cases were continued several times until finally in July 1873 the bonds were declared forfeit. *The St. Louis Times* commented, "Buntline is supposed to be somewhere on the plains gathering materials for another play or novel, but nobody knows exactly where."[32]

Buntline had headed east instead of west. His troupe next performed before large audiences at Pike's Opera House in Cincinnati, Ohio, for six days starting Monday, December 31, 1872.[33] One of the actions during the show was a knife fight between two actors, Big Eagle and Wolf Slayer, portrayed by twenty-four-year-old William Halpin. During the Tuesday night performance, Halpin was accidently injured in the stomach during the knife fight. By Thursday, he could not perform. He grew worse, the doctors could do nothing for him, and he died at Cincinnati's St. James Hotel on Tuesday, January 7, 1873.[34]

Before Halpin died, the troupe had left for Louisville, Kentucky. Throughout January, February, and March, they played before packed audiences in twenty-five major cities in Indiana, Ohio, western Pennsylvania, New York, and New England. Cody said when they played at the Boston Theater, they grossed $16,200. During Buntline's spare time, he wrote a dime novel on Texas Jack and a serial about him for the *New York Weekly*, both released in March.[35]

Scouts of the Prairie played before enthusiastic, packed crowds in New York City and Brooklyn from March 31 through April 15. James Bennett's *New York Herald* tore apart the play in its April 1 edition. The reviewer wrote, "The real hero of the piece is Cale Durg, the part represented by Ned Buntline . . . [who] represents the part as badly as it is possible for any human being to represent it and the part is as bad as it was possible to make it." The reviewer blasted Buntline's temperance address as ludicrous. As for Cody and Texas Jack, he wrote, "The Hon. William F. Cody . . . is a good looking fellow, tall and straight as an arrow, but ridiculous as an actor. Texas Jack . . . is not quite so good-looking, not so tall, not so straight and not so ridiculous." The writer mentioned, "Buffalo Bill was called before the curtain at the end of the first act, when he made a speech that was neat and appropriate, as well as short." Summing up the show, the reviewer wrote, "To describe the play and its reception is alike impossible. The applause savored of derision, and the derision of applause. Everything was so wonderfully bad that it was almost good."[36]

The troupe spent the remainder of April performing before crowds in Trenton, New Jersey, Philadelphia, Pennsylvania, and Baltimore, Maryland. Cody was becoming more confident on stage. By the time they reached Washington, DC, Bessie Sudlow replaced Giuseppina Morlacchi. Attendance at the opening show at Wall's Opera House was disappointing, but after people heard multiple gunshots and war whoops coming from the theater, attendance skyrocketed.[37]

During the first part of May, the troupe played in Virginia and Delaware. By May 21, they were back in Philadelphia. Cody had brought his family along, but left them in New York City when the tour headed south. On May 22, he was in West Chester, Pennsylvania, visiting his relatives and decided it would be a good place to relocate his family. The *West Chester News* interviewed him reporting, "He has informed us he is about to take up his residence in West Chester, or rather he will locate his family here. He has rented a fine brick dwelling on Washington street, into which he proposes to move his family at once."[38]

On May 26, *Scouts of the Prairie* played in Lancaster, Pennsylvania, but Cody was missing due to Louisa being ill. Throughout the rest of May and into June, they performed in six more Pennsylvania cities and more than ten New York cities, ending the tour in Port Jervis, on June 28, 1873.[39]

Cody knew the show had been a success, saying, "There was not a single city where we did not have crowded houses." He learned a few lessons. People enjoyed seeing good marksmanship and costumed actors walking around town. He needed a competent manager to plan the tour route and line up theaters. Cody and Omohundro knew they could perform onstage again, but next time, it would be without Ned Buntline. No reason was given for the split and there seemed to be no animosity on either side. Possibly, Cody and Omohundro thought Buntline had been stingy in sharing the profits. Cody wrote in his autobiography, "when I counted up my share of the profits I found that I was only $6,000 ahead. I was somewhat disappointed, for, judging from our large business, I certainly had expected a greater sum."[40]

While in New York City, Cody met with Elijah P. "George" Greene, son-in-law of the rifle manufacturer Philo Remington. Greene had been one of the members of the Chicago hunting party the previous November. Greene asked Cody to guide his friends and him on a buffalo hunt that summer. Cody was happy to agree. Texas Jack was invited along as well as Greene's friends Eugene Overton and James Scott, "The Hatter," a well-known Chicago hat maker.[41]

They had a pleasant trip by rail on their way to Fort McPherson. On July 17, the hunting party stopped for the night in Omaha. Both Cody and Texas Jack had new Remington rifles that Philo Remington had given them. In contrast to Cody writing he had made only $6,000 while touring with Buntline, the *Omaha Bee* reported "Buffalo Bill, Texas Jack, and Ned Buntline each cleared $30,000 during the past eight months. Bill thinks this more remunerative than the honor of being a Nebraska legislator, while Texas Jack is of the opinion that financially it eclipses buffalo hunting and scouting." The *Bee* continued, "Both men are looking exceedingly well and sport considerable jewelry."[42]

They told the *Bee* their plan was to begin hunting buffalo July 20, and be out two weeks. At the end of the hunt, Cody said, "Texas Jack and I spent several weeks in hunting . . . at the end of our vacation we felt greatly re-invigorated and ready for another theatrical campaign."[43]

By August 4, Cody and Texas Jack were back in West Chester. Cody moved his family to Rochester, New York, where he bought a house. Meanwhile, Texas Jack Omohundro and Giuseppina Morlacchi, who had been in love since first meeting in Chicago, were married in Rochester's St. Mary's Roman Catholic Church on August 31, 1873.[44]

While Cody and Omohundro were buffalo hunting in western Nebraska, they must have been thinking about their next show. When they had stopped in Omaha, they mentioned future possibilities to the *Bee*: "Next fall Buffalo Bill and Texas Jack will appear in an equestrian drama, entitled 'Alexis in America,' the grand feature of which we suppose, will be the grand duke's buffalo hunt when he was in Nebraska."[45]

However, as Cody and Omohundro discussed what they would do, they moved away from that idea and decided to produce their own stage play. Giuseppina Morlacchi rejoined them in a starring role, and they hired her manager, "Major" John Burke, to help. Burke continued to be Morlacchi's manager while handling the troupe's publicity. Burke was also an actor and took a part in the cast as Arizona John.[46]

Cody hired Hiram Robbins to be the troupe's manager. Robbins was also tasked with writing a new play for Cody's troupe. In the meantime, Cody and his actors performed Fred Maeder's play

Buffalo Bill. Maeder revised the play for Cody, making it bigger and better; and Cody played himself as Buffalo Bill.[47]

Cody called his troupe the Buffalo Bill Combination. A combination was a group of actors who presented only one play, whereas a stock company was a group of actors who presented a variety of plays. Cody and Omohundro continued to be the main stars along with Giuseppina Morlacchi. Two cast members were the popular actor Frank Mordaunt and an actor who would stay with Cody for years, J. V. Arlington. Even Fred Maeder would get into the act as Old Vet, and his wife Rena, a popular actress, would play Kitty Muldoon.[48]

The Buffalo Bill Combination needed someone to take Ned Buntline's place on stage. Cody wrote, "Thinking that Wild Bill would be quite an acquisition to the troupe, we wrote him at Springfield, Missouri, offering him a large salary if he would play with us that winter."[49]

After leaving Topeka, Kansas, Wild Bill Hickok went to Springfield, Missouri, where he spent the first few months of 1873. Newspapers began publishing reports Hickok had been killed.[50]

The *Abilene Weekly Chronicle* noted on February 20, 1873, "It was stated that Wild Bill was murdered in Galveston, Texas, about two weeks ago, by some of Phil Cole's [*sic*] friends, who it will be remembered by our citizens, Bill shot in a fracas, while he was marshal of Abilene. Cole's friends vowed vengeance and finally accomplished it. So they go." Another account related revenging Texans killed Hickok at Fort Dodge, Kansas.[51]

Hickok had fun with his reported death. The March 11, 1873 *Kansas City Times* reported, "The celebrated 'Wild Bill' publishes this statement in the Springfield *Advertiser*: 'For the benefit of the Kansas City papers, I hereby acknowledge that I am dead.' Funny William! What a pity he lies in such a grave—way."[52]

On March 13, 1873, Hickok wrote from Springfield, Missouri, to St. Louis's *Missouri Democrat*:

TO THE EDITOR OF THE DEMOCRAT*:*
Wishing to correct an error in your paper of the 12th, I will
state that no Texan has, nor ever will "corral William." I wish
you to correct your statement on account of my people.
  Yours as ever.
  J. B. Hickok
  OR "Wild Bill."
  P.S. I have bought your paper in preference to all others,
since 1857.

The *Missouri Democrat* replied in print, "'Wild Bill,' or any other man killed by mistake in our columns, will be promptly resuscitated upon application by mail."[53]

In another letter to the *Missouri Democrat* and reprinted on April 11, 1873, by the Mendota, Illinois, *Bulletin*, Hickok continues his good-natured banter.

SPRINGFIELD, MO., March 26, 1873
I wish to call your attention to an article published in your
paper of the 19th in regard to my having been killed by Tex-
ans. You say when I was murdered it was fulfilling a prophesy
that all men of my kind should die with their boots on. Now I
would like to know the man that prophesies how men shall die,
or classes of men, so that the public may know who is right and
who is wrong. I never have insulted man or woman in my life
but if you knew what a wholesome regard I have for damn
liars and rascals they would be liable to keep out of my way.
  J. B. HICKOK, OR WILD BILL
  From LaSalle County, Ill.
  N. B. Ned Buntline of the New York Weekly has been try-
ing to murder me with his pen for years; having failed he is
now, so I am told, trying to have it done by some Texans, but
he has signally failed so far.[54]

Hickok's reference to Buntline trying to murder him with his pen was in reference to Buntline's dime novel *Buffalo Bill, The King of the Border Men* in which Wild Bill was portrayed as Buffalo Bill's sidekick. Buntline killed off Wild Bill in the story. After Wild Bill killed Dave Tutt, Tutt's lover, Ruby Blazes, stabbed Wild Bill in the heart.[55]

During the month of May, the Atlantic and Pacific Railroad invited financial and business dignitaries on an excursion from New York City to the West. They arrived in Springfield, Missouri, where a reception was held for them with the governor, state legislators, and prominent citizens as well as Wild Bill Hickok. Some of the delegation had a lengthy talk with Hickok and were impressed. A *New York Daily Herald* reporter traveling with the delegation wrote, "a splendid specimen of a man. He is tall, sinewy, lithe, graceful in his every movement: has a keen gray eye and steady hand. . . . He expresses himself as not at all pleased with the practice some scouts adopt of going to the Eastern cities to exhibit themselves as showmen. 'I want none of it,' exclaimed Bill. 'When they come to me I turn the deck head down and pass.' Bill is a true son of the West, a fearless fellow and one who is ever ready to help a friend with the same characteristic energy as he would 'get square' on an enemy."[56]

The front page of the June 24, 1873 *Galveston Daily News* displayed a private letter recounting how a Texan had hunted for Wild Bill Hickok and when he found him in a Salina, Kansas, saloon, he shot Hickok in the head, killing him. The unidentified writer ended his missive with, "As there have been several accounts published of this affair, and as most of them are erroneous, I thought I would write and tell you how Wild Bill passed in his checks."[57]

However, Wild Bill Hickok was still very much alive in Springfield that summer when he received a letter from Buffalo Bill Cody offering him a job to act on stage with the Buffalo Bill Combination. Hickok was apprehensive of audiences and told

Cody he had no confidence in his acting abilities; however, the large salary Cody offered enticed Hickok to New York City. It looked like Hickok would have to eat his words about being a showman in the East.[58]

Buffalo Bill Cody would be playing himself in Fred Maeder's *Buffalo Bill* at New York City's Bowery Theatre. It was advertised as different from the original with "Novel effects, Startling Tableaux, Thrilling Realistic Situations and a powerful cast." On August 28, 1873, Cody portrayed himself for the first time and thereafter through September 6, after which the Buffalo Bill Combination would take the play on the road.[59]

Cody told a story about Wild Bill Hickok's arrival in New York City. Cody had informed Hickok he was staying at the Metropolitan Hotel and Hickok should come there when he reached the city. Hickok arrived at night and, being unfamiliar with the city, hired a hack to take him to the hotel. When they arrived, Hickok asked the driver what he owed him.

"Five dollars, sir," the driver replied.

"And you wouldn't accept anything less, would you?" Hickok asked.

"No sir, that's the charge and nothing less."

Hickok handed the driver $5, then struck him in the face, knocking him in the gutter. A policeman arrived and hauled Hickok to jail. Cody learned of the incident, bailed Hickok out, and paid his $10 fine.[60]

Hickok was reluctant to perform, telling Cody they would never make an actor out of him. On Thursday, September 4, he appeared on stage with Cody to demonstrate rapid pistol shooting and trick shots.[61]

Cody gave Hickok a few speaking lines. There was only time for a few rehearsals before Hickok appeared onstage. It was at Hickok's first performance and his first appearance onstage where he sat with Texas Jack and Buffalo Bill around a fake campfire.

They were each to take a swig of whiskey from a bottle, tell a story, then pass the bottle on to the next person who would take a swig and tell another tall tale. Cody had the bottle filled with tea. Texas Jack took a drink from the bottle and told a story, then Buffalo Bill took a drink and told a tale. He handed the bottle to Wild Bill who placed it to his lips taking big gulps, then stopped. He spit out a stream of tea and shouted, "You must think I'm the worst fool east of the Rockies, that I can't tell whisky from cold tea. This don't count, and I can't tell a story under the temptation unless I get real whisky." The audience cheered as Cody tried to reason with him, until he realized the whole scene was a big hit with the crowd. Cody said, "I therefore sent out for some whisky, which Bill drank, and then told his story with excellent effect."[62]

The Buffalo Bill Combination took the show on the road. Their first performance was on September 8, 1873 at Greer's Hall in New Brunswick, New Jersey. A large crowd arrived before the doors opened. It was standing room only. The audience whistled and shouted when the three scouts walked onto the stage. The people loved the show.[63]

The combination traveled to West Chester, Pennsylvania, where they played on September 9. It might have been here where Cody broke a rib while performing a fight scene. The combination returned to New York City for three days, then spent the rest of the month performing in Columbus and Cincinnati, Ohio, winding up in Lexington, Kentucky.[64]

Hickok did not have a good stage voice. Cody said, "Although he had a fine stage appearance and was a handsome fellow, and possessed a good strong voice, yet when he went upon the stage before an audience, it was almost impossible for him to utter a word. He insisted that we were making a set of fools of ourselves, and that we were the laughing-stock of the people." Cody told him he didn't care as long as they bought tickets.[65]

During October, after playing three days in Louisville, Kentucky, the Buffalo Bill Combination performed in Hamilton and Dayton, Ohio. They crossed into Indiana, playing in Terre Haute,

Indianapolis, Lafayette, and Fort Wayne, then back to Ohio for a show in Toledo, then back to Indiana to take the stage in Fremont. When Buffalo Bill, Texas Jack, and Wild Bill were not performing, they wore their buckskin stage costumes out on the streets where they were followed by young and old alike. Crossing back into Ohio once again, the combination rounded out the month playing in Sandusky, Cleveland, and Akron.[66]

Hiram Robbins said, "Wild Bill was really the character . . . he was always under the influence of liquor, for it seemed he could not do without a stimulant, yet, he was far from being drunk, and was always modest and respectful until something occurred to claim his warlike attention."[67]

In November, the combination was in northwestern Pennsylvania. After playing at New Castle and Meadville, they arrived in the oil town of Titusville for a show on November 6.[68]

When they were signing in at their hotel, the owner asked Cody to keep the troupe members out of the barroom as "a party of roughs" from the oil fields was on a drinking spree and they intended to "meet the Buffalo Bill gang and clean them out." To please the hotel owner, Cody met with the troupe in the hotel parlor and explained the situation. Hickok wanted to fight them at once, but Cody persuaded him against that.[69]

However, later in the day, Hickok couldn't resist the temptation and went into the barroom. As he stepped into the room, one of the bruisers put his hand on Hickok's shoulder saying, "Hello, Buffalo Bill! We have been looking for you all day."

"My name is not Buffalo Bill; you are mistaken in the man," Hickok replied.

"You are a liar," the bruiser said. Hickok knocked him to the floor, picked up a chair and used it to knock four or five of the men to the floor. The rest ran out.

The hotel owner told Cody there was a fight, but by the time he got there he met Hickok walking out of the barroom whistling a lively tune. Cody said he thought Hickok had promised not to go in there.

"I did try to follow that trail, but I got lost among the cañons, and then I ran in among the hostiles," he said. "But it is all right now. They won't bother us anymore. I guess those fellows have found us." Cody said they had no more trouble with oil workers.[70]

The Buffalo Bill Combination traveled to New York performing in Jamestown and Buffalo. On November 13, they presented at St. James Hall the premier of their new five-act play *Scouts of the Plains* written by Hiram Robbins.[71]

The plot involved Jim Dawes, "a first class renegade and horse thief," who murdered Buffalo Bill's friend and his wife then kidnapped their daughters. Buffalo Bill vowed revenge, and the following scenes and acts revolved around gun battles with Indians and hardcases. There were narrow escapes and finally justice brought to Dawes and his partner in crime, Tom Doggett.[72]

The next day, the *Buffalo Evening Post* reviewed *Scouts of the Plains*: "We think that Buffalo Bill, Texas Jack, Wild Bill and M'lle Morlacchi appear to better advantage in it than in the drama that preceded. We understand that some of the scenes are true to the experiences of the scouts and are made interesting on that account."[73] It must have been a packed house; the *Buffalo Commercial* printed a one-liner, "The Buffalo Bill party did a good business here this week."[74]

They returned to Pennsylvania spending the rest of November playing to packed audiences in Erie, Pittsburgh, Johnstown, Williamsport, Wilkes-Barre, and Scranton. In Williamsport, they played for twelve hundred people; the *Williamsport Gazette & Bulletin* called it "an unparallel success," but there were newspaper critics too.[75]

Cody was having problems with Hickok, who amused himself playing tricks on cast members. He especially enjoyed tormenting the supernumeraries or extras. When they had their battles firing blanks at each other, they were all supposed to shoot over each other's heads, but occasionally, Hickok would run up to a "super" and fire his blank close to his leg. The discharged powder would singe the man's leg, making him jump and forget about falling over dead. The supers complained to Cody, who was paying them to fall over. He would order Hickok to stop shooting at them. Hickok would laugh and promise not to do it again. However, he soon was back to his old tricks, and Cody would have to make him promise again not to shoot at the supers' legs. Cody said, "Wild Bill continued his pranks, which caused us considerable annoyance, but at the same time greatly amused us."[76]

That December, the Buffalo Bill Combination played at Port Jervis and Poughkeepsie, New York, then headed to New Jersey performing in Newark and Trenton. They crossed the Delaware into Pennsylvania, playing in Bethlehem, Easton, Pottsville, Reading, Lancaster, and Harrisburg. From there, the combination put on two shows in Baltimore. They took time off for Christmas from December 24 to 28. After their respite, they performed in Philadelphia from December 29 through the New Year to January 3, 1874.[77]

Wild Bill Hickok was disruptive one night in Philadelphia. The combination had rented a calcium light, also known as a limelight device. When lime was heated to incandescence, light was produced, and a beam of light could be projected onto the stage to illume an actor. Hickok believed when the limelight shone on Cody and Texas Jack, they had more light on them than when the light was shone on him. He climbed the ladder to where the limelight operator was and asked to have more intense light on him. When the operator refused, Hickok pulled his revolver threatening to shoot him. When Hickok appeared onstage in front of the audience, the man, fearful for his life, turned the full force of the beam on Hickok. Blinded, Hickok shouted, "Turn the blamed thing off!"[78]

Buffalo Bill Cody hired Frank Mordaunt as director and Harry Miner as agent. From January 6 through January 27, 1874, the Buffalo Bill Combination played in Bridgeport, New Haven, Waterbury, Middletown, and Hartford, Connecticut; Providence, Rhode Island; and Taunton, New Bedford, and Cambridge, Massachusetts.[79]

Among the many plays being produced was one called *Davy Crockett*. The January 24, 1874 edition of the *Boston Post* announced, "Among the celebrities to attend upon the matinee performance of 'Davy Crockett' at the Boston Theater to-day, will be Wild Bill, Buffalo Bill, and Texas Jack."[80] There was no information on what they thought of the production.

A story was making the rounds that Buffalo Bill had killed Texas Jack. In Rochester, New York, the January 10 edition of the *Democrat and Chronicle* reported, "There is a story abroad that on the 23rd day of last December, somewhere in Kentucky, Buffalo Bill quarreled with Texas Jack and shot him dead. The story has, however, been denied, and we are reluctantly obliged, therefore, to set aside the two or three columns of regret prepared for this day's paper. Which, all things considered, is exasperating."[81]

On January 29 and 30, the Buffalo Bill Combination was playing in Portland, Maine. One night, Hickok was trying to sleep in his room. In an adjoining room, Hickok could hear a group of loud men enjoying themselves as they played cards. Hickok shouted through the wall several times for them to keep it down, but either they ignored or didn't hear him. Hickok got out of bed, walked to their room, and knocked on the door with the intention of throwing them out.[82]

When the door opened, he was surprised to see the cardplayers were Portland businessmen he had met. They invited him to join their poker game. He accepted, saying he might as well since he was not getting any sleep. He pretended to not know much about the game, making bad moves and letting the others win. However, as the game progressed, he played for keeps. By the next morning, he had won $700. As he rose from the table to leave, he advised the players to never wake a man and then invite him to play poker.[83]

Cody later recalled Hickok's advice to him about gambling—don't do it. Gambling would only lead to trouble. Cody said when Hickok believed cheating was going on during a card game, he would act like he was drunk or half-asleep until he caught the cheat in the act and then draw his pistol. Hickok told Cody, "When you play against a stacked deck, make sure you've got a hand to beat theirs" and then touched the butt of his revolver.[84]

The Buffalo Bill Combination's schedule was unrelenting. They continued to play before packed houses. January 31, they were in Bath, Maine, then traveled to other Maine cities: Augusta, Bangor, Lewiston, and again Portland. They were in Dover, Concord, and Manchester, New Hampshire; Haverhill, Lawrence, Lowell, Worcester, Springfield, Pittsfield, and North Adams, Massachusetts; then on to Troy, New York, rounding out February in Albany.[85]

Apparently, the scouts were targets for theft. The *Boston Post* reported, "Somebody stole Buffalo Bill's pocket-book containing $140 and the diamond pin given him by Alexis, in Worcester the other night."[86]

They continued making money. A reporter for the *Pittsfield Sun* said, "Buffalo Bill, Wild Bill, and Texas Jack gave a fine representation of border life at the Academy, Saturday evening to a very good house, considering the weather."[87]

There was good-natured joking among combination members. One Indian actor lamented the Indians got killed all the time. Why couldn't they kill Buffalo Bill? Hickok and Cody knew they were no actors and joked about their lack of ability.[88]

In March, the combination performed in Schenectady, Utica, Oswego, and Syracuse, New York.[89] Rochester's *Democrat and Chronicle* reported on the Buffalo Bill Combination stating, "This drama has been played by them with remarkable success all over the country."[90]

Rumors abounded there would be an Indian war. General Sheridan and Lieutenant Colonel Custer made statements that the three scouts would soon be needed on the frontier. Some would be happy to see them go. The Honesdale, Pennsylvania, *Wayne County Herald* stated in its March 5, 1874 edition, "Buffalo Bill, Wild Bill, and Texas Jack have been engaged by Gen. Custer to head scouting parties on the plains, and they have left the stage.

Let Oregon Bill be added to their ranks, and then, if some wandering tribe of Indians wants to receive the thanks of the present generation, and deserve that of millions yet to be, let them take the scalps of the whole four, and end this King-of-the-border-men 'drama' business forever."[91]

The Buffalo Bill Combination arrived in Rochester, New York, with performances on March 10 and 11. Cody happily reunited with Louisa and the children. He wanted to make a good impression on the community, and Hickok agreed to not play any tricks.[92]

The first night was a success. The *Democrat and Chronicle* reported, "The sight in and around the opera house last night during the performance given by Morlacchi, Wild Bill, *et al.* was simply astonishing. Probably the auditorium of that building was never stormed by so large a crowd of people before. We have seen it packed full, when it appeared impossible to get another person in it, but last night was certainly ahead of anything ever seen there before. Hundreds went disappointed away as they were unable to get inside the door. The seats, boxes, gallery, stools, aisles, stairs, railings and every possible inch of standing room was occupied. The doors on the side of the dress circle were opened, and many at once took up their position in the halls, standing on stools and peering over the heads of the audience to try to catch a glimpse of the stage."[93]

The writer praised Giuseppina Morlacchi performance, then continued, "The drama of 'Scouts of the Plains' is of the highest sensational order, and aside from the distinguished men who present it has but little attraction. The sight of three such men as Wild Bill, Buffalo Bill, and Texas Jack is enough to draw out a crowd. These men appear on the stage with great ease and of course bring out the scenes of border life with great power and naturalness. Their acting is very good. The *physique* of Wild Bill is splendid, and, indeed, the same may be said of them all. They appear again tonight, and probably the same scenes in regard to the crowd will be repeated."[94]

On March 11, the Buffalo Bill Combination took a break to attend the wedding of two of their own, Walt Fletcher, a popular comedian, and Lizzie Hollis, a leading lady of the troupe. They were married by a justice of the peace at the Osborne House, the hotel where many combination members were staying. Many friends in the troupe attended including Hickok, Texas Jack, Giuseppina Morlacchi, as well as Cody and his family. The *Democrat and Chronicle* mentioned, "and little Kit Carson Cody, too."[95]

The second night performance saw another packed crowd. Agnes Lake was in town and came to the evening performance. According to Cody, Hickok often talked about how he admired Agnes. Cody spied her in the audience and between the first and second act, reunited her with Hickok. They spent a brief time together before the second act. In Buel's *Heroes of the Plains*, Cody said Hickok professed his love for Agnes and proposed to her. She replied it was very sudden, and she needed at least two years to put her affairs in order. She also wondered if it was proper for her to remarry.

"I don't want to insist," Hickok responded, "But at the same time you suit me to a dot, and I'd give my eyes to marry you; therefore I'll give you time to consider. I've got to go on the stage now to kill a few Indians to please this congregation, but when the show is out, maybe I might see you over at the Osborne House."[96]

If this conversation happened, it could not have been this spontaneous after only a brief encounter in Abilene. They likely kept in touch and may have seen each other, but there is no record. Maybe Hickok was inspired by the wedding of Walt Fletcher and Lizzie Hollis he had witnessed a few hours earlier.

Piecing together what Louisa and Buffalo Bill later wrote, it appears a frustrated Wild Bill Hickok lost his temper during the second act.

Louisa sat in a wing offstage. Hickok had stuttered and stammered while reciting his lines. Leaving the stage, he said to her, "Ain't this foolish? Ain't it now? What's the use of getting out there and making a show of yourself? I ain't going to do it!"[97]

On cue, Hickok went back onstage during a fight with Indian supernumeraries. Instead of shooting over their heads, he was back to his old tricks shooting at and singeing their legs. After the curtain fell at the end of act two, the supers complained to Cody. Angry, Cody told Hickok to either stop shooting the supers or leave the combination. Hickok made no reply.[98]

Cody had to return onstage. Hickok went to the dressing room and changed into his street clothes. Cody was onstage when he saw Hickok "elbowing his way through the audience and out of the theater." When he finished the scene and walked offstage, the stage carpenter said to him, "That long-haired gentleman, who passed out a few minutes ago, requested me to tell you that you could go to thunder with your old show."[99]

After the performance, Cody found Hickok at the Osborne House. Cody said, "By this time he had recovered from his mad fit and was in as good humor as ever." Hickok said he was through and heading west the next day. Cody tried to persuade him to stay for the rest of the engagements and then they would go west together, but Hickok was adamant. Cody paid Hickok what was due him, and he and Texas Jack gave Hickok a $1,000 cash present.[100]

The next day, March 12, the Buffalo Bill Combination left for its evening performance in Lockport, New York, and Hickok remained in Rochester. A *Democrat and Chronicle* reporter caught up with him on the street that afternoon as a cold wind blew and the snow fell. The reporter asked Hickok why he was still in town. Hickok told him he had received a call to return to the frontier where his services were required. There was talk of trouble with the Sioux at the Red Cloud and Spotted Tail agencies, and General Sheridan believed they might go on the warpath in the next few weeks. "At this time and amid such scenes, as these the services of Wild Bill will be invaluable to United States troops. It is this, together with a longing desire to return to the free, the wild life he loves so well that has called our hero away." However, Hickok said first he needed to go to New York City, to conduct some business that would take several days before heading west.[101]

Hickok talked about his fellow scouts: "Buffalo Bill, Texas Jack and the other scouts did not like to have him leave, but when he said he must go, the noble hearted fellows presented him with $500 a piece and each gave him a splendid revolver. . . . He had nothing but kind words to speak of the boys as he familiarly termed the other scouts. He wished them all manner of good fortune, and was sure they would receive it."[102]

The reporter wrote, "Wild Bill is a noble fellow, a true-hearted child of nature—one of those men which one occasionally comes in contact with and ever after retains a place in his memory. We shook hands with the hero, bade him good-bye and wished him a pleasant journey to his far western home. He left at 12:15 this morning [March 13, 1874] for New York."[103]

CHAPTER 14

"LIVING HEROES" (1874–1876)

After Wild Bill Hickok left Rochester, New York, on March 14, 1874, he arrived in New York City. One reason he left the Buffalo Bill Combination to go to New York must have been Agnes Lake. Agnes and her daughter Emma were staying at New York's posh St. Nicholas Hotel for a week. Agnes had sold her circus and planned to remain with Emma until Emma was married. In the interim, Agnes was concentrating on furthering Emma's career. Emma would soon be called the country's premier equestrienne. During the late nineteenth century, horse and rider performances were the main circus attraction, and Emma was the best.[1]

Hickok rendezvoused with Agnes in New York, and even though there was chemistry between the two, she would not consider marriage until Emma was married. Hickok and Agnes's correspondence would increase after their reunion.[2]

At the end of a week, Agnes and Emma left New York, and Hickok was on his own. According to Buffalo Bill Cody, Hickok lost all his money playing faro.[3]

Whether he needed to recoup his losses or wanted to strike out on his own, Hickok was hired by John Stevens to appear in his new play *Daniel Boone*. Stevens would portray Daniel Boone and Hickok would play himself.[4]

After a short stint in New York City, Stevens took his show on the road into northeastern Pennsylvania. The first performance was Thursday evening, April 30, at Liberty Hall in Honesdale, Pennsylvania. An advertisement in the *Wayne County Herald* advertised Hickok as part of the show: "WILD BILL (J. B. Hickok) KING OF THE PLAINS, Whose marvelous courage and daring achievements for twenty-six years as a scout, stands unequaled in Romance or History."[5] False advertising at its best; Hickok was thirty-seven years old at the time, so according to the advertisement, he started scouting when he was eleven years old.

Stevens used Hickok as the drawing card for his play. "Wild Bill" was the lead banner in each advertisement, but Hickok probably did little more than appear onstage. When reviewers wrote about the play, little or no mention was made of Hickok. Stevens got all the attention. In an article leading up to the play in Wilkes-Barre, Pennsylvania, the *Daily Record of the Times* stated, "Wild Bill—This renowned scout and Indian fighter will appear in Music Hall, Tuesday evening, accompanied by a full troupe." That was it concerning Wild Bill. However, when the article repeated a review by the *Brooklyn Eagle*, it gushed, "Mr. John A. Stevens, from the boards of the Western circuit, appeared as the hero, assisted by the full company of the house. Mr. Stevens is an American, a good reader, and appeared to advantage in this play." No mention of Wild Bill was made.[6]

The troupe was to perform *Daniel Boone* on Tuesday, May 5 in Wilkes-Barre but for some unnamed reason the play was postponed. The *Daily Record of the Times* announced, "Wild Bill will not perform this evening as advertised yesterday—the performance has been postponed to Thursday and Friday evenings of this week, when, with popular prices and a first class entertainment, he hopes to draw a big crowd."[7] Maybe Stevens was charging too much for tickets and selling fewer than expected, so they were reducing to "popular prices."

The May 8, 1874 issue of the *Daily Record of the Times* commented, "Music Hall has been the scene of a variety of entertainments lately; but not one . . . gave greater satisfaction than that played last night by Mr. Stevens and his company. The drama is original and patriotic. The pioneer Daniel Boone, as played by Mr. Stevens, shows the model man, lover and husband, while Wild Bill is the personification of real friendship, unencumbered by lust. His almost brotherly and unobtrusive protection of the beautiful little Ada even after she became the wife of his friend, pictured a phase in life not very common, but nevertheless one to be met with occasionally."[8]

Hickok became disgruntled with Stevens and his play. Cody said, "As a 'star' Wild Bill was not a success; the further he went, the poorer he got." Hickok believed he was making a fool of himself again. This might have been the cause for what the *Carbondale Leader* mentioned in its May 9, 1874 issue: "'Wild Bill' a symmetrical son of the border, and the troupe with which he is connected, gave two performances at Nelson's Hall recently. 'Wild Bill' was much admired by some for his well-built person; by others, perhaps for his precise profanity."[9]

Hickok left *Daniel Boone* most likely right after demonstrating his "precise profanity." The show's next performances were to be at the Opera House in Scranton, Pennsylvania, on the evenings of May 12 and 13, 1874. Stevens had advertised "WILD BILL (J. B. Hickok)" would be onstage. Stevens would have Wild Bill there one way or another. He got one of his actors to wear a long-haired, blonde wig and portray Wild Bill not only on stage, but to also impersonate him offstage around town. Hickok got wind of the deception and sent a message to Stevens to have his actor cease and desist; but Stevens had his actor continue the charade.[10]

Hickok went to the performance and sat near the stage. "Bill . . . watched the performance until the bogus Wild Bill appeared," Cody said. "He then sprang upon the stage, knocked the actor clear through one of the scenes, and grabbing the manager [Stevens] by the shoulders he threw him over the foot-lights into the orchestra. The other actors screamed and yelled police."

Rochester's *Democrat and Chronicle* picked up the story relating what happened next: "It was a genuine opera-house tragedy, and the fiends in the gallery, not to mention those in the dress circle, shrieked with delight and proposed to carry Wild Bill on their shoulders to a whisky saloon attached to the opera-house; but the police put in an appearance, and the hero passed the night in jail and afterward paid $5 for his freedom."[11]

Hickok never acted onstage again.

The Buffalo Bill Combination left Rochester on March 12, 1874, for their performance in Lockport, New York, that evening.[12] Even though Buffalo Bill Cody and Texas Jack Omohundro missed their friend Wild Bill Hickok, they and the rest of the troupe probably were relieved they didn't have to worry about what Hickok's next shenanigan would be. For the rest of March, they played almost every night in fourteen major cities in western New York, northwestern Pennsylvania, northern Ohio, and southern Michigan.[13]

The *Detroit Free Press* praised the combination in its March 24, 1874, edition: "the performance at the Opera House yesterday evening was unique in character. . . . 'The Scouts of the Plains'— was a wonderful triumph. To be sure 'Wild Bill' did not show up at all, but Bison William and Lone-Star-John, otherwise known as 'Buffalo Bill' and 'Texas Jack,' were there, and the crowded gallery was fairly rampant with enthusiasm when the stage (at least once in each act) was strewn with Indian dead and the air heavy with sulfurous smoke."[14]

In April, the Buffalo Bill Combination played in Kalamazoo, Michigan, South Bend, Indiana, and thirteen major cities in Illinois and Iowa. Newspaper announcements continued to display that Hickok was with the troupe up until at least April 7.[15] An advertisement in the *South Bend Tribune* was typical using the phrases, "The Originals. Living Heroes. Links Between Civilization and Savagery. BUFFALO BILL, Hon. William F. Cody. TEXAS JACK, J. B. Ornhundro [*sic*]. WILD BILL, J. B. Hickok.

Will appear on the above named evening in their New Sensational Play. . . ."[16] Some newspapers commented on the absence of Hickok and some speculated whether Cody and Omohundro were the real Buffalo Bill and Texas Jack. Cody began printing in the newspaper details of his life and gave reporters interviews.[17]

The *Daily Davenport Democrat*'s reviewer raved about *Scouts of the Plains* in the April 23, 1874 edition, "For rollicking, pure, unadulterated enjoyment, . . . we have never equaled last night, at Hill's Opera House. . . . The wonderful melodramas of old times are eclipsed by it—where they had one death, this has twenty; where they used their popping iron in the cause of crime, this fires a whole volley in the interests of virtue. . . . Death, war dances, fires and defiance, war whoops and death songs lie round promiscuous; and the entire company must have been killed three times over. We tallied till the slain got up to thirty-seven, and then gave it up, dead beat. . . . Buffalo Bill is handsome as an Adonis, and plays as he fights, with all the nonchalance of a western gentleman scout. . . . outrageous as the whole thing is, we would not have missed it for a $10 bill, and recommend all of our friends to be on hand to-night."[18]

The Buffalo Bill Combination spent May playing in Madison, Milwaukee, and Racine, Wisconsin; a week in Chicago; followed by Saginaw and Bay City, Michigan; and then they went international, playing in London, Hamilton, and Toronto, Canada.[19]

The May 12, 1874, edition of the *Chicago Tribune* was complimentary in a roundabout way: "This house [Academy of Music] is in the possession of 'The Scouts of the Plains,' otherwise known as Buffalo Bill and Texas Jack, and every night this week it will resound with the crack of their gleaming rifles, and smell very badly indeed of powder. . . . They opened last evening to a very large audience, the gallery being crowded to suffocation with a class of men and boys whose taste for literary pursuits comes to an abrupt conclusion after they have gone through a dime novel course and a little heavier blood-and-thunder reading. The lower tiers contained the usual theatrical audience. . . . 'The Scouts of the

Plains' bears but little resemblance to the piece of the same name [Buntline's play] which was presented here by the same performers some time ago, being much better in every respect."[20]

Before the Buffalo Bill Combination's theater season ended in June 1874, they performed for three days in Montreal, Quebec; then in Lowell, Lawrence, Salem, Lynn, and Boston, Massachusetts. The final performances were in New York City on June 29 and 30.[21]

The theatrical season ended on a high note with a good review in the *New York Herald*: "Buffalo Bill conducted himself on all occasions with that quiet, subdued manner which belongs to men who are truly brave in moments of danger. . . . Buffalo Bill has a fine presence, and moves about the stage with an ease and grace which at once wins the heart of the audience. . . . At the conclusion of his present engagement Mr. Cody . . . will depart for the plains, to resume his old profession as guide and scout. . . . The play, too, is full of movement, and suits admirably that portion of the public who love pictures of heroes overcoming obstacles by flood and field. In spite of the warm weather the house was filled and the audience remained in their seats until the curtain dropped. When the state of the weather yesterday is considered, this is the highest praise that we can bestow."[22]

Texas Jack left for Denver to guide the Earl of Dunraven on his hunt. Cody met Thomas Medley, a wealthy businessman from London, England, who hired him to guide him and a few friends on a series of western hunting trips. Medley would pay Cody $1,000 per month. Cody planned to visit his family in Rochester and then meet Medley in Corrine, Utah. Medley asked Cody to find additional scouts and he contacted Hickok, who agreed to join them.[23]

No information has been found concerning what Wild Bill Hickok did right after he left the Scranton jail, but on June 21,

1874, the *Kansas City Journal of Commerce* reported Hickok was back in Kansas City.[24] It must have been a brief visit; the June 26 edition of Paola, Kansas's the *Western Spirit* announced, "Wild Bill was in Kansas City the other day. His greatness has departed."[25]

On July 8, 1874, a reporter for Rochester's *Democrat and Chronicle* interviewed Buffalo Bill Cody. During the interview, Cody mentioned his upcoming big game hunts guiding Thomas Medley and friends. Cody said Hickok who was in Yosemite Valley, California, would be joining them for the hunts and meet them in Corrine, Utah.[26] However, the reporter must have gotten the facts wrong. It was Medley who went to California and would later join Cody and other scouts. California newspapers had Medley in Carlin, Nevada, on July 16 and Sacramento, California, on July 17. There was no mention of Hickok.[27]

Hickok was still in Kansas. Topeka's *Commonwealth* reported on July 23, "Wild Bill passed through North Topeka on Saturday, on his way to Cheyenne, where he is expected to join Buffalo Bill and Texas Jack, and proceed with a party of English tourists to the Yellowstone country. Wild Bill is suffering with an affection [*sic*] of the eyes, caused by the colored fire used during his theatrical tour."[28]

Had stage lighting hurt Hickok's eyes? During the Buffalo Bill Combination Philadelphia performance at the end of December 1873, intense limelight had blinded Hickok. Did that cause a lingering eye problem? Ed Moore, a friend of Hickok, told author William Connelley, "in 1873 or 1874, one of the lamps of the footlights exploded and nearly burned Bill's eyes out. He . . . was compelled to wear thick-lensed glasses until his eyes began to regain their strength." Buel mentioned in *Heroes of the Plains* that in 1875, Hickok had an attack of ophthalmia, an inflammation of the eyes. He returned to Kansas City where "Dr. Thorne treated him for several months with such success that his eyesight . . . was partially restored, but he never again regained his perfect vision."[29]

On July 8, 1874, a reporter for the *Democrat and Chronicle* wanting to know more about Buffalo Bill Cody's life visited him at his Rochester home "and found him suffering from a slight attack of chills and fever which, however, was not sufficient to confine him to his room. He received his visitor with much cordiality, and submitted to his close questioning with much patience."[30]

Cody told the reporter he was spending a few days with his family before heading west. "Next week he goes west to assume the charge of a hunting expedition undertaken by Thomas Medley, the famous millionaire of London, England. He will be joined by Wild Bill and some of his other friends. . . ."They planned to meet at Corinne, Utah, then head to Fort Bridger, Wyoming, where they would hunt bear. Next, they would travel to Fort Saunders to hunt mountain sheep and elk and from there travel to Sidney Plains and Fort McPherson to hunt buffalo. "Mr. Medley has given orders to Buffalo Bill to spare neither pains nor expense in fitting out the expedition, saying he is willing to expend $20,000 to beat the famous expedition of Grand Duke Alexis."[31]

On July 17, 1874, Cody arrived in Omaha and spent the night. The *Omaha Bee* reported, "Buffalo Bill left Saturday for Corinne, where he will meet a party of four wealthy Englishmen, to pilot them through a six weeks hunt, Mr. Thomas Medley, the head of the party, is one of the richest gentlemen in England . . . 'Wild Bill' who has been killed so often by the newspapers, but who yet lives, will aid Buffalo Bill in entertaining the English millionaires, who will undoubtedly liberally compensate them for the service thus rendered."[32]

Arriving at Fort McPherson, Cody wrote a letter, dated July 20, 1874, to Rochester's *Democrat and Chronicle*, saying the hunt plans had been modified. He would meet Medley and friends as well as Hickok in Cheyenne instead of Corinne. They planned to return to the North Platte and McPherson area to hunt buffalo as large herds were grazing there. Colonel Anson Mills with a company of the Third Cavalry would provide an escort for the hunters.[33]

Cody wrote his letter while sitting in the local saloon and described being interrupted: "since I commenced the letter the 'boys' have been engaged in a little customary exercise, in which six-shooters, extension pistols, and tangle-foot whiskey have played the prominent parts. I have stood New York whiskey and Overtour [*sic*] and Blair's hash, but this little game is decidedly the richest encounter yet, and one in which, from the want of experience, I have not been very successful, but after 'fixin' one belligerent chap and treating several times, I have been enabled to resume my writing. (This is the way the boys celebrated an old comrade's return, you know.)"[34]

Cody met Medley and friends and Hickok at Cheyenne. He wrote to the *Democrat and Chronicle* saying, "The first hunt took place from Cheyenne, and we succeeded in getting away with any number of elk, antelope, deer, etc., besides 'hooking' a number of mountain trout from the beautiful streams in that vicinity."[35]

Thomas Medley impressed Cody who noted Medley did not bring along any servants and luxuries, but "he wished to rough it just as I would do—to sleep on the ground in the open air, and kill and cook his own meat." Medley worked around camp never asking anyone to do anything for him. Cody said, "Mr. Medley proved to be a very agreeable gentleman and an excellent hunter."[36]

When they reached North Platte for the buffalo hunt, "Doc" William Carver joined them for several days. Carver had a reputation for being a good shot with a rifle.[37] He had just finished a two-day buffalo hunt around the bluffs of O'Fallon's Station where they found thousands of buffalo.[38]

In Cody's letter to the *Democrat and Chronicle* he wrote about the buffalo hunt: "From this place [North Platte] our party proceeded to the Medicini [*sic*], a tributary of the Republican, where we encountered large numbers of Buffalos. For six days Mr. Medley and party enjoyed one of the grandest and most successful hunts ever participated in in this section. We found large numbers of Buffalos, and I could recount many exciting scenes that occurred, but a want of time prevents. The hunt we had planned for the Dismal River had to be abandoned on account of the hostile attitude of the noble red man. The entire available force of soldiers have been ordered to take to the field."[39]

Concerns affecting the Lakotas were coming to a head. One of the provisions of the 1868 Fort Laramie Treaty established the Great Sioux Reservation, an area encompassing what is now western South Dakota. The eastern border was the Missouri River, and the southern border was Nebraska's northern state line. The northern and western boundaries were undefined and the area was called "unceded Indian territory" stretching to the summits of Wyoming's Big Horn Mountains.[40]

Other treaty provisions guaranteed annuities for the tribes and established agencies for government administration. The Indians had the right to hunt buffalo in the unceded territory "so long as the buffalo may range thereon in such numbers as to justify the chase." They also had the right to hunt buffalo north of the North Platte River and on the Republican Fork of the Smoky Hill River. General William Sherman never liked this provision. He had written General Phil Sheridan, "I think it would be wise to invite all the sportsmen of England & America there this fall for a Grand Buffalo hunt, and make one grand sweep of them all. Until the Buffaloes & Indians are out from between the [rail] Roads we will have collisions & trouble."[41]

The federal government had established two agencies outside the reservation's southern border on Nebraska's White River, Red Cloud Agency and Spotted Tail Agency. Through the winter of 1874, there were problems with the distribution of beef to tribal members at these two agencies. In some cases, the beef did not arrive, and in other cases, the animals were of inferior quality. Tribal leaders had enough of what they believed was government corruption. On February 9, 1874, the chief clerk at Red Cloud Agency was killed in a dispute, and in a separate incident, an army officer and corporal out of Fort Laramie were killed the same day.

At the Spotted Tail Agency, Lakotas took control of the beef distribution from the agent and threatened to kill him if he tried to stop them. On March 1, 1874, the army stepped in and took control of the agencies, causing resentment among the Lakotas. At Spotted Tail Agency, the Army suspended supplies distribution, trying to force a tribal member census. The tribes remained sullen. The Army established a camp near Red Cloud Agency called Camp Robinson, named after the recently killed officer; and in September 1874 the Army would establish Camp Sheridan near Spotted Tail Agency.[42]

On March 21, 1874, federal commissioners arrived at Spotted Tail's camp with demands: a tribal member census; a relocation of the agency; the Lakotas must allow a survey of the Nebraska state line to pass through their land; surrender of murderers; and the end of the Lakotas' treaty-given rights to hunt buffalo in the Republican River territory. Controlling his anger, Spotted Tail refused the demands. He stated his own position: Two years earlier, President Ulysses Grant had told him he could select where he wanted to locate his agency; the president had promised one hundred wagons and either horses or mules so the Lakotas could freight their own goods and not rely on white traders—this promise had not been kept; and Spotted Tail wanted the murderers of Whistler apprehended. Spotted Tail believed the soldiers' presence at the agency was a treaty violation. He did not want them chopping down the Lakotas' trees and their horses eating the Lakotas' grass. He did not want the boundary survey, and he would not give up the Lakota hunting rights.[43]

Unknown to any of the Lakotas, General Sheridan believed there needed to be another fort located in or near the Black Hills to further contain the Lakotas and other tribes. According to the 1868 Fort Laramie Treaty, the Black Hills were part of the Great Sioux Reservation and off limits to whites. There had always been rumors of paying quantities of gold in the Black Hills. Prospectors and speculators wanted the Black Hills opened to search for the yellow metal, but the Lakotas opposed any entry. In the spring of 1874,

Sheridan directed Lieutenant Colonel George Custer to explore the Black Hills and determine a site for a future military post, survey and map the area, and record the topography and geology.[44]

Custer based his expedition out of Dakota Territory's Fort Abraham Lincoln on the west bank of the Missouri River. His command consisted of ten companies of the Seventh Cavalry, two infantry units, white scouts, and seventy Indian scouts, as well as geologists and botanists, a photographer, newspaper reporters, and two experienced miners. On July 2, 1874, Custer and his thousand men set out in a southwesterly direction. The expedition crossed the treeless prairie, arriving at the northern Black Hills and entering them on July 24. They slowly journeyed on a southerly route, finding flower-filled valleys, swift-flowing creeks, and large stands of pines.[45]

On August 2, miners Horatio Ross and William McKay announced they had panned profitable amounts of gold from French Creek. The next day, Custer sent the scout Lonesome Charlie Reynolds south to Fort Laramie with his report mentioning they had found gold. The journalists gave Reynolds their dispatches sensationalizing the discovery of gold. Soon newspapers nationwide were proclaiming the new find. The August 12, 1874 edition of Dakota Territory's *Bismarck Tribune* headlined "GOLD!" and predicted the Black Hills would "become the El Dorado of America."[46]

The Custer expedition left the Black Hills on August 15, reaching Fort Abraham Lincoln on August 30. Gold seekers would soon be illegally rushing to the Black Hills. The Army tried to stop them but could not keep them all out.[47]

There were reports of Indian attacks in Wyoming's Powder River country. The Army was organizing the Big Horn Expedition to Wyoming at Fort McPherson. According to Chicago's *Inter Ocean*, the expedition was "to rid the country of all wandering Indians, who murder and pillage every summer." Captain Anson Mills of the Third Cavalry was leading the expedition consisting of three of his companies, two companies of the Second Cavalry, one company of the Fourth Infantry, and one company of the Thirteenth Infantry, totaling 408 officers and men. In addition, there were four Pawnee Scouts, two white guides, twenty-two mule packers, and twenty-three teamsters along with twenty-nine wagons and 148 wagon mules and twenty pack mules.[48]

Cody was offered the position of chief of scouts. He told the *Democrat and Chronicle*, "I joyfully accepted." He said they were heading to the Powder River country, which was believed to be the Sioux stronghold where they left their families "when they don their war-paint and take the war-path to commit depredations upon the unprotected and unsuspecting settler. The commanding generals of the army recognizing the importance of placing a larger number of soldiers in the heart of the enemy's country, to intimidate the growing war feeling among the Indians, and to have troops in a position to strike them a blow if not checked, is the evident object of this expedition." The Powder River country was part of the 1868 Fort Laramie Treaty's unceded territory; the Lakotas had a right to be there.[49]

The Army hired Cody as chief of scouts on August 7, 1874. The members of the Powder River Expedition were transported by rail to Rawlins, Wyoming, where they detrained. From there, they marched north roughly sixty miles to Independence Rock on the Sweetwater River where Mills established his supply camp. Mills left the infantry to guard the camp while he led the cavalry north toward the Big Horn Mountains.[50]

One morning, while the expedition was still in the headwaters of the Powder River basin, they spotted a solitary horseman approaching. Cody recognized an old scouting acquaintance, Moses "California Joe" Milner.[51]

During General Sheridan's 1868 advance on the Cheyennes and Kiowas, Custer had appointed Milner chief of scouts. He did well until one morning when he was found stinking drunk. Custer demoted Milner but kept him on.[52]

Cody introduced California Joe to Captain Mills. When Milner was asked why he was out there alone, he responded he was out for a morning ride. Cody soon learned California Joe had been prospecting in the Big Horn foothills. Milner stayed with the expedition and after several days, Mills told Cody he might as well put California Joe on the payroll as scout at $5 a day.[53]

The expedition scouted along the Powder River, Crazy Woman's Fork, and Clear Fork. Cody said, "we finally surprised Little Wolf's band of Arapahoes and drove them into the agencies." The expedition climbed into the Big Horn Mountains where on September 1, Captain Mills said it snowed for thirty-six hours, the snow piling up to two feet. They lost a total of twenty-three horses due to the storm.[54]

Mills wrote, "the mountains looked quite formidable to our front, so I sent, early, Cody to the southwest, who soon returned and reported a pass to a stream of water seven miles distant." On September 5, the expedition crossed through the mountains following the pass to the western slopes. They were trying to head north and keep the Big Horns between them and their supposed Indian village target. Mills sent Cody to find a route, but everything he found would take them too far west. Mills had the troops turn and head due east. He wrote, "Cody and I while riding in advance with the Indians [Pawnee Scouts] came abruptly upon a she-bear and two cubs, all of which we dispatched in less than two minutes." The expedition ran into several formidable dead ends and obstacles during their descent of the eastern slopes to the foothills.[55]

Two days later, Mills sent the scouts east to Pumpkin Buttes, the reported location of the Indian village. When the scouts arrived at the site, they determined it had been abandoned about six weeks earlier.[56]

The Big Horn Expedition continued searching the Powder River country for Indians but found none. On September 28, Mills wrote, "the men of Major [brevet rank] Moore's company encountered a bear . . . [they] wounded and chased him into a clump of Willows on the creek when Private Miller dismounted and entered the willows against the remonstrances of California Joe, . . . when he [Miller] was seized by the bear and horribly mangled. . . ." One rider got too close to the bear, which took a swipe of flesh out of the horse. It took three shots to kill the bear. They took Miller back to Fort McPherson where he died of his wounds.[57]

On September 25, General Ord, the department commander, issued an order to end the expedition since it had determined the Indians had left the Powder River Basin. Mills wrote in his report, "Mr. Cody (Buffalo Bill) sustained his reputation as an excellent and invaluable guide. . . ." Cody arrived in Cheyenne, Wyoming, on October 1 and was discharged on October 2. The October 14 edition of the *Buffalo Express* reported he had returned home to Rochester.[58]

San Francisco's *Daily Examiner* reprinted an interview Cody gave the *Buffalo Express* on October 13, 1874. He talked about the expedition and expressed his opinion on the current affairs of the northern plains. "He says the white buffalo hunters create a great deal of trouble among the Indians by killing buffalo for their hides only, and leaving the carcasses to rot on the plains. The Indians do not like this promiscuous slaughter of what they consider their rightful property, and resent it at every opportunity by taking the scalps of the hunters. Mr. Cody is thoroughly convinced that there is gold in large quantities among the Black Hills, and that it will be a difficult matter to keep miners and adventurers from going there. A number of soldiers had already left their commands for the Black Hills country. General Sheridan will do all in his power to prevent persons from entering the coveted territory, but considers it hardly possible to keep all out."[59]

Wild Bill Hickok had stayed in Cheyenne, Wyoming, after assisting Cody in guiding Thomas Medley and friends. Upton Lorentz said by September, Hickok's good friend Colorado Charley Utter had joined Hickok and the two of them frequented the Gold

Room, a combination theater, dance hall, saloon, and gambling hall near the Union Pacific Railroad.[60]

J. W. Buel related a story about a confrontation Hickok had with a faro dealer named Boulder. Hickok had been steadily losing money. Then for several plays, the cards Boulder drew did not affect the faro board card Hickok had laid his bet on and he kept increasing his bet until it reached $50. When Boulder drew the losing card, it was Hickok's bet, and Boulder took Hickok's $50. Hickok laid another $50 on a card and won when Boulder drew the winning card. Instead of paying Hickok $50, Boulder only paid him $25, not a full $50 as it should have been. When Hickok told Boulder he owed him another $25, Boulder replied the betting limit was $25 even though Hickok had laid down $50. Hickok replied if that was the case Boulder should not have taken $50 from him on the losing bet. Their argument became heated. Hickok hit Boulder on the head with a cane. Several bouncers came at Hickok who fought them off with the cane. Backed into a corner, he drew his pistols leveling them at his attackers. The bartender ran in shouting, "Look out, boys, that's Wild Bill!" Realizing who he was, they backed off and let him alone. "On the following day," Buel wrote, "Boulder, although still nursing a badly damaged head, called on Bill and producing champagne and cigars, the two settled their difference amicably."[61]

Bat Masterson, buffalo hunter, lawman, and gambler, arrived in Cheyenne in 1876, just after Hickok left town. In a fictionalized account of Masterson's life, *The Sunset Trail*, author and friend of Masterson, Alfred Henry Lewis, wrote an account of Hickok's confrontation with Boulder whom he called Bowlby. Lewis wrote the confrontation happened when Hickok first arrived in Cheyenne. Hickok had tucked his long hair up under his hat; bright lights hurt his eyes, so he wore dark goggles; a long dark coat hid his pistols; and he carried a rosewood billiard cue as a cane. As Hickok tussled with the bouncers, his hat and goggles were knocked off and that was when they realized they were dealing with Wild Bill.[62]

Buel told the tale that two weeks after Hickok arrived in Cheyenne, a brother of Phil Cole [*sic*] named Jim and a companion had vowed to kill Hickok. Hickok was sitting in a saloon reading when the two men walked in and up to the bar. Jim Cole ordered a drink. Hickok heard his voice, which sounded exactly like Phil Cole's. Hickok was armed with a small double-barreled pistol loaded with only one shot. The two men knew it was Hickok sitting behind them. With pistols drawn, they swung around, but before they could fire, Hickok shot, killing Cole. He threw the pistol in the face of the other man, grabbed him and threw his head against the counter, breaking his neck. After the coroner's examination, Hickok was released as it was justifiable homicide.[63] No other sources collaborate Buel's story.

The *Cheyenne Daily News* October 7 edition reported, "Wild Bill is among the number that will shortly go to Laramie Peak country exploring for gold." Whether he went out and returned, or never left, the same newspaper commented on December 3, "Wild Bill is still in the city. He is a noble specimen of Western manhood."[64]

Even if Hickok wasn't doing anything notable, he was good newspaper material. The October 28, 1874 edition of Kansas's *Wichita Weekly Beacon* reprinted a *Boston Journal* article. The lead-off sentence was, "It was Wild Bill who said there was 'no Sunday west of Junction City, no law west of Hays City, and no God west of Carson City;' and his remarks bids fair to go into history as thoroughly representative of an epoch which is just past."[65]

When Buffalo Bill Cody returned to his family in Rochester, New York, mid-October, he went to work organizing his performance for the 1874–1875 theatrical season. Texas Jack was unavailable; he was acting as the Earl of Dunraven's hunting guide. Cody hired a professional company to perform *Scouts of the Plains*, and he worked on the play's publicity. His opening production was at New York's Bowery Theater on November 1, 1874.[66]

Newspapers such as Pennsylvania's the *Morning Republican: Scranton* in its November 25 edition advertised, "The great original and only 'BUFFALO BILL,' or Hon. William F. Cody. This popular hero has just returned from the BLACK HILLS where he acted as guide to the famous BIG HORN EXPEDITION, establishing his popularity greater than ever. He will appear in the startling and romantic drama, founded on facts and incidents in his own life, entitled 'Buffalo Bill,' or the Scout of the Plains, supported by JOHNSTON'S DRAMATIC COMPANY."[67]

During November and December of 1874, Buffalo Bill's Combination played in major cities throughout New York, Pennsylvania, and New England.[68] People continued to attend and enjoy the show. The *Morning Republican: Scranton* reprinted a review of the play by the *Syracuse Courier*: "It was a large audience that attended Wieting Opera House, last evening, to see Mr. Cody in his great character of 'Buffalo Bill' in the 'Scouts of the Plains.' There was plenty of enthusiasm, plenty of powder and a sufficient number of dead Indians. The entertainment passed off to the satisfaction of all present, and 'Buffalo Bill' can count on a cordial reception every time he comes to Syracuse."[69]

When Texas Jack returned to the East after guiding the Earl of Dunraven, he and Giuseppina decided not to go on tour but remain at her farm in Massachusetts. Cody needed another scout for his performance and found an actor, possibly William A. Carson, from Wheeling, West Virginia. Carson's stage name was Kit Carson Jr. He was no relation to the famous frontiersman Kit Carson, but newspapers portrayed him as such. Rochester's *Democrat and Chronicle* stated, "In the company is the daring young scout, Kit Carson, Jr., a relative of the famous frontiersman." Kit Carson Jr.'s name first appeared as part of the show on December 4, 1874, in Wilmington, Delaware.[70]

The United States was still in the midst of a depression called the Panic of 1873. The January 2, 1875 issue of New York City's *Spirit of the Times* reported on the state of theatrical companies in general: "traveling companies are faring very badly during the present season, and a careful overlook of all on the road shows a great falling off in numbers during the past few weeks. Only those of strong merit or those presenting some popular star meet with paying patronage." Buffalo Bill's Combination must have provided the people a good show; they were willing to spend their meager cash to see it, as the play continued to show a profit.[71]

During January 1875, the Buffalo Bill Combination played throughout New England and New York. It was scheduled to play in Rochester from February 9 through 13. J. Clinton Hall, who was with Rochester's Corinthian Hall, asked Cody to have a new play when he arrived in town. Cody asked Hiram Robbins to write the new play titled *Life on the Border*.[72]

Cody worked with Robbins to tone down the killing and melodrama common in other plays of this type. One of Buffalo Bill's stage speeches was more sympathetic to the Indians: "It is not they who are to blame for these difficulties . . . there's a class of bad white men on this border who disguise themselves as Indians and commit depredations for which the Indians are, of course, blamed. Then away goes your military after them, and that brings on war."[73]

There were those who believed *Life on the Border* was a far better play than *Scouts of the Plains*. The February 18, 1875 edition of Worcester, Massachusetts's *Evening Gazette* said the dialogue was "free from the stilted twaddle of the dime novel," and "the action was toned down within the range of human probability, while preserving all the dash, danger and devil-may-care elements of the traditional life in the backwoods."[74]

In addition to the lingering financial depression of the Panic of 1873, the United States experienced natural disasters. During the summer of 1874, hordes of grasshoppers devoured everything in their path from the Rocky Mountains to the Missouri River, from Texas to Dakota Territory. Henry and Rosie Ise, farming in western Kansas, wrote what many experienced, "millions and billions of them—soon covered the ground in a seething, fluttering mass, their jaws constantly biting and testing all things."

Conditions were dry, and anything remaining could ignite causing prairie fires. Settlers had no choice but leave. One farmer displayed a sign on his wagon, "From Kansas where it rains grasshoppers, fire and destruction." Another said after the grasshoppers left his place he had "nothing but the mortgage."[75]

Government and charity organizations offered some relief to devastated farmers, but there was need for more. After the Buffalo Bill Combination performances in Rochester, Cody donated the proceeds to help those in need from the grasshopper devastation.[76]

After the Buffalo Bill Combination left Rochester, the *Democrat and Chronicle* wrote: "The celebrated character, Buffalo Bill, supported by Kit Carson, Jr., and his large dramatic company, leaves to-day for Batavia. After playing there they go to Albion and thence to Lockport. It is needless to advise the citizens of those places to go and see this troupe, as they never fail to draw immense audiences."[77]

Through the winter and into the spring of 1875, Cody's troupe continued to perform before large audiences in major Midwest and Northeast cities. On April 24, 1875, Buffalo Bill's Combination was playing at Ford's Opera House[78] in Washington, DC. The *National Republican* reported: "This afternoon and evening affords the last opportunities to see Buffalo Bill and Kit Carson, Jr. The play of 'Life on the Border' will be the attraction. Since Buffalo Bill was here last season he has made great advances in the histrionic art, and is beginning to develop decided talent as an actor. In May Mr. Cody (Buffalo Bill) will act as the guide of a party of English gentlemen, headed by Mr. Thomas P. Medley, who remains on the plains, hunting and sight-seeing for three or four months. In September he goes to London to produce his dramas there. The matinee performance will be specially adapted for ladies and children, and the latter will be particularly interested in the great bear fight. Last evening many army officers were present, and a large representation from the best circles of theater-goers."[79] The planned hunt with Medley did not happen, and Cody continued to act on stage in New York City and Brooklyn throughout May and June.[80]

The federal government was trying to buy the Black Hills from the Lakotas. It invited nine Lakota leaders and warriors from the Cheyenne River Agency to Washington, DC. After discussions, their interpreter William Fielder escorted them to New York City on a sightseeing trip where they stayed at the Grand Central Hotel. On June 6, Fielder and Buffalo Bill Cody took the Lakota delegation to visit Gilmore's Garden (today's Madison Square Garden).[81]

The next day at noon, the Lakotas met in the hotel with Fielder, Cody, Texas Jack, Kit Carson Jr., and a couple of reporters. After they smoked cigars, they talked. One Lakota concern was that the Indian agents were not treating them right. They were also concerned if they sold the Black Hills they would not be paid its true worth. One leader, Long Mandan, said, "Would the white people be satisfied to take all of our land and leave us to wander among them and beg from door to door? I don't think this is what they wish, and if it is not, I wish they'd force Congress to do right."[82]

The last of the delegation to speak was a young warrior named Sitting Bull, not to be confused with the Hunkpapa leader Sitting Bull, who was a middle-aged man. The *New York Sun* reported his speech:

> *"I am only a young warrior," he said. "I have met the whites in battle often, and am surprised to meet a man here whom I have met in battle."*
>
> *"He means Bill," said the interpreter, pointing to Mr. Cody.*
>
> *"He can tell you what kind of a man I am," continued the warrior, "and I know what kind of a man he is. He is a good man in battle. When we meet here, we meet as friends. When we meet on the plains I hope it will be as friends. But if he ever comes to get gold from our country I shall not meet him as a friend. I have formed a different opinion of the whites from what I had. I have done."*

Then Mr. Sitting Bull and Mr. Buffalo Bill shook hands
and compared wounds. Cody has a wound in the leg and a
hole in his head made by Sitting Bull's bullets in a fight on the
Loupe River.[83]

That evening, Cody and other whites planned to take the
Lakotas to the Olympic Theatre. As they reached the hotel's cor-
ridor, they were met by a large crowd. The Lakotas greeted the
people with "How" as they walked the short distance to the theater. The number of people around them grew so large it was hard
for them to pass through.[84]

The Lakotas enjoyed the show. They did not understand English but appreciated the music and dancing. When comedians performed comedic actions, the Lakotas laughed heartily, and some
threw their blankets over their heads as they laughed out loud.
After the performance Cody and the others took the Lakotas back
to the hotel followed by a large crowd.[85]

Cody's possible visit to London did not materialize. The Army
had no scouting jobs for him that summer, so he spent his time
with his family in Rochester.[86]

During 1875, Cody began writing in his spare time. *Vickery's
Fireside Visitor* was a monthly magazine publishing good-quality
stories for middle-class readers. In the April 1875 issue appeared a
short story called "The Haunted Valley; or, A Leaf from a Hunter's
Life" by Buffalo Bill. His first dime novel, *The Pearl of the Prairies;
or, The Scout and the Renegade* was published in the *New York Weekly*
in serial form starting August 9, 1875, and would be followed by
more fictional stories over the years.[87]

As the limelight on Buffalo Bill intensified, the light on Wild
Bill dimmed. There is little information on his movements during 1875. The first part of the year, he most likely spent time in
Cheyenne. The February 8, 1875 issue of the *Dispatch: St. Louis*
and countless other newspapers reprinted a one-liner attributed to

the *Springfield Register*, "'Wild Bill' now goes through the dreary duties of United States Marshal at Cheyenne, W. T."[88] That's it; nothing more.

Black-Hillers, prospectors attempting to reach the Black Hills, headed for French Creek where Custer's 1874 expedition had discovered gold. The first group into the Black Hills, called the Gordon Party, originated out of Sioux City, Iowa. It consisted of twenty-six men, one woman, Annie Tallent, her husband, D. G. Tallent, and their son Robert. On December 23, 1874, the Gordon Party reached Custer's old encampment on French Creek and built cabins and a stockade. The Army had learned of the Gordon Party, sending several expeditions to find and bring them back. Captain John Mix, leading a detachment of the Second Cavalry out of Fort Laramie, found them, and on April 10, 1875, the troops escorted the Gordon Party out of the Black Hills to Fort Laramie where Mix released them and they were given transportation to Cheyenne, Wyoming.[89]

Buel, writing in *Heroes of the Plains*, claimed soon after Hickok had been in Cheyenne, he and two friends left for the Black Hills. When they came to the Cheyenne River, they followed it until they arrived at French Creek where they built a cabin. During the winter, they succeeded in finding gold. One evening in early April 1875, Hickok was away from the cabin. When he returned, he found the cabin ablaze, his friends dead and scalped, and a war party of twenty or more Indians.[90]

Before they spotted Hickok, he left on foot heading southwest toward Fort Fetterman, Wyoming. On the second evening, he discovered the Indians were on his trail. They caught up with him on the third day. He fought them off and jumped over a cliff into a stream, making his escape. He followed the stream through the night. The next day, he heard a rumbling noise coming from upstream; he quickly climbed the bank as a torrent of water and ice tore everything before it. Hickok saw his pursuers, carried away by the flood. After four days traveling on foot, Hickok made it to Fort Fetterman.[91] There is no evidence to corroborate Buel's story.

Black-Hiller Annie Tallent wrote about her encounter with Wild Bill Hickok as she walked with a friend on one of Cheyenne's principal streets during the summer of 1875. A long-haired, large man approached them from the opposite direction, stopped, doffed his sombrero, and in good English asked, "Madam, I hope you will pardon my seeming boldness, but knowing that you have recently returned from the Black Hills, I take the liberty of asking a few questions in regard to the country, as I expect to go there myself soon. My name is Hickok." He explained he was known as Wild Bill and said, "I suppose you have heard nothing good of me."

"Yes," Tallent answered, "I have often heard of Wild Bill, and his reputation at least is not at all creditable to him, but perhaps he is not so black as he is painted."

"Well as to that," Hickok replied, "I supposed I am called a red-handed murderer, which I deny. That I have killed men, I admit, but never unless in absolute self-defense, or in the performance of an official duty. I never, in my life, took any mean advantage of an enemy. Yet, understand, I never allowed a man to get the drop on me. But perhaps I may yet die with my boots on."

Tallent allowed Hickok to question her about the Black Hills. When they were through, Hickok gave her a gracious bow and proceeded on his way.[92]

Cheyenne had always been a rowdy town, but with an influx of prospectors hoping to enter the Black Hills and gamblers and others hoping to relieve them of their cash, city officials tried to get individuals they believed to be vagrants to leave town. Vagrants did not necessarily have to be homeless and down-and-out but could be gunfighters and those who earned their living gambling—individuals such as Wild Bill Hickok. On June 17, 1875, Hickok was charged with vagrancy and a warrant issued for his arrest. Bail was set at $200 and the trial was set for November. When November rolled around, a continuance was ordered, and then again, and finally dismissed after his death. While Hickok remained in town, no legal actions were taken against him; it was considered a minor infraction. Cheyenne marshal John Slaughter later stated in the *Daily Sun* that Hickok was never ordered to leave town.[93]

Buffalo Bill Cody worked to make his combination better than ever for the 1875–1876 season. Kit Carson Jr. left to start his own combination. Texas Jack Omohundro and Giuseppina Morlacchi rejoined the troupe. This season they would perform both *Scouts of the Plains* and *Life on the Border*.[94]

They opened on September 2 in Albany, playing in all New York cities for the month including three days in Rochester. In October they performed in Pennsylvania, New Jersey, and in southern states: Virginia, North Carolina, and Georgia.[95]

The reviewer for Wilmington, North Carolina's *Daily Journal* wrote, "our pleasure was profound . . . Buffalo Bill sustained the character he assumed with remarkable effect and the audience was delighted with his fine acting and the same may be said for Texas Jack. . . . We can recommend the troupe to the support of our citizens and we hope they will have a large house as they surely deserve it."[96]

In November and December, the Buffalo Bill Combination continued touring through the South: South Carolina, Georgia, Tennessee, Alabama, Louisiana, and Texas. The combination ended the year playing in Evansville, Indiana, New Year's Eve.[97]

The reviewer for Mobile, Alabama's *Daily Tribune* gave the troupe backhanded compliments: "The Buffalo Bill matinee had a large attendance yesterday. . . . Nobody understands why they drew such splendid houses as their performances are rough and unpolished and the actors in them do not lay claim to dramatic merit. Certain it is that the Buffalo Bill combination captured the popular heart, as no dramatic company of real merit has been able to do this year in Mobile. Perhaps the roughness which they displayed on and off the stage was the lodestone which attracted some of the most refined people of this city to their performances."[98]

Developing events would affect the lives of Cody, Hickok, and countless others.[99] The Army attempted to keep whites off the Great Sioux Reservation and out of the Black Hills, but it could not find and evict them all. In July 1875, General George Crook took command of the Department of the Platte which included the Black Hills. Touring the Hills, Crook found twelve hundred prospectors and ordered them to leave. It's not known if any listened to him.[100]

The federal government sent a commission to meet with Lakota leaders. Its mission was to buy the Black Hills from the Lakotas, get them to cede the Big Horn Mountains, and have them grant the government rights of way through unceded territory east of the Big Horns. The commission didn't have an authorized dollar amount to offer the Lakotas, but they were to assure the tribes they would receive a "fair equivalent." Congress would have to approve anything agreed to before it could go into effect.[101]

The commission led by US senator from Iowa William Allison began meeting with the tribes near Red Cloud Agency on September 20. Many Lakotas were fighting angry. Some staged mock charges on the commissioners and their cavalry escort. Allison estimated five thousand people attended. Tribal leaders did not agree to the commission's proposal.[102]

The commission finally proposed the government lease the Black Hills for $400,000 per year, but if the Lakotas were willing to sell, the government would pay them $6 million in fifteen payments. The Lakotas counteroffered, they would exchange the Black Hills for the government taking care of their needs including the best food, mules, cattle, and wagons for the next seven generations. The commissioners thought it extravagant and unrealistic. Angry and frustrated, they returned to Washington, DC, reporting to Congress that the government should offer a "fair equivalent" for the Black Hills and tell the Lakotas they must take it.[103]

By the fall of 1875, fifteen thousand whites were estimated to be in the Black Hills. On November 3, President Ulysses Grant met with General Phil Sheridan, General George Crook, Interior Secretary Zachariah Chandler, and Commissioner of Indian Affairs Edward Smith. They agreed the government would continue to declare it illegal for whites to enter the Black Hills, but the Army would stop evicting trespassers. Non-agency tribes along the Big Horn Mountains and the Yellowstone River needed to report to the agencies; if they did not, Sheridan would instruct the Army to begin a winter campaign against them.[104]

Indian Bureau Inspector Erwin Watkins filed a report on Sitting Bull's band and others considered hostile. He said they had the best hunting ground in the United States and did not want government aid. He wrote attempts to reason with these "wild and untamable" Indians had failed and recommended the Army "send troops against them in winter—the sooner the better—and whip them into subjection." Interior Secretary Chandler sent the report to Sheridan and instructed his agents "to notify Sitting Bull's band, and other wild and lawless bands of Sioux Indians" to report to the agencies by January 31, 1876 or the Army would force them there.[105]

Sheridan prepared for a winter campaign against the Lakotas and Cheyennes. Scouts learned Sitting Bull's village was on the Little Missouri River in Dakota Territory, and Sheridan planned to have Custer's Seventh Cavalry march west from Fort Abraham Lincoln to attack them. Colonel John Gibbon's column would march east along the Yellowstone River from Forts Ellis and Shaw in Montana. Both columns were in the Department of Dakota, which included Dakota and Montana Territories and under the command of General Alfred Terry. General Crook, commander of the Department of the Platte, which included Wyoming Territory, would lead a column north from Fort Fetterman to the Powder River. Sheridan wanted the troops to attack before spring when the bands would scatter.[106]

On December 22, 1875, a directive to Standing Rock's agent arrived, stating tribes needed to report to the agency by January 31, 1876, or be considered hostile. Messengers were sent out, but the winter was harsh and Sitting Bull's band was 240 miles away. There is no record if a messenger reached his camp. The certain thing is Sitting Bull did not arrive at Standing Rock Agency by January 31 and was considered a fair target for the Army.[107]

On February 7, 1876, Secretary of the Interior Chandler authorized Sheridan to proceed against the bands that had not reported to the agencies. When Sheridan notified Terry to move against Sitting Bull's people, Terry replied the Seventh Cavalry could not head out until spring; severe weather and deep snow made travel impossible.[108]

On March 17, Gibbon's Montana Column began its trek through deep snow downriver along the Yellowstone, establishing its base camp at the mouth of the Big Horn River.[109]

General Crook's column left Fort Fetterman, Wyoming, on March 1. The nine-hundred-man column consisted of ten cavalry companies, two infantry companies, and scouts. They marched northward through snowstorms and subzero temperatures to reach the Powder River across the border in Montana on March 16.[110]

Scouts spotted two hunters and believed they were returning to a village. Crook sent Colonel Joseph Reynolds with three hundred men to attack the village. They followed the hunters' trail to a village of about a hundred lodges, possibly seven hundred to one thousand people. The village was situated in timber beneath bluffs along a dry riverbed.[111]

The morning of March 17, the troops initiated a surprise attack on the village. Warriors grabbed their weapons and hurried the women and children to the bluffs or to protective cover along the river. From those positions they fired on the soldiers. The scouts believed it was the Oglala leader Crazy Horse's village, but it was a Cheyenne camp with a few Oglala lodges. The troops captured over seven hundred horses and set fire to the lodges. The warriors counterattacked; Reynolds panicked and left the village, failing to take with him the bodies of four dead soldiers. In all the shots fired, one warrior was killed.[112]

That night, Cheyenne and Oglala warriors recovered their horses from Reynolds who failed to place guards over the herd. When Crook learned what had happened, he was furious. The column returned to Fort Fetterman where Crook filed court-martial charges against Reynolds. Crook would need to regroup and resupply before taking to the field again.[113]

During the fall of 1875 and into the winter of 1876, little is known of Wild Bill Hickok's movements. He most likely remained in Cheyenne doing nothing worthy of note. In March things changed.

Back on November 16, 1875, Agnes Lake's daughter Emma married Gil Robinson, the son of a circus owner; Agnes believed she was now free. In January 1876, she traveled to San Francisco to visit circus friends. On her return from California, she stopped in Cheyenne to visit old friend and lion tamer Minnie Wells who was living with Sylvester "Wes" Moyer.[114]

Several versions tell the story of how Hickok and Agnes met in Cheyenne. One story had it Hickok was surprised when a friend told him Agnes was in town, another version claimed she pursued him there to marry him even though he was not that interested.[115] The most likely explanation is a simple one: If they were writing to each other, they coordinated their meeting in Cheyenne.

They were quickly engaged and married on March 5, 1876. The wedding took place in Wes and Minnie's home. It was a small affair with a few friends attending. The Methodist minister W. F. Warren married them; in the church register, he wrote the cryptic note "Don't think the[y] meant it."[116]

Agnes later wrote to Hickok's mother, Polly, "I loved James for three years before I married him."[117] In a letter from Hickok to Agnes, he ended it with:

one Thousand kises [sic] to my wife Agnes[.]
From Your ever loving
Husband
J. B. Hickok
Wild Bill
By By[118]

The newlyweds lied on the marriage certificate. Hickok claimed he was forty-five years old; he was thirty-eight. Agnes said she was forty-two; she was almost fifty. The March 7, 1876 *Cheyenne Daily Leader* announced their marriage, and their wedding news was published in newspapers from coast to coast.[119]

The Hickoks left Cheyenne by train the evening of March 6 and traveled to St. Louis where they spent a few days with Agnes's brother, Joseph Mersman, his wife, and eight children. Joseph was a successful businessman in partnership with Charles Orthwein, buying corn and grain and selling it to St. Louis breweries including Anheuser-Busch.[120]

Hickok and Agnes traveled to her Cincinnati home where daughter Emma, now pregnant, was staying. Emma's husband, Gil Robinson, was on the road during circus season, so Agnes planned to stay with Emma during her pregnancy and help when the newborn child arrived.[121]

Hickok and Agnes made plans for their future. Agnes wanted a ranch where she could raise and train horses; Hickok wanted it to be someplace where he could live in obscurity. Even though Agnes had property she could sell, they needed additional money to accomplish their dreams. Hickok wanted to be the provider and didn't want to live off Agnes's money. They believed the best way Hickok could make money was for him to travel to the Black Hills where he could acquire enough gold for them to live the life they wanted.[122]

Hickok planned to organize and lead an expedition to the Black Hills. He would first go to Cheyenne to make arrangements, then travel to St. Louis to recruit party members. Hickok stayed with Agnes and Emma for two weeks and then took the train west to begin organizing the Black Hills party. Agnes planned to join him that fall, once he was settled.[123]

Hickok stopped in Homer, now being called Troy Grove, Illinois, to visit his mother and relatives. He was back in Cheyenne by March 23. A *Cheyenne Leader* reporter wrote, "He is a trifle pale now because of a recent illness," but did not elaborate what Hickok's illness was. Hickok talked about his plans to head to the Black Hills: "he spoke of the prospects in the new El Dorado as soon as the weather opens." On April 14, the *Leader* sarcastically commented on Hickok's efforts to form a party for the Black Hills: "Wild Bill is still with us and the same may be said of winter. He is in his element nowadays and makes a business of stuffing newcomers and tenderfeet of all descriptions with tales of his prowess, his wonderful discoveries of diamond caves, etc., which he describes as located 'up north.'"[124]

Winter stayed in Cheyenne longer than Hickok. The *St. Louis Dispatch* said Hickok arrived in St. Louis on April 15 and was in town to organize a party to lead to the Black Hills. The article continued, "A DISPATCH reporter noticed a gentleman standing on the corner of Fourth and Olive streets this morning [April 18, 1876], having long hair, partially covered by a white sombrero. On closer inspection he recognized the individual as 'Wild Bill' notwithstanding the fact that Bill presents only a shadow of his former self. Engaging him in conversation, he said that his gaunt, thin appearance was owing to the fact that he had been entirely blind for the last two years, but is now rapidly recovering his sight. He married about five weeks ago, having lived the life of a celebate [*sic*] for nearly forty-five years. He had a 'brush' with the Indians on the Powder River a short time ago and was run out of the country. . . . Bill is used to this, and is determined to possess some of the gold, which he says abounds in the hills, before he abandons the territory entirely. He knows every inch of that country, and is therefore a valuable guide to those on a pilgrimage to that new Eldorado."[125]

It's interesting to note several things. Hickok was in poor health, losing lots of weight. He admitted his eyesight was so bad, he considered himself blind for two years. He continued to tell people he was forty-five years old instead of thirty-eight, and he had a "brush" with Indians in the Powder River country which could relate back to Buel's tale of Indians chasing him out of the Black Hills.

The April 17, 1876, edition of the *St. Louis Globe Democrat* contained an announcement by E. A. Ford, Missouri Pacific Railroad general passenger agent: "The Missouri Pacific Railroad is prepared to transport people to that country ['the Black Hills and Big Horn country'] at extremely low rates, and is now arranging for a large expedition, to leave St. Louis and Kansas City about May 10, under the guidance of the celebrated scout and experienced leader 'Wild Bill,' who is now in the city. Mr. Hickok (Wild Bill) has no doubt of the existence of gold in that country, and will pilot his expedition to where it can be found in paying quantities."[126]

However, the expedition did not leave May 10. While Hickok was in St. Louis, he had circulars printed and also published in newspapers concerning the Black Hills expedition such as this one in the *St. Louis Globe-Democrat* May 6, 1876 edition:

> *WANTED—340 more men to join Wild Bill's Black Hills and Big Horn Expedition, which leaves St. Louis, positively May 17. Wild Bill, the commander, is at headquarters—old Pacific Depot, corner of Seventh and Poplar streets—from 9 a.m. till 8 p.m. Call and see him, or write to him. He can tell you all about the gold region, its prospects, etc. We want good men, who are willing to work, and go to stay. The expedition is fast filling up, and, as only a limited number will be taken, all who intend to join should call or send at once, be registered and get their certificates.*
>
> *G. V. TOMS, Manager*[127]

Hickok sent the expedition circulars and posters to Cheyenne where both the *Daily Sun* and the always critical *Leader* covered the planned expedition in depth. The *Kansas City Journal of Commerce* May 18, 1876 edition reported, "William Hickok better known in the West as Wild Bill, came in from St. Louis last night with a large party of Black Hillers, and will escort them as guide into the gold country. The party will outfit at Custar [*sic*] City."[128]

Hickok's expedition to the Black Hills may have been delayed until June 1. The May 29, 1876 edition of the *St. Louis Republican* printed an advertisement that there was still room on the expedition for eighty-five more men and it would leave St. Louis on June 1. Those interested were to inquire at the expedition headquarters at the old Pacific Depot. There was no indication Hickok had returned to St. Louis.[129] However, he must have left Cheyenne for some reason as the *Leader* observed in its June 8 edition, "Wild Bill is among us again."[130]

The reason for the delay has not been discovered. Possibly Hickok was sick. On June 30, 1876, Agnes wrote a letter to Hickok's sister Celinda. She wrote James delayed his expedition until June 1. She then continued, "I have not heard from him since and I feel so bad about it that I can not sleep at night, but the only consolation that I have is that he is where he can not communicate[,] iff [*sic*] I was sure it was that I would not feel so bad. But I am afraid he is sick: and if so he will not write nor alow [*sic*] anyone else to do so."[131]

Information on what happened to Wild Bill's Black Hills and Big Horn Expedition is muddled. Historian William Connelley wrote that on April 12, 1876, Hickok left Cheyenne with his expedition of about two hundred men, most hailing from St. Louis and Kansas City. They reached the Black Hills goldfields in early May, then Hickok left them returning to Cheyenne.[132]

Connelley's date of April 12 for when the expedition left Cheyenne is wrong based on newspaper advertisements that stated the expedition would leave St. Louis on May 17. The *Kansas City Journal of Commerce* reported the evening of May 17, Hickok arrived in town from St. Louis with "a large party of Black-Hillers" he was guiding to Custer City, on French Creek in the southern Black Hills. It is possible they continued their railroad trip to Cheyenne and from there Hickok led them along the trail to Custer. The distance between the two towns was approximately 260 miles, and a round-trip would take roughly two weeks.[133] It's possible Hickok could have taken them to the Black Hills and been back in Cheyenne for the *Leader* to mention he was back in town on June 8.

There were continued newspaper advertisements for Hickok's Black Hills expedition beyond May 17. Possibly he planned to take a second group to the Black Hills. However, he may have realized it was something he didn't want to do again, or he could not find enough people to go. Maybe he became sick and couldn't do it. There is no record Wild Bill's Black Hills and Big Horn Expedition was ever disbanded.

The year 1876 started out good for Buffalo Bill's Combination. After playing New Year's Day in Evansville, Indiana, the troupe performed for five days in St. Louis. The *St. Louis Republican* was surprised by the show:

> *The Buffalo Bill and Texas Jack combination which filled the week at De Bar's proved more attractive and did a far better business than any body expected. The galleries were of course the big end of their houses, but their dress-circle patrons were quite numerous and increased very perceptibly as the week went on. There was so much powder burnt at each general explosion of fire-arms that the shooting lost its terrors for timid ears. It resolved itself into a rattle of musketry or riflery, which was in turn drowned out by the tumultuous applause of the galleries. Buffalo Bill and Texas Jack are emphatically "shooting stars.". . . "Buffalo Bill" and "Texas Jack" have introduced quite a new thing in dramatic presentation. They are the*

first heroic examples of the veritable heroes playing their own heroism on stage. They are not actors, but the simon-pure characters themselves, and this fact constitutes the whole novelty of their performances.[134]

The rest of January, Buffalo Bill's Combination crisscrossed Iowa, Illinois, Ohio, and Indiana. February and March were more of the same, night after night, playing in Illinois, Indiana, Kentucky, West Virginia, Ohio, Pennsylvania, and Michigan, ending the last week of March in Ontario, Canada.[135]

The *Decatur Daily Republican* reprinted what the Springfield, Illinois *Journal* wrote about the combination: "Buffalo Bill, Texas Jack and their excellent combination met with a perfect ovation this trip. Their audience at the Saturday matinee was large, and in the evening as on Friday night, the opera house was packed."[136]

April 1876, Buffalo Bill's Combination was back in New York, playing in Buffalo, Syracuse, and Cody's new hometown, Rochester on April 10, 11, and 12.[137]

Rochester's *Democrat and Chronicle* reported, "An immense audience packed the opera house last evening to see the noted western scouts, Buffalo Bill and Texas Jack, who, with Mlle. Morlacchi and a full company, performed the thrilling drama 'Life on the Bordea [*sic*]' . . . although there are five acts in the play, the audience did not seem to be fatigued with the length. The people always get their money's worth when they go see Buffalo Bill, which accounts for his large houses."[138]

After leaving Rochester, the combination arrived in Springfield, Massachusetts, to perform for two nights. Cody was about to go onstage when he received a telegram telling him his three children had scarlet fever and of the three, five-year-old Kit Carson Cody was dangerously ill. He finished the first act, told the audience what was going on, and had John Burke take his part, as he caught the next train to Rochester.[139]

Cody arrived at the Rochester train station at 10:00 a.m. the next morning where Moses Kerngood met him and drove him to his home. Cody wrote, "I found my little boy unable to speak but he seemed to recognize me and putting his little arms around my neck he tried to kiss me. We did everything in our power to save him, but it was of no avail. The Lord claimed his own, and that evening at six o'clock my beloved little Kit died in my arms. We laid him away to rest in the beautiful cemetery of Mount Hope amid sorrow and tears."[140]

CHAPTER 15

ENCOUNTERS ON THE PRAIRIE (JUNE 1876–JULY 1876)

The Lakotas' Paha Sapa, Hills Black, are sacred to them. The forested mountains form a rough oval stretching north to south approximately 110 miles and east to west approximately 70 miles. The rugged mountains' highest summit, Black Elk Peak, rises 7,244 feet, one of the highest points east of the Rocky Mountains.[1]

After Custer's 1874 Black Hills Expedition discovered gold, prospectors flocked to the Hills. During the summer of 1875, Custer City, along French Creek, was the first major gold camp in the southern Black Hills. In February 1876, Hill City bloomed to life in the central Hills, but quickly faded as rich placer deposits of gold found along Whitewood Creek in the northern Black Hills turned out to be more abundant. Deadwood and outlying gold camps popped into existence along Whitewood Creek, but didn't boom until the spring when an influx of miners and those who mined the miners rushed in to make money. Deadwood had no government. There was no law enforcement. Each person was a law unto himself and most carried weapons.[2]

All these prospectors were trespassers. All these gold camps were illegal. The Army originally attempted to expel whites, but the federal government soon told it to ignore the violators. The

Lakotas were incensed at the invasion of their territory. Although Red Cloud, Spotted Tail, and other Lakota leaders tried to stop warriors from leaving the agencies, many left, as well as large numbers of family groups, heading toward the unceded lands on their annual buffalo hunts. Sitting Bull, Crazy Horse, and other Lakota and Northern Cheyenne leaders who did not recognize the Fort Laramie Treaty of 1868 were living in the unceded lands from the Powder River to the Rosebud and other tributaries south of the Yellowstone River.[3]

General Crook's March 17, 1876 attack on the Cheyenne camp brought the hunting bands the hard reality that the Army was willing to attack a camp in frigid conditions just to destroy it. The attack angered Lakotas and Cheyennes including many who were living at the agencies. Chiefs who had been peaceful advocated war.[4]

Sitting Bull's village was in Montana Territory at Chalk Butte on the divide between the Powder River and the Little Missouri River. On April 1, the refugees from the destroyed Cheyenne village, along with Crazy Horse's Oglala camp, arrived at Sitting Bull's Hunkpapa village and remained with them.[5]

The Lakotas and Cheyennes held a council. They believed the Army would attack again and their best defense was to stay together. Sitting Bull was reconfirmed leader of the Lakotas and Dakotas and the Cheyennes were united under their war chief Two Moons. They sent messengers to all the hunting bands suggesting they join Sitting Bull and Two Moons for mutual protection. The Lakotas, Dakotas, and Cheyennes all looked to Sitting Bull for leadership. Over the next few months, Sitting Bull's camp would become massive [6]

The Lakotas and Cheyennes were right. General Sheridan's plan of three columns of troops converging on the hunting bands in the unceded lands was still in place. General John Gibbon's Montana Column consisting of six companies of the Seventh Infantry, four companies of the Second Cavalry, and twenty-five Crow scouts had been in place on the Yellowstone River at the mouth of the Big Horn River in Montana Territory since March.[7]

General Alfred Terry led the Dakota Column westward out of Fort Abraham Lincoln on May 17. The Dakota Column was almost one thousand men strong, consisting of forty Arikara scouts, a few white scouts, three infantry companies, and twelve companies of the Seventh Cavalry led by Lieutenant Colonel George Custer.[8]

After refitting and augmenting his force at Fort Fetterman, General George Crook marched north toward the Powder River again on May 29. Crook's Big Horn and Yellowstone Expedition consisted of ten companies of the Third Cavalry, five companies of the Second Cavalry, two companies of the Fourth Infantry, and three companies of the Ninth Infantry as well as scouts and civilian teamsters and mule packers. Totaling over one thousand men, it was the largest of the three forces. The columns were converging on where they believed the Lakota and Cheyenne bands would be, and they did not want them to escape.[9]

Little Kit Carson Cody's death devastated Buffalo Bill and Louisa Cody. The two girls would recover. After several days at home, Cody returned to the stage, but his heart was not in it.[10]

Through the rest of April and into May, the Buffalo Bill Combination played to audiences in major cities of Massachusetts, Connecticut, Maine, Rhode Island, and New Jersey. Captain Anson Mills with the Third Cavalry had been writing letters to Cody stating General Crook wanted him to come join his command, but Cody put off Mills, stating he had obligations he had to meet first.[11]

By the end of May, Cody made up his mind to join Crook. He and Texas Jack decided to split up the combination and perform on their own, parting as friends.[12]

The June 1, 1876 edition of Wilmington, Delaware's *Daily Commercial* announced, "Buffalo Bill Combination . . . will appear at the Opera House on Saturday June 3d, for a farewell benefit for Buffalo Bill, who starts Monday morning for the seat of the present Indian war in the Black Hills. He will resume his old position as Chief of Scouts, and will march directly to face the Sioux chiefs, Sitting Bull and Crazy Horse in their strong-holds in the Black Hills."[13]

After performing in Buffalo Bill Combination's final show, Cody hurried home to spend a few days with Louisa and the girls before taking the train west. Louisa later wrote, "We said goodbye at the station once more. Will was going back to the West, and I hoped the West would give him again that old light in his eyes, that the fresh, clean air, the brilliant ruddiness of the sunshine and the glare of the plains would take that pallor from his cheeks, the excitement of the chase once again return the great, happy booming that once had sounded in this voice. My trust in the West was fulfilled."[14]

Cody stopped at Sheridan's Chicago headquarters where he learned Crook was already in the field. He also learned his old comrades, the Fifth Cavalry, were reassigned to the Department of the Platte. Their mission was to contain the Lakotas and Cheyennes at their agencies. The Fifth's headquarters and eight companies were gathering at Fort D. A. Russell outside of Cheyenne, and from there would march to Fort Laramie.[15]

The Fifth's commander, Lieutenant Colonel Eugene Carr, wanted Cody for his guide and chief of scouts. Cody decided to join the Fifth and took the train to Cheyenne. The Chicago headquarters sent a telegram to Carr telling him Cody was on his way. When Cody arrived on June 9, Carr had sent First Lieutenant Charles King to meet him at the Cheyenne train station with a horse for his use. Together, they rode out to the fort.[16]

Upon their arrival, one of the soldiers shouted, "Here's Buffalo Bill!" The men of the regiment gave him three cheers. The officers and men were glad to see Cody, and he was glad to see them. Carr immediately appointed Cody his guide and chief of scouts.[17]

Private Daniel Brown, assigned to headquarters, wrote, "All the old boys in the regiment seeing General [brevet rank] Carr and Cody together, exchanged confidences, and expressed themselves to the effect that with such a leader and scout they could get away with all the Sitting Bulls and Crazy Horses in the Sioux tribe."[18]

The next day, Cody was signed up on the Army payroll, and on June 11, Carr led the Fifth Cavalry to Fort Laramie, roughly ninety-eight miles to the north. They reached the fort on June 14. The evening of that same day, General Sheridan arrived accompanied by Colonel James Fry and Major James Forsyth.[19]

Sheridan wanted to see for himself the situation at Red Cloud Agency and Spotted Tail Agency to the northeast along the White River. He was happy to see Buffalo Bill was a scout again. The morning of June 15, Sheridan, Fry, and Forsyth, with a Fifth Cavalry company as escort as well as Cody, left to inspect the agencies and their Army camps. Sheridan found everything peaceful. He believed reports of large war parties leaving the agencies were exaggerations. Sheridan, Cody, and the rest of the party returned to Fort Laramie on June 18.[20]

Based on what Sheridan learned, he instructed Carr to scout westward along the Powder River trail to turn back any Indians traveling west and to block any returning from the west. The Powder River trail ran from the two White River agencies to the Powder River country running north of Fort Laramie and south of the Black Hills. On the morning of June 22, 1876, Carr, leading the Fifth Cavalry, headed north on the road toward the Black Hills [21]

That same day, a courier from General Crook arrived at Fort Fetterman. Crook had prepared a telegram to be sent to General Sheridan who was now back at his Chicago headquarters. The telegram informed Sheridan that on June 17, the Big Horn and Yellowstone Expedition had been attacked on the upper reaches of the Rosebud River. Crook wrote the Indian force was large enough that it could have defeated his column. He was able to repulse them and returned to his base camp on Goose Creek (near modern-day Sheridan, Wyoming) to care for his wounded. He was also ordering five additional companies of infantry join him before continuing his march against the Indians.[22]

With that information and additional telegrams from Crook arriving, Sheridan ordered Carr to stop his advance and encamp on the Powder River trail where it intersected with the Black Hills road at the South Fork of the Cheyenne River, just to the west of the southern Black Hills. From June 26 to July 3, the Fifth Cavalry would be encamped there. Carr sent out scouting parties in search of Indians. Occasionally, small groups were spotted, but they were too far away and vanished when pursued.[23]

The commander of the Fifth Cavalry was actually Colonel William Emory. For years, Emory had not been in the field to command, effectively leaving Carr in charge. Emory was retiring and his replacement was based solely on seniority. Carr was not the next in line; it was Lieutenant Colonel Wesley Merritt of the Ninth Cavalry who received the position of commander of the Fifth Cavalry.[24]

Carr was disappointed, writing to his wife Mary, "It is of course, an humiliation to me to have him [Merritt] come in and take command. It seems curious that the Government should find it necessary to spend large amounts of money and some blood to teach Terry, Crook and Merritt how to fight these Prairie Indians when there are others who know better how to do it."[25]

Cody later wrote, "I was sorry the command was taken from General [brevet rank] Carr, because under him it had made its fighting reputation. However, upon becoming acquainted with General [brevet rank] Merritt, I found him to be an excellent officer.[26]

Merritt arrived at Fort Laramie in late June, knowing he would be taking over command of the Fifth on July 1. On June 28, Merritt with an escort of the Second Cavalry's Company K and Buffalo Bill Cody as guide, rode north to the Fifth Cavalry's camp on the South Fork of the Cheyenne, arriving there on July 1 to assume command.[27]

At sunrise on the morning of July 3, a report came in from the scouts that twelve Indians leading pack animals were headed up the Powder River trail from the direction of the agencies. Merritt ordered Company K, commanded by Captain Julius Mason and Lieutenant Charles King to mount up and intercept the Indians. As they rode out of the cottonwood trees, they saw Buffalo Bill waving his hat and telling them, "This way Colonel, this way" as he turned his horse and they followed him up a dry streambed.[28]

Captain Sanford Kellogg's Company I joined Company K on its left and slightly behind as they galloped up the streambed and then onto a grassy slope. King wrote, "As we near the ridge and prepare to deploy, excitement is subdued but intense—Buffalo Bill plunging along beside us on a strawberry roan, sixteen hands high, gets a trifle of a lead, but we go tearing up the crest in a compact body, reach it, rein up, amazed and disgusted—not an Indian to be seen for two miles across the intervening 'swale.'"[29]

Other scouts ahead signaled that the troops needed to ride to the left toward the Cheyenne River. There they spotted Indians racing west. Even though the troops were far behind the Indians, they continued the chase. The scouts got close enough to exchange a few shots and force the Indians to abandon several pack animals loaded with supplies. After a thirty-mile chase, the cavalry horses were spent. Two dropped dead. The Indians continued to race toward the Powder River country, as the troops returned to their encampment.[30]

Merritt believed the Indians at the agencies now knew his troops were encamped on the South Fork of the Cheyenne River. He decided to move camp to a new location. He sent out two patrols, one eastward and the other westward, while the companies which had given chase to the Indians rode their worn-out horses to Sage Creek, the location of an Army stockade to protect travelers on the road to the Black Hills. They encamped at the stockade where the troops sent out on patrol would join them. Neither patrol found Indians, but the westward patrol led by Major John Upham discovered the bodies of two Black-Hillers killed by Indians.[31]

On July 6, a courier from Fort Laramie rode north on the Black Hills road with a message for Lieutenant Colonel Merritt. Cody intercepted the courier and escorted him to the Fifth

Cavalry's camp where he delivered the letter to Merritt. Lieutenant King wrote about what happened next: "A party of junior officers were returning from a refreshing bath in a deep pool in the stream, when Buffalo Bill came hurriedly towards them from the general's tent. His handsome face wore a look of deep trouble, and he brought us to a halt in stunned, awe-stricken silence with the announcement, 'Custer and five companies of the Seventh wiped out of existence. It's no rumor—General Merritt's got the official dispatch.'"[32]

On June 25, 1876, Lieutenant Colonel George Armstrong Custer, leading the Seventh Cavalry, had attacked Sitting Bull's massive village on the Little Big Horn River in Montana Territory. Lakota, Dakota, and Cheyenne warriors fighting to defend their families killed Custer and 268 of his men.[33]

In June 1876, Wild Bill Hickok's expedition to the Black Hills and Big Horn Mountains was over. Hickok planned to head to the Black Hills with Colorado Charlie Utter. Utter and his partners, who included his brother Steve, Richard "Bloody Dick" Seymour, and a man named Ingalls, planned to start up the Pioneer Pony Express that would deliver mail between Fort Laramie and Deadwood. The partners believed the mail could be delivered in forty-eight hours.[34]

Hickok and Utter's party started out to be the two of them as well as Steve Utter and a friend of Hickok's only known as Pie. The Utters were taking a four-horse team and wagon to haul supplies, and Hickok and Pie bought a light two-horse wagon.[35]

As they were preparing for their journey, Hickok ran into an old friend, Joseph "White Eye" Anderson. Anderson was called White Eye because a burning buffalo chip had scorched one eyebrow that grew back white. Hickok and Anderson had known each other since meeting years earlier at Fort McPherson.[36]

The first thing Wild Bill said to White Eye was, "Touch flesh, my boy," and they shook hands. Anderson had arrived in Cheyenne with his brother Charlie. They planned to travel to Deadwood and were looking for a party to join. Hickok introduced Anderson to the Utters and Pie by saying, "This is my boy, the white-eyed kid." Since Anderson was a friend of Hickok's, Colorado Charlie invited the brothers to join their party.[37]

The Andersons bought two riding horses. The Utters had plenty of room in their wagon and told the Andersons they would haul their belongings for them. The six men bought provisions for the journey and planned to share meals together. Hickok bought a five-gallon keg of whiskey, believing it should last him and his friends until Deadwood.[38]

Most likely on June 27, 1876, after completing their outfitting, the Hickok-Utter party headed north on the road to Fort Laramie, ninety-eight miles away.[39]

On June 29, they camped two miles south of Jack Hunton's Ranch at Bordeaux, sixty-seven miles north of Cheyenne. Hunton and Hickok were friends. Hunton later wrote Hickok stopped at his ranch long enough to say "How," and when he left, Hickok said, "So long Jack." A few hours later, one of Hunton's men, Waddie Bascom, rode into the ranch saying he met Hickok who said he had left his cane at last night's campsite. Hickok described the cane's location and asked if Hunton would find it and send it to him in Deadwood. Hunton sent one of his men to the site and retrieved Hickok's cane.[40]

It was probably July 1 when Hickok and friends reached Fort Laramie, filled with officers and enlisted men making it a beehive of activity. The six men met with the officer-of-the day who told them since there was increased danger of Indian attacks, they needed to join a party of one hundred or more for mutual protection. The officer told them to continue north sixteen miles to the Government Farm where Black-Hillers were gathering to form a party. Government Farm was the site of an abandoned experimental Army farming operation.[41]

The officer-of-the-day had a request. There was a young woman in the guardhouse; he asked them to take her with them.

White Eye said, "It was just after payday and she had been on a big drunk with the soldiers and had been having a hell of a time of it. When they put her in the post guard house she was very drunk and near naked. Her name was Calamity Jane."[42]

Calamity Jane's real name was Martha Canary. At the time, she was twenty years old and already notorious. She was born near Princeton, Missouri, in 1856. Her family moved west, and by 1867, she and her siblings were orphans. The children were most likely divided up among families to raise. Calamity grew up in Wyoming mining boomtowns, Army forts, and railroad hell-on-wheels towns. By 1870, she was in Cheyenne and had already received her nickname. There were various accounts on how she received it.[43]

By 1874, Calamity was working at the Three Mile road ranch southwest of Fort Laramie. At Three Mile, soldiers and travelers could buy drinks and supplies, get a meal, and spend the night. The road ranch owners hired ten prostitutes, one of whom was Calamity Jane.[44]

The government sent a scientific expedition into the Black Hills to evaluate its mineral resources. The expedition led by geologists Walter Jenney and Henry Newton accompanied by a four-hundred-man Army escort, left Fort Laramie on May 25, 1875. Along with the expedition went Calamity Jane disguised as a soldier. After entering the Black Hills, officers discovered her identity and sent her back to Fort Laramie with a returning supply train.[45]

By 1876, Calamity had made her way to Fort Fetterman where she worked at the Fetterman and Six Mile road ranches. She again disguised herself and went with General Crook's March expedition to the Powder River country and back.[46]

In April, she made the journey to Custer City in the Black Hills where she was noted for her teamster abilities and hard drinking. She returned to Cheyenne where she was arrested on May 22 accused of stealing women's clothing. After a three-week stay in jail, a jury found her not guilty, and she was a free woman again on June 8.[47]

Calamity Jane knew of General Crook's Big Horn and Yellowstone Expedition and returned to Fort Fetterman, then made her way to Crook's camp on Goose Creek between June 15 and 18. She was found out and sent back to Fort Fetterman with the wounded on June 21. She traveled to Fort Laramie where she went on a drinking spree and wound up in the guardhouse.[48]

The officer-of-the-day took Wild Bill Hickok and friends to the guardhouse where Calamity Jane was being held. Steve Utter knew her and said he would take care of her. The officer gave Calamity Army-issue underwear, and, between the six men, they gave her a buckskin shirt and pants and a broad-brimmed hat. White Eye said, "When she got cleaned up and sober she looked quite attractive."[49]

"Calamity Jane had a wonderful command of profanity, that is she could cuss to beat the band," Anderson said. "She was also a good shot with a rifle and six-shooter and could skin mules for further order. I believe it was the first time that Wild Bill had met her and he surely did not have any use for her. She looked to be about twenty-five years of age [she was twenty] and was as tough as they came. She laid up with Steve Utter and ate her meals with us during the trip."[50]

The Hickok-Utter party, now numbering seven souls, headed north to Government Farm where they found other travelers gathering to head north. Their numbers quickly grew to over one hundred people with roughly thirty wagons and plenty of livestock. Anderson remembered there were 130 people saying, "Our wagon train consisted mostly of westerners: prospectors, gamblers, saloon men, bartenders, and wholesale liquor men. There were thirteen or fourteen ladies of easy virtue in the train."[51]

The people needed to elect a captain to lead the wagon train. They wanted that person to be Wild Bill Hickok, but he was not well and didn't want the position, so Colorado Charlie Utter was elected captain and Charlie Anderson was elected wagon boss. The wagon train was soon bound north for Custer City.[52]

"At night there would be a bunch of us around the campfires telling stories," White Eye wrote. "We had a lot of fun and some lively times. Bill Hickok never had much to say, but you can bet there was something doing when Calamity Jane was around. I think she told some of the toughest stories I ever heard and there would always be a big crowd come over to the campfire to hear her talk."[53]

Hickock was generous with his five-gallon barrel of whiskey. Every morning a crowd of men gathered around his wagon to sample his liquor. Hickok would say to White Eye, "Fill her up my boy and pass her around again." They were about half-way to Deadwood when Hickok's whiskey barrel went dry. He refilled the barrel from a wholesale whiskey seller who was hauling a load. He told his friends from then on it was his private stock and they were not to give any whiskey to anyone outside their group except for sickness or snake bite.[54]

Calamity Jane was one of the heavy hitters of the whiskey keg, but she always first asked Hickok for a tin cup saying, "Mr. Hickok, I'm dry again." One time he responded by telling her to go slow, others were dry too.[55]

They saw one band of about forty Indians south of Hat Creek. The warriors started to tangle with the wagon train's advance guard, but when the Indians saw how many members were in the wagon train, they rode off.[56]

On July 6, the wagon train arrived at the Army stockade at Sage Creek, also known as Hat Creek. Buffalo Bill Cody was encamped there with the Fifth Cavalry, and he and Hickok soon found each other.[57]

White Eye Anderson had known Cody since the Fort McPherson days. When Cody saw Anderson he said, "By God, it's the White-Eye Kid" and shook hands with him. Cody tried to get White Eye and others, possibly including Hickok, to sign on with the Army, but they were after gold, not Indians.[58]

White Eye said, "Cody and Hickok had some words over a manuscript they were interested in together, but it was settled peacefully."[59]

Every few days Hickok would shoot at targets. He usually did that in private. White Eye related: "Wild Bill's eyes, which were diseased, concerned him. He was going blind, and knew it. His sight was perfect up to twenty-five steps, but beyond that distance, things became blurred. By shooting at targets he checked them every few days to see if they were any worse."

Hickok asked White Eye to look after him at night once they got to town. "Lights bother me at night," Hickok told White Eye. "People say I'm moonblind but it's worse than that." [60]

The wagon train entered Red Canyon in the southern Black Hills where they found the shallow grave of a man who had been recently killed by Indians. The body had been dug up and dismembered, and coyotes were eating body parts. The travelers dug a deep grave and buried the remains, placing rocks overtop to hopefully keep the coyotes from digging into the grave.[61]

The next day, the wagon train arrived in Custer City on French Creek in the southern Black Hills. This was the final destination for some of their party. After a brief stay, the wagon train continued north. The road was bad from Custer to Deadwood and the going was slower.[62]

It was July 12 when the wagon train reached the outskirts of Deadwood and stopped. Wild Bill Hickok and Colorado Charlie Utter borrowed the Anderson brothers' horses to ride into town. They were going to find a camping location for the wagon train. Charlie Utter's partner, Bloody Dick Seymour was now with them, and rode along. Steve Utter and Calamity Jane were not going to be left behind and found horses, joining the party.[63]

Twenty-year-old Richard Hughes, who had worked as a printer for the Nebraska *West Point Republican* and taught school for one term, had caught gold fever and was working a claim outside Deadwood. He was in town the day Hickok, Seymour, the Utter brothers, and Calamity Jane arrived. Hughes said, "The party above described, entered Deadwood and rode the entire length of Main Street, mounted on good horses and clad in complete suits of buckskin, every suit of which carried sufficient fringe to make a considerable buckskin rope."[64]

Harry Young, who Hickok had helped get a start in Hays City back in 1868 and had had several chance meetings with Hickok over the years, was tending bar in the Number 10 Saloon. Hickok and Utter's cavalcade attracted a large crowd. Young later commented, "They were mounted and a more picturesque sight could not be imagined than Wild Bill on horseback."[65]

Hickok and Utter were both friends of Carl Mann, one of the owners of the Number 10 Saloon. They reined up in front of the saloon, dismounted, and entered, followed by a crowd that packed into the barroom.[66]

Hickok spied Young and said, "Kid, here you are again, like the bad penny, but I am awfully glad to see you." Hickok turned to Carl Mann who was standing beside him and said, "I first met this kid in Hayes [sic] City, Kansas, and wherever I go, he seems to precede me or to follow me, for I have met him in Abilene, Ellsworth, Cheyenne, and now again here; but he is a good boy and you can trust him. Take my word for that." Mann was happy to see Hickok and Utter, telling them they could make his saloon their headquarters. Young said, "This meant money to Mann, as Bill would be a great drawing card." Wild Bill Hickok and Colorado Charlie Utter agreed to make Number 10 Saloon their headquarters.[67]

CHAPTER 16

INCIDENT AT WARBONNET CREEK (JULY 1876–AUGUST 1876)

After Wild Bill Hickok's wagon train continued north toward Custer City, Buffalo Bill Cody and the Fifth Cavalry remained at Sage Creek until July 12, 1876. General Phil Sheridan sent Colonel Wesley Merritt orders to take the Fifth Cavalry back to Fort Laramie where it was to reequip, then ride northwest to Fort Fetterman. From there, they were to head northwest to Crook's encampment on Goose Creek at the foot of the Big Horn Mountains' eastern slopes, near present-day Sheridan, Wyoming. Even though Crook had over one thousand men, he would not move against the Lakotas and Cheyennes until the Fifth Cavalry and other troops arrived.[1]

The evening of July 12, the Fifth Cavalry endured a thunderstorm lasting most of the night. Men, their mounts, and equipment were soaked. By the time they made camp on July 13, they had ridden thirty-four miles south toward Fort Laramie; and again, they were hit by an intense thunderstorm. That evening, Merritt received a message from Major Edwin Townsend, the Fort Laramie commander, who relayed information from Captain William Jordan, the Camp Robinson commander, that hundreds of Cheyennes planned to leave the agency for the north.[2]

On the morning of July 14, Merritt directed his column to leave the road to Fort Laramie and ride cross-country to the southeast. By noon, they reached the road between Fort Laramie and Camp Robinson where he stopped. Even though he had orders to proceed to Fort Laramie, Merritt believed if the Cheyennes were leaving Red Cloud Agency, his duty was to stop them. He sent Major Thaddeus Stanton accompanied by an escort to Camp Robinson to relay back information on the developing situation.[3]

Stanton arrived at Camp Robinson that evening and sent back a message to Merritt, in addition to a message from Captain Jordan confirming what Jordan had originally written as well as new information. The garrison at Camp Robinson was too weak to prevent Indians from leaving the Red Cloud Agency. Many Lakota warriors had already left for the north after learning of Custer's defeat, and now eight hundred Cheyennes, 150 of whom were fighting men, had left the agency. The warriors had been busy buying as many cartridges as they could get. One piece of information benefiting Merritt was that the Indians believed the Fifth Cavalry was still at Sage Creek and they could easily ride past the cavalry without being detected.[4]

Even though Merritt had orders to return to Fort Laramie, he made a field decision to ride north in the opposite direction to intercept the Cheyennes and turn them back to the agency. He sent a message to Stanton to return to the command at once. He sent another message to Fort Laramie to be telegrammed to General Sheridan informing him of his intentions.[5]

At 1:00 p.m. on July 15, Merritt began the Fifth Cavalry's forced march back to Sage Creek. The Fifth's supply wagons under the command of their temporary quartermaster, First Lieutenant William Hall, with an escort of the Ninth Infantry from Fort Laramie, would follow behind as fast as they could.[6]

By 10:00 p.m. the Fifth Cavalry stopped at the Niobrara River crossing, where Merritt allowed the horses and men a brief rest. They had traveled thirty-five miles in nine hours. At midnight, Hall and the supply wagons caught up with the cavalry, and at 5:00 a.m. on July 16, Merritt's command continued its advance, reaching the Sage Creek stockade at 10:00 a.m. The men and horses rested there until Hall's wagons reached them. Merritt had the men draw three days' rations and as many carbine and revolver cartridges as they could carry. He wanted the supply wagons to follow, but he knew where he would be going they would lag far behind. He also reinforced the supply wagons' guard by including three companies of the Twenty-Third Infantry stationed at Sage Creek.[7]

After a little more than an hour, Merritt led the Fifth Cavalry out of Sage Creek continuing to follow the road toward Custer City. The initial stretch of the road led almost straight east and into Nebraska. When the road turned north again, the cavalry continued eastward across the prairie. By sundown, they reached the trail leading from the agencies to the Powder River country where it crossed Warbonnet Creek, flowing to the north toward the Cheyenne River. The scouts who had been out ahead reported no Indians in sight.[8]

The troops camped for the night along the creek. They had traveled eighty-five miles in thirty-one hours. Merritt hoped their forced march had paid off and they were out ahead of the Cheyennes.[9]

At 4:00 a.m. on July 17, the troops were awakened. No fires were permitted. The men ate a cold breakfast. Merritt sent Cody to scout the trail to the southeast toward Red Cloud Agency to try to locate the Cheyenne camp.[10]

Cody was dressed as if he would appear on stage. Lieutenant Charles King said his clothes looked like a Mexican vaquero outfit. He wore a red silk shirt, and black velvet pants that flared at the bottom with buttons on the outside seams. Strapped around his waist was an oversized belt with a huge square buckle. On his head was a broad-brimmed beaver fur hat.[11]

To the east of the camp rose two conical buttes, one three hundred yards away and the other four hundred yards. Lieutenant King, who was in charge of picket duty, had stationed Private

Christian Madsen[12] on the northern, closer-to-camp, butte, while King and Corporal Thomas Wilkinson stood watch on the more distant butte.[13]

It was about 4:25 a.m.; the sky was beginning to lighten in the east. Wilkinson pointed to a ridge to the southeast saying, "Look, lieutenant—there are Indians!" About two miles away, a small group of warriors were riding westward toward them. They were advance scouts from Morning Star's band of Cheyennes. Morning Star was leading his people to the Powder River country. They had camped for the night about seven miles to the southeast of Warbonnet Creek and had sent out the scouts to look for soldiers. Merritt's troops were obscured from their view, but they did see Hall's wagon train approaching from the west.[14]

At the same time King sent his report to Merritt, Cody arrived in camp and informed him he had found the Cheyennes who were breaking camp and preparing to resume their journey. Merritt and several officers rode to King's position and climbed the butte.[15]

It was now about 5:00 a.m., and many more warriors had joined the first few on the ridge, all watching the wagon train as it advanced toward them. Merritt instructed Carr to have the seven companies mount up but remain concealed.[16]

Cody and two of the scouts, Johnathan "Buffalo Chips" White and another named Tate, joined the officers on the butte. Cody noticed sudden activity among the Indians, some of them motioning toward the wagon train. Looking in that direction, Cody and the others saw two riders heading in their direction. They were Privates Harry Anderson and Gordon Keith carrying dispatches to be delivered to Merritt informing him Company C, which had been on detached duty, was on its way to rejoin them.[17]

Fifteen to twenty mounted warriors began racing to intercept the couriers. Merritt was concerned if he sent his troops to intercept those warriors, it would alert the entire band and they would slip away. Cody suggested to Merritt he allow him to take a few men out between the small group of warriors and the rest on the ridge and cut them off. Merritt agreed to the plan. Cody took the two scouts and selected six men from Company K and waited for the signal to spring the trap. Merritt left King on the Butte to watch the small band of warriors; when he saw they were close, he was to signal for Cody and his men to go.[18]

King waited until the warriors were about ninety yards from Cody's position then shouted, "Now, lads, in with you!"[19]

Cody raced his horse out in front of the others in his party. The warriors saw them coming. The lead warrior was well armed with weapons and a shield; his clothing and other articles included a warbonnet, a yellow-haired scalp, arm bands, and a cotton American flag as a breechcloth. The warrior raced his horse toward the oncoming Cody. Their horses were at a full gallop and about thirty yards apart when both men fired simultaneously. The warrior's shot went wide, missing Cody. Cody's shot passed through the warrior's leg, killing his horse.[20]

Cody's horse hit an animal hole and went down. Cody hit the ground and sprang to his feet. The warrior had cleared himself from his dead horse and was taking aim at Cody. They were about twenty paces apart. The warrior shot and missed. Cody fired his rifle, hitting the warrior in the chest, killing him.[21]

Cody claimed he drove a knife into the warrior's heart, though no one else mentioned it. However, they did see him scalp the warrior. The remaining warriors rode toward Cody, but when they saw his companions charging, they turned and raced away. As cavalrymen rode past Cody, he waved the warrior's scalp and warbonnet shouting, "The first scalp for Custer."[22]

Meanwhile, the rest of the Cheyenne warriors started forward to join in the fight. Merritt ordered Major Julius Mason to form three companies into line and charge the warriors. Seeing the cavalry for the first time, the warriors turned their horses and headed back the way they had come. The cavalrymen chased them for three miles, then halted and waited for Merritt to bring up the rest of the troops.[23]

Cody's first scalp for Custer

The warrior who Cody shot was the only one killed during the skirmish. Cody took a few moments to collect some of the warrior's weapons, his warbonnet, and other items.[24]

Merritt intended to pursue the Cheyennes and had the men draw two days' rations from the supply wagons. They then joined Mason and his troops and followed after the Cheyennes. The people in Morning Star's camp had heard the gunfire and had already packed their belongings and were heading back to Red Cloud Agency.[25]

Merritt and his troops followed Morning Star's Cheyennes twenty-five miles toward Red Cloud Agency where they saw that the Cheyennes' trail continued on to the Spotted Tail Agency. Merritt believed he had accomplished his goal, preventing the Cheyennes from leaving the agencies, and could now continue to Fort Laramie to reprovision and march to join Crook.[26]

The day after the Fifth Cavalry arrived at Red Cloud Agency, Lieutenant King wrote, "Quite a number of Cheyennes, our antagonists the day before" had arrived at the agency to visit with the troops. "One and all they wanted to see Buffalo Bill, and wherever he moved they followed him with awe-filled eyes. He wore the same dress in which he had burst upon them in yesterday's fight, a Mexican costume of black velvet, slashed with scarlet and trimmed with silver buttons and lace—one of his theatrical garbs."[27]

At Red Cloud Agency, Cody learned the name of the warrior he had killed was Yellow Hand. However, that was a mistranslation: It was actually Yellow Hair. The father of Yellow Hair, a chief of the Cheyennes named Cut Nose, learned Cody had his dead son's weapons and other possessions. Cut Nose sent a white interpreter to offer Cody four mules for his son's warbonnet, weapons, and other possessions. Cody replied he would like to do that but declined. He had plans to later display Yellow Hair's items to promote his shows.[28]

In a letter dated July 18, 1876, addressed from Red Cloud Agency, Cody wrote Louisa, who he called Lulu:

My Darling Lulu
We have come here for rations. We have had a fight. I killed
Yellow Hand a Cheyenne Chief in a single-handed fight. You
will no doubt hear of it through the paper. I am going as soon
as I reach Fort Laramie [to] . . . send the war bonnet, shield,
bridle, whip, arms and his scalp to Kerngood to put up in his
window. I will write Kerngood to bring it up to the house so
that you can show it to the neighbors. . . . My health is not
good. I have worked myself to death. Although I have shot at
lots of Indians I have only one scalp I can call my own that
fellow I fought single handed in sight of our command and the
cheers that went up when he fell was deafening. . . . Good-bye
my Lulu, a thousand kisses to all from your hubby,
    Willie.[29]

Later in 1876, Cody would embellish the story of his fight at Warbonnet Creek and present it as a new show called *The Red Right Hand; or Buffalo Bill's First Scalp for Custer*. He also included the incident in his 1879 autobiography.[30]

At 2:30 p.m. on July 18, the Fifth Cavalry left Red Cloud Agency marching southwest toward Fort Laramie, arriving there on July 21. After resting and resupplying, they began their march west toward Fort Fetterman at 6:00 a.m. on July 23 and arrived at the fort without incident by midafternoon on July 25.[31]

The Fifth Cavalry stayed there one night, picked up additional soldiers and officers who were waiting to travel with Merritt's troops, and left the following morning at 8:00 a.m., heading north along the eastern slopes of the Big Horn Mountains toward General Crook's encampment along Goose Creek.[32]

On August 1, the column was between Crazy Woman Fork and Clear Fork when it came upon small buffalo herds. Merritt gave permission for Cody to lead a few officers and men on a buffalo hunt to provide the troops with fresh meat.[33]

The Fifth Cavalry arrived at Crook's Goose Creek camp on the afternoon of August 3, 1876. Crook was pleased to be reunited with his old comrades from his Arizona Apache campaigns.[34] Now Crook felt confident to move out against the Lakotas and Cheyennes.

CHAPTER 17

WILD BILL DEAD IN DEADWOOD (JULY 1876–AUGUST 2, 1876)

After Wild Bill Hickok and his friends visited Deadwood's Number 10 Saloon on July 12, 1876, they needed to attend to their original business for coming to town—find a campsite. They found a location outside town along Whitewood Creek about 150 yards above its confluence with Deadwood Creek. They had to cut a road into the spot then clear the brush before they could set up camp. White Eye Anderson said, "It was a nice flat in a grove of spruce and pine trees and made a beautiful summer camp."[1]

Colorado Charlie Utter pitched a large tent he and his brother Steve slept in. Hickok slept in his canvas-covered wagon. The Anderson brothers and Pie also camped with them. After a few days' stay, Charlie Anderson and Pie decided to leave and returned to Cheyenne, and from there went to Colorado.[2]

After they had settled into their campsite, Calamity Jane asked the men for a loan to buy women's clothing. She said she couldn't compete against the other women since she only had buckskin to wear. All the men chipped in. Hickok gave her $20 on the condition she wash behind her ears. After she returned with women's clothing, she asked Steve Utter to wash her in the creek with perfumed soap. After she put on her new clothes, Steve said,

"Ain't she a dove?" They all admitted she could give the other girls a run for their money. A few days later, Calamity returned to repay her debts. Hickok wouldn't take her money saying, "At least she looks like a woman now." Calamity continued to visit their camp whenever she was hungry.[3]

White Eye Anderson said people were always stopping by their camp: old friends, people who had traveled with them from Fort Laramie, and strangers out of curiosity.[4]

Wild Bill Hickok ran into his old friend California Joe Milner. Milner and his son Charley had been prospecting in the Black Hills and came to Deadwood to buy more provisions. They stopped in Number 10 Saloon and saw Hickok standing at the bar surrounded by a crowd of men. Hickok was happy to see his old friend and invited the Milners to make his camp their headquarters while they were in town.[5]

Each morning, the first thing Hickok would do was shoot his revolvers in target practice. He would cut pieces of paper into one-inch squares and pound a tack in the center to attach them to a board propped against a tree. He then stepped back twenty-five paces and fired at the targets, many times making center hits. Others in their party shot too, and Hickok gave White Eye lessons on shooting quickly.[6]

Hickok used cap and ball pistols instead of the more recent cartridge revolvers. Back in Abilene, Charles Gross had seen Hickok fire his pistols early in the morning and asked Hickok, "Did you get your guns damp yesterday, Bill?"

"No," Hickok replied, "But I ain't ready to go yet, and I am not taking any chances when I draw and pull I must be sure." Moisture in a chamber could cause a misfire.[7]

After firing, cleaning, and reloading his pistols, Hickok would take a drink of whiskey and be ready for breakfast.[8]

Hickok and California Joe had shooting contests for drinks. California Joe usually beat Hickok with a rifle, but Hickok would win against California Joe with a revolver.[9]

Hickok went out on a three-day hunt with California Joe and also prospected for gold. When not prospecting, he could be found having a few drinks and gambling in the Senate, Shingle's Number 3, and Mann's Number 10 saloons.[10]

White Eye Anderson said Hickok did well at poker. However, he told White Eye not to play poker or faro because he was not smart enough to beat the game. Hickok would give money from his winnings to people who were down and out. After one big win, he took everyone from their camp out to eat at one of Deadwood's restaurants. Hickok bought a sheet iron stove and food for everyone in camp.[11]

Harry Young, when bartending at Number 10 Saloon, took note of Hickok's mannerisms. When Hickok was at the bar, he poured a drink with his left hand, keeping his right hand ready in case he needed to reach for his revolver. He faced those he was drinking with and never let anyone get behind him. When playing cards, he always sat with his back to the wall. Young said, "I have often thought of the constant uneasiness that he must have felt at all times."[12]

There were plenty of tales about Hickok's stay in Deadwood and confrontations he may or may not have had never making it into the newspapers. By all accounts, Hickok tried to maintain a low profile and avoid trouble, but put a few drinks in him and he could tell tales.[13]

Harry Young said Hickok was a great storyteller and crowds would gather round to listen to his yarns. One of Hickok's tales was about the time he was out alone scouting for Custer in southwestern Kansas. He found a narrow opening into a box canyon and entered the passage wide enough for only one person at a time. A band of Indians tracked him there and came at him. He shot them one at a time until he discharged all six cylinders from both pistols. He drew his knife and was backed up against the far canyon wall as the open space became crowded with Indians. Hickok then stopped talking. One listener asked what did he do?

He said, "What could I do? There were many of them, well armed, and I had only my knife."

"Well then," the same man said, "What did they do?"

Hickok gave a long sigh and said, "By God, they killed me, boys!"

The crowd was silent for a moment, then realizing the joke they all laughed.[14]

Deadwood was an illegal town. It was within the Great Sioux Reservation where whites were not supposed to be. There was no town government, no law, no order. Rumors floated the more respectable citizens wanted to hire Hickok to maintain a semblance of order. The criminal element in town got wind of the possibility, and there were rumors of plots to take his life. According to Charley Milner, when Hickok's friends told him about the threats he laughed saying, "There's no one here going to shoot me. I would not take the marshal's job."[15]

On July 17, he wrote a poorly punctuated, poorly spelled letter to Agnes:

MY OWN DARLING WIFE AGNES. I have but a few moments left before this letter Starts I never was as well in my life but you would laughf to see me now Just got in from Prospecting will go a way again to morrow will write In the morning but god nowse when It will start my friend will take this to Cheyenne if he lives I don't expect to hear from you but it is all the same I no my agnes and only live to love hur never mind Pet we will have a home yet then we will be so happy I am all most shure I will do well hear the man is huring me Good by Dear wife love to Emma
    J B HICKOK
    WILD BILL[16]

Journalist Leander Richardson had left Fort Laramie on July 22 on his journey to Deadwood. At Bowman's ranch on Hat Creek, he met Steve Utter on his way back to Cheyenne. Utter gave Richardson a letter of introduction to brother Colorado Charlie. When Richardson reached Deadwood on July 31, he located Utter who invited him to stay at his camp. Along the way, they met Hickok.[17]

Richardson recalled, "It was about the middle of a bright sunny afternoon, and we found Wild Bill sitting on a board, which was lying on the ground in front of a saloon. His knees were drawn up in front of him as high as his chin, and he was whittling at a piece of wood with a large pocketknife.

'Get up Bill,' said Utter. 'I want you to shake hands with a friend of mine.'

Wild Bill slowly arose. He came up like an elevator, and he came up so high that I thought he was never going to stop. He was unusually tall, and quite spare as to flesh, but very brawny and muscular. His skin was pallid from the use of powerful mineral drugs, and his grayish eyes, which were just beginning to regain their power after almost being blinded altogether by a terrible illness, were rather dull and expressionless in repose. One day afterward I saw them glitter with sudden ferocity that was strangely luminous, and I realized what this man must have looked like when his blood was up. But, at our meeting, when he folded my hand in his big, strong fingers, his face was almost expressionless in repose."[18]

Richardson wrote about life in Utter and Hickok's camp. Referring to Hickok he said, "Bill was less finicky about his quarters. He slept in a big canvas covered wagon, rolled up in an army blanket. Every morning, just before breakfast, he used to crawl out, clad in his shirt, trousers, and boots, tie his hair in a knot at the back of his head, shove his big revolver down inside the waistband of his trousers, and run like a sprinter down the gulch to the nearest saloon. In a few minutes he would come strolling back, with a cocktail or two stowed away where it would do the most good, and would complete his toilet."[19]

The evening of July 31 Colorado Charlie walked into camp and reported a rumor that there were those who were out to assassinate Hickok. Utter suggested they leave town on a little trip.

"Will you go?" Utter asked.

"Not by a d—d foot," Hickok replied.

"Why not?"

"Well, those fellows over across the creek have laid it out to kill me, and they're going to do it, or they ain't. Any way, I don't stir out of here, unless I'm carried out."

Richardson wrote, "That was when I saw the quick flash of ferocity in Wild Bill's eyes. The conversation ended at this point. Everybody knew it was useless to argue with Wild Bill when his mind was set, and so everybody went about his business as before."[20]

People began to notice Hickok seemed depressed. He talked as if he knew he was going to die in the Black Hills. South Dakota historian O. W. Coursey claimed when Hickok had first seen Deadwood Gulch, he said to Charlie Utter, "I have a hunch that I am in my last camp and I will never leave this gulch alive."[21]

Cheyenne's *Daily Leader* would later publish on August 26, 1876:

Wild Bill's Presentiment

A week before Wild Bill's death he was heard to remark to a friend, "I feel that my days are numbered; my sun is sinking fast; I know that I shall be killed here, something tells me I shall never leave these hills alive; somebody is going to kill me. But I don't know who it is or why he is going to do it. I have killed many men in my day, but I never killed a man yet but what it was kill or get killed with me. But I have two trusty friends, one is my six-shooter and the other is California Joe.[22]

Harry Young said on the morning of July 31, Hickok was in Number 10 Saloon, looking dejected. Young told him he didn't look well.

"No," Hickok replied, "I have a feeling something is going to happen to me."

"You are drinking too much," Young replied.

"No, that has nothing to do with it. I have had this feeling for two weeks, but know I will never be killed by anyone in front of me and if it does come, it will be from the back. Now, I want you to do something for me, step out here and walk backward until I tell you to stop."

Young complied with Hickok's request until he told him to stop. Hickok told Young his eyesight was failing him and then said, "Two steps before you stopped, I could plainly recognize you, after which I could see nothing but a blur. Don't mention this circumstance to any one as I do not care to have it known."[23]

O. W. Coursey said on the evening of August 1, Tom Dosier, one of Hickok's friends, saw him appearing downcast and leaning against the Number 10 Saloon's doorjamb. When Dosier asked him what was wrong, Hickok said, "Tom, I have a presentiment that my time is up and that I am soon going to be killed."[24]

Earlier that day, Hickok had written to his wife, "Agnes Darling, if such should be we never meet again, while firing my last shot, I will gently breathe the name of my wife—Agnes—and with wishes even for my enemies I will make the plunge and try to swim to the other shore."[25]

Later on the night of August 1, Hickok was in Number 10 Saloon playing poker. One of the players was twenty-five-year-old Jack McCall, also known as Bill Southerland. Late that night, bartender Harry Young's shift began. Gamblers kept their poke sacks of gold dust behind the bar for safekeeping. Young recalled Hickok asked him how much gold dust McCall had in his sack. Young weighed the gold dust and called the amount to Hickok.

"You have overplayed yourself by $10," Hickok said to McCall.

"All right, I will make it good next Saturday night," McCall replied as the game ended.

"I have not got money enough to buy my breakfast," McCall said. Hickok gave him seventy-five cents and told him to go eat and if he needed more later on, he would help him. Hickok bought drinks for both of them, then McCall left.[26]

Charley Milner said his father California Joe, Hickok, Charlie Utter, and he planned to leave town on a prospecting trip. California Joe and Charley Milner rode north leading pack mules to Crook City. Hickok and Utter would join them later down the trail after Utter had concluded his business in town.[27]

Charlie Utter's business was the Pioneer Pony Express. August 2, 1876 was an important day for Utter and his partners. They were in a promotional race against a competitor named Clippinger to determine who had the faster delivery service. The race was two hundred miles long from Fort Laramie to Deadwood and was estimated to take three days. The express riders were expected to arrive in Deadwood sometime on August 2.[28]

Early that afternoon, Wild Bill Hickok and Colorado Charlie Utter walked into Number 10 Saloon. Carl Mann; Charlie Rich, a young gambler; and William Massie, a riverboat captain whom Hickok had beaten in cards the night before, sat at a round table, playing poker.[29] Mann invited Hickok to join them. There was one open stool for Hickok. Rich had the stool with his back to the wall. Hickok asked Rich to move so he could sit there. Rich stood to give his seat to Hickok, but Massie said he preferred Hickok sit across from him saying, "No one is going to shoot you in the back." The others good-naturedly said the same thing.

"All right you old grouch," Hickok said to Massie and pulled out the unoccupied stool with his foot, "I will sit here."[30]

Rich sat on Hickok's right, Mann to his left, and Massie across from him. Hickok could keep an eye on the front door, but he could not see anyone coming in the back door. Utter pulled up a stool and sat behind Hickok.[31]

Jack McCall entered the front door of Number 10 Saloon and walked to the far end of the bar. It was around 3:00 p.m.; Hickok was losing to Massie. Harry Young and George Shingle worked behind the bar. Hickok called to Young and asked him to bring over $50 of his checks to him.

"Bill, I will go and get something to eat," Utter said standing and walking out the door.[32]

Young brought $50 of checks to Hickok. As Young stood between Mann and Hickok, he laid the checks in front of Hickok who looked up at him and said, "The old duffer [Massie] broke me on the hand."[33]

Massie reached across the table to grab Hickok's checks. McCall acted quickly, gliding along the bar until he was a few feet behind Hickok. McCall drew his pistol, pointed the muzzle at the back of Hickok's head, and pulled the trigger. The pistol fired, killing Wild Bill Hickok instantly.

"Damn you!" McCall shouted, "Take that!"

Hickok's body fell forward onto the table, then slumped to the floor. The bullet had passed through the base of his brain, out his right cheek between the jaws, and smashed into Massie's left wrist.[34]

As McCall backed toward the rear door, he pointed his pistol at a stunned Carl Mann and said, "Come on ye sons of bitches." Rich and Massie ran out the front door, Massie shouting Wild Bill had shot him. As Shingle and Young tried to run out the door, McCall swung the pistol in Shingle's direction and pulled

The assassin Jack McCall

the trigger—a misfire. He next pointed it at Young and pulled the trigger—another misfire.[35]

Running out the back door, McCall approached a saddled horse at the hitching rail. He began to mount the horse, but the saddle swung under the horse's belly, throwing McCall to the ground. The cinch was loose, and McCall, being in a hurry, had failed to check it.[36]

A crowd gathered. Men were shouting, "Wild Bill is shot!" and "Wild Bill is dead!" The crowd pursued McCall down the street. White Eye Anderson was at a tailrace a short distance away. He drew his pistol and ran after McCall but could not get a clear shot as there were too many people in the way. He estimated fifty guns were drawn in the crowd, but no one could shoot for fear of hitting others. McCall tried to shoot into the crowd, but his pistol did not fire. The caps were bad. McCall was cornered in a butcher shop and captured.[37]

"Bring a rope!" someone shouted. The mob was ready to hang McCall right then and there. They found a pine tree with a stout limb and then a rope. The hanging was interrupted when a Mexican on a galloping horse raced up Main Street from the north, swinging the severed head of an Indian and shouting Indians were attacking Crook City. The mob forgot about McCall; some left to investigate the attack while others followed the Mexican with the severed head from saloon to saloon, congratulating him and enjoying alcoholic refreshments.[38]

Fortunately for McCall, cooler heads prevailed, believing there needed to be a trial. They hustled McCall off to a cabin, locked him inside, and posted a guard. Prominent citizens held a coroner's inquest and determined Hickok had been killed by a bullet fired by Jack McCall.[39]

That night, the citizens selected a judge, prosecutor, defense attorney, sheriff for the trial, a deputy, and twelve guards. The next day, a jury was empaneled, and the trial held at the Deadwood Theater. Witnesses were called and when McCall was asked to defend himself, he said, "Well men, I have but few words to say.

Wild Bill killed my brother, and I killed him. Wild Bill threatened to kill me if I crossed his path. I am not sorry for what I have done. I would do the same thing over again."[40]

Despite the testimonies of Carl Mann, Charlie Rich, and Harry Young that McCall shot Hickok in the back of the head, the jury's verdict was not guilty. McCall was freed. However, Hickok's friends made it clear Deadwood was not a safe place for McCall, and he soon left.[41]

CHAPTER 18

SCOUTING FOR CROOK
(AUGUST 1876–SEPTEMBER 1876)

When Buffalo Bill Cody and the Fifth Cavalry joined General George Crook and his Yellowstone and Big Horn Expedition late on the afternoon of August 3, 1876, Crook and his men had been encamped at their Camp Cloud Peak along the South Fork of Goose Creek ever since returning from their fight with the Lakotas and Cheyennes on June 17, 1876. At the end of that day, Crook's thirteen hundred men held the field of battle at the headwaters of Rosebud Creek, and Crook declared it a victory. His troops had two days of rations left. They had carried one hundred thousand rounds of ammunition, expending twenty-five thousand rounds. Ten of Crook's men had been killed and more than twenty wounded, and a few of them were not expected to live. They found 13 Indian bodies and 150 dead horses on the field. There was no telling how many dead and wounded the Indians had carried off. Crook believed he needed reinforcements and resupplies, as well as care for his wounded, before he could pursue the Lakotas and Cheyennes.[1]

While waiting for reinforcements and supplies, Crook left his encampment on expeditions into the Big Horn Mountains—hunting and fishing expeditions. Soldiers played baseball and panned for gold. Crook himself shot plenty of game. One day he caught seventy trout.[2]

Crook's aide-de-camp Lieutenant John Bourke wrote, "My note-books about this time seem to be almost the chronicle of a sporting club, so filled are they with the numbers of trout brought by different fishermen into camp." Later he added, "General Crook started out to catch a mess [of trout], but met with poor luck. He saw bear tracks and followed them, bringing in a good-sized 'cinnamon,' so it was agreed not to refer to his small number of trout. Buffalo and elk meat were both plenty, and with the trout kept the men well fed."[3]

On July 10, Crook was out hunting in the Big Horn Mountains when two civilian scouts, Louis Richard and Ben Arnold, arrived at Camp Cloud Peak with dispatches from General Sheridan informing Crook of Lieutenant Colonel George Custer's demise at the Little Big Horn. A detachment was sent out and found Crook eighteen miles away. When Crook entered camp later that day, he and his hunting party were hauling the meat from fourteen elk they had shot. After being resupplied and reinforced with the Fifth Cavalry, Crook finally felt comfortable enough to pursue the Lakotas and Cheyennes.[4]

Late on the afternoon of August 3, 1876, the Fifth Cavalry reached Crook's camp. With the arrival of the Fifth's headquarters and ten companies, totaling 535 men, Crook was happy. "There was no doubting the sincerity of his welcome as he recognized with genial smiles and words of cordial greetings the officers and men who had served with him in his brilliant Apache campaigns," George Price wrote in the Fifth's regimental history.[5]

Cody's old comrades, the Third Cavalry, were part of Crook's command. Lieutenant Colonel William Royall introduced Cody to Crook then to Frank Grouard, Crook's chief scout. Grouard was of mixed race, white and Hawaiian. Sitting Bull had adopted him as a brother, and he lived for years in Sitting Bull's camp but eventually left after he lied to Sitting Bull.[6]

The reporters were excited about Cody's arrival. Joe Wasson, correspondent for the *New York Tribune*, wrote Cody "will be a command unto himself." Reuben Davenport, reporter for the *New York Herald*, wrote, "William Cody, the inimitable 'Buffalo Bill,' arrived with Colonel Merritt, and is undoubtedly alone a strong reinforcement of the intelligent efficiency of the force in the field. In the recent scout after the Cheyennes, who were attempting to join Sitting Bull, he displayed all the old bravery and deadly prowess which have made him a hero in the hearts of worshippers of melodrama and tales of adventure. He and Frank Gruard [*sic*] are probably the finest scouts now in active service."[7]

The next day, August 4, Cody was officially made chief scout with the Big Horn and Yellowstone Expedition receiving pay at $150 per month. Crook now had 25 companies of cavalry, 10 companies of infantry, 250 Indian scouts, 44 white scouts, and other civilians making a total force of roughly 2,200 hundred men. Crook decided he could travel faster after the Indians if he left his wagon train behind. Two hundred and fifty mules hauled his supplies, which amounted to fifteen days' rations for the men as well as extra ammunition. All tents were left behind. Crook believed he would be able to resupply at a temporary Army depot established on the Yellowstone River to the north.[8]

All during that day and into the night, Indians set fire to the prairie. Davenport wrote, "The atmosphere was clouded by dense masses of foul smoke hanging close to the earth and constantly augmented by the wind, which blew from the prairies, burning along the base of the mountains."[9]

That evening Wasson wrote, "Crook feels confident of meeting the Sioux within three days." If not three days, the troops would encounter them within a week, and if that didn't happen, then the Lakotas and Cheyennes would have scattered.[10]

After repelling Custer's surprise attack on June 25, 1876, Sitting Bull's massive village of Lakotas and Cheyennes continued to follow the buffalo herds up the Little Big Horn River to the foothills of the Big Horn Mountains. Small bands and families continued to join the village as others left based on their individual needs and desires. Some wished to hunt on their own while others began their return to the agencies.[11]

During July, the village moved eastward to Rosebud Creek, then to the Tongue, and on to the Powder River near its confluence with the Yellowstone River. In August the village began to shrink. For hunting purposes, it was not practical for such a large group of people to stay together. Many had accumulated what they needed for meat and hides and were returning to their agencies for the winter. Some hunting bands crossed the Yellowstone River heading north for the Missouri River, others turned south following the Powder River, while some bands, including Crazy Horse's, traveled south along the Little Missouri River. Sitting Bull continued to lead the large village made up mostly of Hunkpapa, Sans Arc, and Miniconjou Lakotas north and downriver on the Little Missouri River toward Killdeer Mountain. From there they would travel southeast to Twin Buttes at the headwaters of the Grand River in Dakota Territory.[12]

General Alfred Terry with his Dakota Column had not been much more active than Crook. Back on the morning of June 27, 1876, his column reached the site of the Little Big Horn battle joining Major Marcus Reno and the rest of the Seventh Cavalry survivors. After burying the dead, most of whom had been stripped and horribly mutilated, the Dakota Column returned to the Yellowstone River where they encamped at the mouth of the Big Horn River. Terry sent the most seriously wounded downriver to Fort Abraham Lincoln aboard the steamboat *Far West*.[13]

On July 27, Terry started his troops marching down the Yellowstone River to the mouth of the Rosebud where they encamped. After being reinforced and resupplied, he renamed his seventeen-hundred-man command the Yellowstone Column. On

August 8, Terry marched the Yellowstone Column south up Rosebud Creek.[14]

At 5:00 a.m. on August 5, 1876, General Crook's Big Horn and Yellowstone Expedition began its march north. Buffalo Bill Cody, Frank Grouard, and a small group of scouts had ridden out earlier and remained well in advance of troops. General Terry had sent Crow scouts to Crook to inform him he believed the hostile Indians' trail lay somewhere to the north of Crook's Goose Creek camp. The expedition marched along Prairie Dog Creek to the Tongue River, making twenty miles.[15]

The next day, the expedition continued following the Tongue River twenty-five miles to the north, having to cross the twisting river seventeen times. It was hot; some believed the temperature reached as high as 105 degrees F.[16]

On August 7, Crook's men crossed from the Tongue River westward to Rosebud Creek, reaching it ten miles downstream and to the north of the June 17 battlefield site. John Finerty, correspondent for the *Chicago Times*, wrote, "The hills were on fire all around us and we could see nothing."[17]

The next morning, August 8, the expedition awoke to find thick fog and smoke lasting through most of the day. The scouts discovered the site of an immense abandoned Indian camp, and then about noon, they found a location with good grass for the horses and mules. The troops rested there while the scouts rode farther down the Rosebud Valley. About seven miles beyond the position of the resting troops and livestock, the scouts found an immense Indian trail that followed the river for another eight miles and then turned east toward the Tongue River. Cody said, "we struck the main Indian trail, leading down this stream [Rosebud]. From the size of the trail, which appeared to be about four days old, we estimated that there must have been in the neighborhood of seven thousand Indians who had made the broad trail."[18]

Early on the morning of August 9, two couriers arrived from Fort Fetterman; one was Cody's friend Captain Jack Crawford. Crawford, whose title Captain was honorific, was an early Black Hills pioneer, correspondent for the *Omaha Daily Bee*, and was called the Poet Scout of the Black Hills. Crawford and the other man, John Graves, arrived with a pack animal loaded down with two thousand letters and papers for the members of the expedition.[19]

Crawford found Cody and handed him a letter from General Phil Sheridan to Colonel Wesley Merritt recommending Merritt hire Crawford as a scout. Cody fed Crawford a breakfast of coffee, bacon, hardtack, and cold beans, then took him to meet Merritt and General Crook.[20]

Besides letters and papers, Crawford carried a gift for Cody from his friend G. M. Jones, owner of the Railroad Hotel in Cheyenne. Crawford, who was a teetotaler, told Cody it was a bottle of bourbon whiskey. Cody later wrote, "I placed my hand over his mouth and told him to keep still, and not whisper it even to the winds, for there were too many dry men around us; and only when alone with him did I dare to have him take the treasure from his saddle-pockets."[21]

However, Cody did not want to drink alone and told his friend Lieutenant Colonel Eugene Carr about it. The two of them rode with the bottle to a secluded spot and dismounted. As they began to sample the whiskey, up rode Barbour Lathrop, a reporter for the *San Francisco Evening Bulletin*. Cody said about Lathrop, "he having, with the true nose of a Reporter, smelt the whiskey from afar off, and had come to 'interview' it. He was a good fellow withal, and we were glad to have him join us."[22]

That same day, Crook's expedition continued its march down the Rosebud Valley for twenty miles, passing hills with smoldering fires. Outcrops of coal seams studded this area and when the Indians had set fire to the vegetation, it was hot enough for the coal formations to catch fire. There was little grass left for the horses and mules to eat.[23]

A cold north wind began to blow, and a chilling rain pelted the men and animals. They found a side canyon where the Indian fires had not consumed the grass and camped there for a cold, wet night.[24]

On the morning of August 10, the Big Horn and Yellowstone Expedition continued its march north along the Rosebud. Four miles downstream, the men came upon what Lieutenant Frederick Schwatka, who also doubled as a reporter for the *Chicago Inter Ocean*, called "remnants of an immense Indian village" that "was about two miles to two and a half long and probably filled the entire valley, about a mile and a half wide." The village had been the site of a Lakota and Cheyenne sun dance back in June.[25]

Around noon, Crook's column halted. They were roughly thirty miles from where the Rosebud emptied into the Yellowstone River. The troops were a short distance from where the massive Indian trail left the valley and turned east, spreading out like a fan.[26]

Buffalo Bill rode out ahead of the troops. From a high hilltop, he used his binoculars to scan the countryside. An immense cloud of dust rose in the northern sky. He sent a fellow scout back to Crook to report the possibility of approaching Indians. Cody first believed the dust cloud was made by the Indians they had been chasing. Then he thought maybe they were troops, but when he saw mounted Indians approaching his position, he thought it might be the massive Lakota village. As he further studied the figures and their actions through his binoculars, he realized it was a column of soldiers marching up the valley toward him.[27]

The correspondent John Finerty, with Crook's main body of troops, discussed with several officers what the dust cloud meant: "We observed a mighty column of dust indicating a large body of men and animals in motion, in our front, about three miles down the Rosebud.

"'They are Sioux!' exclaimed some of our officers. 'If so, you will immediately hear music,' others replied. Just then 'a solitary horseman' separated himself from our vanguard and rode like the devil in a gale of wind down the river. It was 'Buffalo Bill' the most reckless, and the handsomest, of all frontiersmen. 'He's going to reconnoitre [*sic*],' remarked Col. Royall. 'That's Bill's style, you know.' . . . Within a few minutes 'Buffalo Bill' his long hair streaming on the wind, came galloping madly back to our lines. 'What is it Bill?' asked Col. Royall. 'Terry and his outfit,' replied the scout. 'He's got wagons enough to do an army corps. Were we to catch Indians with such lumber as that,' and he dashed off to see Crook."[28]

General Alfred Terry's Yellowstone Column was on its second day's march, August 9. As it passed through abandoned Indian village sites, the troops were hit by a sudden drop in temperature and pelted by a heavy downpour. The column stopped when Crow and Arikara scouts, who had been out to find General Crook and deliver dispatches, raced their horses back to join the troops, saying a large body of Lakota warriors were preparing to attack. Two companies of the Seventh Cavalry were sent ahead with the scouts to be a buffer against an attack as the column prepared its defense. However, it turned out to be a false alarm.[29]

The morning of August 10, Terry asked the Crow and Arikara scouts to again attempt to deliver the dispatches to Crook, but they refused. However, they did say thirty of them would scout in advance and try to determine the number of Lakota warriors ahead of them.[30]

By 11:00 a.m., the Yellowstone Column had advanced nine miles when the Crow and Arikara scouts raced back to the column, shouting large groups of Lakotas were coming. This time, it was not considered a false alarm as a large cloud of dust billowed into the sky two miles to the south and figures were seen on distant bluffs.[31] James O'Kelly, *New York Herald* correspondent with Terry's troops, wrote what happened next:

By general consent these were pronounced Sioux. The troops were immediately formed in line of battle, and the scene suddenly became animated in the extreme. One battalion of the Seventh Cavalry, under Captain Weir, formed a mounted skirmish line at full gallop, aided by the Second Cavalry, drawn up in column on their flank, under Major Brisbin, and Lieutenant Low's battery of three [ordnance] guns. The trains were closed up, and the companies of the Fifth Infantry under Colonel Miles, the Sixth, under Major Moore, and Twenty-second, under [Lieutenant] Colonel Otis, were extended along the flanks, and moved in the rear as supports. For a few moments all was expectation and anxiety.

A single horseman advanced from the timber and there was a muttered exclamation from many mouths, "there they come." As we strained our ears for the report of the first gun the horseman advanced toward the skirmishers making signs of friendship and was allowed to approach. It proved to be Cody, the scout, better known as Buffalo Bill, dressed in the magnificence of border fashion. He announced that we were in front of General Crook's command and might put off all bloody thoughts for the day.[32]

Cody was amused as he watched the Yellowstone Column's defensive maneuvers take place. He wrote, "Having enjoyed the situation to my heart's content, I galloped down towards the skirmish line, waving my hat and when within about one hundred yards of the troops, Colonel [brevet rank] Weir, of the Seventh Cavalry, galloped out and met me. He recognized me at once, and accompanied me inside the line; then he sang out 'Boys, here's Buffalo Bill. Some of you old soldiers know him; give him a cheer!' Thereupon the regiment gave three rousing cheers, and it was followed up all along the line."[33]

Captain Thomas Weir took Cody to meet General Terry and inform him General Crook's troops were in his front. Terry asked

Cody to accompany him along with his officers and they rode five miles to meet Crook.[34]

That night both columns camped on the Rosebud. Terry invited Crook and his officers to dine with them and plan a joint operation to follow the massive Indian trail to the east. The combined column was now over four thousand men. Terry was the senior commander but did not impose his will on Crook. Crook insisted Terry command the two armies, even though he wanted to be separate from Terry.[35]

Cody observed Terry's column was opulent compared to Crook's: "He had large wall tents and portable beds to sleep in, and large hospital tents for dining-rooms. His camp looked very comfortable and attractive, and presented a great contrast to that of General Crook, who had for his headquarters only one small fly tent. . . . When I compared the two camps, I came to the conclusion that General Crook was an Indian fighter; for it was evident that he had learned that, to follow and fight Indians, a body of men must travel lightly and not be detained by a wagon train or heavy luggage of any kind."[36]

Terry must have been a fast learner. The next day, August 11, he ordered provisions to be loaded on mules and the wagons sent back down the Rosebud to the Yellowstone River. He ordered Colonel Nelson Miles to lead the Fifth Infantry to escort the wagon train and the two artillery pieces to the Yellowstone, where he was to board his men on the riverboat *Far West* and patrol the Yellowstone River as far downriver as the mouth of the Powder River to prevent Indians from crossing the river to the north. By 11:00 a.m., Terry and Crook's combined columns marched east eleven miles over rough country to the Tongue River.[37]

Finerty wrote, "That night a terrific storm of wind and rain came up. We had no tents and had to sleep in the puddles. You can imagine how we passed the night. Water saturated us at every point, and the rain kept pouring down until the afternoon of the succeeding day, retarding our march, and making every man of the command feel as if possessed of a devil."[38]

From August 12 through 14, the columns marched north down the Tongue River following the largest Indian trail until about forty miles from the mouth of the Tongue on the Yellowstone where the trail turned eastward. The march was rough on the horses. Finerty said they lost horses every mile.[39]

On August 15, the combined column followed the Indian trail east to the Powder River. From there, they followed the Powder downriver until on August 17, the Indian trail turned east toward the Little Missouri River. The Indians had been continuously burning the prairie to reduce the forage for the army's livestock. The scouts estimated the trail now to be nine days old.[40]

The horses were failing rapidly. Finerty wrote, "Our whole line of march from the Rosebud to this point is dotted with dead or abandoned horses."[41]

Crook was low on rations and needed resupply, so the columns abandoned the Indian trail and continued downriver to the Yellowstone where they waited to be resupplied by riverboats. They had a long wait. The river's water level had dropped making it difficult for the boats to reach them.[42]

Finerty wrote: "I close this letter with a feeling of disgust and disappointment. Incertitude is the order of the day at present. Many camp followers, including some of the correspondents, are leaving the expedition. I have not yet made up my mind what is best for me to do. I hate to leave at this stage of the futile campaign, and, yet by remaining I shall see very little else than mud, misery, and tough country. . . . But I fear very much that the last shot of this section of the campaign has been fired."[43]

Colonel Nelson Miles and the Fifth Infantry, aboard the riverboat *Far West* commanded by Captain Grant Marsh, arrived at the mouth of the Powder River at 5:00 p.m. on August 17. Terry wanted to know if Indians had crossed the Yellowstone to the north bank between the Powder River and Glendive Creek seventy-five miles downriver and was sending Miles and his men aboard the *Far West* the next morning. Buffalo Bill Cody and another of Crook's scouts, Louis Richard, were assigned to go with Miles.[44]

Early on the morning of August 18, Cody and Richard boarded the *Far West*. Miles surprised them when he told them to bring their horses as they might have need of them. As the riverboat steamed downriver, Richard and Cody stood in the pilothouse and scanned the riverbanks for any sign of Indian crossings. Cody said it was pleasant duty.[45]

The *Far West* reached Glendive Creek without sighting any Indians other than a few scaffolds with bodies on them. Miles had sent troops to the mouth of Glendive Creek where they established an encampment. The encampment's commander, First Lieutenant Edmund Rice, reported to Miles that the day before, Indians had attacked but were repulsed.[46]

The *Far West* would return upriver the next day, but Miles wanted to report on his finding to Terry sooner than it would take the steamboat to return. He asked Cody to carry the dispatches to Terry for him. Concerned about the recent Indian attack on the Glendive encampment, Captain Marsh warned Cody, "Bill, don't try it. You'll never get through alive." However, Cody accepted the assignment.[47]

Cody said, "At his [Miles] request I took the dispatches and rode seventy-five miles that night through the bad lands of the Yellowstone, and reached General Terry's camp next morning [August 19], after having nearly broken my neck a dozen times or more."[48]

General Crook was impatient to be resupplied and continue his march, hoping the large Indian camp would remain together. However, he did not consult about his plans with his staff who became dismayed or with his scouts who became angry. [49]

Joe Wasson, correspondent for the *Daily Alta California*, did not have a high opinion of General Terry. When mentioning the march of the combined Terry and Crook columns, he called it "the funeral procession in search of Sitting Bull."[50]

On August 21, the Indians with the columns had enough of the lack of action against the Lakotas. James Talbot, correspondent for the *New York World*, wrote: "The first incident of importance that occurred . . . was the departure of the Indians for home on the 21st inst. Several small parties of them had left on various pretexts before . . . in disgust. . . . The remaining Indians, numbering 250 or 300 Utes, Snakes, Rees [Arikaras], Crows and Shoshones, finding that they had only long marches, short rations and a hard time generally, with very little prospect of anything better in the future, finally became discontented with what was to them the unprofitable monotony of the campaign, . . . resolved to return to their reservations." Finerty wrote that Ute John was the only Indian left.[51]

Others held the same opinion. Lieutenant Charles King said as long as they were under Terry's leadership, the two columns "would never catch, kill or scare 40 Indians. . . . The caution of Headquarters surpasses everything."[52]

"It has reached beyond a joke that we should be kept out and exposed because two fools [Terry and Crook] do not know their business," Lieutenant Colonel Eugene Carr wrote. "I would leave the expedition today, if I could."[53]

Buffalo Bill Cody did just that. Having had enough of inaction and poor leadership, he resigned on August 22, writing, "There being little prospect of any more fighting, I determined to go East as soon as possible to organize a new 'Dramatic Combination,' and have a new drama written for me, based upon the Sioux war." Finerty wrote, "'Buffalo Bill' has given up all hope of a fight, and is going down the river on a steamboat."[54]

Many of those who could, including some correspondents, joined Cody aboard the *Yellowstone* that was heading downriver on August 24. That same day, Terry and Crook's rain-soaked columns slogged back up the Powder River to continue following the old Indian trail they had abandoned a week before.[55]

The *Yellowstone* had traveled downriver about twenty miles when it met the *Josephine* steaming upriver. The two boats pulled up to the riverbank to exchange news. The *Josephine* was transporting reinforcements for Terry, companies of the Fifth Infantry under the command of Lieutenant Colonel Joseph Whistler. Cody was happy to find Texas Jack Omohundro onboard the *Josephine*. The *New York Herald* had hired him to carry dispatches.[56]

Whistler had dispatches from General Phil Sheridan for General Terry outlining a new strategy. Sheridan was ordering Terry to keep troops in the Yellowstone River Valley and build a winter camp at the mouth of the Tongue. Whistler asked Cody to deliver the dispatches to Terry for him. At first, Cody declined. Whistler persisted, saying it would only take Cody a few hours. As an incentive, Whistler offered the use of his thoroughbred horse he had onboard. Cody agreed and rode the horse across forty miles of rough country to the Powder River Valley where he found Terry's encampment that evening and delivered Sheridan's dispatches.[57]

After Cody finished eating a meal, Terry asked him to take dispatches back to Whistler, which Cody agreed to do since he had to return that way. Whistler's horse was exhausted from the day's ride. Terry's aide-de-camp offered Cody his horse, which Cody said turned out to be an excellent animal. He left that night for the *Josephine*, reaching it at 1:00 a.m. on August 25.[58]

While Cody was gone, Indians had appeared on the hills and skirmished with the troops during the day. Whistler needed to get the information about the attacks to Terry, but he was unable to find anyone who was willing to make the dangerous ride. He asked Cody and said he would pay him well. Cody agreed to do it.[59]

Whistler gave his message for Terry to Cody who decided to continue to ride the same horse he had just ridden. Leaving the *Josephine* at 2:00 a.m., he retraced his ride reaching Terry's camp at 8:00 a.m. just as Terry's men were about to resume their march. Cody had ridden 120 miles in twenty-two hours.[60]

After reading Whistler's message that told of the attack on the *Josephine*, and that up to three hundred Lakotas had attempted to cross the Yellowstone at Glendive Creek and had had a fight with Lieutenant Rice's men, Terry ordered the troops to halt.[61]

He wanted to confer with Crook, whose camp was eight miles ahead. Accompanied by a small cavalry escort and Cody, Terry rode to Crook's camp. The two leaders decided to split from each other. Crook would follow the large Indian trail that continued to lead straight east toward the Little Missouri River, and Terry would backtrack to the Yellowstone and follow it downriver to prevent any tribes from crossing to the north and escaping.[62]

On August 27, Terry's troops used the steamboats *Carroll* and *Yellowstone* to cross to the north bank of the Yellowstone downriver at O'Fallon's Creek. Terry planned to march north toward the Big Dry Fork of the Missouri River and asked Cody to accompany his column to which Cody agreed. After three days of marching north to the buffalo ranges, they saw evidence Indians had been hunting, but no signs of any large bands.[63]

General Terry had dispatches for Lieutenant Rice at the Glendive Creek camp, eighty miles to the south. Terry asked Cody to carry those dispatches and he agreed to do it. He left camp at 10:00 p.m. during a drizzling rain, riding through unfamiliar country. By daylight, he had ridden thirty-five miles and found a grove of ash trees in a ravine where he and his horse could remain concealed and rest. He took care of his horse, ate a cold meal of hardtack and bacon, had a smoke, then using his saddle as a pillow, fell asleep.[64]

He awoke to a roaring, rumbling sound. Grabbing his gun and tying his horse in a hidden spot, he climbed the steep bank and peered over the top. In the distance was a large herd of running buffalo being chased by twenty to thirty Indians. He watched as they killed ten to fifteen animals and then returned to butcher them. After about two hours work, they loaded the meat on their horses and headed south in the direction Cody needed to ride. Their camp must have been located between him and Lieutenant Rice's Glendive Creek encampment. Cody waited until nightfall to resume his journey. He headed east and made a wide circle around where the Indian village might be and then continued his ride south toward Glendive Creek, arriving at Rice's camp at daybreak.[65]

Lieutenant Rice informed Cody almost every day he had been having fights with Indians and wanted General Terry to know

that. Cody agreed to deliver the message to Terry. After spending the day at Rice's camp, Cody left and found Terry's column at
Deer Creek. Terry was on his way to Glendive Creek but was too
far east. Terry asked Cody to guide the column in the right direction, which he did.[66]

There is one problem with Cody's account of his ride from
Terry's command to Rice's camp at Glendive Creek and back. He
probably had a fellow scout along whom he failed to mention in
his autobiography. Lieutenant Edward Settle Godfrey wrote in
his diary entry for Wednesday, August 30, 1876, "Marched to a
creek said to empty opposite Glendive crk. Here Buffaloe Bill and
Herndon [George Herendeen] scouts who had been sent to Glendive on 28th, rejoined us. . . ."[67]

On September 6, 1876, Captain H. J. Nowlan, with the Seventh Cavalry, acting assistant quartermaster, paid Cody $200 for
his scouting services with General Terry. Cody said farewell to
the officers and his friends and boarded the *Far West* on its trip
down the Yellowstone to the Missouri River and on to Bismarck,
Dakota Territory.[68]

While the *Far West* stopped at Fort Buford, Dakota Territory,
a correspondent for the *Chicago Tribune* interviewed Cody who
had no kind words for Crook and Terry:

> *His opinion, however was outspoken, and he denounced the
> powers that controlled matters in and out of the field, in no
> measured terms, which is surprising when we remember he
> is the "chief scout" of the Lieutenant-General [Phil Sheri-
> dan] and draws a salary of $10 per diem. He said plainly
> that the soldiers did not want or intend to fight; that he had
> worn himself out finding Indians; that when he did discover
> their whereabouts, there was no one ready to "go for them." To
> use his language, it was evident to him that no one connected
> with the army had lost any Indians, and consequently they
> were not going to hunt any. He said he had pointed out fresh
> trails, and they had been pooh-poohed as old; and when he*

had reported bodies of the enemy, no troops could be got ready until all hope of successful pursuit had faded away. This, and much more to the same effect, fell from the lips of the noted scout, who seemed untiring and outspoken in his denunciation of the entire business. Were his stories uncorroborated, there would be some excuse for passing them by, or attributing them to excess or vindictiveness consequent on some real or imaginary affront; but, unfortunately, they are fully confirmed by the Indian scouts employed,—Crows, Rees, and Mandans. These all tell the same tale: that they found "much Sioux" often, and that there was no fighting.[69]

The *Far West* continued steaming down the Missouri River to Bismarck, where Cody disembarked and boarded a train to return to his family in Rochester, New York.[70]

Cody sent Louisa a telegram letting her know he was on his way. When he reached the Rochester train station on Saturday, September 16, a large number of friends were there to welcome him.[71]

The next evening, a reporter for the Rochester *Democrat and Chronicle* visited Cody in his home and had a pleasant conversation with him as Louisa and the children sat and listened. Cody recounted his experiences with the Fifth Cavalry, his fight with Yellow Hand [Hair], and joining Crook's command. Cody said Crook was rapidly gaining ground on Sitting Bull's band until they met General Terry's column. Cody had nothing good to say about it: "General Terry took command and wasted a day and a half in council. It ruined the expedition entirely, as the Indians could not be over hauled when they were given so much advantage. . . . There was a great difference between Generals Crook and Terry. . . . General Crook slept on his blanket, made his own coffee and broiled his own bacon. General Terry had a bed brought with him, a portable cooking range and an extension table. 'We could not travel fast enough to catch the Indians as we would break the dishes,' says Bill, which is a whole volume of criticism on the campaign."[72]

Cody said there should be no more large columns but smaller detachments that would start together from the west and drive the Indian bands toward the Missouri River.[73]

"At the time of Wild Bill's death one of the evening papers said you and he were bitter enemies, and were looking for each other on the plains. Is that so?" the reporter asked.

"That is a bad error," Cody said. "Bill and I were friends always. There was but one time when he felt hard towards me, and that was from jealousy, when I was appointed chief of scouts over him by General Sheridan. I used to be under him as chief, and naturally he felt it a little. No, Bill and I were the best of friends." Cody went into a long monologue about Wild Bill's exploits, riding the Pony Express and fighting the "McCandless gang." As he continued on, he said, "He had been in a great many fights and killed a great many men, but I never knew of his killing a man when the law and justice were not on his side. I met him on his way to the Black Hills just before he was killed and he said he did not expect to come out again alive. He was killed at Deadwood; but I don't know the circumstances. When I met him, we were nooning on Sage creek, and we talked for two hours telling of old times."[74]

The reporter ended the article with Cody's plans: "If it is thought best to raise a force of frontiersmen to do service in the Indian country during the winter, probably Bill will be at their head, but if not he will play as usual during the winter months. He goes to New York to day [sic] [September 18, 1876] to make arrangements for a new drama embodying the main points of the Indian campaign."[75]

Buffalo Bill Cody never again scouted for the Army.[76] In September 1876, he was thirty years old and would have forty more active years of life.

CHAPTER 19

THE END OF THE TRAIL

After Wild Bill Hickok was killed on August 2, 1876, the Number 10 Saloon was locked with his body inside. Colorado Charlie Utter arrived at the saloon with his brother Steve and the Anderson brothers. They asked a barber, Doc Ellis Peirce, to help with the body.[1]

The men loaded Hickok's body into a one-horse express wagon owned by a man named Rutherford and took the body to their camp. They pitched a teepee under a large tree and laid Hickok's body within it. Charley Anderson, Doc Peirce, and Colorado Charlie removed Hickok's boots and made his body look presentable.[2]

They found a carpenter to make a coffin out of rough pine lumber. White Eye Anderson said, "The coffin was covered with black cloth on the outside and white cloth on the inside and it looked pretty good for a homemade coffin. We put Bill's old buffalo rifle in the coffin with him and Charlie Utter put in a few other trinkets." A *Chicago Inter Ocean* correspondent also mentioned Hickok's rifle: "Beside him in the coffin lay his trusty rifle which the deceased prized above all other things, and which was to be buried with him in compliance with a long expressed desire."[3]

That evening, Colorado Charlie had Deadwood's *Black Hills Pioneer* print an announcement:

FUNERAL NOTICE

Died, in Deadwood, Black Hills, August 2, 1876, from the effects of a pistol shot J. B. Hickok, (Wild Bill) formerly of Cheyenne, Wyoming.

Funeral Services will be held at Charles Utter's Camp, on Thursday afternoon, August 3, 1876, at 3 o'clock P.M.

All are respectfully invited to attend.[4]

The morning of August 3, many people came to Utter's camp to pay their respects and view Hickok's body. The *Chicago Inter Ocean* correspondent wrote, "in a handsome coffin . . . lay Wild Bill, a picture of perfect repose. His long chestnut hair, evenly parted over his marble brow, hung in waving ringlets over the broad shoulders; his face was cleanly shaved except for the drooping mustache, which shaded a mouth in death almost seemed to smile, but which in life was unusually grave."[5]

The funeral service was held that afternoon. Harry Young said, "The funeral was a very large one, and very impressive; all the stores, saloons and dance halls being closed out of respect for the greatest character of his day."[6]

The *Chicago Inter Ocean* correspondent continued, "A clergyman read an impressive funeral service, which was attentively listened to by the audience, after which the coffin lid hid the well-known face of Wild Bill from the prying gaze of the world forever."[7]

They placed the coffin in Rutherford's wagon and took it to a spot in Deadwood Gulch being used as Deadwood's cemetery, later known as Ingleside. White Eye said among the mourners were six or seven women including Tid Bit, Dirty Em, and Calamity Jane who gathered a bouquet of little blue flowers and threw them into the grave on top of the coffin.[8]

A large stump stood at the head of the grave and on its side was cut the inscription "A brave man; the victim of an assassin—J. B. (Wild Bill) Hickok, aged 48 years; murdered by Jack McCall, August 2, 1876."[9]

Later, Utter had a wooden headboard placed there. The inscription read, "Wild Bill. J. B. Hickok. Killed by the assassin Jack McCall in Deadwood Black Hills. August 2nd 1876. Pard we will meet in the Happy Hunting ground to part no more. Good Bye. Colorado Charlie. C. H. Utter."[10]

Deadwood was growing rapidly; more space was needed for homes. A new cemetery named Mount Moriah was established overlooking the town, and bodies were being disinterred and reburied there. Hickok's grave's headboard was vandalized and had to be replaced four times. Colorado Charlie Utter bought a burial plot in Mount Moriah Cemetery, and on August 3, 1879, he had Hickok's body disinterred and reburied there, where it remains today.[11]

There were reports Hickok's body had hardened, appearing to be petrified in a perfect state of preservation, and Hickok's carbine was still there. The weight of the casket was estimated to be between four hundred and five hundred pounds.[12]

Several stone monuments were erected over Hickok's gravesite. Each was chipped at and vandalized over the years. Today, Hickok's current monument has an iron railing around it.

Buffalo Bill Cody was in Deadwood at least four times and visited Hickok's grave at least twice. In one photo, Cody stands by the grave with three men and a woman. The photo was taken about 1906. In a second photo taken about 1915, he stands by the grave with five men.[13]

Jack McCall, Wild Bill Hickok's assassin, did not leave Deadwood right after the jury had acquitted him. Many believed McCall was a paid assassin and the jury had been rigged to let him off.[14]

At the trial's end, the prosecuting attorney, Colonel George May, announced he learned two hundred ounces of gold dust had been given to jury members, and he declared he would pursue McCall until justice was done. White Eye Anderson later recalled the jury was packed with McCall's friends, a rough crowd.[15]

The *Chicago Inter-Ocean* correspondent reported in the August 17, 1876 edition, "The prisoner was at once liberated, several of the model jurymen who had played their parts in this burlesque upon justice, and who had turned their bloodthirsty tiger loose on the community, indulged in a sickening cheer which grated harshly upon the ears of those who heard it. All lawabiding [*sic*] citizens feel that a terrible injustice has been done, and realize the fact that their only protection now is forming 'vigilantes.'"[16]

It was rumored Tim Brady and Johnny Varnes, members of Deadwood's criminal element, had approached Jack McCall. If he would assassinate Hickok, they would pay him up front $25 in gold dust and an additional $175 after the murder was committed. White Eye Anderson said he heard McCall had been paid $1,000 to murder Hickok.[17]

Leander Richardson reported in the *Denver News,* reprinted in St. Paul, Minnesota's *Pioneer Press* on September 8, 1876, "There were a dozen or more men in Deadwood who wanted to kill Wild Bill because he would not 'stand in' with them on any 'deadbeat' games, but not one man among them all dared to pick a quarrel with him. They were all waiting to get a chance to shoot him in the back. And it was this clique who got Sutherland [McCall] clear of the charge, whereupon he took the first opportunity of getting out of town."[18]

However, McCall did not leave Deadwood right away. He must have believed he was safe while in town.[19]

The day Jack McCall murdered Hickok, California Joe Milner had ridden north to Crook City. While there, Milner's dog spooked one of his horses, which kicked Milner in the side, severely injuring him. When he learned McCall had murdered Hickok, he vowed vengeance, but his injury was too severe to leave Crook City right away.[20]

California Joe was well enough to return to Deadwood on August 5. Colorado Charlie Utter told him the particulars of Hickok's murder and that Jack McCall was still in town. The August 26, 1876 issue of the *Cheyenne Daily Leader* reported what happened next: "California Joe . . . walked down to McCall's cabin, and called him out asked him if he didn't think the air about there was rather light for him. McCall's cheeks blanched, and he feebly answered he thought it was. 'Well, I guess you had better take a walk then,' said Joe, and seating himself on the side of the hill he watched the retreating figure out of sight."[21]

After the trial, the court had appointed an escort to see McCall out of town, believing Hickok's friends would seek revenge.[22] McCall quickly made use of the escort after his encounter with California Joe.

Once McCall left the relative safety of Deadwood, California Joe went after him, leaving town on August 6. Milner's search eventually led him to Laramie, Wyoming. McCall had been arrested there and was behind bars. Milner told the jailer he would save everyone the cost of a trial if he could have half a minute with McCall. The jailer refused to let him in.[23]

Others had vowed to bring McCall to justice, one of whom had been the prosecuting attorney at McCall's trial, Colonel George May. McCall was not quiet about murdering Hickok. He boasted about the murder to a reporter and confessed to him Hickok had not killed his brother. George May located McCall in Laramie, notified authorities about McCall's murder of Hickok, and they issued a warrant for his arrest. On August 29, 1876, US Marshal St. Andre Durand Balcombe and May overheard McCall bragging about killing Hickok, and Balcombe promptly arrested McCall.[24]

When taken before Judge Jacob Blair, McCall admitted to killing Hickok and that Hickok had not killed his brother. The government did not recognize the Deadwood trial as a legal proceeding, as the miners' court was not sanctioned by Dakota Territory. McCall was sent to Yankton, the territorial capital, for trial.[25]

McCall was indicted for the murder of Wild Bill Hickok on October 18, 1876. Realizing he was in a bad predicament, he tried to make a deal with the prosecution. He told them Johnny Varnes and Tim Brady had paid him to assassinate Hickok. The court sent a US deputy marshal and a five-man posse to Deadwood to locate Varnes and Brady, but they had vanished.[26]

There is no information on Tim Brady, but there is on Johnny Varnes. It appears he had had two run-ins with Hickok in the past. The following story appeared in the November 11, 1876 issue of Deadwood's *Black Hills Weekly Pioneer*:

> *Some time ago, Wild Bill and Varnes had a difficulty in Denver and the animosity between the two was augmented by a dispute over a game of poker at the "Senate" saloon in this city, a short time previous to the death of Wild Bill, at which time Wild Bill interfered in a dispute between Varnes and another man. Bill covered Varnes with his pistol and arrogated to himself the position of umpire, after which friends interfered and ended the difficulty.*[27]

Wild Bill's brother Lorenzo attended McCall's trial and was allowed to visit McCall in his cell. McCall intimated he had been paid to kill Hickok but would say nothing more about that or show remorse to Lorenzo's disgust.[28]

McCall received his just payment from the law. On March 1, 1877, Jack McCall was hanged by the neck until dead.

After Buffalo Bill Cody served as chief of scouts for General George Crook in 1876, the thirty-year-old Cody would live an abundant life for the next forty years. His many and varied experiences are beyond the scope of this book. However, here is a brief summary.

After Cody spent a short time with his family in Rochester, New York, his Buffalo Bill Combination was performing a new play, *Red Right Hand; or, Buffalo Bill's First Scalp for Custer*. This time he took the show into the West as far as California. It was a hit. Cody realized people didn't care about the plots of the plays; they just wanted to see real western characters, so he made sure to include actual Indians, not white actors portraying Indians.[29]

In 1877, Cody and his old scouting companion Frank North purchased a ranch sixty-five miles north of North Platte, Nebraska. They bought cattle in Ogallala, Nebraska, branded them, and drove them to their ranch.[30]

The Codys decided to build a house on a separate property they owned just north of North Platte. Louisa moved there in February 1878 and supervised the construction of the house while Cody was on the road performing.[31]

That spring, Cody participated in the local cattle roundup and was impressed with the cowboys' skill and hard work. He wrote, "In this cattle driving business is exhibited some most magnificent horsemanship, for the 'cow-boys,' as they are called, are invariably skillful and fearless horsemen—in fact only a most expert rider could be a cow-boy, as it requires the greatest dexterity and daring in the saddle to cut a wild steer out of the herd."[32]

In 1879, Buffalo Bill Cody's autobiography, *The Life of Hon. William F. Cody*, was published. Controversy has continued over the years whether Cody wrote it or someone else. Cody biographer Don Russell believed Cody was the author stating, "No self-respecting professional writer of the nineteenth century could have written the straightforward, unpretentious recital that was Cody's original autobiography." The book was filled with misspelled names and date errors. Cody was not good at spelling, and Russell believed the spelling and date errors pointed to Cody writing the book from memory. As further proof, its style was consistent with his handwritten manuscripts and letters. That is not the case with later versions where more stories were added and original stories embellished, many times without Cody's involvement.[33]

In 1882, Cody assisted North Platte with its Fourth of July celebration. Cowboys and Indians were invited to participate. Cody included roping and riding contests in the festivities. The show had many components that would become part of *Buffalo Bill's Wild West*.[34]

Cody wanted to present an exhibition of large animals, riders, and western action scenes outside in an arena, and he partnered with William Frank "Doc" Carver to present *Cody and Carver's Wild West* in Omaha on May 17, 1883.[35]

Over the years, Cody's partners in the exhibition would change, but the exhibition would always have "Wild West" in its name. Cody never liked the word *show* and never used it. To Cody, the *Wild West* was more than a show. It was an educational exhibition—an authentic portrayal of the West.[36]

The first exhibition had fifty-one performers—cowboys, Mexican vaqueros, and Pawnee and Lakota Indians. Notable people included Frank North, who had led the Pawnee Scouts; and Captain Adam Bogardus, a well-known marksman alongside Carver and Cody. There was Cody's old scouting friend John Nelson and his family, and a big Texas cowboy named Buck Taylor. Gordon Lillie, known as Pawnee Bill, stayed with Cody for the first two seasons; he left to form his own Wild West exhibition and would again team up with Cody twenty-five years later. Another member of the exhibition was thirteen-year-old Johnny Baker, who Cody took under his wing and taught to shoot. Baker was the same age as Cody's dead son Kit Carson would have been, and Cody treated him like his own son, nicknaming him The Cowboy Kid. Baker stayed with Cody for the rest of Cody's life.[37]

Cody acquired a Concord stagecoach that had been used on the Cheyenne to Deadwood trail. It remained one of the most popular *Wild West* attractions for thirty years.[38]

The first performances were held at Omaha's driving park on Saturday May 19 and Sunday May 20, 1883. It was a success with an audience of eight thousand people the first day and the same number the second day. The opening parade featured a twenty-piece band, Indians, buffalo, elk, cowboys, Buffalo Bill and Doc Carver, the Deadwood stagecoach pulled by six mules, as well as the Fourth Infantry band.[39]

After the parade, a dozen Indians participated in a horse race. There was a Pony Express ride, Indian attack on the Deadwood stage, a fifty-yard dash between a horseback rider and an Indian on foot, and rifle-shooting exhibitions on foot and on horseback by Carver, Bogardus, and Cody. The *Omaha Daily Bee* listed "Cowboys' fun, riding, lassoing, and the introduction of the famous bucking ponies." There were chases after and lassoing of buffalo and Texas steers. The final event was "The Indians on the warpath. Grand closing equestrian act. Furious finale."[40]

The *Omaha Daily Bee* wrote:

> *The illustration of the Pony Express was enthusiastically received, and the skillful rider was greeted with abundant applause; but the great and crowning feature on both days was the stage coach scene, which the crowd yesterday encored until it was repeated . . . the historic Deadwood coach . . . appears upon the scene drawn by six mules. The passengers, who in this instance, were all well known Nebraska people, got aboard at the grand stand, and after a warning from the agent went whirling away on its trip. After three-quarters of the track were traversed a band of red men emerged from ambush and set out in pursuit, yelling like fiends. They closed about the coach and revolver shots were exchanged with startling effect. About the time they seemed to have victory in their hands Buffalo Bill and Dr. Carver appeared with a rescuing party and routed the Indians. This feature is a thrilling and dramatic one, and it is no wonder that the immense audience went nearly wild over it.*[41]

The *Omaha Daily Bee* continued, "The 'Wild West' is undoubtedly destined to make a big hit in the east. . . . The company left about 11 o'clock last night [May 20] on a special train for Des Moines, being billed for that place to-day and to-morrow, and then making a jump to Davenport."[42]

The *Wild West* toured for six months. There was friction between Carver and Cody, and Carver didn't get along with other members of the exhibition. Cody said, "the enterprise was not a complete financial success during the first season, though everywhere our performances were attended by immense audiences."

When they returned to Omaha at the end of the season, Cody and Carver agreed to separate. They split the exhibition's physical assets by flipping a coin for each item. Fortunately for Cody, he won the Deadwood stage.[43]

Cody had problems during this time and drank heavily. He attempted to ride Monarch, a big bull buffalo, who tossed him high into the air. Cody hit the ground so hard he wound up in the hospital for a couple of weeks.[44]

The Codys' eleven-year-old daughter, Orra Maude, became ill and died on October 24, 1883. Two children remained, Arta who had been born in 1866 and the infant Irma Louisa born February 6, 1883.[45] Orra Maude's death renewed marital difficulties between Cody and Louisa that began back in 1877 when at the end of the play season, Louisa caught him giving parting kisses to four actresses.[46]

Buffalo Bill Cody was happy to see Doc Carver go. Cody teamed up with the well-known actor Nate Salsbury for the 1884 season. Salsbury was a good businessman and manager. With John Burke doing an excellent job at promotion, Salsbury's business know-how, and Cody's enthusiasm and popularity, the new *Buffalo Bill's Wild West* became what Burke called "America's National Entertainment."[47]

Buffalo Bill's Wild West was a success throughout the Northeast. Mark Twain wrote to Cody, "I have now seen your Wild West show two days in succession, and have enjoyed it thoroughly. It brought back vividly the breezy, wild life of the great plains and the Rocky Mountains and stirred me like a war song. Down to its smallest details the show is genuine—cowboys, vaqueros, Indians, stagecoach, costumes and all; it is wholly free from sham and insincerity, and the effects produced upon me by its spectacles were identical with those wrought upon me a long time ago by the same spectacles on the frontier."[48]

By October 1884, instead of ending for the season, Cody and Salsbury continued touring through Kentucky, Tennessee, and Mississippi with a goal of performing at the World's Industrial and Cotton Exposition in New Orleans. On December 9, a Mississippi riverboat was transporting *Wild West* members, animals, and props downriver when it sank. The people survived, but the animals were lost. The only prop salvaged was the Deadwood stage.[49]

They bought more animals, built new props, and were back in business opening their exhibition in New Orleans on December 23. However, circumstances worked against the *Wild West*. First, a streetcar strike limited attendance, then it rained straight for forty-four days. Captain Bogardus quit and Cody became discouraged. By the time the *Wild West* left New Orleans on April 11, 1885, it was $60,000 in debt.[50]

The addition of two new people brought Cody out of his funk and helped save the *Wild West*—Annie Oakley and Sitting Bull.[51]

Annie Oakley was already a well-known markswoman. She remained with the *Wild West* for the next fifteen years and became almost as famous as Buffalo Bill. Cody supported equal rights for women. He was quoted as saying, "Let them do any kind of work they see fit, and if they do it as well as men, give them the same pay."[52]

Sitting Bill was the famous Hunkpapa Lakota leader who had led the resistance against white intrusion and was one of the last Lakota leaders to surrender in 1881. Cody wanted him to join the exposition. Federal bureaucrats denied Cody's request, but eventually he received enough high-powered support, they relented. The next step was to get Sitting Bull to agree. He had seen Annie Oakley perform, and they had met. When he learned she was part of the *Wild West*, he agreed to join and brought his family along.[53]

The *Wild West* toured over forty major cities of the Northeast, Midwest, and Canada. The 1885 advertisements were changed to include the phrases, "Larger and Greater Than Ever" and "the renowned Sioux Chief Sitting Bull."[54]

When the show arrived in a city, the performers paraded down the main street. Buffalo Bill rode first, then behind him rode Sitting Bull wearing his eagle feather headdress and buckskin clothing. Sitting Bull would begin the performance by riding around the arena once as the announcer informed the crowd, "Here he comes! The Napoleon of the Plains! Chief Sitting Bull, ladies and gentlemen!"[55]

Even though the performances reenacted violent encounters between white men and Indians, Cody promoted reconciliation using Sitting Bull and himself as the focal point as his advertising material proclaimed, "Foes in '76—Friends in '85."[56]

Cody respected Indians, and his time spent with Sitting Bull and other Indians made him their advocate. The Indians Cody employed received good pay, had an opportunity to leave the reservation, and were able to share their culture with the world. He frequently referred to them as, "The Americans" as a sign of respect. He told one Toronto newspaper, "In nine cases out of ten when there is trouble between white men and Indians, it will be found that the white man is responsible. Indians expect a man to keep his word. They can't understand how a man can lie. Most of them would as soon cut off a leg than lie." Cody also told the newspapers, "The defeat of Custer was not a massacre. The Indians were being pursued by skilled fighters with orders to kill. . . . They had their wives and little ones to protect and they were fighting for their existence."[57]

Sitting Bull participated in only one *Wild West* season. When he and Cody parted, they exchanged gifts. Sitting Bull gave Cody a bear claw necklace representing strength, as the bear was the ally of the greatest warriors. Cody gave Sitting Bull a horse he was fond of and a sombrero.[58] Sitting Bull said about the hat, "My friend Long Hair [Cody] gave me this hat. I value it very highly, for the hand that placed it upon my head had a friendly feeling for me."[59] Cody said of Sitting Bull, "He won my friendship and sympathy; he impressed me as a deep thinker; conscientious as to the proper rights to the lands of their fathers."[60]

At the end of the 1885 season, *Buffalo Bill's Wild West* was a success, grossing over a million dollars with a profit of $100,000. Attendance estimates totaled over a million people.[61]

New features were added including an Indian attack on a settler's cabin, the destruction of a village by a cyclone, and the Battle of the Little Big Horn, also known as "Custer's Last Stand," where Cody often portrayed Lieutenant Colonel George Custer valiantly dying.[62]

In 1887, Cody took his *Wild West* to Great Britain, performing in front of packed crowds. On May 11, *Buffalo Bill Cody's Wild West* gave a command performance before Queen Victoria who wrote in her journal, "we saw a very extraordinary & interesting sight, a performance of 'Buffalo Bill's Wild West.'" Cody, Salsbury, Annie Oakley, and other performers were introduced to the queen. Cody said after the queen attended "the people considered it *the thing* to go to the show, and thousands were turned away from the enormous pavilions." By his return to the United States in May 1888, Buffalo Bill Cody had become one of the most popular and recognizable people in the United States if not the world.[63]

By 1888, commercial hide hunters had decimated the buffalo herds. It was estimated only about 256 remained in captivity and 285 in the wild. Cody's twenty buffalo were the third largest herd in captivity. He began to work with others in buffalo restoration efforts. Cody spoke out against hide hunting and advocated the establishment of a hunting season.[64]

Cody and the *Wild West* toured Europe in 1889 through much of 1890, playing before massive crowds in France, Italy, and Germany.[65]

In 1893, Cody and Nat Salsbury expanded the exhibition, calling it *Buffalo Bill's Wild West and Congress of Rough Riders of the World*, adding famous horseback riders from around the world—Cossacks, Arabs, and gauchos, and European cavalry.[66]

The World's Columbian Exposition in Chicago from May 1 to October 30, 1893, was the all-time peak performance of *Buffalo Bill's Wild West*. Officials would not accept the *Wild West* as part of the exposition, so Salsbury leased land near its entrance and siphoned off large numbers of those heading to the exposition. A Chicago city editor who Cody biographer Don Russell knew told him he considered *Buffalo Bill's Wild West* the greatest show he had ever seen in his life. Major General Hugh Scott, who had served with the Seventh Cavalry, said, "That was the most realistic show I have ever seen."[67]

The *Wild West* had large audiences and had to turn people away. There were twenty main events starting with the playing of "The Star-Spangled Banner." Past events continued to be performed such as the attack on the Deadwood stage and the buffalo hunt. Stars such as Annie Oakley, Johnny Baker, and Buffalo Bill gave their performances. The Indians were ever popular as well as "Cowboy Fun. Picking Objects from the Ground [while on a racing horse], Lassoing Wild Horses, Riding the Buckers." There were new additions such as a horse race between a Cowboy, a Cossack, a Mexican, an Arab, and an Indian. There was *"Military Evolutions* by a Company of the Sixth Cavalry of the United States Army; a Company of the First Guard Uhlan Regiment of His Majesty King William II, German Emperor, commonly known as the 'Potsdamer Reds'; a Company of French Chasseurs (Chasseurs a Cheval de la Garde République Francais); and a company of the 12th Lancers (Prince of Wales' Regiment) of the British Army." It's estimated *Buffalo Bill's Wild West's* profits were between $700,000 and $1 million.[68]

Cody helped found the town of Cody, Wyoming, in the spring of 1896.[69] He developed irrigated agriculture, bought the TE Ranch, owned the Irma Hotel named after his daughter, built the Pahaska Tepee hunting lodge near Yellowstone National Park's East Entrance, and established way stations on the road to the park. In his will, Cody stated he wanted to be buried on Cedar Mountain overlooking his town.[70]

Cody used his money to buy more ranchland in the North Platte area and invest in Wyoming and Arizona mining ventures. Many of these investments were failures, and Cody never recouped his funds. He was generous, lending money to people with little hope of getting it back. All this combined to stress the Codys' finances.[71]

However, life dealt Cody several major blows. On December 24, 1902, Nate Salsbury died. He and Cody had made a good team, and the *Wild West* would miss his business savvy. Then, the Codys' oldest daughter, Arta, died from meningitis on January 30, 1904. Louisa accused Cody of breaking Arta's heart. After years of fighting, Cody filed for divorce. Louisa didn't want it. It wound up in court and got ugly. Newspapers had a field day. The judge denied the divorce on March 23, 1905. Years later, in 1911, Cody and Louisa would reconcile and reunite.[72]

Cody had never been religious. His sister Julia, a Christian, told him she was concerned about him. He didn't care about matters of faith until after the divorce proceedings, when he saw the light. On June 14, 1905, he wrote Julia, "And it's in my old age I have found God—And realize how easy it is to abandon sin and serve him. When one stops to think how little they have to give up—to serve God. It's a wonder so many don't do it. A person only has to do right."[73]

By 1909, the *Wild West*'s ticket sales had dropped off, so Cody combined his *Wild West* with the show of a competitor, Gordon Lillie, known as Pawnee Bill, who had originally worked for Cody.[74]

In 1913, low on funds and without telling Pawnee Bill, Cody obtained a six-month $20,000 loan from Denver entrepreneur Harry Tammen. Tammen wanted Cody's *Wild West* to join his show, the Sells-Floto Circus, and publicly made that announcement. Cody denied ever having agreed to such a thing, but Pawnee Bill was furious with Cody's perceived commitment to abandon their partnership. Tammen bought another outstanding loan of Cody and Pawnee Bill's show, and when they couldn't repay, Tammen foreclosed on the show selling their assets. Cody reluctantly performed in Tammen's Sells-Floto Circus into 1915 hoping he could accumulate enough finances to bring back his *Wild West*, but Tammen was so ruthless, Cody couldn't take it and quit.[75]

While Buffalo Bill Cody was visiting his sister in Denver, he died on January 10, 1917. Harry Tammen wanted Cody's body

Buffalo Bill and his Wild West

buried on Lookout Mountain, Golden, Colorado, and requested permission from Louisa. In Cody's original will, he stated he wanted to be buried on Cedar Mountain overlooking his town of Cody, Wyoming. However, in a second more recent will, Cody left everything to Louisa, and it was interpreted his Cedar Mountain burial request could be ignored. Louisa agreed to have Cody buried on Lookout Mountain. The people of Cody, Wyoming, were furious.[76]

Before burial, Cody's body was laid in state in the Colorado Capitol rotunda; it was estimated twenty-five thousand people came to pay their respects. Many people eulogized Cody including President Woodrow Wilson, Theodore Roosevelt, and General Nelson Miles.[77]

Annie Oakley said, "He was the kindest, simplest, most loyal man I ever knew. He was the staunchest friend. He was in fact the personification of those sturdy and lovable qualities that really made the West, and they were the final criterion of all men, East and West. Like all really great and gentle men he was not even a fighter by preference. His relations with everyone he came in contact with were the most cordial and trusting of any man I ever knew."[78]

It was over. Buffalo Bill Cody had been gracious to many people during his life and had given the world a good show.

Wild Bill Hickok has received lots of attention from writers. An immense amount of material has been written about him, much of it fiction; and much that is considered nonfiction has elements of fiction in it.

One of the many Wild Bill legends is that he had an affair with Calamity Jane. There is no evidence for this. They did not meet until Hickok and friends agreed to take her with them to Deadwood and during that time, she was with Steve Utter. The legend of a Wild Bill and Calamity Jane affair developed years after Hickok's death.

Another Wild Bill legend is the Dead Man's Hand, the cards he held when Jack McCall killed him. No one mentioned the cards he was holding until years later when "Doc" Ellis Peirce wrote about it. Peirce was called Doc because he claimed to have studied medicine for two years. Peirce was working as a barber in Deadwood on August 2, 1876, when Hickok was shot in Number 10 Saloon. Colorado Charlie Utter asked Peirce to help prepare Hickok's body. Along with Utter and Hickok's friends, Peirce entered the saloon. Frank Wilstach in his 1926 book *Wild Bill Hickok: The Prince of the Pistoleers* included an extract from a letter he received from Peirce:

> *When they unlocked the door for me to get his body, he was lying on his side, with his knees drawn up just as he slid off his stool. We had no chairs in those days—and his fingers were still crimped from holding his poker hand. Charlie Rich, who sat beside him, said he never saw a muscle move. Bill's hand read "aces and eights"—two pair, and since that day aces and eights have been known as "the dead man's hand" in Western country.*[79]

Joe Koller, a reporter for the *Rapid City Journal*, interviewed Doc Peirce in Hot Springs, South Dakota, in 1915. Koller said Peirce was "a rare character" known for being "a practical joker."[80] No one else ever mentioned Hickok's poker hand. Did Peirce tell the truth or was it one of his practical jokes?

Colonel George Ward Nichols gave Hickok national exposure in the February 1867 edition of *Harper's New Monthly Magazine* in its lead article "Wild Bill." Over the next several months, newspapers reprinted the story. Whether he liked it or not, Wild Bill Hickok became a national figure.[81]

Dime novelists realized a character like Wild Bill was great material. In July 1867, *DeWitt's Ten Cent Romances* published the first Wild Bill dime novel, *Wild Bill, the Indian Slayer*. It must have made *DeWitt's* money since a few months later *DeWitt's* published *Wild Bill's First Trail*. For the next couple of years, Hickok was safe from the dime novelists until Ned Buntline got his hands on him. In December 1869, Buntline published his dime novel *Buffalo Bill, The King of the Border Men* in which Wild Bill was portrayed as Buffalo Bill's sidekick. However, Buntline killed off Wild Bill. After Wild Bill killed Dave Tutt, Tutt's lover, Ruby Blazes, stabbed Wild Bill in the heart.[82]

Dime novels continued to be released after Hickok's death. In 1880, Buntline struck again with *On the Death-Trail; or, The Last of Wild Bill*. In this dime novel, Buntline described Wild Bill as a hardened desperado who had "killed at least one man for every year of his life."[83]

The Hickok family was outraged. Hickok's brother Horace sent a letter to the publisher requesting it be forwarded to Buntline. The publisher printed the letter. It's not known if Buntline responded. In part, Horace wrote:

> *The author basely slanders the dead, and says of Wild Bill what, I do not think, he would dare publish if Wild Bill were living: and all, as I think, to gratify a petty spite . . . Buntline seems to be trying to make Bill out a regular desperado, with all that the word implies, and . . . a cowardly one at that—I allude to the fainting scene and the attack made upon a woman. . . . There are hundreds of people living here that have known James, or Wild Bill, from his boyhood, and when any one says that Wild Bill was a coward, or that he ever once in his life picked a quarrel with anyone, is either mistaken, or willfully says that which is not true. . . . As an officer he did his duty, no matter what the odds against him were. He had a pleasant, good disposition; was slow to anger, but when aroused and obliged to fight he fought to the death. Bill Cody (Buffalo Bill) and James Hickok (Wild Bill) were friends, and Cody knows what I say is true; and I know, Ned Buntline knows, he had not written the truth of my brother. I do not expect a work of fiction to be true in every respect, but it ought to have a faint resemblance to it, and not be slanderous.*[84]

Buffalo Bill Cody saw Horace Hickok's letter and wrote him on March 23. He was glad Horace had corrected Buntline's statements about Wild Bill's character. Cody said he planned to write his own dime novel with Hickok as the hero. He ended by writing, "My long and intimate association with Wild Bill will enable me to found my story on solid facts, and correcting errors regarding his life and character, is a pleasure to me, as well as a duty I owe to his memory, for he was ever in good or evil times a tried and true friend of mine." Cody never found the time in his busy schedule to work in his Wild Bill dime novel.[85]

The nineteenth-century dime novels became twentieth-century comic books, and Wild Bill Hickok continued to be portrayed in those in the 1950s and 1960s.

In 1880, J. W. Buel, a St. Louis newspaper reporter, published *The Life and Marvelous Adventures of Wild Bill, the Scout, Being a True and Exact History of All the Sanguinary Combats and Hair-Breathe Escapes of the Most Famous Spy America Ever Produced*. It quickly sold out, then in 1881, he produced an expanded version: *Heroes of the Plains: or, Lives and Wonderful Adventures of Wild Bill, Buffalo Bill, Kit Carson, Capt. Payne, "White Beaver," Capt. Jack, Texas Jack, California Joe* . . . [the title goes on and on].[86]

Buel wrote in his introduction to *Heroes of the Plains*: "In compiling these personal histories, I have adhered strictly to facts without florid coloring. I was well acquainted with Wild Bill for several years before his death, and in 1879 wrote a pamphlet sketch of his life, but discovered afterward that while it contained comparatively few of his adventures, there were several mortifying errors, a correction of which influenced me to write another sketch of the famous scout, and this labor developed into "HEROES OF THE PLAINS." I was fortunate in securing Wild Bill's diary from his widow Mrs. Agnes Lake Hickok, of Cincinnati, from which I have drawn my facts concerning him, that there might be no mistakes or omissions in recounting the marvelous exploits of his life in this publication."[87] If Hickok's diary did exist, it hasn't been found. Some of Buel's accounts cannot be verified and others he embellished.

Later biographers used Buel as a source—Frank Wilstach, William Elsey Connelley, Joseph Rosa, and me. Whenever I've told a story that is strictly Buel's, I've noted that. There are three Wild Bill Hickok books I recommend: James McLaird's *Wild Bill Hickok and Calamity Jane*, Bob Boze Bell's *The Illustrated Life and Times of Wild Bill Hickok*, and Joseph Rosa's classic *They Called Him Wild Bill: The Life and Adventures of James Butler Hickok*.

When motion pictures began to be produced, Wild Bill Hickok was an early subject. The first known film about Hickok was made in 1915 titled *In the Days of '75 and '76, or the Thrilling Lives of Wild Bill and Calamity Jane*, which had no basis in fact. In 1923, the popular silent screen actor William Hart wrote the screenplay for *Wild Bill Hickok* and portrayed him. It was far-fetched and irritated the Hickok family.[88]

There were more silent screen portrayals of Hickok, and then he was brought along into the talkies. In 1936, Cecil B. DeMille was making a movie based on Hickok's life called *The Plainsman* starring Gary Cooper as Hickok. DeMille planned to have Hickok marry Calamity Jane. The Hickok family was upset. They got him to drop it, but then he planned to have Hickok, Calamity, and Buffalo Bill ride off into the sunset together. The Hickok family was against that. DeMille finally decided to have Calamity Jane kiss Hickok on the lips after he was killed.[89]

There were plenty more films and television shows with Wild Bill Hickok in them. Bob Boze Bell has counted seventy actors who portrayed Hickok.[90] I'm not a film critic, I know movies are for entertainment, and I have not seen all the Hickok films, but I just haven't seen any that portray Hickok correctly and that goes for the HBO series *Deadwood* too—just my opinion.

If you want to learn more about Wild Bill Hickok and view some of the items that might have been his, the Adams Museum in Deadwood, South Dakota, has several said to have belonged to or were associated with Hickok as well as an original N. C. Wyeth pencil sketch portrait of Hickok. Darrel Nelson, exhibits director for Deadwood History, Inc., said, "The most notable and controversial Wild Bill artifacts we display are his 1860 Army Colt revolver, holster, cartridges, belt and buckle. The city bought these at auction, and they are on loan to the Adams for display. Another small case holds Charlie Utter's pistol, Wild Bill's razor, his lucky stone (which obviously did not work), and five cards that might have come from the deck that was used when Wild Bill was killed." Nelson said the cards are the queen of hearts, ace of clubs, ace of diamonds, eight of hearts, and eight of spades. "The city also has letters from Hickok's siblings which are indisputably genuine," Nelson said.[91]

If lots of material has been written about Wild Bill Hickok, even more has been written about Buffalo Bill Cody. Much is fiction. As to nonfiction, there are those who strive to defend him, and others who work to lessen his reputation.

Buffalo Bill was featured in a vast number of dime novels starting with Buntline's December 1869 *Buffalo Bill, the King of the Border Men*. Twenty-four dime novels were signed "by Buffalo Bill." Cody biographer Don Russell believed Cody wrote the first dime novels attributed to him; but later, they were written by Colonel Prentiss Ingraham and other ghostwriters. Russell determined there were 557 original Buffalo Bill dime novels and 1,143 reprints.[92]

As with Wild Bill, Buffalo Bill was carried over into the comic book era. Kellen Cutsforth, author of *Buffalo Bill and the Birth of American Celebrity*, says, "Comic books are one of the most lucrative genres in entertainment and publishing today. Buffalo Bill is considered by many, including myself, as an example of America's first superheroes. Larger than life, heroic, and in many instances, he seems to possess almost superhuman capabilities."

Back to nineteenth-century books: In J. W. Buel's *Heroes of the Plains*, it appears Buel used Cody's autobiography embellishing those stories. Early books about Cody were filled with fiction such as Ingraham's 1881 book *Adventures of Buffalo Bill from Boyhood to*

Manhood. Ingraham had little Billy Cody riding a buffalo through a buffalo herd.[93]

In 1888, *Story of the Wild West and Camp Fire Chats by Buffalo Bill (Hon. W. F. Cody), A Full and Complete History of the Renowned Pioneer Quartette, Boone, Crockett, Carson and Buffalo Bill* was published. Cody wrote in the preface that he had researched government records to find Kit Carson's true story, "which I find frequently conflicts with the statements of those who in writing his life have made facts subservient to wild exaggerations, just as many romancers have done while soberly pretending to record the incidents in my own life."[94]

Most likely the only part of the book Cody wrote was the preface. Someone else must have taken already-published stories and embellished them, and Cody must not have read the final version. The writer got the Battle of Summit Springs wrong. His version did not match Cody's original autobiography or other known accounts of the battle. *Story of the Wild West* was one of the most successful Cody books supposedly signed "by Buffalo Bill."[95]

Plenty of books added to and embellished his autobiographical material. Others who knew Cody wrote books about him. His wife Louisa, with help from Courtney Riley Cooper, a circus press agent, and both sisters Julia and Helen wrote their versions of his life. Some stories were fiction, and others embellished.

I recommend the following books on Buffalo Bill Cody. The first is his own autobiography, but be careful. Read the first one, the original he wrote in 1879, *The Life of Hon. William F. Cody.* There were other Cody autobiographies over the years, and many of them were added onto by other people. The next is Joseph Rosa and Robin May's book *Buffalo Bill and His Wild West*, then Steve Friesen's *Buffalo Bill: Scout, Showman, Visionary,* Sandra Sagala's *Buffalo Bill on Stage* is an excellent book covering his acting years, and finally Don Russell's classic, *The Lives and Legends of Buffalo Bill.*

Buffalo Bill Cody was fascinated with moving pictures. In 1912, Pawnee Bill Lillie and he formed the Buffalo Bill/Pawnee

Bill Film Company producing the moderately successful *Life of Buffalo Bill*. Their second film was a documentary, *The Indian Wars*, filmed and released the next year. General Nelson Miles gave Cody permission to use soldiers and the Department of the Interior allowed Lakotas from the Pine Ridge Reservation to participate. Many veteran warriors and soldiers participated in the filming.[96]

Wikipedia lists twenty-three movies and television shows about Buffalo Bill or in which he is a character. *Hidalgo* is a fictional story about a rider named Frank Hopkins. Buffalo Bill and Annie Oakley are portrayed in it. It's a fun movie, but purely fiction. Other than that, there are no good Buffalo Bill movies. Someone needs to make one.

Denver's Buffalo Bill Museum and Grave maintains Cody's gravesite at Lookout Mountain Park, and the museum there holds a large collection of Buffalo Bill's items. Johnny Baker began the museum with Buffalo Bill memorabilia, and Louisa Cody provided personal Cody family items.[97] The five museums of the Buffalo Bill Center of the West in Cody, Wyoming, are an amazing experience. The Buffalo Bill Museum displays Cody's possessions and memorabilia. The Plains Indian Museum has a large Native American collection. The Cody Firearms Museum has over four thousand firearms. The Draper Natural History Museum presents the Yellowstone region ecosystems. The Whitney Western Art Museum features artwork by Charlie Russell, Frederic Remington, Albert Bierstadt, and other traditional and contemporary artists.[98]

After reviewing the accounts of Wild Bill Hickok and Buffalo Bill Cody's lives and trying to determine what was real and what was fiction, I have a deeper appreciation of who they were. I like them. They were two regular people trying to make a go of it on the frontier. Both men were good at scouting. They could read the land, finding water, game, and locating the best routes and campsites. Both men had compassion on those down-and-out and gave freely.

Hickok had a strong sense of honor and always stood on what he thought was the side of right. He was fearless and deadly with a gun. A combination of good eyesight, fast reflexes, keeping his weapons in top-notch working order, and having the will to fight to the death, kept away those who wanted to test him, until Jack McCall shot him from behind.

Cody was fearless, racing toward danger and not away from it. He was an excellent shot and hunter. He was honorable and treated opponents fairly.

In one respect, they were different. Cody sought publicity; Hickok had no desire for it. When he was dismissed as Abilene's marshal, he never sought a law enforcement position again; and after being on the stage with Cody, he said they were making fools of themselves.

Both men were top-notch scouts, the best of the best plainsmen. However, Cody stands out from Hickok due to what he did after scouting. He brought the West to the world and his actions live on today.

Imagine what it would have been like if one dark night you could have sat at a blazing campfire with Wild Bill Hickok and Buffalo Bill Cody. You pull out a bottle of whiskey and pass it to them, lean back against a cottonwood log, and listen to them spin their yarns and then contradict each other: "Wait a minute, that's not the way I remember it. This is how it actually happened...."

Hickok was a leg-puller and Cody was an embellisher—but they were lovable.

ACKNOWLEDGMENTS

Thanks to Buffalo Bill Cody, I got to wear one of his hats! Thanks to the Buffalo Bill Center of the West for allowing people that experience. I've had the opportunity to visit Buffalo Bill's Iowa home and stand by his grave in Golden, Colorado. I've been to Wild Bill's grave countless times at Mount Moriah Cemetery in Deadwood, South Dakota. Thank you to Wild Bill and Buffalo Bill for living extraordinary lives. Thanks to the folks who remembered and spoke about these two plainsmen, to those who recorded those memories, and to those who preserve the records.

Erin Turner, Sarah Parke, Meredith Dias, Joshua Rosenberg, and the rest of the folks at TwoDot and Rowman & Littlefield, thank you for the opportunity to write this book and your support. Jim Hatzell, thanks for your outstanding illustrations. Thank you to wordsmith Barry Keith Williams for manuscript polishing and fact checking.

Thanks to Joseph Rosa for his research into the life of Wild Bill. I had the opportunity to sit alongside him during a book signing at the 2003 South Dakota Festival of Books in Deadwood. Kellen Cutsforth, thanks for fact-checking and finding grammatical errors! Monty McCord, thanks for your leads on the murder of Whistler by "Wild Bill of the Blue." Nancy Shoup, thank you for your review. Mike Pellerzi, thanks for providing your horsemanship expertise and cowboy point-of-view. Thank you to Steve Haberman, reference archivist with the Greene County Archives and Records Center in Springfield, Missouri. His assistance with the coroner's inquest into Davis Tutt's death and the *State of Missouri v. William Haycock (Hickok)*, Greene County Circuit Court, manslaughter indictment for the death of Davis Tutt exceeded my expectations. Thank you Jessica Tubis and those who helped her in the Access Services Department of the Beinecke Rare Book and Manuscript Library, Yale University, for locating Albert Barnitz's July 21 and 22, 1865 journal entries, concerning the Hickok and Tutt fight. Their efforts exceeded my expectations. Thanks to Ollie Reed and Don Bullis for help with terrain nomenclature around Santa Fe. Thank you to Park Superintendent I Michaela Clemens and Park Superintendent Jeff Bargar at the Rock Creek Station State Historical Park for your insight into the incident at Rock Creek Station, Nebraska. Steve Friesen, former director of the Buffalo Bill Museum and Grave in Golden, Colorado, thanks for your guidance and advice on the Bill Cody and Bill Comstock buffalo hunting contest. Tom Rizzo, thank you for the correct name for Jules Beni. Doug Ellison, John Wesley Hardin historian, thanks for your insight on Hickok and Hardin in Abilene! Thank you Sandy Sagala, author of *Buffalo Bill on Stage*, for your help in deciphering the murky details of Buffalo Bill and Wild Bill's stage performances and your suggested changes! Thanks to Mariah Emmons, registrar with the Wyoming State Museum, for information on Wild Bill Hickok's cane. Thank you, Candy Moulton and Elanna "Quackgrass Sally" Skorupa for help with historic trails. Thanks to the late James McLaird for his friendship and comments on Wild Bill and Calamity Jane. Thank you to Carolyn Weber, executive director, and Darrel Nelson, exhibits director, from Deadwood History, Inc. for your help and review of Hickok's time in Deadwood.

A big thank-you to my wife, Liz, for putting up with my long hours in the basement plunking away on the computer keyboard, and traveling along to obscure places on my research trips. Thanks to my entire family for their continued support. Most of all, thanks to the Lord for giving me this opportunity and for the ability to think and write.

NOTES

INTRODUCTION

1. *Leavenworth Times* (Leavenworth, KS, March 1, 1870), 4, Newspapers .com, March 6, 2021, https://www.newspapers.com/image/96075446/?terms =%22Wild%20Bill%22%20%245.00%20Topeka&match=1.

CHAPTER 1: EARLY LIFE (1837–1857)

1. Joseph Rosa, *They Called Him Wild Bill: The Life and Adventures of James Butler Hickok* (Norman: University of Oklahoma Press, 1974), 11, 12.
2. Ibid., 12.
3. Ibid., 13.
4. Ibid.
5. Ibid., 10, 13.
6. J. W. Buel, *Heroes of the Plains* (Philadelphia: Historical Publishing Co., 1881), 24; Rosa, *They Called Him Wild Bill*, 13, 14.
7. Buel, *Heroes*, 23; Rosa, *They Called Him Wild Bill*, 14.
8. Rosa, *They Called Him Wild Bill*, 14.
9. Ibid.
10. Ibid., 15.
11. Ibid., 15–16.
12. Buel, *Heroes*, 24.
13. Rosa, *They Called Him Wild Bill*, 15.
14. Ibid., 16.
15. Rosa, *They Called Him Wild Bill*, 16; Buel, *Heroes*, 25.
16. Rosa, *They Called Him Wild Bill*, 16; Buel, *Heroes*, 25.
17. Joseph Rosa, *Wild Bill Hickok: The Man and His Myth* (Lawrence: University Press of Kansas, 1996), 4; Rosa, *They Called Him Wild Bill*, 17, 20–21.
18. Rosa, *They Called Him Wild Bill*, 17.
19. Ibid.
20. Ibid.
21. An 1859 Kansas Territory census shows James arrived in 1855; however in a September 28, 1856 letter to his mother he wrote "it has been more than three months since I left home." Rosa, *They Called Him Wild Bill*, 16–17.
22. Rosa, *They Called Him Wild Bill*, 17–18.

23. Ibid., 18, 21–22.

24. Ibid., 18, 22.

25. Russell, Majors & Waddell owners constantly formed partnerships among themselves and other investors.

26. Don Russell, *The Lives and Legends of Buffalo Bill* (Norman: University of Oklahoma Press, 1960), 35; Rosa, *They Called Him Wild Bill*, 22.

27. Russell, *Buffalo Bill*, 3–4.

28. Julia Cody Goodman, Elizabeth Jane Leonard, and James William Hoffman, eds., *Buffalo Bill: King of the Old West* (New York: Library Publishers, 1955), 25, 27; Russell, *Buffalo Bill*, 4–5.

29. Writers state Mary was from Derby, Pennsylvania. There is no Derby. They must mean Darby, Pennsylvania.

30. Russell, *Buffalo Bill*, 5.

31. Goodman, Leonard, and Hoffman, *Buffalo Bill*, 28; Russell, *Buffalo Bill*, 5.

32. Goodman, Leonard, and Hoffman, *Buffalo Bill*, 28; Russell, *Buffalo Bill*, 5. William Cody was never good with dates. In his first autobiography, he said he was born in 1845, but he corrected it in later editions. Russell, *Buffalo Bill*, 5–6.

33. Goodman, Leonard, and Hoffman, *Buffalo Bill*, 29; Russell, *Buffalo Bill*, 6.

34. Goodman, Leonard, and Hoffman, *Buffalo Bill*, 30–31; Russell, *Buffalo Bill*, 7.

35. Goodman, Leonard, and Hoffman, *Buffalo Bill*, 38.

36. Goodman, Leonard, and Hoffman, *Buffalo Bill*, 31, 36–37; Russell, *Buffalo Bill*, 8.

37. William F. Cody, *The Life of Hon. William F. Cody, Known as Buffalo Bill, the Famous Hunter, Scout, and Guide: An Autobiography* (Lincoln: University of Nebraska Press, 1879), 20; Goodman, Leonard, and Hoffman, *Buffalo Bill*, 38–39; Russell, *Buffalo Bill*, 8.

38. Laura Ella was also called Nellie and Helen. Russell, *Buffalo Bill*, 10.

39. William Frederick Cody, *An Autobiography of Buffalo Bill (Colonel W. F. Cody)* (New York: Cosmopolitan Book Corporation, 1920), 4; Russell, *Buffalo Bill*, 9, 10.

40. Cody, *Autobiography*, 4–5; Russell, *Buffalo Bill*, 11.

41. Cody, *Autobiography*, 5; Goodman, Leonard, and Hoffman, *Buffalo Bill*, 42–43. Russell, *Buffalo Bill*, 11.

42. Goodman, Leonard, and Hoffman, *Buffalo Bill*, 45; Russell, *Buffalo Bill*, 11.

43. James Crutchfield, Candy Moulton, and Terry Del Bene, eds., *The Settlement of America: Encyclopedia of Western Expansion from Jamestown to the Closing of the Frontier*, Vol. 1 (Armonk, NY: M. E. Sharp, Inc., 2011), 203–4.

44. The dragoons were the forerunner of the cavalry.

45. Cody, *Autobiography*, 5–6; Russell, *Buffalo Bill*, 11.

46. Cody, *Autobiography*, 7; Russell, *Buffalo Bill*, 11.

47. John S. Grey, "Fact Versus Fiction in the Kansas Boyhood of Buffalo Bill," *Kansas History: A Journal of the Central Plains*, Vol. 8, no. 1, Spring 1985, 4; Russell, *Buffalo Bill*, 11.

48. Cody, *Life of*, 31–34, 37; Russell, *Buffalo Bill*, 12.

49. Russell, *Buffalo Bill*, 12, 27.

50. Cody, *Autobiography*, 10; Russell, *Buffalo Bill*, 13.

51. Russell, *Buffalo Bill*, 13.

52. Cody, *Autobiography*, 9–10.

53. Goodman, Leonard, and Hoffman, *Buffalo Bill*, 54–55; Russell, *Buffalo Bill*, 12.

54. Some accounts say Willie Cody was with Isaac, but in Cody's first autobiography, *The Life of Hon. William F. Cody*, he doesn't mention he was with his father.

55. Cody, *Life of*, 40–41; Russell, *Buffalo Bill*, 14.

56. Cody, *Life of*, 40–42; Russell, *Buffalo Bill*, 14.

57. Cody, *Life of*, 41–42; Russell, *Buffalo Bill*, 14.

58. Louis S. Warren, *Buffalo Bill's America: William Cody and the Wild West Show* (New York: Random House, Inc., 2005), 10.

59. Russell, *Buffalo Bill*, 15.

60. Ibid., 14.

61. Goodman, Leonard, and Hoffman, *Buffalo Bill*, 58–59; Cody, *Life of*, 48; Russell, *Buffalo Bill*, 15.

62. Russell, *Buffalo Bill*, 16.

63. Goodman, Leonard, and Hoffman, *Buffalo Bill*, 63; Russell, *Buffalo Bill*, 16.

64. Russell, *Buffalo Bill*, 17.

65. Russell, *Buffalo Bill*, 19; Jesse A. Hall and Leroy T. Hand, "Miscellaneous Items in Leavenworth County, Kansas History," *History of Leavenworth County, Kansas* (Topeka, KS: Historical Publishing Company, 1921), November 8, 2020, http://history.rays-place.com/ks/lea-misc.htm.

66. James M. McPherson, *Battle Cry of Freedom: The Civil War Era* (New York: Ballantine Books, 1988), 148.

67. Russell, *Buffalo Bill*, 19.

68. Ibid., 20.

69. Goodman, Leonard, and Hoffman, *Buffalo Bill*, 59–60; Cody, *Life of*, 48, 50–52; Russell, *Buffalo Bill*, 20–21.

70. There were various versions of the stories as well as timelines depending on which family member told the story.

71. Cody, *Life of*, 43–44, 45–46.

72. Russell, *Buffalo Bill*, 21.

73. Russell, *Buffalo Bill*, 25: Goodman, Leonard, and Hoffman, *Buffalo Bill*, 71–72.

74. Russell, *Buffalo Bill*, 27.

75. Cody, *Life of*, 57.

76. Goodman, Leonard, and Hoffman, *Buffalo Bill*, 73.

77. Alexander Majors, *Seventy Years on the Frontier, Pony Express & Overland Stage: Two Accounts of the Opening of the American Western Frontier* (Driffield, Great Britain: Leonaur, 2017), 180; Russell, *Buffalo Bill*, 27, 28; Goodman, Leonard, and Hoffman, *Buffalo Bill*, 74.

78. Majors, *Seventy Years on the Frontier*, 181.

79. Russell, *Buffalo Bill*, 29.

80. Ibid.

81. Cody, *Life of*, 53–55; Russell, *Buffalo Bill*, 29–30.

82. Cody, *Life of*, 55–56; Russell, *Buffalo Bill*, 30.

83. Cody, *Life of*, 56–57; Russell, *Buffalo Bill*, 30.

84. Crutchfield, Moulton, and Del Bene, *Settlement of America*, Vol. 1, 199–200.

85. Russell, *Buffalo Bill*, 31.

86. Russell, *Buffalo Bill*, 31; Cody, *Life of*, 57, 73–74. Cody wrote this incident happened on a later bull train, but Willis remembered it happening on his bull train.

87. George Walton, *Sentinel of the Plains: Fort Leavenworth and the American West* (Englewood Cliffs, NJ: Prentice-Hall, Inc., 1973), 80; James Crutchfield, Candy Moulton, and Terry Del Bene, *The Settlement of America: Encyclopedia of Western Expansion from Jamestown to the Closing of the Frontier*, Vol. 2 (Armonk, NY: M. E. Sharp, Inc., 2011), 479.

88. Walton, *Sentinel*, 80, 82.

89. Jim DeFelice, *West Like Lightning: The Brief, Legendary Ride of the Pony Express* (New York: HarperCollins Publishers, 2018), 27; David L. Bigler and Will Bagley, *The Mormon Rebellion: America's First Civil War, 1857–1858* (Norman: University of Oklahoma Press, 2011), 244.

90. Cody, *Autobiography*, 16.

91. Ibid., 16–17.

92. Cody, *Autobiography*, 17. Other versions of the oath appear in books. I used Cody's version.

93. Ibid., 17, 18.

94. Ibid., 18.

95. Ibid., 19.

96. Ibid., 19–20.

97. Buel, *Heroes*, 244; Cody, *Autobiography*, 20; Russell, *Buffalo Bill*, 32.

98. Cody, *Autobiography*, 21; Russell, *Buffalo Bill*, 33.

Chapter 2: The Utah War (1857–1860)

1. Cody, *Life of*, 72.

2. Bigler and Bagley, *Mormon Rebellion*, 212.

3. Bigler and Bagley, *Mormon Rebellion*, 212; Russell, *Buffalo Bill*, 34–35; Cody, *Autobiography*, 22–24.

4. Cody, *Autobiography*, 24–25.

5. Rosa, *They Called Him Wild Bill*, 23–26.

6. Ibid., 24.

7. It was erroneously believed James and Mary Jane married, but copies of James's letters home prove otherwise. Rosa, *They Called Him Wild Bill*, 26–27.

8. Rosa, *They Called Him Wild Bill*, 21–22, 26, 27.

9. Buel, *Heroes*, 29; Rosa, *They Called Him Wild Bill*, 27.

10. Rosa, *They Called Him Wild Bill*, 27.

11. Rosa, *They Called Him Wild Bill*, 31; Russell, *Buffalo Bill*, 41.

12. Richard E. Lingenfelter, *Bonanzas & Borrascas: Gold Lust and Silver Sharks, 1848–1884* (Norman: University of Oklahoma Press, 2012), 85; Robert Wallace, *The Miners* (Alexandria, VA: Time-Life Books, 1976), 19, 21.

13. Ralph Moody, *Stagecoach West* (New York: Thomas Y. Crowell Company, 1967), 154–55, 171, 176; Mark Dugan, *Tales Never Told Around the Campfire: True Stories of Frontier America* (Athens: Swallow Press/Ohio University Press, 1992), 47.

14. Rosa, *They Called Him Wild Bill*, 28.

15. Cody, *Autobiography*, 25; Russell, *Buffalo Bill*, 36.

16. Cody, *Autobiography*, 25.

17. Douglas C. McChristian, *Fort Laramie: Military Bastion of the High Plains* (Norman: University of Oklahoma Press, 2008), 123.

18. Cody, *Autobiography*, 25–26, 28.

19. Ibid., 27.

20. Ibid.

21. Cody, *Autobiography*, 28.

22. Cody, *Autobiography*, 28; Russell, *Buffalo Bill*, 38–39.

23. Cody, *Autobiography*, 29.

24. Ibid., 29–30.

25. Page Smith, *The Nation Comes of Age*, 565; Crutchfield, Moulton, and Del Bene, eds., *The Settlement of America*, Vol. 2, 480.

26. Buel, *Heroes*, 250–52; Cody, *Autobiography*, 30–32.

27. Cody, *Autobiography*, 32–33.

28. Buel, *Heroes*, 253; Cody, *Autobiography*, 33–34: Cody, *Life of*, 86.

29. Buel, *Heroes*, 253; Cody, *Autobiography*, 34.

30. Russell, *Buffalo Bill*, 38; Goodman, Leonard, and Hoffman, *Buffalo Bill*, 80–81.

31. Cody, *Life of*, 89; Russell, *Buffalo Bill*, 41.

32. Cody, *Life of*, 90; Russell, *Buffalo Bill*, 41.

33. Russell, *Buffalo Bill*, 41.

34. Ibid., 48.

35. Ibid., 41.

36. Goodman, Leonard, and Hoffman, *Buffalo Bill*, 84.

37. Ibid., 101–3.

38. Goodman, Leonard, and Hoffman, *Buffalo Bill*, 100–101; Russell, *Buffalo Bill*, 41.

39. Russell, *Buffalo Bill*, 41.

40. Moody, *Stagecoach*, 156–57, 162; Cody, *Life of*, 93.

41. In a later version, a bear attacked the ox. Harrington shot the bear wounding it. Billy had a lucky shot in the dark killing the bear. Cody, *Autobiography*, 37–38.

42. Cody, *Life of*, 93; Russell, *Buffalo Bill*, 42.

43. Cody, *Life of*, 94.

44. Ibid.

45. Ibid., 97.

46. Many believed Rain-in-the-Face killed Custer, but this was later disproved. Russell, *Buffalo Bill*, 42.

47. Josephine Waggoner, *Witness: A Hunkpapa Historian's Strong-Heart Song of the Lakotas* (Lincoln: University of Nebraska Press, 2013), 43, 436.

48. Cody, *Life of*, 97.

49. Ibid., 97–98.

50. Ibid., 98–99.

51. Ibid., 99, 100.

52. Ibid., 101.

53. Ibid.

54. Ibid., 102.

CHAPTER 3: PONY EXPRESS (APRIL 3, 1860–JUNE 1, 1861)

1. Moody, *Stagecoach*, 170, 175, 176.

2. Ibid., 170, 171.

3. Ibid., 178–79, 183.

4. Ibid., 183.

5. Ibid., 184, 185.

6. Jim DeFelice, *West Like Lightning*, 66.

7. DeFelice, *West Like Lightning*, 87, 288; Moody, *Stagecoach*, 177.

8. DeFelice, *West Like Lightning*, 88.

9. Moody, *Stagecoach*, 178; DeFelice, *West Like Lightning*, 88.

10. Moody, *Stagecoach*, 178; DeFelice, *West Like Lightning*, 88.

11. Bill O'Neal, *Encyclopedia of Western Gunfighters* (Norman: University of Oklahoma Press, 1979), 286–87.

12. Rosa, *They Called Him Wild Bill*, 32, 33.

13. Majors, *Seventy Years on the Frontier*, 143.

14. Majors, *Seventy Years on the Frontier*, 180; Moody, *Stagecoach*, 183.

15. Russell, *Buffalo Bill*, 48–49.

16. Majors, *Seventy Years on the Frontier*, 142; Moody, *Stagecoach*, 183.

17. Russell, *Buffalo Bill*, 49, 50; Majors, *Seventy Years on the Frontier*, 143.

18. Russell, *Buffalo Bill*, 50.

19. Ibid., 51.

20. Ibid.

21. Ibid., 52.

22. Ibid.

23. Ibid., 53.

24. Ibid.

25. Frank J. Wilstach, *Wild Bill Hickok, the Prince of Pistoleers* (Garden City, NY: Doubleday, Page & Company, 1926), 34.

26. Joseph Rosa, *Wild Bill Hickok, Gunfighter: An Account of Hickok's Gunfights* (Norman: University of Oklahoma Press, 2003), 71.

27. J. W. Buel wrote in *Heroes of the Plains*, p. 36, Hickok was "passing through the Soccoro range" when this incident occurred implying he was close to Santa Fe to be taken there for treatment. There is no Soccoro Range near Santa Fe. I asked journalist Ollie Reed Jr. about the Soccoro Range. After conferring with fellow New Mexico journalist Don Bullis, Ollie wrote, "Like me, the only mountains Don knows of that might be referred to as the Socorro Range are near the town of Socorro, which is 72 miles south of Albuquerque. If Bill [Hickok] got mauled by a bear down that way, there would be places closer than Santa Fe to take him for treatment."

28. Buel, *Heroes*, 36.

29. Ibid.

30. Ibid., 37.

31. Ibid., 38.

CHAPTER 4: INCIDENT AT ROCK CREEK STATION (MAY 1861–JULY 1861)

1. Everyone called the Central Overland California & Pikes Peak Express Company the Overland Stage Company.

2. Today, the site is Nebraska's Rock Creek Station State Historical Park with reconstructed station buildings.

3. Dugan, *Tales*, 48.

4. Ibid., 32, 33.

5. Ibid., 31, 34, 40.

6. Ibid., 40, 41.

7. Ibid., 41.

8. Ibid.

9. Ibid., 41–43.

10. Ibid., 44.

11. Ibid., 48.

12. Ibid., 43, 44.

13. Charles Dawson, *Pioneer Tales of the Oregon Trail and of Jefferson County* (Topeka, KS: Crane & Company, 1912), 203, 204.

14. Dugan, *Tales*, 44.

15. Ibid.

16. Ibid., 45.

17. Ibid., 46–47.

18. Ibid., 47.

19. Ibid.

20. Rosa, *They Called Him Wild Bill*, 51.

21. Rosa, *They Called Him Wild Bill*, 51; Dugan, *Tales*, 48.

22. Rosa, *They Called Him Wild Bill*, 44; Dugan, *Tales*, 48–49.

23. Dugan, *Tales*, 51.

24. Dugan, *Tales*, 49.

25. William Monroe McCanles, "The Only Living Eye Witness," *Nebraska Historical Magazine*, Vol. 10, no. 2 (April-June 1927): 48; Dugan, *Tales*, 49.

26. Dawson, *Pioneer Tales*, 215.

27. Rosa, *Wild Bill Hickok, Gunfighter*, 74, 75.

28. McCanles, "Eye Witness," 48.

29. Dugan, *Tales*, 44–45.

30. Ibid., 49.

31. Ibid., 51–52.

32. McCanles, "Eye Witness," 49.

33. Ibid., 48.

34. Ibid., 49.

35. Dugan, *Tales*, 53.

36. McCanles, "Eye Witness," 48; Dugan, *Tales*, 53.

37. McCanles, "Eye Witness," 48.

38. McCanles, "Eye Witness," 48; Dugan, *Tales*, 53.

39. McCanles, "Eye Witness," 49.

40. Dugan, *Tales*, 53.

41. Dawson, *Pioneer Tales*, 219–20.

42. Dugan, *Tales*, 53–54.

43. Ibid., 54.

44. Ibid., 54–55.

45. Rosa, *Wild Bill Hickok,* 233.

CHAPTER 5: CIVIL WAR (1861–1865)

1. Walton, *Sentinel*, 119–20, 122.

2. Ibid., 123–24, 127.

3. Shelby Foote, *The Civil War, A Narrative: Fort Sumter to Perryville* (New York: Random House, 1986), 92; E. B. Long, *The Civil War Day by Day: An Almanac: 1861–1865* (Garden City, NY: Doubleday & Company, Inc., 1971), 107; Rosa, *They Called Him Wild Bill*, 53.

4. Foote, *Civil War, A Narrative: Fort Sumter to Perryville*, 92.

5. Foote, *Civil War, A Narrative: Fort Sumter to Perryville*, 92–93; Long, *Civil War Day by Day*, 107.

6. Foote, *Civil War, A Narrative: Fort Sumter to Perryville*, 94; Long, *Civil War Day by Day*, 107.

7. H. D. Hickok, "He Collaborates Col. Ed. Little," *Mail and Breeze* (Topeka, KS, September 27, 1901), 2, Newspapers.com, December 26, 2020, https://www.newspapers.com/image/366205895; Rosa, *Wild Bill Hickok,* 238.

8. George W. Hance, "The Truth About Wild Bill," *Mail and Breeze* (Topeka, KS, December 20, 1901), 5, Newspapers.com, December 27, 2020, https://www.newspapers.com/image/366208009; Rosa, *They Called Him Wild Bill*, 53; Russell, *Buffalo Bill*, 58; Cody, *Life of*, 131.

9. Cody, *Life of*, 125; Goodman, Leonard, and Hoffman, *Buffalo Bill*, 124.

10. Goodman, Leonard, and Hoffman, *Buffalo Bill*, 125.

11. Cody, *Life of*, 12526.

12. Ibid.

13. Ibid., 126–27.

14. Ibid., 127. Chandler's Jayhawkers continued their thieving ways after Cody left. Captain A. W. Williams with the Eighth Regiment of Kansas Volunteers reported November 24, 1861, they had chased but failed to capture twenty-four Kansas Jayhawkers "commanded by one Chandler, who had stolen some twenty-five horses, clothing, silver spoons, etc."; Walton, *Sentinel*, 127; Chandler was killed in late January 1862. Russell, *Buffalo Bill*, 58.

15. McPherson, *Battle Cry*, 353; Long, *Civil War Day by Day*, 124.

16. Cody, *Life of*, 131.

17. Ibid.

18. Ibid., 131–32.

19. Ibid., 132.

20. Goodman, Leonard, and Hoffman, *Buffalo Bill*, 128; Cody, *Life of*, 134.

21. Rosa, *They Called Him Wild Bill*, 54; Christopher Phillips, "Jennison, Charles R.," *Civil War on the Western Border: The Missouri-Kansas Conflict, 1854–1865*, Kansas City Public Library, Monday, December 28, 2020, https://civilwaronthewesternborder.org/encyclopedia/jennison-charles-r; Wilstach, *Wild Bill Hickok*, 79–80. I placed this attack on Hickok's bull train as the incident was recorded in the November 17, 1861 issue of the *Leavenworth Daily Times* although the newspaper doesn't identify the wagon master. George Hance writes about the incident in the *Topeka Mail and Breeze*, December 20, 1901, that it occurred early spring of 1862. To me, the earlier date makes more sense.

22. Rosa, *They Called Him Wild Bill*, 54.

23. Ibid., 54–55.

24. Ibid., 55.

25. Hance, "The Truth About Wild Bill," 5.

26. Ibid.

27. Rosa, *They Called Him Wild Bill*, 53.

28. Foote, *Civil War, A Narrative: Fort Sumter to Perryville*, 280; McPherson, *Battle Cry*, 404.

29. Foote, *Civil War, A Narrative: Fort Sumter to Perryville*, 278; McPherson, *Battle Cry*, 404.

30. Foote, *Civil War, A Narrative: Fort Sumter to Perryville*, 281, 282–84; Rosa, *They Called Him Wild Bill*, 56.

31. McPherson, *Battle Cry*, 404–5.

32. Rosa, *They Called Him Wild Bill*, 56.

33. Foote, *Civil War, A Narrative: Fort Sumter to Perryville*, 286–87; Rosa, *They Called Him Wild Bill*, 56.

34. McPherson, *Battle Cry*, 405.

35. "John S. Phelps Papers," *Community and Conflict: The Impact of the Civil War in the Ozarks*, Wilson's Creek National Battlefield, December 29, 2020, https://ozarkscivilwar.org/archives/3549; Rosa, *They Called Him Wild Bill*, 56.

36. Long, *Civil War Day by Day*, 180; McPherson, *Battle Cry*, 405.

37. Rosa, *They Called Him Wild Bill*, 54.

38. Cody, *Life of*, 134; "Civil War: The 9th Kansas Volunteer Cavalry Regiment," *Museum of the Kansas National Guard*, December 30, 2020, https://www.kansasguardmuseum.com/?page_id=2081.

39. Russell, *Buffalo Bill*, 60–61.

40. Ibid., 59.

41. Johnny Fry was killed on October 7, 1863 by William Quantrill's bushwhackers. Russell, *Buffalo Bill*, 60.

42. Cody, *Life of*, 134.

43. Goodman, Leonard, and Hoffman, *Buffalo Bill*, 130; Russell, *Buffalo Bill*, 60. Cody, *Life of*, 135.

44. Cody, *Life of*, 135.

45. Russell, *Buffalo Bill*, 61.

46. Cody, *Life of*, 135.

47. Rosa, *They Called Him Wild Bill*, 54, 62.

48. Rosa, *Wild Bill Hickok*, 230.

49. Rosa, *They Called Him Wild Bill*, 57; Rosa, *Wild Bill Hickok*, 34–35; "The Search for Soldiers," *The Civil War*, National Park Service website, December 31, 2020, https://www.nps.gov/civilwar/search-soldiers.htm#q=%228th%20Regiment,%20Missouri%20State%20Militia%20Cavalry%22.

50. Joseph G. Rosa, "George Ward Nichols and the Legend of Wild Bill Hickok," *Arizona and the West*, Vol. 19, no. 2 (1977), 138, December 31, 2020, http://www.jstor.org/stable/40168620.

51. *History of Greene County, Missouri* (St. Louis: Western Historical Company, 1883), 763–64, January 4, 2021, https://www.google.com/books/edition/History_of_Greene_County_Missouri/p9EyAQAAMAAJ?hl=en&gbpv=1.

52. Rosa, *They Called Him Wild Bill*, 58.

53. Buel, *Heroes*, 53.

54. Rosa, *They Called Him Wild Bill*, 54.

55. Buel, *Heroes*, 53; Rosa, *They Called Him Wild Bill*, 17.

56. Buel, *Heroes*, 54–57; Rosa, *They Called Him Wild Bill*, 60–62; Wilstach, *Wild Bill Hickok*, 82–86.

57. Rosa, *They Called Him Wild Bill*, 65.

58. William Elsey Connelley and Charles Harger, *Wild Bill and His Era: The Life and Times of James Butler Hickok* (New York: The Press of the Pioneer, 1933), 51, 57–58; Rosa, *They Called Him Wild Bill*, 58, 59.

59. Buel, *Heroes*, 63, 66, 68–72.

60. Rosa, *They Called Him Wild Bill*, 62; Rosa, *Wild Bill Hickok,* 227–29; Buel, *Heroes*, 76; Wilstach, *Wild Bill Hickok*, 106.

61. Rosa, *Wild Bill Hickok*, 40.

62. *History of Greene County, Missouri*, 764.

63. Rosa, *They Called Him Wild Bill*, 64, 65.

64. McPherson, *Battle Cry*, 787; Shelby Foote, *The Civil War, A Narrative: Red River to Appomattox* (New York: Random House, 1974), 575–76, 578; Rosa, *They Called Him Wild Bill*, 65.

65. McPherson, *Battle Cry*, 787, 788.

66. Cody, *Life of*, 136; Russell, *Buffalo Bill*, 69.

67. Russell, *Buffalo Bill*, 61–62.

68. Ibid., 62.

69. Brian Steel Wills, *A Battle from the Start: The Life of Nathan Bedford Forrest* (New York: HarperCollins Publishers, 1992), 169.

70. Wills, *Battle from the Start*, 180, 196.

71. Wills, *Battle from the Start*, 214–15; Russell, *Buffalo Bill*, 62.

72. Russell, *Buffalo Bill*, 62, 64.

73. Ibid., 64.

74. Ibid., 64, 65–66.

75. Cody, *Life of*, 136; Russell, *Buffalo Bill*, 68.

76. Russell, *Buffalo Bill*, 66, 67.

77. Cody, *Life of*, 136.

78. Cody, *Life of*, 137; Russell, *Buffalo Bill*, 67.

79. Cody, *Life of*, 137–38.

80. Ibid., 139.

81. Long, *Civil War Day by Day*, 587–88; Russell, *Buffalo Bill*, 67.

82. Foote, *Civil War, A Narrative: Red River to Appomattox*, 583.

83. Cody, *Autobiography*, 77–78. Cody said after Marmaduke had been governor of Missouri, he visited him in London where he was performing his Wild West exhibition.

84. Cody, *Life of*, 139–40.

85. Rosa, *They Called Him Wild Bill*, 69.

86. Foote, *Civil War, A Narrative: Red River to Appomattox*, 585; Cody, *Life of*, 140.

87. Russell, *Buffalo Bill*, 71, 72; Cody, *Life of*, 141.

88. Louisa Frederici Cody and Courtney Ryley Cooper, *Memories of Buffalo Bill* (New York: D. Appleton & Company, 1919), 1–6; Cody, *Life of*, 141.

89. Rosa, *They Called Him Wild Bill*, 68.

90. Buel, *Heroes*, 80–82, 85.

91. Rosa, *They Called Him Wild Bill*, 69–70.

92. Ibid., 70.

93. Ibid.

94. Brevet-Major-General John B. Sanborn, "The Campaign in Missouri in September and October 1864," *Glimpses of the Nation's Struggle*. Third Series. Papers Read Before the Minnesota Commandery of the Military Order of the Loyal Legion of the United States, 1889–1892 (New York: D. D. Merrill Company, 1893), 171.

CHAPTER 6: INCIDENT AT SPRINGFIELD (JULY 1865–JANUARY 1866)

1. *History of Greene County, Missouri*, 763–64.

2. Rosa, *They Called Him Wild Bill*, 73, 75; Rosa, *Wild Bill Hickok, Gunfighter*, 82.

3. Rosa, *They Called Him Wild Bill*, 73; Rosa, *Wild Bill Hickok, Gunfighter*, 82.

4. Rosa, *They Called Him Wild Bill*, 72, 73.

5. Ibid., 73.

6. Rosa, *Wild Bill Hickok, Gunfighter*, 93.

7. Rosa, *They Called Him Wild Bill*, 74; Rosa, *Wild Bill Hickok, Gunfighter*, 86.

8. Rosa, *Wild Bill Hickok, Gunfighter*, 86–87.

9. Rosa, *Wild Bill Hickok, Gunfighter*, 87; Coroner's Inquest, Greene County Circuit Court, Inquest into the Death of Davis Tutt, 1865 [J. W. Orr Testimony], Greene County Archives and Records Center, Springfield, Missouri.

10. *History of Greene County, Missouri*, 764; Bob Boze Bell, *The Illustrated Life and Times of Wild Bill Hickok* (Cave Creek, AZ: Two Roads West, 2017), 46.

11. Coroner's Inquest, Greene County Circuit Court, Inquest into the Death of Davis Tutt, 1865 [Eli Armstrong Testimony]; Rosa, *Wild Bill Hickok, Gunfighter*, 88.

12. Coroner's Inquest, Greene County Circuit Court, Inquest into the Death of Davis Tutt, 1865 [Thomas D. Hudson Testimony]; Rosa, *Wild Bill Hickok, Gunfighter*, 91.

13. Coroner's Inquest, Greene County Circuit Court, Inquest into the Death of Davis Tutt, 1865 [Oliver Scott Testimony]; Coroner's Inquest, Greene County Circuit Court, Inquest into the Death of Davis Tutt, 1865 [Thomas D. Hudson Testimony].

14. Coroner's Inquest, Greene County Circuit Court, Inquest into the death of Davis Tutt, 1865 [F. W. Scholten Testimony].

15. Coroner's Inquest [Eli Armstrong Testimony].

16. Rosa, *Wild Bill Hickok, Gunfighter*, 91.

17. Coroner's Inquest [Eli Armstrong Testimony].

18. Rosa, *Wild Bill Hickok, Gunfighter*, 91, 93.

19. Coroner's Inquest, Greene County Circuit Court, Inquest into the Death of Davis Tutt, 1865 [Lorenza F. Lee Testimony].

20. Rosa, *Wild Bill Hickok, Gunfighter*, 91; Coroner's Inquest [Eli Armstrong Testimony].

21. Coroner's Inquest [F. W. Scholten Testimony].

22. Colonel Albert Barnitz, "Journal of the Operations of the 2nd Regiment, Ohio Cavalry, 1865 Mar 29–Nov 10," Collections: Colonel Albert Barnitz Papers, Series: Diaries, Beinecke Rare Book and Manuscript Library, Yale University, New Haven, Connecticut.

23. Coroner's Inquest, Greene County Circuit Court, Inquest into the death of Davis Tutt, 1865 [Dr. Edwin Ebert report and coroner's jury findings], Greene County Archives and Records Center, Springfield, Missouri.

24. Rosa, *They Called Him Wild Bill*, 76; Rosa, *Wild Bill Hickok*, 117.

25. Rosa, *They Called Him Wild Bill*, 74–75; Lt. Col. A. B. Warfield, Q. M. C., "The Quartermaster's Department, 1861–1864," American Civil War, January 23, 2021, https://www.americancivilwar.com/tcwn/civil_war/QuarterMaster_History.html.

26. Colonel Albert Barnitz, "Journal of the Operations of the 2nd Regiment, Ohio Cavalry, 1865 Mar 29–Nov 10."

27. "John S. Phelps Papers"; Rosa, *They Called Him Wild Bill*, 57.

28. Rosa, *They Called Him Wild Bill*, 75–76.

29. Rosa, *Wild Bill Hickok*, 120; Rosa, *They Called Him Wild Bill*, 77–78.

30. *State of Missouri v. William Haycock (Hickok)*, Greene County Circuit Court, Manslaughter, Indictment for the Death of Davis Tutt, 1865, Greene County Archives and Records Center, Springfield, Missouri; Rosa, *They Called Him Wild Bill*, 77–78.

31. *State of Missouri v. William Haycock (Hickok)*.

32. Rosa, *They Called Him Wild Bill*, 78.

33. "Local Items," *Missouri Weekly Patriot* (Springfield, MO, August 10, 1865), 3, Newspapers.com, January 21, 2021, https://www.newspapers.com/image/671306199.

34. *History of Greene County, Missouri*, 763.

35. Rosa, *They Called Him Wild Bill*, 81, 84; Rosa, *Wild Bill Hickok*, 47, 48.

36. Rosa, *Wild Bill Hickok*, 49.

37. *History of Greene County, Missouri*, 766–67.

38. Ibid., 767.

39. Rosa, *They Called Him Wild Bill*, 85, 86.

CHAPTER 7: SCOUTS (JULY 1865–AUGUST 1867)

1. Russell, *Buffalo Bill*, 71, 72; Cody, *Life of*, 141.

2. Cody and Cooper, *Memories*, 1–6; Cody, *Life of*, 141.

3. Russell, *Buffalo Bill*, 71–72; Cody, *Life of*, 141; Cody and Cooper, *Memories*, 36.

4. Cody, *Life of*, 141; Russell, *Buffalo Bill*, 75.

5. Russell, *Buffalo Bill*, 75.

6. Cody and Cooper, *Memories*, 36; Cody, *Life of*, 141–42.

7. Cody, *Life of*, 142.

8. Cody and Cooper, *Memories*, 37–38.

9. Cody, *Life of*, 142–43.

10. Cody and Cooper, *Memories*, 39–41; Cody, *Life of*, 143–44.

11. Goodman, Leonard, and Hoffman, *Buffalo Bill*, 142; Cody, *Life of*, 144.

12. Helen Cody Wetmore, *Buffalo Bill, Last of the Great Scouts: The Life Story of Colonel William F. Cody* (Lincoln: University of Nebraska Press, 1965), 136; Cody, *Life of*, 144–45.

13. Wetmore, *Buffalo Bill*, 136.

14. Cody, *Life of*, 144–45.

15. Rosa, *They Called Him Wild Bill*, 86.

16. "History of Fort Riley and the 1st Infantry Division," US Army Fort Riley, January 25, 2021, https://home.army.mil/riley/index.php/about/history; Jeffry D. Wert, *Custer: The Controversial Life of George Armstrong Custer* (New York: Simon & Schuster, 1996), 244.

17. "Great Fire at Fort Riley—A Million Dollars of Property Destroyed," *Junction City Weekly Union* (Junction City, KS, January 27, 1866), 3, Newspapers .com, January 25, 2021, https://www.newspapers.com/image/76652619; Rosa, *They Called Him Wild Bill*, 86; "Letter Signed O. J. Hopkins, Capt. And Commissary," *Junction City Weekly Union* (Junction City, KS, February 17, 1866), 3, Newspapers.com, January 25, 2021, https://www.newspapers.com/ image/76652647/?terms=%22O.%20J.%20Hopkins%22.

18. George W. Hance, "The Truth About Wild Bill," *Mail and Breeze* (Topeka, KS, December 20, 1901), 5, https://www.newspapers.com/image/366208009; Rosa, *They Called Him Wild Bill*, 87–88; *Facing the Frontier: The Missions, the Soldiers, and Civilians of Fort Leavenworth*, Kansas (Fort Leavenworth, KS: Frontier Army Museum), 42, January 25, 2021, https://www.armyupress.army .mil/Portals/7/educational-services/frontier-army-museum/FTF%20Book.pdf.

19. Rosa, *They Called Him Wild Bill*, 88.

20. Hance, "The Truth About Wild Bill," 5.

21. Rosa, *They Called Him Wild Bill*, 88, 90.

22. Ibid., 90.

23. Robert G. Athearn, *William Tecumseh Sherman and the Settlement of the West* (Norman: University of Oklahoma Press, 1956), 45–46; Crutchfield, Moulton, and Del Bene, *The Settlement of America*, Vol. 2, 432.

24. Walter R. Borneman, *Rival Rails: The Race to Build America's Greatest Transcontinental Railroad* (New York: Random House, 2010), 49; Rosa, *They Called Him Wild Bill*, 90–91.

25. Rosa, *They Called Him Wild Bill*, 91.

26. Ibid., 92.

27. Russell, *Buffalo Bill*, 74–75.

28. Warren, *Buffalo Bill's America*, 79.

29. Warren, *Buffalo Bill's America*, 79. Russell, *Buffalo Bill*, 74–75.

30. Athearn, *William Tecumseh Sherman*, 19.

31. Ibid., 21–22.

32. James Florant Meline, *Two Thousand Miles on Horseback, Santa Fé and Back: A Summer Tour Through Kansas, Nebraska, Colorado, and New Mexico, in the Year 1866* (New York: Hurd and Houghton, 1867), 17.

33. Ibid., 299–300.

34. "Julia Rockwell's Story," *Kansas City Star* (Kansas City, MO, December 14, 1947), 47, Newspapers.com, January 26, 2021, https://www.newspapers.com/ image/655666374/?terms=%22Wild%20Bill%20Hickok%22&match=1; Rosa, *They Called Him Wild Bill*, 92–93.

35. "7th Cavalry Regiment," Wikipedia, January 27, 2021, https://en.wikipedia .org/wiki/7th_Cavalry_Regiment; Wert, *Custer*, 244.

36. Wert, *Custer*, 245; Rosa, *They Called Him Wild Bill*, 92–93.

37. Borneman, *Rival Rails*, 49.

38. "Capt. Richard Bentley Owen," Find a Grave, January 27, 2021, https:// www.findagrave.com/memorial/44968453/richard-bentley-owen.

39. Cody, *Life of*, 145; Cody and Cooper, *Memories*, 49, 50.

40. Connelley and Harger, *Wild Bill*, 96.

41. Connelley and Harger, *Wild Bill*, 96. Rosa, *Wild Bill Hickok*, 135.

42. Rosa, *Wild Bill Hickok*, 26.

43. Colonel George Ward Nichols, "Wild Bill," *Harper's New Monthly Magazine*, Vol. XXXIV, no. CCI, February 1867, Reprint (Springfield, MO: Greene County Archives & Records Center, n.d.), 274.

44. Ibid.

45. Ibid., 275–77.

46. Ibid., 277.

47. Ibid., 277–79.

48. Ibid., 279.

49. Ibid.

50. Ibid., 279–80.

51. Ibid., 280.

52. Ibid., 281–82.

53. Ibid., 282.

54. Ibid.

55. Ibid., 282–84.

56. Ibid., 285.

57. Ibid.

58. "'Wild Bill,' Harper's Monthly and 'Colonel' G. W. Nichols," *Missouri Weekly Patriot* (Springfield, MO, January 31, 1867), 2, Newspapers.com, January 28, 2021, https://www.newspapers.com/image/671310085.

59. Rosa, *Wild Bill Hickok*, 41.

60. "'Wild Bill,' Harper's Monthly and 'Colonel' G. W. Nichols," 2.

61. Ibid.

62. Rosa, *Wild Bill Hickok*, 4.

63. Rosa, *They Called Him Wild Bill*, 83.

64. Rosa, *Wild Bill Hickok*, 158–59.

65. Rosa, *They Called Him Wild Bill*, 105.

66. "Wild Bill," *Daily Bulletin* (Leavenworth, KS, February 13, 1867), 1, Newspapers.com, January 29, 2021, https://www.newspapers.com/ image/364881458/?terms=%22Wild%20Bill&match=1.

67. Nyle H. Miller and Joseph W. Snell, *Why the West Was Wild: A Contemporary Look at the Antics of Some Highly Publicized Kansas Cowtown Personalities* (Norman: University of Oklahoma Press, 1963), 182.

68. "Local Matters," *Weekly Free Press* (Atchison, KS, March 2, 1867), 3, News papers.com, January 30, 2021, https://www.newspapers.com/image/480028411.

69. Indian Annie lived in a shack behind Ellsworth's Grand Central Hotel, working at the hotel. She married Ben Wilson. They had a daughter Birdie. After Wilson's death, Indian Annie supported Birdie and herself doing odd jobs and fortune-telling. Indian Annie died in a poorhouse in 1883. Rosa, *They Called Him Wild Bill*, 225.

70. Buel wrote Hickok left Mary Logan at the Niobrara cabin. She married a St. Louis man named Rogers. She ran into Hickok and they rekindled their romance and had extensive correspondence. Rogers found Hickok's love letters and threatened to kill him. Mary prevented Rogers from carrying out his threat by killing him, lacing his coffee with poison. Mary then disappeared. Buel, *Heroes*, 86–90.

71. George Armstrong Custer, *My Life on the Plains or, Personal Experiences with Indians* (Norman: University of Oklahoma Press, 1962), 44–45.

72. Elizabeth B. Custer, *Following the Guidon* (Norman: University of Oklahoma Press, 1966), 160–61.

73. Ibid., 162.

74. Wert, *Custer*, 253.

75. Glen Tucker, *Hancock the Superb* (Dayton, OH: Morningside House, Inc., 1960), 13; Wert, *Custer*, 253.

76. Paul Andrew Hutton, ed., *The Custer Reader* (Lincoln: University of Nebraska Press, 1992), 118; Wert, *Custer*, 253. Connelley and Harger, *Wild Bill*, 97, 99.

77. Hutton, *Custer Reader*, 118; Wert, *Custer*, 253.

78. *Harper's Weekly* and *Harper's New Monthly Magazine* were two different publications by the same company.

79. Rosa, *They Called Him Wild Bill*, 106–7, 110.

80. Ibid., 107. If a writer wanted to make someone appear to be a hick, they used poor spelling and grammar.

81. Rosa, *They Called Him Wild Bill*, 108–9.

82. Custer, *Life on the Plains*, 29.

83. Rosa, *They Called Him Wild Bill*, 109–10.

84. Custer, *Life on the Plains*, 29; Wert, *Custer*, 253.

85. Hutton, *Custer Reader*, 119; Custer, *Life on the Plains*, 29, 30; Wert, *Custer*, 254.

86. Dee Brown, *Bury My Heart at Wounded Knee: An Indian History of the American West* (New York: Henry Holt and Company, 1970), 151, 152; Wert, *Custer*, 254.

87. Brown, *Bury My Heart*, 152; Wert, *Custer*, 254.

88. Crutchfield, Moulton, and Del Bene, *Settlement of America*, Vol. 2, 420.

89. Brown, *Bury My Heart*, 153; Wert, *Custer*, 254.

90. Brown, *Bury My Heart*, 154, 156; Wert, *Custer*, 254.

91. Brown, *Bury My Heart*, 156; Wert, *Custer*, 254.

92. Brown, *Bury My Heart*, 156.

93. Custer, *Life on the Plains*, 34–35; Wert, *Custer*, 254.

94. Custer, *Life on the Plains*, 36–42.

95. Connelley and Harger, *Wild Bill*, 98; Custer, *Life on the Plains*, 43–44.

96. Custer, *Life on the Plains*, 48.

97. Ibid., 48–52.

98. Connelley and Harger, *Wild Bill*, 99, 100.

99. Ibid., 100.

100. Custer, *Life on the Plains*, 53; Wert, *Custer*, 255.

101. Custer, *Life on the Plains*, 57; Wert, *Custer*, 255.

102. Custer, *Life on the Plains*, 57; Brown, *Bury My Heart*, 157.

103. Custer, *Life on the Plains*, 64; Rosa, *They Called Him Wild Bill*, 111.

104. Hutton, *Custer Reader*, 123–24.

105. Custer, *Life on the Plains*, 65, 73; Connelley and Harger, *Wild Bill*, 101.

106. Wert, *Custer*, 258.

107. Miller and Snell, *Why the West Was Wild*, 184.

108. Ibid., 185.

109. Colonel George A. Armes, *Ups and Downs of an Army Officer* (Washington, DC: Privately Published, 1900), 232–33. Google Books, February 3, 2021, https://www.google.com/books/edition/Ups_and_Downs_of_an_Army_Officer/2xeZNAlSn8AC?hl=en&gbpv=1&printsec=frontcover.

110. Armes, *Ups and Downs*, 233.

111. Rosa, *They Called Him Wild Bill*, 116.

112. Cody, *Life of*, 145.

113. Cody and Cooper, *Memories*, 51–54.

114. Russell, *Buffalo Bill*, 78, 84; Warren, *Buffalo Bill's America*, 559n36.

115. Cody, *Life of*, 145.

116. Ibid., 145–47.

117. "Fort Fletcher, Kansas," Santa Fe Trail Research Site, February 5, 2021, http://www.santafetrailresearch.com/spacepix/fort-fletcher.html; Cody, *Life of*, 145.

118. Armes, *Ups and Downs*, 236, 237; Cody, *Life of*, 147.

119. Armes, *Ups and Downs*, 237.

120. Ibid., 239.

121. Cody, *Life of*, 147–48; Armes, *Ups and Downs*, 240, 242.

122. Brown, *Bury My Heart*, 157.

Chapter 8: Buffalo (August 1867–May 1868)

1. The Union Pacific Railroad, Eastern Division officially became the Kansas Pacific Railroad in 1869. Borneman, *Rival Rails*, 58.

2. "Our History," City of Ellsworth website, February 6, 2021, https://www.ellsworthks.net/pview.aspx?id=21044&catid=29; Rosa, *They Called Him Wild Bill*, 116, 118.

3. Rosa, *They Called Him Wild Bill*, 95.

4. Miller and Snell, *Why the West Was Wild*, 185–86.

5. Miller and Snell, *Why the West Was Wild*, 186; Rosa, *They Called Him Wild Bill*, 117.

6. Rosa, *They Called Him Wild Bill*, 116.

7. Miller and Snell, *Why the West Was Wild*, 186; Rosa, *They Called Him Wild Bill*, 118.

8. Cody, *Life of*, 149.

9. Ibid.

10. Ibid., 150.

11. Warren, *Buffalo Bill's America*, 50.

12. Warren, *Buffalo Bill's America*, 50; Cody, *Life of*, 150.

13. Cody and Cooper, *Memories*, 55–64; Cody, *Life of*, 151; "From Western Kansas," *Kansas State Journal* (Lawrence, KS, March 5, 1868), 2, Newspapers.com, February 14, 2021, https://www.newspapers.com/image/489028477/?terms=%22Wild%20Bill%22%201868%20KS&match=1.

14. Warren, *Buffalo Bill's America*, 50; Cody and Cooper, *Memories*, 78.

15. Cody, *Life of*, 152.

16. Ibid., 153.

17. Cody, *Life of*, 153; William Edward Webb, *Buffalo Land* (Cincinnati: E. Hannaford & Company, 1872), 149–50, Google Books, February 10, 2021, https://www.google.com/books/edition/Buffalo_Land/8_E0AAAAIAAJ?hl=en&gbpv=1.

18. Cody, *Life of*, 153.

19. Webb, *Buffalo Land*, 194; Cody, *Life of*, 153, 154, 172, 173; Russell, *Buffalo Bill*, 85.

20. Steve Friesen, *Buffalo Bill: Scout, Showman, Visionary* (Golden, CO: Fulcrum Publishing, Inc., 2010), 15; Cody, *Life of*, 154; Russell, *Buffalo Bill*, 86; "Famous Guns: Lucretia Borgia," Firearms History, Technology & Development, February 10, 2021, http://firearmshistory.blogspot.com/2015/12/famous-guns-lucretia-borgia.html. Lucretia Borgia is on display at the Buffalo Bill Center of the West Museum in Cody, Wyoming.

21. Cody, *Life of*, 154.

22. Ibid.

23. Ibid., 155.

24. Ibid., 155–56.

25. Cody, *Life of*, 156–57; Russell, *Buffalo Bill*, 87.

26. Cody, *Life of*, 158; Russell, *Buffalo Bill*, 87.

27. Cody, *Life of*, 158–60.

28. Ibid., 161.

29. Ibid., 161–62.

30. Ibid., 174.

31. Ibid., 161–62.

32. Russell, *Buffalo Bill*, 89.

33. I ran my own calculation. Using all days in each eight months, the total is 243 days. Multiply that by 12 buffalos per day equals 2,916 buffalos, just a little under Russell's number.

34. Cody and Cooper, *Memories*, 113–14.

35. Cody and Cooper, *Memories*, 114; Cody, *Life of*, 162.

36. "The Buffalo Hunt," *Leavenworth Daily Conservative* (November 26, 1867), 1, Newspapers.com, February 11, 2021, https://www.newspapers.com/image/365761820/?terms=November%2028%2C%201867&match=1.

37. Cody and Cooper, *Memories*, 78, 82.

38. Ibid., 84, 85–86.

39. Ibid., 86–87.

40. Ibid., 90–91.

41. Ibid., 93–96.

42. Ibid., 98–99.

43. Ibid., 99.

44. Ibid., 105–7.

45. Ibid., 109, 112, 116–18.

46. Ibid., 118–21.

47. Ibid., 74–76.

48. Cody and Cooper, *Memories*, 108, 121–22; Rosa, *They Called Him Wild Bill*, 95.

49. Rosa, *They Called Him Wild Bill*, 95.

50. Miller and Snell, *Why the West Was Wild*, 187.

51. J. Parks, "From Western Kansas," *Kansas State Journal* (Lawrence, KS, March 5, 1868), 2, Newspapers.com, February 14, 2021, https://www.newspapers.com/image/489028477.

52. Rosa, *They Called Him Wild Bill*, 119.

53. "From the West," *Leavenworth Daily Commercial* (Leavenworth, KS, January 11, 1868), 4, Newspapers.com, February 14, 2021, https://www.newspapers.com/image/425157608/?terms=Cody&match=1.

54. "From Ellsworth and Hays," *Daily Kansas Tribune* (Leavenworth, KS, February 14, 1868), 3, Newspapers.com, February 14, 2021, https://www.newspapers.com/image/60531847/?terms=Cody&match=1; J. Parks, "From Western Kansas," 2.

55. J. Parks, "From Western Kansas," *Daily Kansas State Journal* (Lawrence, KS, March 11, 1868), 1, Newspapers.com, February 15, 2021, https://www.newspapers.com/image/365202378/?terms=Cody&match=1.

56. Ibid.

57. Ibid.

58. J. Parks, "From Western Kansas," *Daily Kansas State Journal* (Lawrence, KS, March 13, 1868), 1, Newspapers.com, February 15, 2021, https://www.newspapers.com/image/365202422/?terms=Cody&match=1.

59. Ibid.

60. J. Parks, "From Western Kansas," *Daily Kansas State Journal* (Lawrence, KS, March 14, 1868), 1, Newspapers.com, February 15, 2021, https://www.news papers.com/image/365202447/?terms=Cody&match=1.

61. Ibid.

62. Ibid.

63. "Hotel Arrivals, Massasoit House," *Daily Free Press* (Atchison, KS, March 12, 1868), Newspapers.com, February 8, 2021, https://www.newspapers.com/image/480034982/?terms=%22Wild%20Bill%22%201868%20KS&match=1; "Massasoit House, Atchison, Kansas," Kansas Memory, Kansas State Historical Society, February 8, 2021, https://www.kshs.org/index.php?url=km/items/view/218699.

64. "Local Matters," *Weekly Free Press* (Atchison, KS, March 21, 1868), News papers.com, February 8, 2021, https://www.newspapers.com/image/480034982/?terms=%22Wild%20Bill%22%201868%20KS&match=1.

65. Rosa, *They Called Him Wild Bill*, 96–97; "Band of Road Men Captured," *Topeka Weekly Leader* (Topeka, KS, April 2, 1868), 3, Newspapers.com, February 8, 2021, https://www.newspapers.com/image/366977912.

66. Cody, *Life of*, 161–62.

67. Cody, *Life of*, 162, 165–66; Russell, *Buffalo Bill*, 95.

68. Cody, *Life of*, 166–67; Russell, *Buffalo Bill*, 95–96.

69. Cody, *Life of*, 167–68.

70. Ibid., 168.

71. Ibid.

72. Ibid., 169.

73. Cody, *Life of*, 175; Borneman, *Rival Rails*, 50, 58. "Sheridan, Kansas," Wikipedia, February 18, 2021, https://en.wikipedia.org/wiki/Sheridan,_Kansas.

74. Paul Andrew Hutton, *Phil Sheridan and His Army* (Norman: University of Oklahoma Press, 1985), 36; Custer, *Life on the Plains*, 65.

75. Russell, *Buffalo Bill*, 92.

76. Cody, *Life of*, 171; Russell, *Buffalo Bill*, 93.

77. Cody, *Life of*, 171; Russell, *Buffalo Bill*, 93.

78. Cody, *Life of*, 172.

79. Ibid., 172–73.

80. Ibid., 173–74.

81. Comstock's scouting partner Abner "Sharp" Grover said Cheyenne warriors attacked them. Comstock was killed while Grover was wounded but escaped. Some believed Grover killed Comstock. After Comstock's death Grover acquired Comstock's profitable hay ranch near Fort Wallace. Susan K. Salzer, "Medicine Bill Comstock—Saga of the Leatherstocking Scout," HistoryNet, February 18, 2021, https://www.historynet.com/medicine-bill-comstock-saga-of-the-leatherstocking-scout.htm.

82. Cody, *Life of*, 175–77.

Chapter 9: Scouting for the Army (May 1868–July 1870)

1. Crutchfield, Moulton, and Del Bene, *Settlement of America*, Vol. 2, 325; L. Robert Pyle, "Cheyenne Chief Tall Bull," Historynet, February 26, 2021, https://www.historynet.com/cheyenne-chief-tall-bull.htm.

2. Hutton, *Sheridan*, 33–34; Crutchfield, Moulton, and Del Bene, *Settlement of America*, Vol. 2, 325; Brown, *Bury My Heart*, 158.

3. Hutton, *Sheridan*, 34.

4. Raymond J. DeMallie, vol. ed., *Plains, Handbook of North American Indians*, Vol. 13, Part 2 (Washington, DC: Smithsonian Institution, 2001), 876; Brown, *Bury My Heart*, 162.

5. Yes, 1868 was a leap year.

6. Philip Henry Sheridan, *Personal Memoirs of P. H. Sheridan*, Vol. 2 (New York: Charles L. Webster & Company, 1888), 288, Google Books, February 23, 2021, https://www.google.com/books/edition/Personal_Memoirs_of_P_H_Sheridan _General/gC8OAAAAIAAJ?hl=en&gbpv=1; Hutton, *Sheridan*, 28, 34–35, 37; Brown, *Bury My Heart*, 163.

7. Cody, *Life of*, 177.

8. Ibid., 178.

9. Hutton, *Sheridan*, 42; Cody, *Life of*, 178.

10. Joseph Rosa places this incident in 1868. Bill Tilghman was born July 4, 1854. Zoe Tilghman, his wife, wrote he was twelve years old when he met Hickok. If it was in 1868, Tilghman was fourteen years old, so I use that.

11. Zoe Agnes Stratton Tilghman, *Marshal of the Last Frontier, Life and Services of William Matthew (Bill) Tilghman* (Glendale, CA: The Arthur H. Clark Company, 1949), 38–40.

12. Harry "Sam" Young, *Hard Knocks: A Life Story of the Vanishing West* (Pierre: South Dakota Historical Society Press, 2005), 41–43.

13. "Excursion to Monument," *Topeka Leader* (Topeka, KS, August 13, 1868), 2, Newspapers.com, February 21, 2021, https://www.newspapers.com/ image/366979929/.

14. "Excursion to Monument," 2; Rosa, *They Called Him Wild Bill*, 121.

15. Brown, *Bury My Heart*, 163; Hutton, *Sheridan*, 38.

16. Sheridan, *Memoirs*, Vol. 2, 292.

17. Salzer, "Medicine Bill Comstock—Saga of the Leatherstocking Scout"; Sheridan, *Memoirs*, Vol. 2, 286–87.

18. Sheridan, *Memoirs*, Vol. 2, 295.

19. Sheridan, *Memoirs*, Vol. 2, 299, 302; Hutton, *Sheridan*, 45.

20. Sheridan, *Memoirs*, Vol. 2, 294.

21. Cody, *Life of*, 178–80.

22. Ibid., 180–82.

23. Ibid., 185, 187.

24. Ibid., 186–87.

25. Ibid., 187–88.

26. Ibid., 188, 189.
27. Ibid., 189–90.
28. Ibid., 191–92.
29. Ibid., 192–93.
30. Ibid., 193.
31. Sheridan, *Memoirs*, Vol. 2, 300.
32. Cody, *Life of*, 193–94.
33. Ibid., 194.
34. Ibid.
35. Ibid., 195–96.
36. Ibid., 197–98.
37. Sheridan, *Memoirs*, Vol. 2, 301; Cody, *Life of*, 198, 199.
38. Sheridan, *Memoirs*, Vol. 2, 301.
39. Rosa, *They Called Him Wild Bill*, 121.
40. Armes, *Ups and Downs*, 272, 273; Russell, *Buffalo Bill*, 101.
41. Armes, *Ups and Downs*, 273.
42. Russell, *Buffalo Bill*, 102, 104.
43. Hutton, *Sheridan*, 46; Brown, *Bury My Heart*, 163.
44. Hutton, *Sheridan*, 47; Brown, *Bury My Heart*, 166.
45. Wert, *Custer*, 267; Hutton, *Sheridan*, 42.
46. Hutton, *Custer Reader*, 145.
47. Hutton, *Sheridan*, 51.
48. Russell, *Buffalo Bill*, 105; Cody, *Life of*, 207; George F. Price, *Across the Continent with the Fifth Cavalry* (New York: D. Van Nostrand, 1883), 133, Hathi Trust Digital Library, March 1, 2021, https://babel.hathitrust.org/cgi/pt?id=uc2.ark:/13960/t2q52tj5v&view=1up&seq=143.
49. Cody, *Life of*, 207.
50. Ibid., 207–8.
51. Price, *Across the Continent*, 132; Cody, *Life of*, 209.
52. Price, *Across the Continent*, 132; Hutton, *Sheridan*, 50.
53. Price, *Across the Continent*, 132; Hutton, *Sheridan*, 50.
54. Jeff Broome, *Indian Raids and Massacres: Essays on the Central Plains Indian War* (Caldwell, ID: Caxton Press, 2020), 385.
55. Price, *Across the Continent*, 132–33; Hutton, *Sheridan*, 51; Cody, *Life of*, 215–16.
56. Cody, *Life of*, 216–17.
57. Connelley and Harger, *Wild Bill*, 113; Armes, *Ups and Downs*, 274, 278.
58. Hutton, *Sheridan*, 49, 383n448.
59. Ibid., 52–53.
60. Ibid., 53.
61. Rosa, *They Called Him Wild Bill*, 124; Connelley and Harger, *Wild Bill*, 220n1; Armes, *Ups and Downs*, 280.
62. Hutton, *Sheridan*, 53; Price, *Across the Continent*, 133.
63. Wert, *Custer*, 271; Hutton, *Sheridan*, 53–54, 63.

64. Armes, *Ups and Downs*, 279, 280.

65. Ibid., 281–82.

66. Bruce A. Clasrud and Michael N. Searles, *Buffalo Soldiers in the West: A Black Soldiers Anthology* (College Station, TX: Texas A&M University Press), 38.

67. Hutton, *Sheridan*, 67; Crutchfield, Moulton, and Del Bene, *Settlement of America*, Vol. 1, 90–91.

68. James Donovan, *A Terrible Glory, The Last Great Battle of the American West* (New York: Little, Brown & Company, 2008), 64; Brown, *Bury My Heart*, 168–69; Hutton, *Sheridan*, 67–68.

69. Two weeks later, Sheridan and Custer visited the site of Black Kettle's village. They found the naked, mutilated bodies of Elliott and his men left where they fell. Donovan, *Terrible Glory*, 64.

70. Wert, *Custer*, 275–76, 278.

71. Luke Cahill, "An Indian Campaign and Buffalo Hunting with Buffalo Bill," *Colorado Magazine*, Vol. IV, no. 4 (August 1927), 127, February 26, 2021, https://www.historycolorado.org/sites/default/files/media/document/2018/ColoradoMagazine_v4n4_August1927.pdf; Russell, *Buffalo Bill*, 110; Price, *Across the Continent*, 133.

72. Cahill, "An Indian Campaign and Buffalo Hunting with Buffalo Bill," 128; Russell, *Buffalo Bill*, 111.

73. Russell, *Buffalo Bill*, 111.

74. Ibid., 111–12.

75. Cahill, "An Indian Campaign and Buffalo Hunting with Buffalo Bill," 129; Cody, *Life of*, 224.

76. Cody, *Life of*, 224–25.

77. Ibid., 225.

78. Hutton, *Sheridan*, 108; Cody, *Life of*, 225.

79. Cody, *Life of*, 226.

80. Hutton, *Sheridan*, 93–94.

81. Russell, *Buffalo Bill*, 113.

82. Cahill, "An Indian Campaign and Buffalo Hunting with Buffalo Bill," 127, 132–34.

83. Ibid., 134.

84. Hutton, *Sheridan*, 108.

85. Connelley and Harger, *Wild Bill*, 121; Rosa, *They Called Him Wild Bill*, 127.

86. Connelley and Harger, *Wild Bill*, 122.

87. Connelley and Harger, *Wild Bill*, 122–23; Rosa, *They Called Him Wild Bill*, 127.

88. Rosa, *They Called Him Wild Bill*, 129–30.

89. Cody, *Life of*, 229.

90. Ibid.

91. Ibid., 230–33.

92. Russell, *Buffalo Bill*, 116; Cody, *Life of*, 233–34.

93. Also spelled Bevans and Blivins. Russell, *Buffalo Bill*, 118.

94. Cody, *Life of*, 234–36.

95. Ibid., 236–37.

96. Ibid., 237.

97. Ibid., 238.

98. Ibid., 238, 241.

99. Ibid., 241.

100. Rosa, *They Called Him Wild Bill*, 130–31.

101. Ibid., 99–100.

102. "Wild Bill," *Daily Commonwealth* (Topeka, KS, September 18, 1869), 2, Newspapers.com, February 28, 2021, https://www.newspapers.com/image/366927699; Rosa, *They Called Him Wild Bill*, 133.

103. "Excursion to Sheridan," *Weekly Union* (Junction City, KS, July 31, 1869), 3, Newspapers.com, February 28, 2021, https://www.newspapers.com/image/76340507.

104. Wert, *Custer*, 286.

105. Custer, *Following the Guidon*, 160–61.

106. Hutton, *Sheridan*, 110.

107. Hutton, *Sheridan*, 110; Russell, *Buffalo Bill*, 121.

108. Price, *Across the Continent*, 135, 584; Russell, *Buffalo Bill*, 121–22; Cody, *Life of*, 245–46.

109. Price, *Across the Continent*, 134–35; Russell, *Buffalo Bill*, 122; Cody, *Life of*, 247–48.

110. Price, *Across the Continent*, 135, 584; Russell, *Buffalo Bill*, 122.

111. Price, *Across the Continent*, 584; Russell, *Buffalo Bill*, 122.

112. Carr was wrong about Cody's horse, Powder Face. He didn't obtain that horse until the Summit Springs battle.

113. Broome, *Indian Raids*, 360.

114. Price, *Across the Continent*, 135; Russell, *Buffalo Bill*, 122.

115. Russell, *Buffalo Bill*, 123.

116. Ibid., 123–24.

117. Jeff Broome, "Death at Summit Springs: Susanna Alderdice and the Cheyennes," *Wild West Magazine* (October 2003), HistoryNet, March 1, 2021, https://www.historynet.com/death-at-summit-springs-susanna-alderdice-and-the-cheyennes.htm; Russell, *Buffalo Bill*, 126–27; Broome, *Indian Raids*, 351, 402.

118. Price, *Across the Continent*, 135, 584; Russell, *Buffalo Bill*, 125–26.

119. Price, *Across the Continent*, 136; Russell, *Buffalo Bill*, 124; Cody, *Life of*, 251.

120. Cody rode Buckskin Joe during his time with the Fifth Cavalry. After Cody left in 1872, Dave Perry bought Buckskin Joe giving him to Cody in 1877. In 1879 when *The Life of Hon. William F. Cody* was published, Cody wrote, "He is now at my ranch on the Dismal river, stone blind, but I shall keep him until he dies." Cody, *Life of*, 252.

121. Donald F. Danker, ed., "The Journal of an Indian Fighter: The 1869 Diary of Major Frank J. North," *Nebraska History* 39 (1958), 133, March 1, 2021, https://history.nebraska.gov/sites/history.nebraska.gov/files/doc/publications/NH1958FJNorth.pdf; Cody, *Life of*, 253.

122. Cody, *Life of*, 252.

123. Brown, *Bury My Heart*, 172–73.

124. Russell, *Buffalo Bill*, 128.

125. Price, *Across the Continent*, 136.

126. Price, *Across the Continent*, 137; Russell, *Buffalo Bill*, 132, 133.

127. Price, *Across the Continent*, 137; Cody, *Life of*, 255.

128. "Our Indian Troubles," *New York Herald* (New York, July 28, 1869), 6, Newspapers.com, May 21, 2021, https://www.newspapers.com/image/21201799.

129. Price, *Across the Continent*, 138; Cody, *Life of*, 255–56.

130. Broome, *Indian Raids*, 337–38; Price, *Across the Continent*, 138; Cody, *Life of*, 256.

131. Price, *Across the Continent*, 138–39.

132. Cody, *Life of*, 256.

133. Price, *Across the Continent*, 139; Cody, *Life of*, 256.

134. Cody wrote Tall Bull was the fastest horse in Nebraska for four years. Cody, *Life of*, 260–61.

135. Russell, *Buffalo Bill*, 141–42, 147; Danker, "The Journal of an Indian Fighter."

136. Russell, *Buffalo Bill*, 147–48; Broome, *Indian Raids*, 340–44.

137. Broome, "Death at Summit Springs."

138. Price wrote in *Across the Continent with the Fifth Cavalry* that Tall Bull and sixty warriors were killed, p. 140.

139. Russell, *Buffalo Bill*, 138.

140. The troops found $1,300 giving $900 to Maria. Price, *Across the Continent*, 140.

141. Broome, "Death at Summit Springs"; Russell, *Buffalo Bill*, 138.

142. Price, *Across the Continent*, 140–41; Cody, *Life of*, 262; Broome, *Indian Raids*, 333–34.

143. Russell, *Buffalo Bill*, 149, 155; Cody, *Life of*, 263.

144. Julia Bricklin, *The Notorious Life of Ned Buntline: A Tale of Murder, Betrayal, and the Creation of Buffalo Bill* (Guilford, CT: TwoDot, 2020), 1, 3–4, 123–26; Cody, *Life of*, 263.

145. Bricklin, *Buntline*, 133; Cody, *Life of*, 264.

146. Cody, *Life of*, 264–65.

147. Ibid., 265.

148. Ibid., 265–66.

149. Price, *Across the Continent*, 141; Russell, *Buffalo Bill*, 156.

150. Price, *Across the Continent*, 141.

151. Danker, "Indian Fighter," 146; Russell, *Buffalo Bill*, 130, 156.

152. Price, *Across the Continent*, 141; Danker, "Indian Fighter," 147n125.

153. Russell, *Buffalo Bill*, 156; Cody, *Life of*, 268.

154. Cody and Cooper, *Memories*, 155, 160–61; Russell, *Buffalo Bill*, 156; Cody, *Life of*, 268.

155. Danker, "Indian Fighter," 153; Russell, *Buffalo Bill*, 157; Cody, *Life of*, 268.

156. Cody was wrong writing Duncan's expedition took place in the spring of 1870 in his book *The Life of*, 271.

157. Price, *Across the Continent*, 142.

158. Nelson would be an important part of Buffalo Bill's Wild West. Russell, *Buffalo Bill*, 157.

159. Cody, *Life of*, 272.

160. Danker, "Indian Fighter," 157.

161. Danker, "Indian Fighter," 158, 158n144; Russell, *Buffalo Bill*, 158.

162. Danker, "Indian Fighter," 158n144; Cody, *Life of*, 274–75.

163. Price, *Across the Continent*, 141–42; Danker, "Indian Fighter," 160n147; Russell, *Buffalo Bill*, 159; Cody, *Life of*, 275.

164. Bricklin, *Buntline*, 134; Russell, *Buffalo Bill*, 160.

165. Cody and Cooper, *Memories*, 196–97, 200–201, 203–4.

166. Alexander Roob, "Van Goghs Favorites III: Arthur Boyd Houghton— Our One-Eyed Artist in America," Melton Pryor Institute for Reportage Drawing & Printing Culture, March 4, 2021, http://www.meltonpriorinstitut .org/pages/textarchive.php5?view=text&ID=14&language=English; Cody, *Life of*, 268.

167. Cody, *Life of*, 269.

168. Russell, *Buffalo Bill*, 162; Cody, *Life of*, 269.

169. Price, *Across the Continent*, 142; Russell, *Buffalo Bill*, 163; Cody, *Life of*, 269–70.

170. Price, *Across the Continent*, 142; Russell, *Buffalo Bill*, 163; Cody, *Life of*, 270.

171. Price, *Across the Continent*, 142, 584; Russell, *Buffalo Bill*, 164.

172. Russell, *Buffalo Bill*, 159, 164.

CHAPTER 10: HAYS CITY (MAY 1869–JULY 17, 1870)

1. Rosa, *They Called Him Wild Bill*, 135–36.

2. *Weekly Union* (Junction City, KS, July 9, 1871), 3, Newpapers.com, March 4, 2021, https://www.newspapers.com/image/76341797/?terms=Hays%20 City&match=1.

3. Rosa, *Wild Bill Hickok, Gunfighter*, 101; Rosa, *They Called Him Wild Bill*, 137, 138.

4. Rosa, *They Called Him Wild Bill*, 138.

5. Rosa, *Wild Bill Hickok, Gunfighter*, 101; Rosa, *They Called Him Wild Bill*, 139.

6. Rosa, *Wild Bill Hickok, Gunfighter*, 99, 104.

7. "State News," *Weekly Union* (Junction City, KS, July 31, 1869), 2, Newspapers.com, March 5, 2021, https://www.newspapers.com/

image/76340504/?terms=Hays%20Webster&match=1; Rosa, *Wild Bill Hickok, Gunfighter*, 102–3.

8. Alonzo Webster would become Dodge City mayor.

9. "State News," 2; "A Scrap of History," *Ford County Republican* (Dodge City, KS: April 20, 1887), 2, Newspapers.com, March 5, 2021, https://www.news papers.com/image/367309332/?terms=Webster&match=1; Rosa, *Wild Bill Hickok, Gunfighter*, 103.

10. "From Hays City," *Times and Conservative* (Leavenworth, KS, August 22, 1869), 3, Newspapers.com, March 5, 2021, https://www.newspapers.com/image /95943875/?terms=Hays&match=1; Rosa, *They Called Him Wild Bill*, 139, 140.

11. Connelley and Harger, *Wild Bill*, 126; Rosa, *They Called Him Wild Bill*, 141.

12. Rosa, *They Called Him Wild Bill*, 144–45.

13. Mulvey was also spelled Mulrey and Melvin.

14. "Arrests—Shootings," *Aitchison Daily Patriot* (Aitchison, KS, August 24, 1869), 1, Newspapers.com, March 5, 2021, https://www.newspapers.com/ image/80353546/?terms=%22Wild%20Bill%22&match=1; Rosa, *Wild Bill Hickok, Gunfighter*, 104–5.

15. Buel, *Heroes*, 116–17.

16. Rosa, *Wild Bill Hickok*, 125.

17. Rosa, *They Called Him Wild Bill*, 143, 144.

18. Ibid., 142–43.

19. Ibid., 141.

20. Ibid., 149.

21. Sandy Barnard, ed., *Ten Years with Custer: A Seventh Cavalryman's Memoirs* (Terre Haute, IN: AST Press, 2001).

22. "Particulars of the Killing of Stranhan at Hays City," *Leavenworth Daily Commercial* (Leavenworth, KS, October 3, 1869), 4, March 6, 2021, https://www.newspapers.com/image/426368652/?terms=%22Hays%20 City%22&match=1; Rosa, *They Called Him Wild Bill*, 147.

23. "Particulars of the Killing of Stranhan, 4"; Rosa, *They Called Him Wild Bill*, 147.

24. Rosa, *They Called Him Wild Bill*, 147.

25. Ibid., 150–53.

26. "From Hays City. A Double Shooting Affray," *Leavenworth Times and Conservative* (Leavenworth, KS, October 13, 1869), 4, Newspapers.com, March 6, 2021, https://www.newspapers.com/image/96072457/?terms=Allmeyer&match=1; Rosa, *They Called Him Wild Bill*, 153–54.

27. Rosa, *They Called Him Wild Bill*, 154.

28. "A Trip Up the Road," *Daily Commonwealth* (Topeka, KS, December 9, 1869), 3, Newspapers.com, March 6, 2021, https://www.newspapers.com/ image/366942740/?terms=%22Wild%20Bill%22&match=1.

29. "A Buffalo," *Daily Commonwealth* (Topeka, KS, December 9, 1869), 3, Newspapers.com, March 6, 2021, https://www.newspapers.com/ image/366944639.

30. "Topeka House," *Daily Commonwealth* (Topeka, KS, December 9, 1869), 1, Newspapers.com, March 6, 2021, https://www.newspapers.com/image/3669276 74/?terms=McMeekin&match=1.

31. Connelley and Harger, *Wild Bill*, 131–32, 134; Buel, *Heroes*, 121; Rosa, *They Called Him Wild Bill*, 156.

32. "Muster Out Roll, Eighteenth Battalion, Cavalry, Kansas Volunteers," volume 5, 4, Kansas Memory, Kansas Historical Society, March 6, 2021, https://www.kansasmemory.org/item/227826/page/4; Rosa, *They Called Him Wild Bill*, 161.

33. "Fined," *Daily Commonwealth* (Topeka, KS, February 8, 1870), 3, News papers.com, March 6, 2021, https://www.newspapers.com/image/366951219/?terms=%22Wild%20Bill%22&match=1.

34. Connelley and Harger, *Wild Bill*, 17.

35. "Wild Bill," *Warrensburg Standard* (Warrensburg, MO, February 24, 1870), 3, Newspapers.com, March 6, 2021, https://www.newspapers.com/image/69458 9272/?terms=McLellan&match=1.

36. *Jefferson Democrat* (Hillsboro, MO, April 1, 1870), 1, Newspapers.com, March 6, 2021, https://www.newspapers.com/image/687524934.

37. "Local Brevities," *Daily Commonwealth* (Topeka, KS, February 8, 1870), 3, Newspapers.com, March 7, 2021, https://www.newspapers.com/image/366959611/?terms=%22Wild%20Bill%22&match=1.

38. Rosa, *They Called Him Wild Bill*, 102, 162; Connelley and Harger, *Wild Bill*, 136–37.

39. Colonel Lewis Granger, "Reminiscences of Colonel Lewis Granger," *Frontier Times*, Vol. 4, no. 1 (Bandera, TX, October 1926), https://archive.org/stream/frontiertimesdev04bandrich/frontiertimesdev04bandrich_djvu.txt.

40. Jeff Broome shows Kile is the correct spelling. It was spelled Kelley, Kelly, and Kyle. On May 16, 1869, Kile, a member of Fifth Cavalry, was with the advance guard at Spring Creek, Nebraska, along with Buffalo Bill Cody in the fight with Indians. On July 8, 1869, Kile and two others were separate from the command and fought off a large war party. Kile received the Congressional Medal of Honor for his actions. Barnard, *Ten Years with Custer*, 122; Rosa, *They Called Him Wild Bill*, 158; Broome, *Indian Raids*, 367, 379, 402, 403.

41. Some versions have the fight taking place in Paddy Welch's saloon.

42. Barnard, *Ten Years with Custer*, 123; Rosa, *They Called Him Wild Bill*, 158–59; Broome, *Indian Raids*, 410.

43. Barnard, *Ten Years with Custer*, 123; Broome, *Indian Raids*, 381, 384, 386–87, 396–97.

44. Barnard, *Ten Years with Custer*, 123.

45. Ibid.

46. Ibid.

47. Barnard, *Ten Years with Custer*, 123; Rosa, *Wild Bill Hickok, Gunfighter*, 122.

48. Lonergan was later court-martialed and sentenced to prison at Fort Leavenworth. After taps, on the night of January 31, 1871, Lonergan was drunk

in the barracks. He kicked a sleeping corporal shouting foul language against "Dutch" soldiers saying he was ready to kill them all. He drew a knife on the first sergeant and later defecated beside the sergeant's bunk. When Captain Frederick Benteen ordered Lonergan's arrest, Lonergan pulled a pocketknife on the first sergeant saying, "If you say another word to me I'll cut the guts out of you." The sergeant pulled out his pistol, ending any further discussion. Broome, *Indian Raids*, 381–82.

49. Barnard, *Ten Years with Custer*, 124n10; Rosa, *Wild Bill Hickok, Gunfighter*, 120.

50. "Brevities," *Daily Commonwealth* (Topeka, KS, July 22, 1870), 4, News papers.com, March 7, 2021, https://www.newspapers.com/image/367008401/ ?terms=Wild%20Bill&match=1.

51. Rosa, *They Called Him Wild Bill*, 156.

52. Custer, *Following the Guidon*, 163–64.

53. Custer, *Life on the Plains*, xxxiii, 45.

CHAPTER 11: THE CHIEF SCOUT AND THE ABILENE MARSHAL (JULY 1870–DECEMBER 1871)

1. "City and Vicinity," *Kansas State Record* (Topeka, KS, October 21, 1870), 4, Newspapers.com, March 8, 2021, https://www.newspapers.com/ image/366138702; Rosa, *They Called Him Wild Bill*, 169.

2. He was not the notorious Billy Thompson, brother to Ben Thompson.

3. Rosa, *They Called Him Wild Bill*, 170; "Singular Appeal," *Leavenworth Daily Commercial* (Leavenworth, KS, July 31, 1870), 4, Newspapers.com, March 8, 2021, https://www.newspapers.com/image/425166567/?terms=%22Emma%20 Williams%22&match=1; "News Items," *Guilford Citizen* (Guilford, KS, August 13, 1870), 2, Newspapers.com, March 8, 2021, https://www.newspapers.com/ image/422283474/?terms=%22Emma%20Williams%22&match=1; Buel, *Heroes*, 145–47.

4. Rosa, *They Called Him Wild Bill*, 180.

5. Russell, *Buffalo Bill*, 164.

6. "The Yale College Expedition of 1870," Yale Peabody Museum of Natural History, March 8, 2021, https://peabody.yale.edu/collections/archives/yale-college-scientific-expedition-1870; Hutton, *Sheridan*, 167.

7. Cody, *Life of*, 279–80; Russell, *Buffalo Bill*, 167; "The Yale College Expedition of 1870."

8. Cody, *Life of*, 275; Russell, *Buffalo Bill*, 160.

9. Cody, *Life of*, 275; Cody, *Autobiography*, 212–13.

10. Cody, *Life of*, 275; Russell, *Buffalo Bill*, 165.

11. Cody, *Life of*, 276; Russell, *Buffalo Bill*, 169; Price, *Across the Continent*, 143, 584.

12. Cody, *Life of*, 276.

13. Cody, *Life of*, 276; Price, *Across the Continent*, 584.

14. Cody, *Life of*, 276.
15. Ibid., 277–78.
16. Hutton, *Sheridan*, 205–7.
17. Hutton, *Sheridan*, 207; "The Buffalo Huntr," *New York Herald* (New York, September 22, 1871), 7, Newspapers.com, March 9, 2021, https://www.news papers.com/image/21563824/?terms=%22General%20Sheridan%22%2028%20 1871&match=1.
18. Henry E. Davies, *Ten Days on the Plains* (New York: Crocker & Co., 1871), 25, Internet Archive, March 9, 2021, https://archive.org/details/GR_1013/ page/n23/mode/2up?q=Buffalo+Bill.
19. Davies, *Ten Days*, 26.
20. Ibid., 29.
21. Ibid., 109.
22. Russell, *Buffalo Bill*, 165.
23. Earl of Dunraven, *Canadian Nights: Being Sketches and Reminiscences of Life and Sport in the Rockies and Prairies, and the Canadian Woods* (New York: Charles Scribner's Sons, 1914), 51–52, 55, https://www.google.com/books/edition/ Canadian_Nights/k1BJAAAAYAAJ?hl=en&gbpv=1&bsq=Buffalo%20Bill.
24. Ibid., 55–56.
25. Ibid., 62–63.
26. Ibid., 66, 67, 71, 82–83.
27. Cody, *Life of*, 290–92.
28. Ibid., 292.
29. Price, *Across the Continent*, 144; Cody, *Life of*, 292.
30. "From Abilene," *Leavenworth Times and Conservative* (Leavenworth, KS, June 25, 1869), 2, Newspapers.com, March 10, 2021, https://www.newspapers .com/image/95943604/?terms=Abilene&match=1; Rosa, *They Called Him Wild Bill*, 172–73; Connelley and Harger, *Wild Bill*, 140.
31. Rosa, *They Called Him Wild Bill*, 175.
32. "From Abilene," 2.
33. Rosa, *They Called Him Wild Bill*, 176.
34. Ibid., 177–78.
35. Ibid., 180.
36. "Abilene in the Early Days," *National Field* (Salina, KS, November 23, 1908), 8, Newspapers.com, March 10, 2021, https://www.newspapers .com/image/485144756/?terms=%22Wild%20Bill%22%20%20Hickok%20 1908%2C%20McCoy&match=1; Rosa, *They Called Him Wild Bill*, 181.
37. Rosa, *They Called Him Wild Bill*, 181, 182.
38. "Gleanings," *Emporia News* (Emporia, KS, May 26, 1871), 1, Newspapers.com, March 10, 2021, https://www.newspapers.com/ image/88952468/?terms=%22Wild%20Bill%22&match=1.
39. Connelley and Harger, *Wild Bill*, 142, 148.
40. "How to Get a Quorum," *Topeka State Record* (Topeka, KS, May 9, 1871), 4, Newspapers.com, March 11, 2021, https://www.newspapers.com/

image/366132465/?terms=%22Wild%20Bill%22&match=1; Rosa, *They Called Him Wild Bill*, 183.

41. "How to Get a Quorum," 4; Rosa, *They Called Him Wild Bill*, 183.

42. "How to Get a Quorum," 4.

43. "Brevities," *Topeka Daily Commonwealth* (Topeka, KS, May 11, 1871), 4; Newspapers.com, March 11, 2021, https://www.newspapers.com/image/366997 016/?terms=%22Columbus%20Carrol%22%20May%2011%201871&match=1.

44. Ibid.

45. George L. Cushman, "Abilene, First of the Kansas Cow Towns," *Kansas Historical Quarterly*, Vol. 9, no. 3, August 1940, 240–58, Kansas Historical Society, March 11, 2021, https://www.kshs.org/p/abilene-first-of-the-kansas-cow -towns/12833; Rosa, *They Called Him Wild Bill*, 184.

46. "Fire Arms," *Abilene Weekly Chronicle* (Abilene, KS, June 8, 1871), 3, News papers.com, March 11, 2021, https://www.newspapers.com/image/384019060.

47. *Abilene Weekly Chronicle* (Abilene, KS, June 22, 1871), 3, Newspapers.com, March 11, 2021, https://www.newspapers.com/image/384019130.

48. "Miscellaneous Ordinances," *Abilene Weekly Chronicle* (Abilene, KS, June 29, 1871), 3, Newspapers.com, March 11, 2021, https://www.newspapers.com/ image/384019163.

49. Ibid.

50. Cushman, "Abilene, First of the Kansas Cow Towns," 240–58; Rosa, *They Called Him Wild Bill*, 184–85.

51. Rosa, *They Called Him Wild Bill*, 185–86; Rosa, *Wild Bill Hickok*, 110.

52. Douglas W. Ellison, *"A Desperado Without a Peer," John Wesley Hardin Invades Kansas, 1871* (Medora, ND: Western Edge Book Distributing, 2021), 1; John Wesley Hardin, *The Life of John Wesley Hardin* (Seguin, TX: Smith & Moore, 1896), 5, 13, 14.

53. Hardin, *Life of*, 17, 18, 21.

54. Ibid., 23, 24, 25, 28, 32.

55. Ibid., 33–34.

56. Ibid., 34, 36, 37, 42, 43.

57. Ibid.

58. Ibid., 44.

59. Ibid.

60. Ibid., 44, 45.

61. Ibid., 45.

62. Hardin, *Life of*, 45; Ellison, *"Desperado,"* 16.

63. Hardin, *Life of*, 46.

64. Ellison, *"Desperado,"* 16–18. "Aibileen Items," *Kansas City Daily Journal of Commerce* (Kansas City, MO: June 24, 1871), 4, May 20, 2021, https://www .newspapers.com/image/666722446.

65. Hardin, *Life of*, 46–49, 50–51.

66. Ibid., 54–56.

67. Ibid., 58.

68. Ibid., 59–60. Hardin died August 19, 1895, in El Paso, Texas. He threatened to kill John Selman and his son John Selman Jr., both law enforcement officers. Hardin was drinking and gambling in the Acme Saloon when the senior Selman walked in, shot Hardin in the back of the head, then fired two more shots into his body. O'Neal, *Encyclopedia of Western Gunfighters*, 130. By 1877, Hardin said he killed twenty-seven men. Ellison, *"Desperado,"* 47.

69. Rosa, *They Called Him Wild Bill*, 186–87.

70. Ibid.

71. "Local News," *Lawrence Daily Journal* (Lawrence, KS, August 10, 1871), 3, Newspapers.com, March 13, 2021, https://www.newspapers.com/image/595174 81/?terms=Abilene&match=1.

72. "Murder," *Abilene Weekly Chronicle* (Abilene, KS, August 17, 1871), 3, Newspapers.com, March 13, 2021, https://www.newspapers.com/image/384019357.

73. Rosa, *They Called Him Wild Bill*, 187.

74. Ellison, *"Desperado,"* 2, 36.

75. Rosa, *They Called Him Wild Bill*, 189. Brace games were rigged faro games. Cappers pretended to be players in the faro game when they were in cahoots with the dealer to rip off unsuspecting players.

76. W. M. Walton and Lisa Lach, annotated, *Life and Adventures of Ben Thompson, the Famous Texan* (Austin, TX: Steck Company Publishers, 2016), 44; O'Neal, *Encyclopedia of Western Gunfighters*, 315–16; Rosa, *They Called Him Wild Bill*, 189, 190, 195; Connelley and Harger, *Wild Bill*, 158.

77. Ibid., x, 159.

78. Rosa, *They Called Him Wild Bill*, 190.

79. Ibid.

80. Connelley and Harger, *Wild Bill*, 154; Rosa, *They Called Him Wild Bill*, 191.

81. "Amusements," *Leavenworth Daily Commercial* (Leavenworth, KS, August 2, 1871), 1, Newspapers.com, March 13, 2021, https://www.newspapers.com/image/425163647/?terms=Abilene%20Lake%27s%20circus&match=1; Bell, *Illustrated Life and Times of Wild Bill Hickok*, 60; Connelley and Harger, *Wild Bill*, 155.

82. "Amusements," *Leavenworth Daily Commercial*, 1; Connelley and Harger, *Wild Bill*, 155; Rosa, *They Called Him Wild Bill*, 191.

83. "An Ordinance Related to Dance Houses," *Abilene Weekly Chronicle* (Abilene, KS, September 7, 1871), 3, Newspapers.com, March 15, 2021, https://www.newspapers.com/image/384019415/; Rosa, *They Called Him Wild Bill*, 192.

84. "Reformation in Abilene," *Abilene Weekly Chronicle* (Abilene, KS, September 14, 1871), 3, Newspapers.com, March 15, 2021, https://www.newspapers.com/image/384019461/.

85. Rosa, *They Called Him Wild Bill*, 92.

86. Ibid., 194.

87. Ibid.

88. Ibid., 195, 196.

89. Walton and Lach, *Ben Thompson*, 161.

90. "Shooting Affray," *Abilene Weekly Chronicle* (Abilene, KS, October 12, 1871), 3, Newspapers.com, March 15, 2021, https://www.newspapers.com/image/384019547.

91. *Junction City Union* (Junction City, KS, October 7, 1871), 3, Newspapers.com, March 16, 2021, https://www.newspapers.com/image/76341971/?terms=Junction%20City%20Union&match=1.

92. "Shooting Affray," 3.

93. Rosa, *They Called Him Wild Bill*, 196.

94. "Shooting Affray," 3; *Junction City Union*, 3.

95. "Shooting Affray," 3; Rosa, *They Called Him Wild Bill*, 196.

96. Mike Williams was not one of Hickok's deputies, but a special deputy hired by the Novelty Theater to maintain order in the establishment. Rosa, *They Called Him Wild Bill*, 196n57.

97. "Shooting Affray," 3; *Junction City Union*, 3.

98. "Shooting Affray," 3; Rosa, *Wild Bill Hickok, Gunfighter*, 142–43.

99. Rosa, *They Called Him Wild Bill*, 196–97.

100. Connelley and Harger, *Wild Bill*, 160; Rosa, *They Called Him Wild Bill*, 197; Rosa, *Wild Bill Hickok, Gunfighter*, 143.

101. Rosa, *They Called Him Wild Bill*, 197.

102. "Shooting Affray," 3.

103. Rosa, *They Called Him Wild Bill*, 200.

104. *Junction City Union*, 3.

105. Rosa, *They Called Him Wild Bill*, 201.

106. "Attempt to Kill Marshal Hickok," *Abilene Weekly Chronicle* (Abilene, KS, November 30, 1871), 3, https://www.newspapers.com/image/384019822.

107. Rosa, *They Called Him Wild Bill*, 203–4.

108. Ibid., 204.

109. Ibid., 205.

110. "To Cattle Drovers," *Abilene Weekly Chronicle* (Abilene, KS, February 22, 1872), 3, Newspapers.com, March 11, 2021, https://www.newspapers.com/image/384020156/?terms=Abilene%20Chronicle&match=1.

111. "How Abilene Was Made in Early Days," *Topeka Daily Capital* (Topeka, KS, August 30, 1908), 11, https://www.newspapers.com/image/63718564/?terms=McCoy&match=1.

Chapter 12: Life on the Plains (January 1872–November 1872)

1. Hutton, *Sheridan*, 208, 213; Russell, *Buffalo Bill*, 174–75.

2. Cody, *Life of*, 295–96; Russell, *Buffalo Bill*, 175.

3. Cody, *Life of*, 295–96.

4. Ibid.

5. Ibid., 296–97.

6. Ibid., 297–98.

7. Ibid., 298–99.

8. Cody, *Life of*, 299; Russell, *Buffalo Bill*, 176.

9. Richmond L. Clow, *Spotted Tail: Warrior and Statesman* (Pierre: South Dakota Historical Society, 2019), 70; "The Imperial Buffalo Hunter," *New York Daily Herald* (New York, January 16, 1872), 7, Newspapers.com, March 29, 2021, https://www.newspapers.com/image/329391462.

10. "Telegraphic. At It. Alexis on the Untamed Bison's Native Heath," *Kansas City Times* (Kansas City, KS, January 14, 1872), 1, Newspapers.com, March 28, 2021, https://www.newspapers.com/image/649207846/?terms=%22Wild%20 Bill%22%20Boston&match=1; "The Grand Duke's Hunt," *New York Daily Herald* (New York, January 14, 1872), 7, Newspapers.com, March 28, 2021, https:// www.newspapers.com/image/329390726/?terms=Grand%20Duke&match=1.

11. "The Grand Duke's Hunt," 7.

12. "Telegraphic. At It. Alexis on the Untamed Bison's Native Heath," 1.

13. "The Grand Duke's Hunt," 7; "The Imperial Buffalo Hunter," 7.

14. "The Imperial Buffalo Hunter," 7.

15. Cody, *Life of*, 300–301.

16. "The Imperial Buffalo Hunter," 7.

17. I'm sure Cody wasn't pleased when the grand duke dropped Lucretia Borgia.

18. Cody, *Life of*, 301.

19. "The Imperial Buffalo Hunter," 7; Cody, *Life of*, 301–2.

20. "Alexis' Grand Hunt," *New York Daily Herald* (New York, January 17, 1872), 7, Newspapers.com, March 29, 2021, https://www.newspapers.com/ image/329391901.

21. "Alexis' Grand Hunt," 7.

22. "Alexis' Grand Hunt," 7; Cody, *Life of*, 302.

23. "Bos Americanus!" *New York Daily Herald* (New York, January 18, 1872), 3, Newspapers.com, March 29, 2021, https://www.newspapers.com/ image/329392088.

24. Ibid.

25. Ibid.

26. Cody, *Life of*, 304–5.

27. Cody, *Life of*, 305–6. Russell, *Buffalo Bill*, 180.

28. Cody, *Life of*, 306.

29. Russell, *Buffalo Bill*, 180.

30. Cody, *Life of*, 307–8.

31. Ibid., 308.

32. Ibid.

33. Ibid.

34. Ibid., 308–9.

35. Ibid., 309.

36. "New York," *Chicago Tribune* (Chicago, February 24, 1872), 4, Newspapers .com, March 30, 2021, https://www.newspapers.com/image/466368828/?terms =%22Buffalo%20Bill%22%20Chicago&match=1.

37. Bricklin, *Buntline*, 50–51, 60.

38. Cody, *Life of*, 310; "The Liederkranz Ball," *New York Daily Herald* (New York, February 16, 1872), 7, Newspapers.com, March 30, 2021, https://www .newspapers.com/image/329400315/?terms=Liederkranz&match=1.

39. "The Liederkranz Ball," 7.

40. "The Liederkranz Ball," 7; Cody, *Life of*, 310.

41. "The Liederkranz Ball," 7.

42. Warren, *Buffalo Bill's America*, 153; "Bowery Theatre—'Buffalo Bill,'" *New York Daily Herald* (New York, February 21, 1872), 5, Newspapers.com, March 10, 2021, https://www.newspapers.com/image/329401795/?terms=%22Buff alo%20Bill%22&match=1; Sara Marian and Clio Admin., "The Bowery Theatre, 1826–1929," Clio: Your Guide to History. December 3, 2017, March 10, 2021, https://theclio.com/entry/21656.

43. "Amusements," *New York Daily Herald* (New York, February 20, 1872), 9, Newspapers.com, March 30, 2021, https://www.newspapers.com/image/ 329401641/?terms=Buffalo%20Bill&match=1.

44. "Bowery Theatre—'Buffalo Bill,'" 5; Cody, *Life of*, 310.

45. "Bowery Theatre—'Buffalo Bill,'" 5.

46. "Bowery Theatre—'Buffalo Bill,'" 5; T. Allston Brown, *A History of the New York Stage: From the First Performance in 1732 to 1901*, Vol. 1 (New York: Dodd, Mead and Company, 1902), 151, Google Books, March 10, 2021, https://www .google.com/books/edition/A_History_of_the_New_York_Stage_from_the/ RwnuuuBfJvkC?hl=en&gbpv=1.

47. Cody, *Life of*, 312.

48. Ibid.

49. Russell, *Buffalo Bill*, 182–83.

50. "Buffalo Bill," *Intelligencer Journal* (Lancaster, PA, February 26, 1872), 2, Newspapers.com, March 29, 2021, https://www.newspapers.com/image/556648 638/?terms=Philadelphia%20%22Buffalo%20Bill%22&match=1.

51. Russell, *Buffalo Bill*, 186; Cody, *Life of*, 313.

52. "Letter from Captain Charles Meinhold to 1st Lieutenant J. B. Johnson, April 27, 1872," The William F. Cody Archive, The Papers of William F. Cody, March 31, 2021, https://codyarchive.org/texts/wfc.css00665.html; Russell, *Buffalo Bill*, 186; Cody, *Life of*, 313.

53. "Letter from Captain Charles Meinhold"; Russell, *Buffalo Bill*, 186; Cody, *Life of*, 313.

54. "Letter from Captain Charles Meinhold"; Russell, *Buffalo Bill*, 186–87; Cody, *Life of*, 313–14.

55. "Letter from Captain Charles Meinhold"; Russell, *Buffalo Bill*, 187; Cody, *Life of*, 314–15.

56. "Letter from Captain Charles Meinhold"; Russell, *Buffalo Bill*, 187; Cody, *Life of*, 315.

57. "Letter from Captain Charles Meinhold"; Russell, *Buffalo Bill*, 187; "Buffalo Bill's Medal Restored," *New York Times* (New York, July 9, 1989), *New York Times* Archives, June 2, 2021, https://www.nytimes.com/1989/07/09/us/buffalo-bill-s-medal-restored.html.

58. Russell, *Buffalo Bill*, 188; Cody, *Life of*, 315.

59. Russell, *Buffalo Bill*, 188.

60. Cody, *Life of*, 316; Russell, *Buffalo Bill*, 188.

61. Cody, *Life of*, 316; "Our Sportsmen," *Chicago Tribune* (Chicago, November 23, 1872), 3, Newspapers.com, March 31, 2021, https://www.newspapers.com/image/466193858/?terms=Chicago%20Heath%20%26%20Milligan&match=1; "Local Brevities," *Chicago Evening Post* (Chicago, November 15, 1872), 1, Newspapers.com, March 31, 2021, https://www.newspapers.com/image/667952334/?terms=Chicago%20%22Alexander%20Sample%22&match=1; "Elijah Priest Greene," Gazlay Family History, March 31, 2021, https://gazlayfamilyhistory.org/book.php?person=4703.

62. Cody, *Life of*, 317; Russell, *Buffalo Bill*, 189.

63. Cody, *Life of*, 318.

64. Ibid.

65. Russell, *Buffalo Bill*, 190–91.

66. Cody, *Life of*, 320.

67. Ibid., 321.

68. Russell, *Buffalo Bill*, 192.

69. Cody and Cooper, *Memories*, 233–34.

70. Rosa, *They Called Him Wild Bill*, 217; "Local Chips" and "Amusements," *Kansas City Times* (Kansas City, KS, January 19, 1872), 4, Newspapers.com, March 26, 2021, https://www.newspapers.com/image/649207914/?terms=%22Wild%20Bill%22%20Boston&match=1.

71. "An Altercation Between Two Reporters," *Saint Joseph Daily Gazette* (St. Joseph, MO, January 31, 1872), 4, Newspapers.com, March 26, 2021, https://www.newspapers.com/image/558869754/?terms=%22Wild%20Bill%22&match=1.

72. *Weekly Journal* (Salina, KS, January 18, 1872), 3, Newspapers.com, March 26, 2021, https://www.newspapers.com/image/72155272.

73. Rosa, *They Called Him Wild Bill*, 218–19.

74. Buel, *Heroes*, 153–54.

75. Rosa, *They Called Him Wild Bill*, 163, 165–67.

76. Rosa, *They Called Him Wild Bill*, 167–68; "The Buffalo Hunt at the Falls," *Buffalo Commercial* (Buffalo, August 29, 1872), 3, Newspapers.com, March 27, 2021, https://www.newspapers.com/image/264590571/?terms=%22Niagara%20Falls%22%20%22Wild%20Bill%22&match=1.

77. "Bos Americanos," *New York Herald* (New York, August 29, 1872), 7, Newspapers.com, March 27, 2021, https://www.newspapers.com/image/9058054/?terms=%22Wild%20Bill%22&match=1.

78. "The Buffalo Hunt at the Falls," 3.

79. Rosa, *They Called Him Wild Bill*, 168.

80. Buel, *Heroes*, 155–56.

81. "A Myth Is Born," Kansas City Public Library, March 27, 2021, https://kchistory.org/week-kansas-city-history/myth-born.

82. "New Advertisements," *Aitchison Daily Champion* (Aitchison, KS, September 1, 1872), 3, Newspapers.com, March 27, 2021, https://www.newspapers.com/image/103847274.

83. Bill Markley, *Billy the Kid and Jesse James: Outlaws of the Legendary West* (Guilford, CT: TwoDot, 2019), 40–42.

84. "Domestic: The Kansas City Fair," *Daily Commonwealth* (Topeka, KS, September 28, 1872), 1, Newspapers.com, March 27, 2021, https://www.newspapers.com/image/368699450.

85. "Wild Bill," *Daily Commonwealth* (Topeka, KS, March 1, 1873), 2, Newspapers.com, March 27, 2021, https://www.newspapers.com/image/367004834.

86. Matt Vincent, "Whistler's Murder," *Wild West Magazine*, October 2018, 28–29; Rosa, *They Called Him Wild Bill*, 207.

87. Rosa, *They Called Him Wild Bill*, 208.

88. Ibid., 209.

89. Vincent, "Whistler's Murder," 28–29; Rosa, *They Called Him Wild Bill*, 211.

Chapter 13: The Wild East
(November 1872–March 1874)

1. "Buffalo Bill," *Daily Bee* (Sacramento, December 10, 1872), 2, Newspapers.com, April 1, 2021, https://www.newspapers.com/image/623364023.

2. Cody, *Life of*, 322; Russell, *Buffalo Bill*, 193.

3. Cody, *Life of*, 322; "Amusements," *Chicago Evening Mail* (Chicago, December 12, 1872), 4, Newspapers.com, April 1, 2021, https://www.newspapers.com/image/668331849/?terms=Chicago%20%22Buffalo%20Bill%22&match=1.

4. "Amusements," *New York Times* (New York, November 10, 1872), 7, Newspapers.com, April 1, 2021, https://www.newspapers.com/image/20512289/?terms=%22Buffalo%20Bill%22&match=1.

5. "Academy of Music," *Buffalo Commercial Advertiser* (Buffalo, November 19, 1872), 3, Newspapers.com, April 1, 2021, https://www.newspapers.com/image/264637469.

6. "Buffalo Bill," *Wyandott Herald* (Kansas City, KS, December 12, 1872), 3, Newspapers.com, April 1, 2021, https://www.newspapers.com/image/65960021/?terms=%22Buffalo%20Bill%22%20Omaha&match=1.

7. Cody, *Life of*, 322; Neil Gale, "Nixon's Parisian Hippodrome and Amphitheater in Chicago (1872-1873)," Digital Research Library of Illinois History Journal, April 1, 2021, https://drloihjournal.blogspot.com/2019/12/nixons-parisian-hippodrome-and-amphitheater-in-chicago.html.

8. Cody, *Life of*, 322.

9. Ibid., 322–23.

10. Ibid., 323–24.

11. Ibid.

12. Ibid., 324–25.

13. "The City in Brief," *Chicago Tribune* (Chicago, December 14, 1872), 5, Newspapers.com, April 1, 2021, https://www.newspapers.com/image/371948339.

14. Cody, *Life of*, 325.

15. "The Theatres," *Chicago Evening Post* (Chicago, December 14, 1872), 5, Newspapers.com, April 2, 2021, https://www.newspapers.com/image/667953148.

16. "Amusements," *Chicago Tribune* (Chicago, December 14, 1872), 9, Newspapers.com, April 2, 2021, https://www.newspapers.com/image/371948004/?terms=%22Buffalo%20Bill%22%20Omaha&match=1; Sandra K. Sagala, *Buffalo Bill on Stage* (Albuquerque: University of New Mexico Press, 2008), 20.

17. "Amusements," *Chicago Tribune* (Chicago, December 15, 1872), 9, Newspapers.com, April 1, 2021, https://www.newspapers.com/image/466194836; Sagala, *Buffalo Bill*, 21.

18. Cody, *Life of*, 325–26.

19. "Amusements," *Chicago Inter Ocean* (Chicago, December 17, 1872), 4, Newspapers.com, April 2, 2021, https://www.newspapers.com/image/35055311; Sagala, *Buffalo Bill*, 20–21.

20. Sagala, *Buffalo Bill*, 21; Cody, *Life of*, 326.

21. "Amusements," 4.

22. Sagala, *Buffalo Bill*, 21–22; Cody, *Life of*, 326–27.

23. Sagala, *Buffalo Bill*, 26; Bricklin, *Buntline*, 138; Cody, *Life of*, 327.

24. "The Theatres," *Chicago Evening Post* (Chicago, December 17, 1872), 1, Newspapers.com, April 2, 2021, https://www.newspapers.com/image/667953186.

25. "Amusements," *Chicago Evening Mail* (Chicago, December 17, 1872), 4, Newspapers.com, April 2, 2021, https://www.newspapers.com/image/668332104/?terms=%22Buffalo%20Bill%22%20Omaha&match=1.

26. "Buffalo Bill," *Leavenworth Daily Commercial* (Leavenworth, KS, December 21, 1872), 2, Newspapers.com, April 2, 2021, https://www.newspapers.com/image/425154963/?terms=%22Buffalo%20Bill%22%20Omaha&match=1.

27. "Nebraska Items," *Sioux City Journal* (Sioux City, IA, December 28, 1872), 2, Newspapers.com, April 1, 2021, https://www.newspapers.com/image/416281860/?terms=%22Buffalo%20Bill%22%20Omaha&match=1. On January 14, 1873, Nebraska determined a county in Cody's district had not had its ballots counted as they were sent to the wrong address. When counted those votes placed D. P. Ashburn forty-two votes ahead of Cody. Nebraska's House Committee on Privileges and Elections gave the seat to Ashburn since Cody failed to contest it. Russell, *Buffalo Bill*, 191.

28. Cody and Cooper, *Memories*, 248–50; Sagala, *Buffalo Bill*, 26; Russell, *Buffalo Bill*, 197; Cody, *Life of*, 328.

29. "Arrest of Ned Buntline," *Kansas City Times* (Kansas City, KS, December 29, 1872), 3, Newspapers.com, April 2, 2021, https://www.newspapers.com/image/649178014/?terms=%22Ned%20Buntline%22&match=1.

30. Bricklin, *Buntline*, 66–71.

31. "Arrest of Ned Buntline," 3.

32. "Ned Buntline's Riot," *Daily Press and Herald* (Knoxville, TN, July 24, 1873), 1, Newspapers.com, April 3, 2021, https://www.newspapers.com/image/584940778/?terms=%22Buffalo%20Bill%22&match=1.

33. "Amusements," *Cincinnati Enquirer* (Cincinnati, December 28, 1872), 5, Newspapers.com, April 3, 2021, https://www.newspapers.com/image/30688728/?terms=%22Scouts%20of%20the%20Prairie%22&match=1.

34. "Deaths" and "His Last Stage Fight," *Cincinnati Enquirer* (Cincinnati, January 8, 1873), 5, 8, Newspapers.com, April 3, 2021, https://www.newspapers.com/image/30689220.

35. Sagala, *Buffalo Bill*, 226; Cody, *Life of*, 328; Russell, *Buffalo Bill*, 198.

36. "Amusements," *New York Herald* (New York, April 1, 1873), 12, Newspapers.com, April 3, 2021, https://www.newspapers.com/image/329423266/?terms=%22Buffalo%20Bill%22&match=1; Sagala, *Buffalo Bill*, 226–27.

37. Sagala, *Buffalo Bill*, 37, 38, 227; "The Scouts in Luck," *Missouri Republican* (St. Louis, July 21, 1873), 2, Newspapers.com, April 3, 2021, https://www.newspapers.com/image/666824861/?terms=%22Buffalo%20Bill%22&match=1.

38. Sagala, *Buffalo Bill*, 227; "Buffalo Bill," *Delaware State Journal* (Wilmington, DE, May 24, 1873), 2, Newspapers.com, April 3, 2021, https://www.newspapers.com/image/624811946/?terms=Cody&match=1.

39. Sagala, *Buffalo Bill*, 38, 227.

40. Cody, *Life of*, 328; Sagala, *Buffalo Bill*, 40.

41. Russell, *Buffalo Bill*, 204–5; Mathew Kerns, "James A. Scott," The Dime Library, April 3, 2021, https://www.dimelibrary.com/post/james-a-scott.

42. "The Scouts in Luck," 2.

43. "The Scouts in Luck," 2; Cody, *Life of*, 328–29.

44. Sagala, *Buffalo Bill*, 41; Russell, *Buffalo Bill*, 205; "The Scouts in Luck," 2; Cody and Cooper, *Memories*, 257; "A New Roll," *Inter Ocean* (Chicago, September 3, 1873), 4, Newspapers.com, April 4, 2021, https://www.newspapers.com/image/38403354/?terms=Morlacchi%2C&match=1.

45. "The Scouts in Luck," 2.

46. Russell, *Buffalo Bill*, 202.

47. Sagala, *Buffalo Bill*, 43, 47, 48, 52, 54.

48. Russell, *Buffalo Bill*, 204–5; Sagala, *Buffalo Bill*, 44.

49. Cody, *Life of*, 329.

50. Rosa, *They Called Him Wild Bill*, 220, 248.

51. "Wild Bill," *Abilene Weekly Chronicle* (Abilene, KS, February 20, 1873), 3, Newspapers.com, March 28, 2021, https://www.newspapers.com/image/384017143/?terms=%22Wild%20Bill%22&match=1; Rosa, *They Called Him Wild Bill*, 248.

52. "Playful," *Kansas City Times* (Kansas City, MO, March 11, 1873), 4, Newspapers.com, March 28, 2021, https://www.newspapers.com/image/649206125/?terms=%22Wild%20Bill%22&match=1.

53. Rosa, *They Called Him Wild Bill*, 249.

54. Ibid.

55. Rosa, *Wild Bill Hickok*, 158–60.

56. "The Land of the West," *New York Daily Herald* (New York, May 21, 1873), 13, Newspapers.com, March 28, 2021, https://www.newspapers.com/image/329594388/?terms=%22Wild%20Bill%22&match=1.

57. "How Wild Bill Died," *Galveston Daily News* (Galveston, TX, June 24, 1873), 1, Newspapers.com, March 28, 2021, https://www.newspapers.com/image/24057040/?terms=%22Wild%20Bill%22&match=1.

58. Cody, *Life of*, 329.

59. Sagala, *Buffalo Bill*, 42, 43, 227.

60. Buel, *Heroes*, 160–61.

61. Cody, *Life of*, 329; Sagala, *Buffalo Bill*, 47.

62. Buel, *Heroes*, 161–62.

63. Sagala, *Buffalo Bill*, 47–48.

64. Ibid., 50, 227.

65. Cody, *Life of*, 329.

66. Sagala, *Buffalo Bill*, 227.

67. Ibid., 48.

68. Ibid., 227.

69. Cody, *Life of*, 330.

70. Ibid., 331.

71. Sagala, *Buffalo Bill*, 54, 227.

72. Ibid., 54.

73. "The Scouts of the Plains," *Buffalo Evening Post* (Buffalo, November 14, 1873), 3, Newspapers.com, April 5, 2021, https://www.newspapers.com/image/261423011.

74. "The Drama," *Buffalo Commercial* (Buffalo, November 15, 1873), 4, Newspapers.com, April 5, 2021, https://www.newspapers.com/image/264741853.

75. Sagala, *Buffalo Bill*, 49, 54, 227.

76. Cody, *Life of*, 329–30.

77. Sagala, *Buffalo Bill*, 228.

78. Ibid., 55.

79. Ibid., 55, 228.

80. "Local Summary," *Boston Post* (Boston, January 24, 1874), 3, Newspapers.com, April 9, 2021, https://www.newspapers.com/image/72009371/?terms=%22Buffalo%20Bill%22&match=1.

81. "Current Topics," *Democrat and Chronicle* (Rochester, NY, January 10, 1874), 2, Newspapers.com, April 9, 2021, https://www.newspapers.com/image/135074707/?terms=%22Buffalo%20Bill%22&match=1.

82. Sagala, *Buffalo Bill*, 228; Cody, *Life of*, 331.

83. Cody, *Life of*, 331–32.

84. Rosa, *They Called Him Wild Bill*, 254.

85. Sagala, *Buffalo Bill*, 228.

86. "Personal," *Cincinnati Enquirer* (Cincinnati, February 24, 1874), 4, Newspapers.com, April 9, 2021, https://www.newspapers.com/image/31308684/?terms=%22Buffalo%20Bill%22&match=1.

87. *Pittsfield Sun* (Pittsfield, MA, February 25, 1874), 2, Newspapers.com, April 9, 2021, https://www.newspapers.com/image/531855850/?terms=%22Buffalo%20Bill%22&match=1.

88. Sagala, *Buffalo Bill*, 56–57.

89. Ibid., 228.

90. "Opera House," *Democrat and Chronicle* (Rochester, NY, March 10, 1874), 4, Newspapers.com, April 9, 2021, https://www.newspapers.com/image/135076680/?terms=%22Wild%20Bill%22&match=1.

91. "Personal," *Wayne County Herald* (Honesdale, PA, March 5, 1874), 3, Newspapers.com, April 9, 2021, https://www.newspapers.com/image/362446429/?terms=%22Wild%20Bill%22&match=1.

92. Sagala, *Buffalo Bill*, 228; Cody, *Life of*, 332.

93. "Opera House—'The Scouts,'" *Democrat and Chronicle* (Rochester, NY, March 11, 1874), 4, Newspapers.com, April 9, 2021, https://www.newspapers.com/image/135076717/?terms=%22Wild%20Bill%22&match=1.

94. Ibid., 4.

95. "Marriage," *Democrat and Chronicle* (Rochester, NY, March 12, 1874), 4, Newspapers.com, April 9, 2021, https://www.newspapers.com/image/135076761/?terms=%22Wild%20Bill%22&match=1.

96. Buel, *Heroes*, 162–63.

97. Cody and Cooper, *Memories*, 256.

98. Cody, *Life of*, 333.

99. Ibid.

100. Ibid.

101. "Wild Bill," *Democrat and Chronicle* (Rochester, NY, March 13, 1874), 4, Newspapers.com, April 9, 2021, https://www.newspapers.com/image/135076804/?terms=%22Wild%20Bill%22&match=1.

102. Ibid.

103. Ibid.

Chapter 14: "Living Heroes" (1874–1876)

1. "Wild Bill," 4; Linda A. Fisher and Carrie Bowers, *Agnes Lake Hickok: Queen of the Circus, Wife of a Legend* (Norman: University of Oklahoma Press, 2020), 218, 220, 222.

2. Ibid., 218–19.

3. Cody, *Life of*, 333.

4. "Wild Bill," *Wayne County Herald* (Honesdale, PA, April 30, 1874), 3, Newspapers.com, April 11, 2021.

5. "New This Week," *Wayne County Herald* (Honesdale, PA, April 30, 1874), 2. Newspapers.com, April 11, 2021, https://www.newspapers.com/image/362446820/?terms=%22Wild%20Bill%22&match=1.

6. "Wild Bill," *Daily Record of the Times* (Wilkes-Barre, PA, May 4, 1874), 3, Newspapers.com, April 11, 2021, https://www.newspapers.com/image/390118471/?terms=%22Wild%20Bill%22&match=1.

7. "New Advertisements," *Daily Record of the Times* (Wilkes-Barre, PA, May 4, 1874), 2, Newspapers.com, April 11, 2021, https://www.newspapers.com/image/83166457/?terms=%22Wild%20Bill%22&match=1; "Music Hall," *Daily Record of the Times* (Wilkes-Barre, PA, May 5, 1874), 3, Newspapers.com, April 11, 2021, https://www.newspapers.com/image/83166729/?terms=%22Wild%20Bill%22&match=1.

8. "Daniel Boone," *Daily Record of the Times* (Wilkes-Barre, PA, May 8, 1874), 3, Newspapers.com, April 11, 2021, https://www.newspapers.com/image/83167565/?terms=%22Wild%20Bill%22&match=1.

9. Cody, *Life of*, 333; Rosa, *They Called Him Wild Bill*, 260; "City, County, and Vicinity," *Carbondale Leader* (Carbondale, PA, May 9, 1874), 3, Newspapers.com, April 11, 2021, https://www.newspapers.com/image/639235495.

10. "Amusements," *Morning Republican* (Scranton, PA, May 12, 1874), 2, 3, Newspapers.com, April 12, 2021, https://www.newspapers.com/image/532484237/?terms=%22Wild%20Bill%22&match=1; Cody, *Life of*, 333.

11. "Current Topics," *Democrat and Chronicle* (Rochester, NY, May 26, 1874), 2, Newspapers.com, April 12, 2021, https://www.newspapers.com/image/135079351/?terms=%22Wild%20Bill%22&match=1; Cody, *Life of*, 334–35.

12. "Wild Bill," 4.

13. Sagala, *Buffalo Bill*, 228.

14. "Opera House," *Detroit Free Press* (Detroit, March 24, 1874), 1, https://www.newspapers.com/image/118155312/?terms=%22Wild%20Bill%22&match=1.

15. "Amusements," *Pentagraph* (Bloomington, IL, April 7, 1874), 1, https://www.newspapers.com/image/69149472/?terms=%22Wild%20Bill%22&match=1.

16. "Good's Opera House," *South Bend Tribune* (South Bend, ID, April 1, 1874), 4, Newspapers.com, April 13, 2021, https://www.newspapers.com/image/513469913/?terms=%22Buffalo%20Bill%22&match=1.

17. Sagala, *Buffalo Bill*, 63.

18. "The Scouts of the Plains," *Daily Davenport Democrat* (Davenport, IA, April 23, 1874), 1, Newspapers.com, April 13, 2021, https://www.newspapers.com/image/299024160/?terms=%22Buffalo%20Bill%22&match=1.

19. Sagala, *Buffalo Bill*, 228.

20. "Academy of Music," *Chicago Tribune* (Chicago, May 12, 1874), 8, Newspapers.com, April 13, 2021, https://www.newspapers.com/image/349264974/?terms=%22Buffalo%20Bill%22&match=1.

21. Sagala, *Buffalo Bill*, 228.

22. "Buffalo Bill at Woods Museum," *New York Herald* (New York, June 30, 1874), 7, Newspapers.com, April 13, 2021, https://www.newspapers.com/image/329606695/?terms=%22Buffalo%20Bill%22&match=1.

23. Russell, *Buffalo Bill*, 208; Cody, *Life of*, 337; "Buffalo Bill," *Rochester Democrat and Chronicle* (Rochester, NY, July 9, 1874), 4, Newspapers.com, April 13, 2021, https://www.newspapers.com/image/135075156/?terms=%22Wild%20Bill%22&match=1.

24. "Jottings," *Daily Journal of Commerce* (Kansas City, MO, June 21, 1874), 4, Newspapers.com, April 12, 2021, https://www.newspapers.com/image/666736648/?terms=%22Wild%20Bill%22&match=1.

25. "State News Hashed," *Western Spirit* (Paola, KS, June 26, 1874), 2, Newspapers.com, April 13, 2021, https://www.newspapers.com/image/382883092/?terms=%22Wild%20Bill%22&match=1.

26. "Buffalo Bill," *Democrat and Chronicle* (Rochester, NY, July 9, 1874), 4, Newspapers.com, April 12, 2021, https://www.newspapers.com/image/135075156/?terms=%22Wild%20Bill%22&match=1.

27. "Overland Passengers," *San Francisco Examiner* (San Francisco, CA, July 17, 1874), 3, Newspapers.com, April 12, 2021, https://www.newspapers.com/image/457859673/?terms=Medley%20London&match=1; "Overland," *Sacramento Bee* (Sacramento, July 17, 1874), 3, Newspapers.com, April 12, 2021, https://www.newspapers.com/image/623351079/?terms=Medley%20London&match=1.

28. *Commonwealth* (Topeka, KS, July 23, 1874), 3, Newspapers.com, April 12, 2021, https://www.newspapers.com/image/367309072/?terms=%22Wild%20Bill%22&match=1.

29. Connelley and Harger, *Wild Bill*, 173; Buel, *Heroes*, 181.

30. "Buffalo Bill," 4.

31. Ibid.

32. "Buffalo Bill," *Omaha Bee* (Omaha, July 20, 1874), 4, Newspapers.com, April 13, 2021, https://www.newspapers.com/image/466154769/?terms=%22Wild%20Bill%22&match=1.

33. "From the Plains," *Democrat and Chronicle* (Rochester, NY, August 3, 1874), 3, Newspapers.com, April 14, 2021, https://www.newspapers.com/image/135075913/?terms=%22Wild%20Bill%22&match=1.

34. Ibid.

35. "Buffalo Bill," *Democrat and Chronicle* (Rochester, NY, August 17, 1874), 4, Newspapers.com, April 14, 2021, https://www.newspapers.com/image/135076360/?terms=%22Medley%22%2C%20%22Buffalo%20Bill%22&match=1; Rosa, *They Called Him Wild Bill*, 264.

36. Cody, *Life of*, 337.

37. Ibid.

38. "Buffalo Hunting," *Independent* (Grand Island, NE, July 25, 1874), 4, Newspapers.com, April 14, 2021, https://www.newspapers.com/image/693108025/?terms=Carver&match=1.

39. "Buffalo Bill," 4.

40. Crutchfield, Moulton, and Del Bene, *Settlement of America*, Vol. 1, 202–3; "Transcript of Treaty of Fort Laramie (1868)," Our Documents, August 25, 2019, https://www.ourdocuments.gov/doc.php?flash=false&doc=42&page=transcript.

41. Crutchfield, Moulton, and Del Bene, *Settlement of America*, Vol. 2, 570–71; John D. McDermott, *Red Cloud's War: The Bozeman Trail, 1866–1868*, Vol. 2 (Norman: University of Oklahoma Press, 2010), 497–98.

42. Hutton, *Sheridan*, 282, 287–88, 290.

43. Clow, *Spotted Tail*, 91–92.

44. Hutton, *Sheridan*, 290; Crutchfield, Moulton, and Del Bene, *Settlement of America*, Vol. 1, 158–59; Bill Markley, "Custer's Gold," *True West Magazine*, April 2018, 70.

45. Crutchfield, Moulton, and Del Bene, *Settlement of America*, Vol. 1, 158–59; Paul Horsted, Ernest Grafe, and Jon Nelson, *Crossing the Plains with Custer* (Custer, SD: Golden Valley Press, 2009), 12, 21, 24, 146; Paul Horsted and Ernest Grafe, *Exploring with Custer: The 1874 Black Hills Expedition* (Custer, SD: Golden Valley Press, 2002), 30.

46. Herbert Krause and Gary D. Olson, *Prelude to Glory: A Newspaper Accounting of Custer's 1874 Expedition to the Black Hills* (Sioux Falls, SD: Brevet Press, 1974), 26; Crutchfield, Moulton, and Del Bene, *Settlement of America*, Vol. 1, 158–59; Horsted and Grafe, *Exploring with Custer*, 87–89.

47. Crutchfield, Moulton, and Del Bene, *Settlement of America*, Vol. 1, 158–59; Markley, "Custer's Gold," 74; Robert Utley, *The Lance and the Shield: The Life and Times of Sitting Bull* (New York: Ballantine Books, 1993), 116.

48. "The Big Horn Expedition," *Inter Ocean* (Chicago, September 12, 1874), 5, Newspapers.com, April 15, 2021, https://www.newspapers.com/image/39527212.

49. "Buffalo Bill," *Democrat and Chronicle*, 4.

50. Cody, *Life of*, 337–38.

51. Ibid., 338.

52. Custer, *Life on the Plains*, 192, 198.

53. Cody, *Life of*, 338–39.

54. Cody, *Life of*, 339; Russell, *Buffalo Bill*, 211.

55. Russell, *Buffalo Bill*, 211.

56. Ibid.

57. Ibid., 212.

58. Russell, *Buffalo Bill*, 211–12; "Editorial Notes," *Buffalo Express* (Buffalo, October 14, 1874), 2, Newspapers.com, April 15, 2021, https://www.newspapers.com/image/343726217/?terms=%22Buffalo%20Bill%22&match=1.

59. "Buffalo Bill's Opinion," *Daily Examiner* (San Francisco, October 24, 1874), 1, Newspapers.com, April 15, 2021, https://www.newspapers.com/image/457885360/?terms=%22Buffalo%20Bill%22&match=1.

60. Rosa, *They Called Him Wild Bill*, 271.

61. Buel, *Heroes*, 167–68.

22. Hedren, *Rosebud*, 313; Hutton, *Sheridan*, 313.

23. Hutton, *Sheridan*, 314; Hedren, *First Scalp*, 7, 8, 13.

24. Hedren, *First Scalp*, 13.

25. Ibid.

26. Cody, *Life of*, 341.

27. Hedren, *First Scalp*, 14.

28. Captain Charles King, *Campaigning with Crook* (Norman: University of Oklahoma Press, 1964), 19; Russell, *Buffalo Bill*, 221; Hedren, *First Scalp*, 14.

29. King, *Campaigning with Crook*, 20.

30. Ibid., 20–21.

31. Russell, *Buffalo Bill*, 221; Hedren, *First Scalp*, 15.

32. Russell, *Buffalo Bill*, 221–22; Hedren, *First Scalp*, 17.

33. Bill Markley and Kellen Cutsforth, *Old West Showdown, Two Authors Wrangle Over the Truth About the Old West* (Guilford, CT: TwoDot, 2018), 68.

34. Spring, *Cheyenne and Black Hills Stage*, 155; James D. McLaird, *Wild Bill and Calamity Jane: Deadwood Legends* (Pierre: South Dakota State Historical Society Press, 2008), 47.

35. William B. Secrest, ed., *I Buried Hickok: The Memoirs of White Eye Anderson* (College Station, TX: Creative Publishing Co., 1980), 92.

36. McLaird, *Wild Bill and Calamity Jane*, 47; Rosa, *They Called Him Wild Bill*, 285; Secrest, *Hickok*, 57.

37. Secrest, *Hickok*, 92.

38. Ibid., 92, 94.

39. Ibid., 92.

40. Before Hunton could send the cane, Hickok was killed. In 1921 Hunton sent it to the Wyoming Historical Society. In an April 27, 2021 email to Bill Markley, Mariah Emmons, Registrar, Wyoming State Museum, described it. "The cane is bamboo with three nodes and four internodal sections. The head is the carved root section and ovoid in shape with a slightly larger diameter covered with knots. There are two small nails in the tip. It measures 33.8" long x 1.6" diameter. Per the donor the cane belonged to James B. Hickok ('Wild Bill') whom he knew in 1875. '. . . cane which had belonged to his grandfather in Indiana, and of which he was very fond'"; Rosa, *They Called Him Wild Bill*, 286; Spring, *Cheyenne and Black Hills Stage*, 155.

41. Secrest, *Hickok*, 92; Spring, *Cheyenne and Black Hills Stage*, 118.

42. Secrest, *Hickok*, 92–93.

43. McLaird, *Wild Bill and Calamity Jane*, 73, 75.

44. McLaird, *Calamity Jane*, 30.

45. Ibid., 39.

46. Ibid., 44.

47. Ibid., 46, 47.

48. Ibid., 48, 53, 54.

49. Secrest, *Hickok*, 93.

50. Ibid.

51. Ibid., 93, 102, 108n9.
52. Ibid., 92.
53. Ibid., 95.
54. Ibid., 94.
55. Raymond W. Thorp, "White-Eye, Last of the Old Time-Plainsmen," *True West Magazine*, Vol. 12, no. 4 (March-April 1965), 10.
56. Secrest, *Hickok*, 95.
57. Rosa, *They Called Him Wild Bill*, 287.
58. Rosa, *They Called Him Wild Bill*, 287; Secrest, *Hickok*, 43, 50n5, 95.
59. Secrest, *Hickok*, 95.
60. Thorp, "White-Eye, Last of the Old Time-Plainsmen," 46.
61. Secrest, *Hickok*, 97.
62. Ibid.
63. Richard B. Hughes, *Pioneer Years in the Black Hills* (Rapid City, SD: Dakota Alpha Press, 2002), 122; Secrest, *Hickok*, 97.
64. Ibid., 1, 122, 123.
65. Young, *Hard Knocks*, 213.
66. Ibid.
67. Ibid., 213–14.

CHAPTER 16: INCIDENT AT WARBONNET CREEK (JULY 1876–AUGUST 1876)

1. Hutton, *Sheridan*, 312; Hedren, *First Scalp*, 17.
2. Hedren, *First Scalp*, 18.
3. Ibid., 19.
4. Ibid., 19–21.
5. Price, *Across the Continent*, 158; Hedren, *First Scalp*, 21–22.
6. Hedren, *First Scalp*, 22–23.
7. Ibid.
8. Ibid., 23.
9. Price, *Across the Continent*, 158; Hedren, *First Scalp*, 23.
10. Hedren, *First Scalp*, 25, 26.
11. King, *Campaigning with Crook*, 38.
12. Madsen became a famous Oklahoma peace officer. Russell, *Buffalo Bill*, 223.
13. Hedren, *First Scalp*, 24–25.
14. King, *Campaigning with Crook*, 29; Hedren, *First Scalp*, 25–26.
15. Russell, *Buffalo Bill*, 223–24.
16. Hedren, *First Scalp*, 26.
17. Russell, *Buffalo Bill*, 224; Hedren, *First Scalp*, 27.
18. Cody, *Life of*, 342; Hedren, *First Scalp*, 28.
19. King, *Campaigning with Crook*, 34.
20. Russell, *Buffalo Bill*, 226; Cody, *Life of*, 343; Hedren, *First Scalp*, 36.
21. Russell, *Buffalo Bill*, 226; Cody, *Life of*, 343–44.

22. Cody, *Life of*, 344; Russell, *Buffalo Bill*, 226; Hedren, *First Scalp*, 29.

23. Hedren, *First Scalp*, 29.

24. Ibid., 36.

25. Ibid., 29.

26. Hedren, *First Scalp*, 29, 38–39; Hutton, *Sheridan*, 319.

27. King, *Campaigning with Crook*, 38.

28. Cody, *Life of*, 347; Hedren, *First Scalp*, 39–40.

29. Hedren, *First Scalp*, 40.

30. Ibid., 43.

31. Hedren, *First Scalp*, 41; Russell, *Buffalo Bill*, 237.

32. Russell, *Buffalo Bill*, 237–38.

33. King, *Campaigning with Crook*, 45.

34. Price, *Across the Continent*, 159.

CHAPTER 17: WILD BILL DEAD IN DEADWOOD (APRIL 1876–AUGUST 2, 1876)

1. Secrest, *Hickok*, 99.

2. John McClintock, *Pioneer Days in the Black Hills: Accurate History and Facts by One of the Early Day Pioneers* (Norman: University of Oklahoma Press, 2000), 107; Secrest, *Hickok*, 99.

3. Thorp, "White-Eye, Last of the Old Time-Plainsmen," 46; Secrest, *Hickok*, 99.

4. Secrest, *Hickok*, 104.

5. Joe Milner and Earle Forrest, *California Joe: Noted Scout and Indian Fighter* (Lincoln: University of Nebraska Press, 1935), 243, 247.

6. Secrest, *Hickok*, 104.

7. Ibid., 115n32.

8. Ibid., 104.

9. Milner and Forrest, *California Joe*, 246–47.

10. Milner and Forrest, *California Joe*, 248; Rosa, *They Called Him Wild Bill*, 390.

11. Secrest, *Hickok*, 116.

12. Young, *Hard Knocks*, 215.

13. Rosa, *They Called Him Wild Bill*, 288, 289; Young, *Hard Knocks*, 214.

14. Young, *Hard Knocks*, 216–17.

15. Rosa, *They Called Him Wild Bill*, 289; Milner and Forrest, *California Joe*, 250.

16. Rosa, *They Called Him Wild Bill*, 288–89.

17. Ibid., 291.

18. Leander Richardson, "A Very Lively Camp," *Daily Bee* (Sacramento, January 20, 1894), 6, Newspapers.com, May 1, 2021, https://www.newspapers.com/image/624045034/?terms=%22Leander%20Richardson%22%2C%20%22Wild%20Bill%22&match=1.

19. Ibid.

20. Ibid.

21. Rosa, *They Called Him Wild Bill*, 290; Wilstach, *Wild Bill Hickok*, 280–81.

22. Rosa, *Wild Bill Hickok*, 196.

23. *Hard Knocks*, 218.

24. Wilstach, *Wild Bill Hickok*, 281.

25. Rosa, *Wild Bill Hickok*, 196.

26. Young, *Hard Knocks*, 220; Thad Turner, *Wild Bill Hickok: Deadwood City—End of Trail* (Deadwood, SD: Old West Alive! Publishing, 2001), 125.

27. Milner and Forrest, *California Joe*, 251.

28. Spring, *Cheyenne and Black Hills Stage*, 155–56; Rosa, *Wild Bill Hickok*, 196.

29. The format of the account of Hickok's murder and the first trial of Jack McCall is similar to the account in Bill Markley and Kellen Cutsforth, *Standoff at High Noon: Another Battle over the Truth in the Mythic Wild West* (Guilford, CT: TwoDot, 2021).

30. Young, *Hard Knocks*, 220; Rosa, *They Called Him Wild Bill*, 297.

31. Young, *Hard Knocks*, 220.

32. Young, *Hard Knocks*, 220; Rosa, *They Called Him Wild Bill*, 324–25.

33. Young, *Hard Knocks*, 220.

34. Rosa, *They Called Him Wild Bill*, 297, 299.

35. Ibid., 298.

36. Rosa, *They Called Him Wild Bill*, 298; Young, *Hard Knocks*, 221; Secrest, *Hickok*, 120.

37. Secrest, *Hickok*, 120; McLaird, *Wild Bill Hickok and Calamity Jane*, 53.

38. Secrest, *Hickok*, 120; McLaird, *Wild Bill Hickok and Calamity Jane*, 58; Turner, *Wild Bill Hickok*, 146, 148.

39. Turner, *Wild Bill Hickok*, 149–50.

40. Turner, *Wild Bill Hickok*, 152–53; McLaird, *Wild Bill Hickok and Calamity Jane*, 54.

41. McLaird, *Wild Bill Hickok and Calamity Jane*, 54.

CHAPTER 18: SCOUTING FOR CROOK (AUGUST 1876–SEPTEMBER 1876)

1. Russell, *Buffalo Bill*, 238; Powers, *Killing of Crazy Horse*, 185, 189; Utley, *Lance and the Shield*, 141; Hutton, *Sheridan*, 313; Bourke, *On the Border*, 302–3.

2. Hedren, *Rosebud*, 318, 335; Utley, *Lance and the Shield*, 141, 142–43; Hutton, *Sheridan*, 313; Powers, *Killing of Crazy Horse*, 192; Bourke, *On the Border*, 325, 327, 329; Donovan, *Terrible Glory*, 153.

3. Bourke, *On the Border*, 321–22.

4. Mac Abrams, *Sioux War Dispatches: Reports from the Field*, 1876–1877 (Yardley, PA: Westholme Publishing, 2012), 208; Bourke, *On the Border*, 334; Powers, *Killing of Crazy Horse*, 197; Hedren, *Rosebud*, 349.

5. Price, *Across the Continent*, 159.

6. De Barthe, *Frank Grouard*, 110–13; Utley, *Lance and the Shield*, 94; Cody, *Life of*, 347.

7. Abrams, *Sioux War Dispatches*, 206.

8. Jerome Green, *Slim Buttes, 1876: An Episode of the Great Sioux War* (Norman: University of Oklahoma Press, 1982), 13, 15, 23; Russell, *Buffalo Bill*, 239.

9. Abrams, *Sioux War Dispatches*, 208.

10. Ibid.

11. Gregory Michno, *Lakota Noon: The Indian Narrative of Custer's Defeat* (Missoula, MT: Mountain Press Publishing Company, 1997), 301; Utley, *Lance and the Shield*, 165.

12. Michno, *Lakota Noon*, 301; Utley, *Lance and the Shield*, 165–66; Vestal, *Sitting Bull*, 184.

13. Donovan, *Terrible Glory*, 306, 308–11, 312–13, 325.

14. Alfred Terry, *The Field Diary of General Alfred H. Terry: The Yellowstone Expedition—1876*, 2nd ed. (Bellevue, NE: Old Army Press, 1970), 31; Donovan, *Terrible Glory*, 332; Hutton, *Sheridan*, 320.

15. Paul Hedren, ed., *John Finerty Reports the Sioux War* (Norman: University of Oklahoma Press, 2020), 150; Green, *Slim Buttes*, 25.

16. Green, *Slim Buttes*, 26; Abrams, *Sioux War Dispatches*, 208.

17. Hedren, *John Finerty Reports*, 147; Green, *Slim Buttes*, 26.

18. Green, *Slim Buttes*, 26; Abrams, *Sioux War Dispatches*, 209; Cody, *Life of*, 347.

19. Paul Hedren, ed., *Ho! For the Black Hills: Captain Jack Crawford Reports the Black Hills Gold Rush and Great Sioux War* (Pierre: South Dakota State Historical Press, 2012), 20, 35, 37, 201, 212.

20. Ibid., 199, 201.

21. Hedren, *Ho! For the Black Hills*, 200; Cody, *Life of*, 349.

22. Cody, *Life of*, 350; Oliver Knight, *Following the Indian Wars: The Story of the Newspaper Correspondents Among the Indian Campaigners* (Norman: University of Oklahoma Press, 1960), 251.

23. Green, *Slim Buttes*, 26–27; Hedren, *John Finerty Reports*, 147.

24. Hedren, *John Finerty Reports*, 154.

25. Abrams, *Sioux War Dispatches*, 209, 211.

26. Ibid., 211.

27. Cody, *Life of*, 351.

28. Hedren, *John Finerty Reports*, 155–56.

29. Abrams, *Sioux War Dispatches*, 212; Terry, *Diary*, 31.

30. Terry, *Diary*, 31.

31. Abrams, *Sioux War Dispatches*, 213; Terry, *Diary*, 31.

32. Abrams, *Sioux War Dispatches*, 213.

33. Cody, *Life of*, 351.

34. Cody, *Life of*, 351; Terry, *Diary*, 31.

35. Bourke, *On the Border*, 352; Green, *Slim Buttes*, 28.

36. Cody, *Life of*, 351.

37. Green, *Slim Buttes*, 28; Bourke, *On the Border*, 352; Cody, *Life of*, 352; Terry, *Diary*, 32; Abrams, *Sioux War Dispatches*, 216.

38. Hedren, *John Finerty Reports*, 158.

39. Abrams, *Sioux War Dispatches*, 218; Hedren, *John Finerty Reports*, 159.

40. Abrams, *Sioux War Dispatches*, 218.

41. Hedren, *John Finerty Reports*, 160.

42. Green, *Slim Buttes*, 28.

43. Hedren, *John Finerty Reports*, 162–63.

44. Terry, *Diary*, 32; Hedren, *John Finerty Reports*, 161; Cody, *Life of*, 353.

45. Cody, *Life of*, 353.

46. Cody, *Life of*, 355; Russell, *Buffalo Bill*, 246.

47. Cody, *Life of*, 355; Russell, *Buffalo Bill*, 246.

48. Cody, *Life of*, 355.

49. Green, *Slim Buttes*, 28.

50. Abrams, *Sioux War Dispatches*, 219.

51. Abrams, *Sioux War Dispatches*, 219; Hedren, *John Finerty Reports*, 170.

52. Green, *Slim Buttes*, 30.

53. Hutton, *Sheridan*, 321.

54. Russell, *Buffalo Bill*, 246; Cody, *Life of*, 355; Hedren, *John Finerty Reports*, 170.

55. Green, *Slim Buttes*, 31.

56. Cody, *Life of*, 356; Russell, *Buffalo Bill*, 248.

57. Hutton, *Sheridan*, 322; Russell, *Buffalo Bill*, 248; Cody, *Life of*, 356.

58. Cody, *Life of*, 356.

59. Ibid., 356–57.

60. Ibid., 357.

61. Cody, *Life of*, 357; Hedren, *John Finerty Reports*, 225.

62. Abrams, *Sioux War Dispatches*, 225; Cody, *Life of*, 357; Green, *Slim Buttes*, 31.

63. Russell, *Buffalo Bill*, 250; Cody, *Life of*, 357; Abrams, *Sioux War Dispatches*, 226.

64. Cody, *Life of*, 357–58.

65. Ibid., 358–59.

66. Ibid., 359.

67. Edgar Stewart and Jane Stewart, eds., *The Field Diary of Lt. Edward Settle Godfrey* (Portland, OR: Champoeg Press, 1957), 44; Russell, *Buffalo Bill*, 250.

68. Russell, *Buffalo Bill*, 250; Cody, *Life of*, 359.

69. "An Utter Failure," *Chicago Tribune* (Chicago, September 22, 1876), 5, Newspapers.com, May 6, 2021, https://www.newspapers.com/image/349590200.

70. Cody, *Life of*, 359; Russell, *Buffalo Bill*, 250.

71. "Buffalo Bill," *Democrat and Chronicle* (Rochester, NY, September 18, 1876), 4, Newspapers.com, May 6, 2021, https://www.newspapers.com/image/135076128/?terms=%22Buffalo%20Bill%22&match=1.

72. Ibid.
73. Ibid.
74. Ibid.
75. Ibid.
76. Russell, *Buffalo Bill*, 251.

Chapter 19: The End of the Trail

1. Secrest, *Hickok*, 120.
2. Secrest, *Hickok*, 120; "A Frontier Hero," *Inter Ocean* (Chicago, August 17, 1876), 1, Newspapers.com, May 7, 2021, https://www.newspapers.com/image/32559406/.
3. Secrest, *Hickok*, 121; "A Frontier Hero," 1.
4. Rosa, *They Called Him Wild Bill*, 301.
5. McClintock, *Pioneer Days*, 112; "A Frontier Hero," 1.
6. Young, *Hard Knocks*, 222–23.
7. "A Frontier Hero," 1.
8. Helen Rezatto, *Mount Moriah: The Story of Deadwood's Boot Hill* (Rapid City, SD: Fenwyn Press, 1989), 11; Secrest, *Hickok*, 121.
9. "A Frontier Hero," 1.
10. Rosa, *They Called Him Wild Bill*, 301.
11. Rezatto, *Mount Moriah*, 11–12, 29–30; Rosa, *They Called Him Wild Bill*, 302–3.
12. Rosa, *They Called Him Wild Bill*, 304–6.
13. *Black Hills Weekly Journal* (Rapid City, SD, March 1, 1895), 3, Newspapers.com, May 12, 2021, https://www.newspapers.com/image/351064206; "William F. Cody at Wild Bill Hickok's Grave (2)," Digital Collections, Buffalo Bill Center of the West, May 8, 2021, http://library.centerofthewest.org/digital/collection/BBOA/id/2503; "Buffalo Bill After Indians," *Weekly Pioneer-Times* (Deadwood, SD, November 15, 1906), 3, Newspapers.com, May 8, 2021, https://www.newspapers.com/image/94322371/?terms=%22Buffalo%20Bill%22&match=1; "William F. Cody at Wild Bill Hickok's Grave (1)," Digital Collections, Buffalo Bill Center of the West, May 8, 2021, http://library.centerofthewest.org/digital/collection/BBOA/id/3072/rec/1.
14. A version of this material on Jack McCall appears in Kellen Cutsforth's and my book, *Standoff at High Noon*.
15. Wilstach, *Wild Bill Hickok*, 301; Secrest, *Hickok*, 121.
16. Rosa, *They Called Him Wild Bill*, 317.
17. Wilstach, *Wild Bill Hickok*, 295; Milner and Forrest, *California Joe*, 258; Secrest, *Hickok*, 121.
18. Rosa, *Wild Bill Hickok, Gunfighter*, 164.
19. Rosa, *They Called Him Wild Bill*, 317
20. Milner and Forrest, *California Joe*, 251–52, 257.
21. Milner and Forrest, *California Joe*, 258; Rosa, *They Called Him Wild Bill*, 317–18.

22. Secrest, *Hickok*, 121.

23. Milner and Forrest, *California Joe*, 260.

24. Joseph Rosa, *Alias Jack McCall: A Pardon or Death?* (Kansas City, MO: The Kansas City Posse, The Westerners, 1967), 5; Aaron Woodard, "The Coward Who Shot Wild Bill," *Wild West Magazine*, August 2019, 40–41; Aaron Woodard, *The Revenger: The Life and Times of Wild Bill Hickok* (Guilford, CT: TwoDot, 2018), 117–18.

25. Woodard, "The Coward Who Shot Wild Bill," 41; Woodard, *The Revenger*, 118.

26. Rosa, *Wild Bill Hickok*, 201; Woodard, *The Revenger*, 118–19; Rosa, *Alias Jack McCall*, 8–9.

27. "Wild Bill: A Sequel to the Tragedy," *Black Hills Weekly Pioneer* (Deadwood, SD: November 11, 1876), 4, Newspapers.com, July 19, 2020, https://www.newspapers.com/image/262594576/?terms=%2C%2BWild%2BBill.

28. Rosa, *Wild Bill Hickok, Gunfighter*, 173.

29. Friesen, *Buffalo Bill*, 42, 44.

30. Cody, *Life of*, 361.

31. Ibid.

32. Ibid., 362.

33. Russell, *Buffalo Bill*, 271–72, 274.

34. Joseph Rosa and Robin May, *Buffalo Bill and His Wild West: A Pictorial Biography* (Lawrence: University Press of Kansas, 1989), 60; Friesen, *Buffalo Bill*, 42, 46.

35. Rosa and May, *Buffalo Bill*, 70–71; Friesen, *Buffalo Bill*, 45–46.

36. Friesen, *Buffalo Bill*, 47–48.

37. Ibid., 46–47.

38. Rosa and May, *Buffalo Bill*, 70; Friesen, *Buffalo Bill*, 48.

39. "A Grand Success," *Omaha Daily Bee* (Omaha, May 21, 1883), 8, Newspapers.com, May 12, 2021, https://www.newspapers.com/image/78692515/?terms=Buffalo%20Bill&match=1.

40. Ibid.

41. Ibid.

42. Ibid.

43. Friesen, *Buffalo Bill*, 48; Rosa and May, *Buffalo Bill*, 73.

44. Russell, *Buffalo Bill*, 298.

45. Russell, *Buffalo Bill*, 299; "Irma Louisa Cody Garlow," Find a Grave, June 4, 2021, https://www.findagrave.com/memorial/26937809/irma-louisa-garlow.

46. Rosa and May, *Buffalo Bill*, 73; Russell, *Buffalo Bill*, 257–58.

47. Friesen, *Buffalo Bill*, 50.

48. Ibid., 52.

49. Ibid.

50. Ibid., 53.

51. Ibid.

52. Steve Friesen, "The Man Behind the Legend," *American Cowboy Magazine* (February 13, 2017), May 15, 2021, https://www.americancowboy.com/people/buffalo-bill-man-behind-legend-24354; Friesen, *Buffalo Bill*, 53–56.

53. Friesen, *Buffalo Bill*, 56.

54. Bobby Bridger, *Buffalo Bill and Sitting Bull: Inventing the West* (Austin, TX: University of Texas Press, 2002), 318; Deanne Stillman, *Blood Brothers: The Story of the Strange Friendship Between Sitting Bull and Buffalo Bill* (New York: Simon & Schuster, Inc., 2017), 142, 143.

55. Warren, *Buffalo Bill's America*, 254; Stillman, *Blood Brothers*, 144–45, 155.

56. Bridger, *Buffalo Bill and Sitting Bull*, 318.

57. Markley and Cutsforth, *Old West Showdown*, 85; Bridger, *Buffalo Bill and Sitting Bull*, 318, 319.

58. Stillman, *Blood Brothers*, 183; Vestal, *Sitting Bull*, 251; Donovin Arleigh Sprague, *Images of America Standing Rock* (Charleston, SC: Arcadia Publishing, 2004), 61.

59. Vestal, *Sitting Bull*, 251.

60. Friesen, *Buffalo Bill*, 56.

61. Bridger, *Buffalo Bill and Sitting Bull*, 320.

62. Warren, *Buffalo Bill's America*, 30, 40; Markley and Cutsforth, *Old West Showdown*, 80.

63. Friesen, *Buffalo Bill*, 67; Rosa and May, *Buffalo Bill*, 116, 118, 121; Markley and Cutsforth, *Old West Showdown*, 85.

64. Bridger, *Buffalo Bill and Sitting Bull*, 344, 346; Markley and Cutsforth, *Old West Showdown*, 83.

65. Friesen, *Buffalo Bill*, 73–74, 81.

66. Warren, *Buffalo Bill's America*, 332.

67. Russell, *Buffalo Bill*, 374.

68. Ibid., 374–77.

69. Robert Bonner, *William F. Cody's Empire, the Buffalo Bill Nobody Knows* (Norman: University of Oklahoma Press, 2007), 53.

70. Bridger, *Buffalo Bill and Sitting Bull*, 440–41; Russell, *Buffalo Bill*, 427.

71. Russell, *Buffalo Bill*, 434–35; Markley and Cutsforth, *Old West Showdown*, 81.

72. Friesen, *Buffalo Bill*, 108, 115–16.

73. Ibid., 116.

74. Ibid., 119–22.

75. Bridger, *Buffalo Bill and Sitting Bull*, 428–30; Friesen, *Buffalo Bill*, 138.

76. Bridger, *Buffalo Bill and Sitting Bull*, 443.

77. Ibid., 442.

78. Ibid., 443–44.

79. Wilstach, *Wild Bill Hickok*, 284.

80. Joe Koller, "Doc Peirce—Pioneer Hills Barber Used His Wit, Humor to Save His Scalp," *Rapid City Journal* (Rapid City, SD, May 14, 1950), 3, Newspapers.com, May 8, 2021, https://www.newspapers.com/image/350472431.

81. Rosa, *Wild Bill Hickok*, 26.

82. Ibid., 158–60.

83. Ibid., 164–65.

84. Ibid., 164.

85. Ibid., 165.

86. McLaird, *Wild Bill Hickok and Calamity Jane*, 110.

87. Buel, *Heroes*, 9–10.

88. McLaird, *Wild Bill Hickok and Calamity Jane*, 180–81.

89. Ibid., 183.

90. Bell, *Life and Times of Wild Bill Hickok*, 104.

91. Darrel Nelson, Exhibits Director, Deadwood History, Inc., email communication to Bill Markley, May 13, 2021.

92. Russell, *Buffalo Bill*, 159, 265–66, 415.

93. Ibid., 273.

94. Buffalo Bill (Hon. W. F. Cody), *Story of the Wild West and Camp Fire Chats* (Chicago: Stanton and Van Vliet Co., 1919), v; Russell, *Buffalo Bill*, 274.

95. Russell, *Buffalo Bill*, 274–75; Buffalo Bill, *Story of the Wild West*, 199–201.

96. Friesen, *Buffalo Bill*, 136.

97. Buffalo Bill Museum and Grave website, May 13, 2021, https://www.buffalobill.org/index.html.

98. "Museums," Buffalo Bill Center of the West website, May 15, 2021, https://centerofthewest.org/our-museums.

BIBLIOGRAPHY

MANUSCRIPTS AND PRIMARY SOURCES

Barnitz, Colonel Albert. "Journal of the Operations of the 2nd Regiment, Ohio Cavalry, 1865 Mar 29–Nov 10." Collections: Colonel Albert Barnitz Papers, Series: Diaries. Beinecke Rare Book and Manuscript Library, Yale University, New Haven, Connecticut.

Coroner's Inquest, Greene County Circuit Court. Inquest into the Death of Davis Tutt, 1865 [Eli Armstrong Testimony]. Greene County Archives and Records Center, Springfield, Missouri.

Coroner's Inquest, Greene County Circuit Court. Inquest into the Death of Davis Tutt, 1865 [Dr. Edwin Ebert Report and Coroner's Jury Findings]. Greene County Archives and Records Center, Springfield, Missouri.

Coroner's Inquest, Greene County Circuit Court. Inquest into the Death of Davis Tutt, 1865 [Thomas D. Hudson Testimony]. Greene County Archives and Records Center, Springfield, Missouri.

Coroner's Inquest, Greene County Circuit Court. Inquest into the Death of Davis Tutt, 1865 [Lorenza F. Lee Testimony]. Greene County Archives and Records Center, Springfield, Missouri.

Coroner's Inquest, Greene County Circuit Court. Inquest into the Death of Davis Tutt, 1865 [J. W. Orr Testimony]. Greene County Archives and Records Center, Springfield, Missouri.

Coroner's Inquest, Greene County Circuit Court. Inquest into the Death of Davis Tutt, 1865 [F. W. Scholten Testimony]. Greene County Archives and Records Center, Springfield, Missouri.

Coroner's Inquest, Greene County Circuit Court. Inquest into the Death of Davis Tutt, 1865 [Oliver Scott Testimony]. Greene County Archives and Records Center, Springfield, Missouri.

Emmons, Mariah, Registrar, Wyoming State Museum. Personal email communication to Bill Markley on April 27, 2021, concerning Wild Bill Hickok's cane.

McLaird, James. Personal email communication to Bill Markley, March 28, 2017.

Nelson, Darrel, Exhibits Director, Deadwood History, Inc. Personal email communication to Bill Markley, May 13, 2021.

State of Missouri v. William Haycock (Hickok), Greene County Circuit Court, Manslaughter. Indictment for the Death of Davis Tutt, 1865. Greene County Archives and Records Center, Springfield, Missouri.

Books

Abrams, Mac H. *Sioux War Dispatches: Reports from the Field, 1876–1877*. Yardley, PA: Westholme Publishing, 2012.

Armes, Colonel George A. *Ups and Downs of an Army Officer*. Washington, DC: Privately Published, 1900.

Athearn, Robert G. *William Tecumseh Sherman and the Settlement of the West*. Norman: University of Oklahoma Press, 1956.

Barnard, Sandy, ed. *Ten Years with Custer: A Seventh Cavalryman's Memoirs*. Terre Haute, IN: AST Press, 2001.

Bell, Bob Boze. *The Illustrated Life and Times of Wild Bill Hickok*. Cave Creek, AZ: Two Roads West, 2017.

Bigler, David L., and Will Bagley. *The Mormon Rebellion: America's First Civil War, 1857–1858*. Norman: University of Oklahoma Press, 2011.

Billington, Ray Allen. *Westward Expansion: A History of the American Frontier*. New York: The Macmillan Company, 1949.

Bonner, Robert E. *William F. Cody's Empire, the Buffalo Bill Nobody Knows*. Norman: University of Oklahoma Press, 2007.

Borneman, Walter R. *Rival Rails: The Race to Build America's Greatest Transcontinental Railroad*. New York: Random House, 2010.

Bourke, John G. *On the Border with Crook*. New York: Skyhorse Publishing, 2014.

Bricklin, Julia. *The Notorious Life of Ned Buntline: A Tale of Murder, Betrayal, and the Creation of Buffalo Bill*. Guilford, CT: TwoDot, 2020.

Bridger, Bobby. *Buffalo Bill and Sitting Bull: Inventing the West*. Austin, TX: University of Texas Press, 2002.

Broome, Jeff. *Indian Raids and Massacres: Essays on the Central Plains Indian War*. Caldwell, ID: Caxton Press, 2020.

Brown, Dee. *Bury My Heart at Wounded Knee: An Indian History of the American West*. New York: Henry Holt and Company, 1970.

Brown, T. Allston. *A History of the New York Stage: From the First Performance in 1732 to 1901*, Vol. 1. New York: Dodd, Mead and Company, 1902.

Buel, J. W. *Heroes of the Plains*. Philadelphia: Historical Publishing Co., 1881.

Buffalo Bill (Hon. W. F. Cody). *Story of the Wild West and Camp Fire Chats*. Chicago: Stanton and Van Vliet Co., 1919.

Canary, Martha. *Life and Adventures of Calamity Jane, By Herself*. Ye Galleon Pr., 1979.

Clasrud, Bruce A., and Michael N. Searles. *Buffalo Soldiers in the West: A Black Soldiers Anthology*. College Station, TX: Texas A&M University Press, 2007.

Clow, Richmond L. *Spotted Tail: Warrior and Statesman*. Pierre: South Dakota Historical Society, 2019.

Cody, Louisa Frederici, and Courtney Ryley Cooper. *Memories of Buffalo Bill*. New York: D. Appleton & Company, 1919.

Cody, William Frederick. *An Autobiography of Buffalo Bill (Colonel W. F. Cody)*. New York: Cosmopolitan Book Corporation, 1920.

Cody, William F. *The Life of Hon. William F. Cody, Known as Buffalo Bill, the Famous Hunter, Scout, and Guide: An Autobiography*. Lincoln: University of Nebraska Press, 1978.

Connelley, William, and Charles Harger. *Wild Bill and His Era: The Life and Adventures of James Butler Hickok*. New York: The Press of the Pioneer, 1933.

Crutchfield, James, Candy Moulton, and Terry Del Bene, eds. *The Settlement of America: Encyclopedia of Western Expansion from Jamestown to the Closing of the Frontier*, Vols. 1 and 2. Armonk, NY: M. E. Sharp, Inc., 2011.

Custer, George Armstrong. *My Life on the Plains or, Personal Experiences with Indians*. Norman: University of Oklahoma Press, 1962.

Custer, Elizabeth B. *Following the Guidon*. Norman: University of Oklahoma Press, 1966.

Davies, Henry E. *Ten Days on the Plains*. New York: Crocker & Co., 1871.

Dawson, Charles. *Pioneer Tales of the Oregon Trail and of Jefferson County*. Topeka, KS: Crane & Company, 1912.

DeArment, Robert K. *Bat Masterson: The Man and the Legend*. Norman: University of Oklahoma Press, 1979.

De Barthe, Joe. *The Life and Adventures of Frank Grouard*. St. Joseph, MO: Combe Printing Company, 1894.

DeFelice, Jim. *West Like Lightning: The Brief, Legendary Ride of the Pony Express*. New York: HarperCollins Publishers, 2018.

DeMallie, Raymond J., vol. ed. *Plains, Handbook of North American Indians*, Vol. 13, Part 2. Washington, DC: Smithsonian Institution, 2001.

Donovan, James. *A Terrible Glory, The Last Great Battle of the American West*. New York: Little, Brown & Company, 2008.

Dugan, Mark. *Tales Never Told Around the Campfire: True Stories of Frontier America*. Athens: Swallow Press/Ohio University Press, 1992.

Earl of Dunraven, The. *Canadian Nights: Being Sketches and Reminiscences of Life and Sport in the Rockies and Prairies, and the Canadian Woods*. New York: Charles Scribner's Sons, 1914.

Ellison, Douglas W. "A Desperado Without a Peer," *John Wesley Hardin Invades Kansas, 1871*. Medora, ND: Western Edge Book Distributing, 2021.

Etulain, Richard W. *Calamity Jane: A Reader's Guide*. Norman: University of Oklahoma Press, 2015.

Fisher, Linda A., and Carrie Bowers. *Agnes Lake Hickok: Queen of the Circus, Wife of a Legend*. Norman: University of Oklahoma Press, 2020.

Foote, Shelby. *The Civil War, A Narrative: Fort Sumter to Perryville*. New York: Random House, 1986.

Foote, Shelby. *The Civil War, A Narrative: Red River to Appomattox*. New York: Random House, 1974.

Friesen, Steve. *Buffalo Bill: Scout, Showman, Visionary*. Golden, CO: Fulcrum Publishing, Inc., 2010.

Goodman, Julia Cody, Elizabeth Jane Leonard, and James William Hoffman, eds. *Buffalo Bill: King of the Old West*. New York: Library Publishers, 1955.

Green, Jerome A. *Slim Buttes, 1876: An Episode of the Great Sioux War*. Norman: University of Oklahoma Press, 1982.

Hardin, John Wesley. *The Life of John Wesley Hardin*. Seguin, TX: Smith & Moore, 1896.

Hedren, Paul L. *First Scalp for Custer: The Skirmish at Warbonnet Creek, Nebraska, July 17, 1876*. Lincoln: Nebraska State Historical Society, 2005.

Hedren, Paul L. *Rosebud June 17, 1876: Prelude to the Little Big Horn*. Norman: University of Oklahoma Press, 2019.

Hedren, Paul L., ed. *Ho! For the Black Hills: Captain Jack Crawford Reports the Black Hills Gold Rush and Great Sioux War*. Pierre: South Dakota State Historical Press, 2012.

Hedren, Paul L., ed. *John Finerty Reports the Sioux War*. Norman: University of Oklahoma Press, 2020.

Horsted, Paul, and Ernest Grafe. *Exploring with Custer: The 1874 Black Hills Expedition*. Custer, SD: Golden Valley Press, 2002.

Horsted, Paul, Ernest Grafe, and Jon Nelson. *Crossing the Plains with Custer*. Custer, SD: Golden Valley Press, 2009.

Hughes, Richard B. *Pioneer Years in the Black Hills*. Rapid City, SD: Dakota Alpha Press, 2002.

Hutton, Paul Andrew. *Phil Sheridan and His Army*. Norman: University of Oklahoma Press, 1985.

Hutton, Paul Andrew, ed. *The Custer Reader*. Lincoln: University of Nebraska Press, 1992.

King, Captain Charles. *Campaigning with Crook*. Norman: University of Oklahoma Press, 1964.

Knight, Oliver. *Following the Indian Wars: The Story of the Newspaper Correspondents Among the Indian Campaigners*. Norman: University of Oklahoma Press, 1960.

Krause, Herbert, and Gary D. Olson. *Prelude to Glory: A Newspaper Accounting of Custer's 1874 Expedition to the Black Hills*. Sioux Falls, SD: Brevet Press, 1974.

Larson, Robert W. *Red Cloud: Warrior-Statesman of the Lakota Sioux*. Norman: University of Oklahoma Press, 1997.

Lewis, Alfred Henry. *The Sunset Trail*. New York: A. L. Burt Company, 1905.

Lingenfelter, Richard E. *Bonanzas & Borrascas: Gold Lust and Silver Sharks, 1848–1884*. Norman: University of Oklahoma Press, 2012.

Long, E. B. *The Civil War Day by Day: An Almanac: 1861–1865*. Garden City, NY: Doubleday & Company, Inc., 1971.

Majors, Alexander. Seventy Years on the Frontier, Pony Express & Overland Stage: Two Accounts of the Opening of the American Western Frontier. Driffield, Great Britain: Leonaur, 2017.

Markley, Bill. *Billy the Kid and Jesse James: Outlaws of the Legendary West*. Guilford, CT: TwoDot, 2019.

Markley, Bill. *Geronimo and Sitting Bull: Leaders of the Legendary West*. Guilford, CT: TwoDot, 2021.

Markley, Bill, and Kellen Cutsforth. *Old West Showdown, Two Authors Wrangle Over the Truth About the Old West*. Guilford, CT: TwoDot, 2018.

Markley, Bill, and Kellen Cutsforth. *Standoff at High Noon: Another Battle Over the Truth in the Mythic Wild West*. Guilford, CT: TwoDot, 2021.

McChristian, Douglas C. *Fort Laramie: Military Bastion of the High Plains*. Norman: University of Oklahoma Press, 2008.

McClintock, John S. *Pioneer Days in the Black Hills: Accurate History and Facts by One of the Early Day Pioneers*. Norman: University of Oklahoma Press, 2000.

McDermott, John D. *Red Cloud's War: The Bozeman Trail, 1866–1868*, Vol. 2. Norman: University of Oklahoma Press, 2010.

McLaird, James D. *Calamity Jane: The Woman and the Legend*. Norman: University of Oklahoma Press, 2005.

McLaird, James D. *Wild Bill and Calamity Jane: Deadwood Legends*. Pierre: South Dakota State Historical Society Press, 2008.

McPherson, James M. *Battle Cry of Freedom: The Civil War Era*. New York: Ballantine Books, 1988.

Meline, James Florant. *Two Thousand Miles on Horseback, Santa Fé and Back: A Summer Tour Through Kansas, Nebraska, Colorado, and New Mexico, in the Year 1866*. New York: Hurd and Houghton, 1867.

Michno, Gregory F. *Lakota Noon: The Indian Narrative of Custer's Defeat*. Missoula, MT: Mountain Press Publishing Company, 1997.

Miller, Nyle H., and Joseph W. Snell. *Why the West Was Wild: A Contemporary Look at the Antics of Some Highly Publicized Kansas Cowtown Personalities*. Norman: University of Oklahoma Press, 1963.

Milner, Joe E., and Earle R. Forrest. *California Joe: Noted Scout and Indian Fighter*. Lincoln: University of Nebraska Press, 1935.

Moody, Ralph. *Stagecoach West*. New York: Thomas Y. Crowell Company, 1967.

Nichols, Colonel George Ward. "Wild Bill." *Harper's New Monthly Magazine*, Vol. XXXIV, No. CCI, February 1867. Reprint. Springfield, MO: Greene County Archives & Records Center, n.d.

O'Neal, Bill. *Encyclopedia of Western Gunfighters*. Norman: University of Oklahoma Press, 1979.

Parker, Watson. *Gold in the Black Hills*. Pierre: South Dakota State Historical Press, 1966.

Powers, Thomas. *The Killing of Crazy Horse*. New York: Alfred A. Knopf, 2010.

Price, George F. *Across the Continent with the Fifth Cavalry*. New York: D. Van Nostrand, 1883.

Rezatto, Helen. *Mount Moriah: The Story of Deadwood's Boot Hill*. Rapid City, SD: Fenwyn Press, 1989.

Rosa, Joseph G. *They Called Him Wild Bill: The Life and Adventures of James Butler Hickok*. Norman: University of Oklahoma Press, 1974.

Rosa, Joseph G. *Wild Bill Hickok, Gunfighter: An Account of Hickok's Gunfights*. Norman: University of Oklahoma Press, 2003.

Rosa, Joseph G. *Wild Bill Hickok: The Man and His Myth*. Lawrence: University Press of Kansas, 1996.

Rosa, Joseph G., and Robin May. *Buffalo Bill and His Wild West: A Pictorial Biography*. Lawrence: University Press of Kansas, 1989.

Russell, Don. *The Lives and Legends of Buffalo Bill*. Norman: University of Oklahoma Press, 1960.

Sagala, Sandra K. *Buffalo Bill on Stage*. Albuquerque: University of New Mexico Press, 2008.

Sanborn, Brevet-Major-General John B. "The Campaign in Missouri in September and October 1864." *Glimpses of the Nation's Struggle*. Third Series. Papers Read Before the Minnesota Commandery of the Military Order of the Loyal Legion of the United States, 1889–1892. New York: D. D. Merrill Company, 1893.

Secrest, William B., ed. *I Buried Hickok: The Memoirs of White Eye Anderson*. College Station, TX: Creative Publishing Co., 1980.

Sheridan, Philip Henry. *Personal Memoirs of P. H. Sheridan*, Vol. 2. New York: Charles L. Webster & Company, 1888.

Smith, Page. *The Nation Comes of Age: A People's History of the Ante-Bellum Years*. New York: McGraw-Hill Book Company, 1981.

Smith, Page. *The Rise of Industrial America: A People's History of the Post-Reconstruction Era*. New York: McGraw-Hill Book Company, 1984.

Sprague, Donovin Arleigh. *Images of America Standing Rock*. Charleston, SC: Arcadia Publishing, 2004.

Spring, Agnes Wright. *The Cheyenne and Black Hills Stage and Express Routes*. Lincoln: University of Nebraska Press, 1948.

Stewart, Edgar I., and Jane R. Stewart, eds. *The Field Diary of Lt. Edward Settle Godfrey*. Portland, OR: Champoeg Press, 1957.

Stillman, Deanne. *Blood Brothers: The Story of the Strange Friendship Between Sitting Bull and Buffalo Bill*. New York: Simon & Schuster, Inc., 2017.

Tallent, Annie D. *The Black Hills; or, The Last Hunting Ground of the Dakotahs*. St. Louis: Nixon-Jones Printing Co., 1899.

Terry, Alfred H. *The Field Diary of General Alfred H. Terry: The Yellowstone Expedition—1876*, 2nd ed. Bellevue, NE: Old Army Press, 1970.

Tilghman, Zoe Agnes Stratton. *Marshal of the Last Frontier, Life and Services of William Matthew (Bill) Tilghman.* Glendale, CA: The Arthur H. Clark Company, 1949.

Tucker, Glen. *Hancock the Superb.* Dayton, OH: Morningside House, Inc., 1960.

Turner, Thad. *Wild Bill Hickok: Deadwood City—End of Trail.* Deadwood, SD: Old West Alive! Publishing, 2001.

Utley, Robert M. *The Lance and the Shield: The Life and Times of Sitting Bull.* New York: Ballantine Books, 1993.

Vestal, Stanley. *Sitting Bull Champion of the Sioux.* Norman: University of Oklahoma Press, 1932.

Waggoner, Josephine. *Witness: A Hunkpapha Historian's Strong-Heart Song of the Lakotas.* Lincoln: University of Nebraska Press, 2013.

Wallace, Robert. *The Miners.* Alexandria, VA: Time-Life Books, 1976.

Walton, George. *Sentinel of the Plains: Fort Leavenworth and the American West.* Englewood Cliffs, NJ: Prentice-Hall, Inc., 1973.

Walton, W. M., and Lisa Lach, annotated. *Life and Adventures of Ben Thompson, the Famous Texan.* Austin, TX: The Steck Company Publishers, 2016.

Warren, Louis S. *Buffalo Bill's America: William Cody and the Wild West Show.* New York: Random House, Inc., 2005.

Webb, William Edward. *Buffalo Land.* Cincinnati: E. Hannaford & Company, 1872.

Wert, Jeffry D. *Custer: The Controversial Life of George Armstrong Custer.* New York: Simon & Schuster, 1996.

Wetmore, Helen Cody. *Buffalo Bill, Last of the Great Scouts: The Life Story of Colonel William F. Cody.* Lincoln: University of Nebraska Press, 1965.

Wills, Brian Steel. *A Battle from the Start: The Life of Nathan Bedford Forrest.* New York: HarperCollins Publishers, 1992.

Wilstach, Frank J. *Wild Bill Hickok, the Prince of Pistoleers.* Garden City, NY: Doubleday, Page & Company, 1926.

Woodard, Aaron. *The Revenger: The Life and Times of Wild Bill Hickok.* Guilford, CT: TwoDot, 2018.

Young, Harry "Sam." *Hard Knocks: A Life Story of the Vanishing West.* Pierre: South Dakota Historical Society Press, 2005.

PERIODICALS

Grey, John S. "Fact Versus Fiction in the Kansas Boyhood of Buffalo Bill." *Kansas History: A Journal of the Central Plains*, Vol. 8, no. 1, Spring 1985.

Markley, Bill. "Black Hills Gold." *True West Magazine*, April 2020.

Markley, Bill. "Custer's Gold." *True West Magazine*, April 2018.

McCanles, William Monroe. "The Only Living Eye Witness." *Nebraska Historical Magazine*, Vol. 10, no. 2, April-June 1927.

Rosa, Joseph G. *Alias Jack McCall: A Pardon or Death?* Kansas City, MO: The Kansas City Posse, The Westerners, 1967.

Thorp, Raymond W. "White-Eye, Last of the Old Time-Plainsmen." *True West Magazine*, Vol. 12, no. 4, March-April 1965.

Vincent, Matt. "Whistler's Murder." *Wild West Magazine*, October 2018.

Woodard, Aaron. "The Coward Who Shot Wild Bill." *Wild West Magazine*, August 2019.

INTERNET SOURCES

"Abilene in the Early Days." *National Field* (Salina, KS, November 23, 1908), Newspapers.com.

Abilene Weekly Chronicle (Abilene, KS, June 22, 1871), Newspapers.com.

"Aibileen Items," *Kansas City Daily Journal of Commerce* (Kansas City, MO, June 24, 1871), Newspapers.com.

"Academy of Music." *Buffalo Commercial Advertiser* (Buffalo, November 19, 1872), Newspapers.com.

"Academy of Music." *Chicago Tribune* (Chicago, May 12, 1874), Newspapers .com.

"Alexis' Grand Hunt." *New York Daily Herald* (New York, January 17, 1872), Newspapers.com.

"An Altercation Between Two Reporters." *Saint Joseph Daily Gazette* (St. Joseph, MO, January 31, 1872), Newspapers.com.

"Amusements." *Chicago Evening Mail* (Chicago, December 12, 1872), News papers.com.

"Amusements." *Chicago Inter Ocean* (Chicago, December 17, 1872), Newspapers .com.

"Amusements." *Chicago Tribune* (Chicago, December 14, 1872), Newspapers .com.

"Amusements." *Chicago Tribune* (Chicago, December 15, 1872), Newspapers .com.

"Amusements." *Cincinnati Enquirer* (Cincinnati, December 28, 1872), News papers.com.

"Amusements." *Democrat and Chronicle* (Rochester, NY, February 5, 1875), Newspapers.com.

"Amusements." *Leavenworth Daily Commercial* (Leavenworth, KS, August 2, 1871), Newspapers.com.

"Amusements." *Morning Republican* (Scranton, PA, May 12, 1874), Newspapers .com.

"Amusements." *Morning Republican: Scranton* (Scranton, PA, November 25, 1874), Newspapers.com.

"Amusements." *New York Daily Herald* (New York, February 20, 1872), News papers.com.

"Amusements." *New York Herald* (New York, April 1, 1873), Newspapers.com.

"Amusements." *New York Times* (New York, November 10, 1872), Newspapers .com.

"Amusements." *Pentagraph* (Bloomington, IL, April 7, 1874), Newspapers.com.

"Amusements." *St. Louis Republican* (St. Louis, January 9, 1876), Newspapers
.com.

"Arrest of Ned Buntline." *Kansas City Times* (Kansas City, KS, December 29,
1872), Newspapers.com.

"Arrests—Shootings." *Atchison Daily Patriot* (Atchison, KS, August 24, 1869),
Newspapers.com.

"Attempt to Kill Marshal Hickok." *Abilene Weekly Chronicle* (Abilene, KS,
November 30, 1871), Newspapers.com.

"Band of Road Men Captured." *Topeka Weekly Leader* (Topeka, KS, April 2,
1868), Newspapers.com.

"The Big Horn Expedition." *Inter Ocean* (Chicago, September 12, 1874), News
papers.com.

"Big Injun." *Lancaster Daily Intelligencer* (Lancaster, PA, June 8, 1875), News
papers.com.

"Bio. of O. P. Vickery." *Representative Men of Maine*, Online Biographies
Information.

Black Hills Weekly Journal (Rapid City, SD, March 1, 1895), Newspapers.com.

"Bos Americanos." *New York Herald* (New York, August 29, 1872), Newspapers
.com.

"Bos Americanus!" *New York Daily Herald* (New York, January 18, 1872), News
papers.com.

"Bowery Theatre—'Buffalo Bill,'" *New York Daily Herald* (New York, February
21, 1872), Newspapers.com.

"Brevities." *Daily Commonwealth* (Topeka, KS, July 22, 1870), Newspapers.com.

"Brevities." *Topeka Daily Commonwealth* (Topeka, KS, May 11, 1871), News
papers.com.

Broome, Jeff. "Death at Summit Springs: Susanna Alderdice and the Cheyennes." *Wild West Magazine* (October 2003), HistoryNet.

"A Buffalo." *Daily Commonwealth* (Topeka, KS, December 9, 1869), Newspapers
.com.

"Buffalo Bill." *Daily Bee* (Sacramento, December 10, 1872), Newspapers.com.

"Buffalo Bill." *Delaware State Journal* (Wilmington, DE, May 24, 1873), News
papers.com.

"Buffalo Bill." *Democrat and Chronicle* (Rochester, NY, July 9, 1874), News
papers.com.

"Buffalo Bill." *Democrat and Chronicle* (Rochester, NY, August 17, 1874), News
papers.com.

"Buffalo Bill." *Democrat and Chronicle* (Rochester, NY, February 9, 1875), News
papers.com.

"Buffalo Bill." *Democrat and Chronicle* (Rochester, NY, September 18, 1876),
Newspapers.com.

"Buffalo Bill." *Intelligencer Journal* (Lancaster, PA, February 26, 1872), News
papers.com.

"Buffalo Bill." *Leavenworth Daily Commercial* (Leavenworth, KS, December 21, 1872).

"Buffalo Bill." *Morning Republican: Scranton* (Scranton, PA, November 26, 1874), Newspapers.com.

"Buffalo Bill." *Omaha Bee* (Omaha, July 20, 1874), Newspapers.com.

"Buffalo Bill." *Rochester Democrat and Chronicle* (Rochester, NY, July 9, 1874) Newspapers.com.

"Buffalo Bill." *Wyandott Herald* (Kansas City, KS, December 12, 1872), News papers.com.

"Buffalo Bill After Indians." *Weekly Pioneer-Times* (Deadwood, SD, November 15, 1906), Newspapers.com.

"Buffalo Bill at Woods Museum." *New York Herald* (New York, June 30, 1874), Newspapers.com.

"The Buffalo Bill Combination." *Democrat and Chronicle* (Rochester, NY, April 12, 1876), Newspapers.com.

"Buffalo Bill Combination." *Wilmington Daily Commercial* (Wilmington, DE, June 1, 1876), Newspapers.com.

The Buffalo Bill Museum and Grave website.

"Buffalo Bill Showing Up Gotham to the Siouxs." *Republican Banner* (Nashville, June 8, 1875), Newspapers.com.

"Buffalo Bill's Medal Restored," *New York Times* (New York, July 9, 1989), *New York Times* Archives.

"Buffalo Bill's Opinion." *Daily Examiner* (San Francisco, October 24, 1874), Newspapers.com.

"The Buffalo Hunt." *Leavenworth Daily Conservative* (Leavenworth, KS, November 26, 1867), Newspapers.com.

"The Buffalo Hunt at the Falls." *Buffalo Commercial* (Buffalo, August 29, 1872), Newspapers.com.

"The Buffalo Huntre." *New York Herald* (New York, September 22, 1871), Newspapers.com.

"Buffalo Hunting." *Independent* (Grand Island, NE, July 25, 1874), Newspapers .com.

Cahill, Luke. "An Indian Campaign and Buffalo Hunting with Buffalo Bill." *Colorado Magazine*, Vol. IV, no. 4 (August 1927).

"Capt. Richard Bentley Owen." Find a Grave.

"City and Vicinity." *Kansas State Record* (Topeka, KS, October 21, 1870), News papers.com.

"City, County, and Vicinity." *Carbondale Leader* (Carbondale, PA, May 9, 1874), Newspapers.com.

"The City in Brief." *Chicago Tribune* (Chicago, December 14, 1872), News papers.com.

"Civil War: The 9th Kansas Volunteer Cavalry Regiment." Museum of the Kansas National Guard.

Commonwealth (Topeka, KS, July 23, 1874), Newspapers.com.

"Current Topics." *Democrat and Chronicle* (Rochester, NY, January 10, 1874), Newspapers.com.

"Current Topics." *Democrat and Chronicle* (Rochester, NY, May 26, 1874), Newspapers.com.

Cushman, George L. "Abilene, First of the Kansas Cow Towns." *Kansas Historical Quarterly*, Vol. 9, no. 3, August 1940, Kansas Historical Society.

"Daniel Boone." *Daily Record of the Times* (Wilkes-Barre, PA, May 8, 1874), Newspapers.com.

Danker, Donald F., ed. "The Journal of an Indian Fighter: The 1869 Diary of Major Frank J. North." *Nebraska History* 39 (1958).

"Deaths" and "His Last Stage Fight." *Cincinnati Enquirer* (Cincinnati, January 8, 1873), Newspapers.com.

"Domestic: The Kansas City Fair." *Daily Commonwealth* (Topeka, KS, September 28, 1872), Newspapers.com.

"The Drama." *Buffalo Commercial* (Buffalo, November 15, 1873), Newspapers.com.

"Dramatic." *Decatur Daily Republican* (Decatur, IL, February 7, 1876), Newspapers.com.

"Editorial Notes." *Buffalo Express* (Buffalo, October 14, 1874), Newspapers.com.

"Elijah Priest Greene." Gazlay Family History.

"Excursion to Monument." *Topeka Leader* (Topeka, KS, August 13, 1868), Newspapers.com.

"Excursion to Sheridan." *Weekly Union* (Junction City, KS, July 31, 1869), Newspapers.com.

Facing the Frontier: The Missions, the Soldiers, and Civilians of Fort Leavenworth, Kansas, Fort Leavenworth, KS: Frontier Army Museum.

"Famous Guns: Lucretia Borgia." Firearms History, Technology & Development.

"Fined." *Daily Commonwealth* (Topeka, KS, February 8, 1870), Newspapers.com.

"Fire Arms." *Abilene Weekly Chronicle* (Abilene, KS, June 8, 1871), Newspapers.com.

"Ford's Opera House—Buffalo Bill." *National Republican* (Washington, DC, April 24, 1875), Newspapers.com.

"Fort Fletcher, Kansas." Santa Fe Trail Research Site.

Friesen, Steve. "The Man Behind the Legend." *American Cowboy Magazine* (February 13, 2017).

"From Abilene." *Leavenworth Times and Conservative* (Leavenworth, KS, June 25, 1869), Newspapers.com.

"From Ellsworth and Hays." *Daily Kansas Tribune* (Leavenworth, KS, February 14, 1868), Newspapers.com.

"From Hays City." *Times and Conservative* (Leavenworth, KS, August 22, 1869), Newspapers.com.

"From Hays City. A Double Shooting Affray." *Leavenworth Times and Conservative* (Leavenworth, KS, October 13, 1869), Newspapers.com.

"From the Plains." *Democrat and Chronicle* (Rochester, NY, August 3, 1874), Newspapers.com.

"From the West." *Leavenworth Daily Commercial* (Leavenworth, KS, January 11, 1868), Newspapers.com.

"From Western Kansas." *Kansas State Journal* (Lawrence, KS, March 5, 1868), Newspapers.com.

"A Frontier Hero." *Inter Ocean* (Chicago, August 17, 1876), Newspapers.com.

Gale, Neil, PhD. "Nixon's Parisian Hippodrome and Amphitheater in Chicago (1872–1873)." Digital Research Library of Illinois History Journal.

"Gleanings." *Emporia News* (Emporia, KS, May 26, 1871), Newspapers.com.

"Gold in the Black Hills." *St. Louis Globe-Democrat* (St. Louis, April 17, 1876), Newspapers.com.

"Good's Opera House." *South Bend Tribune* (South Bend, IN, April 1, 1874), Newspapers.com.

"The Grand Duke's Hunt." *New York Daily Herald* (New York, January 14, 1872), Newspapers.com.

"A Grand Success." *Omaha Daily Bee* (Omaha, May 21, 1883), Newspapers .com.

Granger, Colonel Lewis. "Reminiscences of Colonel Lewis Granger." *Frontier Times*, Vol. 4, no. 1 (Bandera, TX, October 1926).

"Great Fire at Fort Riley—A Million Dollars of Property Destroyed." *Junction City Weekly Union* (Junction City, KS, January 27, 1866), Newspapers.com.

Hall, Jesse A., and Leroy T. Hand. "Miscellaneous Items in Leavenworth County, Kansas History." *History of Leavenworth County, Kansas* (Topeka, KS: Historical Publishing Company, 1921).

Hance, George W. "The Truth About Wild Bill." *Mail and Breeze* (Topeka, KS, December 20, 1901), Newspapers.com.

Hickok, H. D. "He Collaborates Col. Ed. Little." *Mail and Breeze* (Topeka, KS, September 27, 1901), Newspapers.com.

"History of Fort Riley and the 1st Infantry Division." US Army Fort Riley.

History of Greene County, Missouri (St. Louis: Western Historical Company, 1883).

"Hotel Arrivals, Massasoit House." *Daily Free Press* (Atchison, KS, March 12, 1868), Newspapers.com.

"How Abilene Was Made in Early Days." *Topeka Daily Capital* (Topeka, KS, August 30, 1908).

"How to Get a Quorum." *Topeka State Record* (Topeka, KS, May 9, 1871), Newspapers.com.

"How Wild Bill Died." *Galveston Daily News* (Galveston, TX, June 24, 1873), Newspapers.com.

"The Imperial Buffalo Hunter." *New York Daily Herald* (New York, January 16, 1872), Newspapers.com.

Jefferson Democrat (Hillsboro, MO, April 1, 1870), Newspapers.com.

"John S. Phelps Papers." *Community and Conflict: The Impact of the Civil War in the Ozarks*, Wilson's Creek National Battlefield.

"Jottings." *Daily Journal of Commerce* (Kansas City, MO, June 21, 1874), News papers.com.

"Jottings." *Kansas City Journal of Commerce* (Kansas City, MO, May 18, 1876), Newspapers.com.

"Julia Rockwell's Story." *Kansas City Star* (Kansas City, MO, December 14, 1947), Newspapers.com.

Junction City Union (Junction City, KS, October 7, 1871), Newspapers.com.

Kerns, Mathew. "James A. Scott." The Dime Library.

Koller, Joe. "Doc Peirce—Pioneer Hills Barber Used His Wit, Humor to Save His Scalp." *Rapid City Journal* (Rapid City, SD, May 14, 1950), News papers.com.

"The Land of the West." *New York Daily Herald* (New York, May 21, 1873), Newspapers.com.

Leavenworth Times (Leavenworth, KS, March 1, 1870), Newspapers.com.

"Letter from Captain Charles Meinhold to 1st Lieutenant J. B. Johnson, April 27, 1872." William F. Cody Archive, The Papers of William F. Cody.

"Letter Signed O. J. Hopkins, Capt. and Commissary." *Junction City Weekly Union* (Junction City, KS, February 17, 1866), Newspapers.com.

"The Liederkranz Ball." *New York Daily Herald* (New York, February 16, 1872), Newspapers.com.

"Local Brevities." *Chicago Evening Post* (Chicago, November 15, 1872), News papers.com.

"Local Brevities." *Daily Commonwealth* (Topeka, February 8, 1870), News papers.com.

"Local Chips." *Kansas City Times* (Kansas City, KS, January 19, 1872), News papers.com.

"Local Items." *Missouri Weekly Patriot* (Springfield, MO, August 10, 1865), Newspapers.com.

"Local Matters." *Weekly Free Press* (Atchison, KS, March 2, 1867), Newspapers .com.

"Local Matters." *Weekly Free Press* (Atchison, KS, March 21, 1868), Newspapers .com.

"Local News." *Lawrence Daily Journal* (Lawrence, KS, August 10, 1871), News papers.com.

"Local Notices." *St. Louis Globe-Democrat* (St. Louis, May 6, 1876), Newspapers .com.

"Local Summary." *Boston Post* (Boston, January 24, 1874), Newspapers.com.

Marian, Sara, and Clio Admin. "The Bowery Theatre, 1826–1929." Clio: Your Guide to History, December 3, 2017.

"Marriage." *Democrat and Chronicle* (Rochester, NY, March 12, 1874), News papers.com.

"Massasoit House, Atchison, Kansas." Kansas Memory, Kansas State Historical Society.

"The Matinee." *Daily Tribune* (Mobile, AL, November 21, 1875), Newspapers .com.

"Miscellaneous." *St. Louis Republican* (St. Louis, May 29, 1876), Newspapers .com.

"Miscellaneous Ordinances." *Abilene Weekly Chronicle* (Abilene, KS, June 29, 1871), Newspapers.com.

"Murder." *Abilene Weekly Chronicle* (Abilene, KS, August 17, 1871), Newspapers .com.

"Museums." Buffalo Bill Center of the West.

"Music Hall." *Daily Record of the Times* (Wilkes-Barre, PA, May 5, 1874), Newspapers.com.

"Muster Out Roll, Eighteenth Battalion, Cavalry, Kansas Volunteers," Vol. 5, Kansas Memory, Kansas Historical Society.

"A Myth Is Born." Kansas City Public Library.

"A Nation's Tawny Wards." *Sun* (New York, June 8, 1875), Newspapers.com.

"Nebraska Items." *Sioux City Journal* (Sioux City, IA, December 28, 1872), Newspapers.com.

"Ned Buntline's Riot." *Daily Press and Herald* (Knoxville, TN, July 24, 1873), Newspapers.com.

"New Advertisements." *Aitchison Daily Champion* (Aitchison, KS, September 1, 1872), Newspapers.com.

"New Advertisements." *Daily Record of the Times* (Wilkes-Barre, PA, May 4, 1874), Newspapers.com.

"A New Roll." *Inter Ocean* (Chicago, September 3, 1873), Newspapers.com.

"News Items." *Guilford Citizen* (Guilford, KS, August 13, 1870), Newspapers .com.

"New This Week." *Wayne County Herald* (Honesdale, PA, April 30, 1874), Newspapers.com.

"New York." *Chicago Tribune* (Chicago, February 24, 1872), Newspapers.com.

"The Opera House." *Daily Journal* (Wilmington, NC, October 26, 1875), Newspapers.com.

"Opera House." *Democrat and Chronicle* (Rochester, NY, March 10, 1874), Newspapers.com.

"Opera House." *Detroit Free Press* (Detroit, March 24, 1874).

"Opera House—'The Scouts.'" *Democrat and Chronicle* (Rochester, NY, March 11, 1874), Newspapers.com.

"An Ordinance Related to Dance Houses." *Abilene Weekly Chronicle* (Abilene, KS, September 7, 1871), Newspapers.com.

"Our History." City of Ellsworth website.

"Our Indian Troubles." *New York Herald* (New York, July 28, 1869), Newspapers .com.

"Our Sportsmen." *Chicago Tribune* (Chicago, November 23, 1872), Newspapers .com.

"Overland." *Sacramento Bee* (Sacramento, July 17, 1874), Newspapers.com.

"Overland Passengers." *San Francisco Examiner* (San Francisco, July 17, 1874), Newspapers.com.

Parks, J. "From Western Kansas." *Daily Kansas State Journal* (Lawrence, KS, March 11, 1868), Newspapers.com.

Parks, J. "From Western Kansas." *Daily Kansas State Journal* (Lawrence, KS, March 13, 1868), Newspapers.com.

Parks, J., "From Western Kansas." *Daily Kansas State Journal* (Lawrence, KS, March 14, 1868), Newspapers.com.

Parks, J. "From Western Kansas." *Kansas State Journal* (Lawrence, KS, March 5, 1868), Newspapers.com.

"Particulars of the Killing of Stranhan at Hays City." *Leavenworth Daily Commercial* (Leavenworth, KS, October 3, 1869), Newspapers.com.

"Personal." *Cincinnati Enquirer* (Cincinnati, February 24, 1874), Newspapers .com.

"Personal." *Wayne County Herald* (Honesdale, PA, March 5, 1874), Newspapers .com.

Phillips, Christopher. "Jennison, Charles R." *Civil War on the Western Border: The Missouri-Kansas Conflict, 1854–1865.* The Kansas City Public Library.

Pittsfield Sun (Pittsfield, MA, February 25, 1874), Newspapers.com.

"Playful." *Kansas City Times* (Kansas City, MO, March 11, 1873), Newspapers .com.

Pyle, L. Robert. "Cheyenne Chief Tall Bull." Historynet.

"Reformation in Abilene." *Abilene Weekly Chronicle* (Abilene, KS, September 14, 1871), Newspapers.com.

Richardson, Leander. "A Very Lively Camp." *Daily Bee* (Sacramento, January 20, 1894), Newspapers.com.

Roob, Alexander. "Van Goghs Favorites III: Arthur Boyd Houghton—Our One-Eyed Artist in America." Melton Pryor Institute for Reportage Drawing & Printing Culture.

Rosa, Joseph G. "George Ward Nichols and the Legend of Wild Bill Hickok." *Arizona and the West*, Vol. 19, no. 2 (1977).

Salzer, Susan K., "Medicine Bill Comstock—Saga of the Leatherstocking Scout." HistoryNet.

"The Scouts in Luck." *Missouri Republican* (St. Louis, July 21, 1873), Newspapers.com.

"The Scouts of the Plains." *Buffalo Evening Post* (Buffalo, November 14, 1873), Newspapers.com.

"The Scouts of the Plains." *Daily Davenport Democrat* (Davenport, IA, April 23, 1874), Newspapers.com.

"A Scrap of History." *Ford County Republican* (Dodge City, KS, April 20, 1887), Newspapers.com.

"The Search for Soldiers." *The Civil War*, National Park Service website.

"7th Cavalry Regiment." Wikipedia.

"Sheridan, Kansas." Wikipedia.

"Shooting Affray." *Abilene Weekly Chronicle* (Abilene, KS, October 12, 1871), Newspapers.com.

"Singular Appeal." *Leavenworth Daily Commercial* (Leavenworth, KS, July 31, 1870), Newspapers.com.

"Some Frontier Peculiarities." *Wichita Weekly Beacon* (Wichita, KS, October 28, 1874), Newspapers.com.

"State News." *Weekly Union* (Junction City, KS, July 31, 1869), Newspapers .com.

"State News Hashed." *Western Spirit* (Paola, KS, June 26, 1874), Newspapers .com.

"Telegraphic. At It. Alexis on the Untamed Bison's Native Heath." *Kansas City Times* (Kansas City, KS, January 14, 1872), Newspapers.com.

"The Theatres." *Chicago Evening Post* (Chicago, December 14, 1872), News papers.com.

"The Theatres." *Chicago Evening Post* (Chicago, December 17, 1872), News papers.com.

"Three Notabilities." *Dispatch: St. Louis* (St. Louis, February 8, 1875), News papers.com.

"To Cattle Drovers." *Abilene Weekly Chronicle* (Abilene, KS, February 22, 1872), Newspapers.com.

"Topeka House." *Daily Commonwealth* (Topeka, KS, December 9, 1869), News papers.com.

"Town Talk." *Democrat and Chronicle* (Rochester, NY, February 15, 1875), Newspapers.com.

"Transcript of Treaty of Fort Laramie (1868)." Our Documents.

"A Trip Up the Road." *Daily Commonwealth* (Topeka, KS, December 9, 1869), Newspapers.com.

"An Utter Failure." *Chicago Tribune* (Chicago, September 22, 1876), News papers.com.

Warfield, Lt. Col. A. B., Q. M. C. "The Quartermaster's Department, 1861–1864." American Civil War.

Weekly Journal (Salina, KS, January 18, 1872), Newspapers.com.

Weekly Union (Junction City, KS, July 9, 1871), Newspapers.com.

"Wild Bill." *Abilene Weekly Chronicle* (Abilene, KS, February 20, 1873), News papers.com.

"Wild Bill." *Daily Bulletin* (Leavenworth, KS, February 13, 1867), Newspapers .com.

"Wild Bill." *Daily Commonwealth* (Topeka, KS, September 18, 1869), News papers.com.

"Wild Bill." *Daily Commonwealth* (Topeka, KS, March 1, 1873), Newspapers .com.

"Wild Bill." *Daily Record of the Times* (Wilkes-Barre, PA, May 4, 1874), News papers.com.

"Wild Bill." *Democrat and Chronicle* (Rochester, NY, March 13, 1874), News papers.com.

"Wild Bill." *St. Louis Dispatch* (St. Louis, April 18, 1876), Newspapers.com.

"Wild Bill." *Warrensburg Standard* (Warrensburg, MO, February 24, 1870), Newspapers.com.

"'Wild Bill,' *Harper's Monthly* and 'Colonel' G. W. Nichols." *Missouri Weekly Patriot* (Springfield, MO, January 31, 1867), Newspapers.com.

"Wild Bill: A Sequel to the Tragedy." *Black Hills Weekly Pioneer* (Deadwood, SD, November 11, 1876), Newspapers.com.

"William F. Cody at Wild Bill Hickok's Grave (1)." Digital Collections, Buffalo Bill Center of the West.

"William F. Cody at Wild Bill Hickok's Grave (2)." Digital Collections, Buffalo Bill Center of the West.

"The Yale College Expedition of 1870." Yale Peabody Museum of Natural History.

INDEX

ABOUT THE AUTHOR

Bill Markley, member of Western Writers of America and staff writer for WWA's *Roundup* magazine, also writes for *True West* and *Wild West* magazines. *Wild Bill Hickok and Buffalo Bill Cody: Plainsmen of the Legendary West* is the fourth in *The Legendary West* series. The first in the series, *Wyatt Earp and Bat Masterson: Lawmen*, examines the lives of those two well-known characters. His second book, *Billy the Kid and Jesse James: Outlaws*, delves into the lives of the famous desperados. Both books are 2020 Will Rogers Medallion Award nonfiction finalists. The third in the series, released in May 2021, is *Geronimo and Sitting Bull: Leaders of the Legendary West*. Coauthor Kellen Cutsforth and Bill wrote *Old West Showdown*, in which they explore controversial Old West stories. *Old West Showdown* was a 2019 Will Rogers Medallion Award nonfiction finalist. They followed *Old West Showdown* with additional controversial stories in *Standoff at High Noon*, released in October 2021. Bill has written additional nonfiction books: *Dakota Epic, Experiences of a Reenactor During the Filming of Dances with Wolves*; *Up the Missouri River with Lewis and Clark*; and *American Pilgrim: A Post–September 11th Bus Trip*. His historical novel, *Deadwood Dead Men*, was selected by Western Fictioneers as a finalist for its 2014 Peacemaker Award in the category Best First Western Novel. Bill and his wife, Liz, live in Pierre, South Dakota, where they raised two children and currently have three grandchildren.

ABOUT THE ILLUSTRATOR

Jim Hatzell is a graduate of the American Academy of Art in Chicago, Illinois, with a degree in Advertising and Design and in Illustration. He has a strong background in acrylic painting, pen-and-ink illustrations, and photography, and volunteers to teach art. Jim was a photographer for *Down Country Roads* magazine, and Books In Motion has used his artwork for over one hundred book covers. Jim has been in the motion picture business since 1989, when he and Bill Markley first met on the set of *Dances with Wolves*. Jim drew quick sketches during the filming, and some illustrate Bill's book *Dakota Epic*. Since *Dances with Wolves* Jim has been involved in films such as *Far and Away, Gettysburg, Geronimo, Crazy Horse, Rough Riders, Ride with the Devil, Skins, Comanche Warriors, National Treasure 2, Black Wood, The Last Son,* and *Murder at Emigrant Gulch*. He is a stagehand in International Alliance of Theatrical Stage Employees Local 731. During two summer seasons, he worked as a park ranger and historic interpreter at the Little Bighorn Battlefield National Monument. Jim created the illustrations for Bill's books *Wyatt Earp and Bat Masterson, Geronimo and Sitting Bull,* and *Billy the Kid and Jesse James*. Jim and his wife, Jacqui, make their home in Rapid City, South Dakota.